BREAKING THE GRID

THE GRID

How to Buy Nothing, Make Everything, and Live Sustainably

Published by Familius LLC, www.familius.com
PO Box 1249, Reedley, CA 93654

Familius books are available at special discounts for bulk purchases, whether for sales promotions or for family or corporate use.
For more information, contact Familius Sales at orders@familius.com.

The publisher and the author advise you to take full responsibility for your safety and know your limits.
This publication is meant as a source of valuable information for the reader, however it is not meant as a substitute for direct expert assistance.
If such level of assistance is required, the services of a competent professional should be sought.

Library of Congress Control Number: 2022930401

Print ISBN 9781641704625
Ebook ISBN 9781641705097

Printed in China

Edited by Shaelyn Topolovec, Michele Robbins, Barbara Seiden, and Spencer Skeen
Cover design by Carlos Guerrero
Book design by Mara Harris

10 9 8 7 6 5 4 3 2 1

First Edition

BREAKING THE GRID

How to Buy Nothing, Make Everything, and Live Sustainably

Dan Martin

FAMILIUS

To Luna, our once wild and crazy burro who opened her home and her heart to us.

Contents

Project List

Introduction

Every product you purchase; every broken part, item, or object; everything you currently have or don't; everything you use or have discarded; everything you need, want, or have ever dreamt about is made by a human. Every job, service, task, or chore is performed by a human just like you. I have a secret to tell you, something they don't want you to know . . . every human is the same. It's true. There's no difference. One person doesn't have more ability than another.

Anyone and everyone can do anything and everything that everyone else does, just as good or better!

Someone may be smarter or stronger or faster, but all that means is that we have to work harder and longer to achieve the same results. You see, humans belong to the Great Ape family of animals, just like a beaver belongs to the *Castoridae* family. Some beavers can build their homes faster than others, but all beavers can build a home of the same standard. For some reason, society has led us to believe that Joe can paint because he was born with that inclination. Maybe, but guess what? Sally can paint better with enough practice, time, and hard work.

There's no reason why you can't deliver the same, if not better, products or services as any other human when given the same know-how. And corporations know this. That's where patents, copyrights, intellectual property, and trade secrets come in. When plans are open source, anyone can duplicate the results.

Anyone and everyone can do anything and everything that everyone else does, just as good or better!

> *A human being should be able to change a diaper, plan an invasion, butcher a hog, conn a ship, design a building, write a sonnet, balance accounts, build a wall, set a bone, comfort the dying, take orders, give orders, cooperate, act alone, solve equations, analyze a new problem, pitch manure, program a computer, cook a tasty meal, fight efficiently, die gallantly. Specialization is for insects.*
> —*Robert Heinlein, author of* Time Enough for Love

Actually, the concept of doing everything yourself isn't new. Humans have always been self-sufficient. But clearing fields, fixing cars, harvesting honey, and baking bread is backbreaking work. Only in today's hectic day-to-day society do we find ourselves specializing and relying. However, technologies and materials have changed. There are more efficient methods of doing things, making it easier—even effortless—to live comfortably, independently, and self-sufficiently. So why don't we?

We are bombarded with endless commercials, endless lines, endless traffic, and endless time on hold. Simply taking the first steps in a different path amidst all this can seem daunting. Society wants everyone to move as a herd because it's easier that way—working, sleeping, and eating together; drowsy drones pushing cogs in a machine for unknown reasons they attribute to their family's comfort. Well, how harmonious is a family with a spouse or parent figure that works over forty hours a week? Why, when there are other simpler, easier, healthier, and better ways to live, do we do this to ourselves?

For years, I sat studying society's monstrous motion, the rat wheel rolling its way through existence. I finally discovered that you can create more time for your family and add years to your life, all while not harming other terrestrial life and the planet in the process, by doing things differently and more *efficiently.*

We hear everywhere at work, "That's not an efficient way to do it." "You're not being efficient, Dave." "We need to be more efficient next quarter, people!" What's the big deal? Efficiency saves ridiculous amounts of time, energy, and money. I'm not talking cents saved by turning off lights. I'm talking profit margin increases of several hundred percent after Cost of Doing Business (CODB) when companies construct new ways of doing things. Unfortunately, this efficiency concept hasn't made its way outside of the workplace.

But why? If doing things more efficiently is, well, a more efficient way of doing things, why don't we do things differently at home? It's because we were raised to think our lives would be a certain way—"When I grow up, I'm going to go to college, get a good job, go to work every day, get a house, have kids, have green grass, and do everything I see on TV"—and we're not willing to waver from that dream. Well, the cost of money is getting expensive. It costs you time without loved ones, energy, and health; that's too expensive for my blood. How about you? Are you ready to try something different, or would you prefer to keep your nose to the grindstone?

Society will have you believe it's not that simple. I'd have you believe it is. The truth will, in the end, be up to you. New ideas will take getting used to. Changes and sacrifices will need to be made. *Changing your mindset will be the biggest challenge.* Is it worth it? Coming from someone who's made the change to self-reliance . . . there's no comparison.

I already did the hard part. Through trial and error, my wife and I figured out what works and what doesn't. It's not hard or complicated, but you do need to think outside the box. Way outside. I'm talking about new ways of thinking about new ways of thinking, outside a box that was once inside the same box.

There's an endless list of ways to do stuff yourself (in this book I've only skimmed the surface); but keep in mind, doing something yourself isn't always about saving time and money—it's about independence and self-reliance. When you do everything yourself, you have purpose, satisfaction, and freedom. And in the end, isn't that what it's all about?

Eventually, when you get to the point that you're doing everything yourself, you become self-reliant. Completely self-sustaining. Self-sufficient. The term applies to not one or a few things but all things—all comforts and essentials in life. Any and all elements that society currently provides for you, you provide for yourself.

People interested in the topic are met with confusion as to the breadth of the definition. To say "I'm self-reliant" is to take the totality of the term upon yourself. Anything less does an injustice to those who are completely self-reliant, similar to installing some faucets, maybe a toilet, or fixing some broken pipes and saying, "I'm a plumber."

The process of becoming self-reliant doesn't need to be difficult or uncomfortable. Over the next few chapters, I'll help with those steps to self-reliance, each bigger than the last, navigating you along a path of least resistance in order to save you the most time, energy, and money by avoiding the many unnecessary steps my wife and I made. Take as many steps as you want to, pick your own level of self-reliance—partially, mostly, or completely. Even just being a little self-reliant is enough to make a huge difference in your life.

Can you do everything yourself? You can do anything yourself, that much I've already proven, but can we do *everything*? Everything that's provided for us today by society, do we have the energy and time to do it all?

When I was writing *Breaking the Grid*, collecting notes from dozens of my handwritten journals, and re-inspecting inventions to see how I'd built them, not only did I realize that one person couldn't retain that much knowledge (I don't even remember how to do everything in my book and it's *my* book!), but the sheer amount of stuff that we find we need in order to be comfortable and happy in today's life is extensive. Much more so than one hundred years ago when our ancestors did it.

So can a person, a couple, a family, do everything themselves? If you'd like to live the high life in a mansion, with four cars, three swimming pools, an 18-hole miniature golf course, a basketball court, and a helicopter, probably not. But if you'd like a middle-class level of self-sufficiency (one pool, a basketball court, a 6-hole mini golf course, no helicopter), with some hard work, perseverance, teamwork, and a little efficiency, absolutely. We did!

And when I say you can do "anything" I mean *anything*! You can build a computer, you can perform surgery, you can build an ultralight aircraft with a lawn mower engine, PVC tubing, and a bunch of tarps *and* fly it if you wanted to. All it takes is knowing how to do it.

Through this book, I intend to prove that you can do anything by showing you how we did it and giving you the needed knowledge in an easy-to-read, step-by-step format. Anything and everything required to be partially or completely self-sufficient, be it in suburbia or cut off from society, off the grid or smack dab in the middle of the city, can be found in this book, along with a whole lot of great stuff that everyone should know. You can start wherever you want to, skip around, or jump on that project you've always wanted to build. And watch out for cross-references; when you're making everything yourself, you'll find that you often don't have to buy your own materials—you can make them!

In today's day and age, with books like this and the internet, with community colleges, trade schools, online courses, and workshops (many of which you can audit or sit in for free), there's no reason not to learn to do everything. In the end I hope to hear you say, "I can do anything, no, *everything* myself!"

To have everything you need to be 100% self-sufficient, this book would have had to be 17,000 pages. Because of space limitations, the majority of this book, over 90% of the content, was cut out. For more projects and self-sufficiency know-how, pick up my other soft cover books, Apocalypse: How To Survive a Global Crisis and The End: Survivors, as well as my upcoming unpublished books, or visit my website diysufficient.com and download any of my hundreds of digital DIY guides. Then dart over and check out my DIY YouTube videos and the "Think About It!" series on my channel (youtube.com/DanMartinHuman). And definitely make sure to attend any of my speaking engagements, seminars and workshops. Or if you'd like me to come check out your site, schedule a consultation with me. Not looking to dive in alone? Join one of my Intentional Communities!"

Chapter 1: Our Experience

Homesteading is the epitome of self-reliance. There are different degrees, sure. At the lighter end of the spectrum, you have living on a farm while going to work every day. In the middle, there are people like the Amish, Quakers, Mennonites, and some indigenous peoples who have some degree of contact with society and rely on and/or purchase goods and materials from them but do many things solely using their community resources. And at the heaviest end, completely cut-off, providing 100% of one's needs and wants, totally separated from society (i.e., stores, phones, TV, internet, people), you have those with the goal to live completely off the grid.

"That's impossible," is the most frequent response I get. On one hand, it's sort of a compliment. The thought that my wife and I managed to do something that's considered "impossible" is pretty cool! We did this amazing thing, sacrificed our life, our friends, our family, and so much more. I hear this so often, it makes me think . . . did we actually do it? I have the memories, but it seems surreal now. I can't believe we did so much, passed through so much, achieved so much, just us, alone in the wild!

"Then why aren't there more people doing it?" some ask. At first, I couldn't answer this and actually wondered about it myself. At the time we heard stories about other young, free spirits leaving society, building wind turbines, living off the grid, collecting rain, building with the earth, but not so much in the last decades. There must be others, but most probably don't come back and write books on the subject or make their story public. It would be nice to hear more couples' experiences to see if they fought through the same challenges we did or had trouble in ways we didn't.

"Well, it's easy if you have money," is another response. We were no different than you and most Americans: a tier 4 tax bracket family who ate out a couple times a week, went to BBQs with friends, and owned cars, a few toys, good clothes, and a decent home. There were a couple fundamental differences in choice, though. We chose not to have children (the average American spends $¼ million a child[1]), and we made some good financial decisions very early. Like most people, we did acquire some stuff and we liked our stuff, but we were able to break free of material things and choose a different life. I share our story, our choices, and how we lived off grid, so you can see it is doable and so you don't repeat the same mistakes we made.

"Why?" Why would anyone in their right mind abandon the comforts of society to have to provide for themselves. For most people, living, working, and raising a family dependent on society is a way of life, the only way of life. What if it didn't have to be? What if you didn't need society in order to exist? Or what if that way of life was drastically disturbed, stripped away, or terminated altogether? Is there another option?

Our Story

We were a newly married couple, each only twenty-five, both with lucrative careers, typical dreams, aspirations, and only one thing on our minds . . . money! We had it, what everyone strives for in life. We were living the American dream. Making lots of money and buying lots of stuff!

But something didn't feel right. One day we realized, we're sick of corporate America, consumerism, capitalism, materialism, greed, the government, and the hassle and bustle of society. So, we cashed in our investments; sold two waterfront homes, the vehicles, boats, and the toys; burned the cell phones, TVs, computers, even money; and left.

It got so bad! I used to be addicted to material possessions, comforts, my phone, the internet, money, and food. I couldn't live without them and didn't want to stop! I realized I had a problem when no matter how much money I made, how much I bought, it never satisfied my need to make more, to buy more. More, more, more! I needed it all, the newer, the better.

Like any addiction, the only way to stop is cold turkey and stay away from other addicts. I could have given it all away, or dropped it off at Goodwill, but that is just enabling someone else's addiction. No. If you're a drug addict, you can't give away or even throw away your drugs, you have to destroy them! You have to throw then into the fire and scream out "No . . . You will no longer have control over me!!" And it works. Burning all your stuff—it's euphoric. Every time I do it, I feel a HUGE weight lifted off my shoulders. Therapists actually employ this type of therapy. It not only destroys the thing you're addicted to or that has a hold over you, it destroys the mental and emotional connection. The process even releases adrenaline and endorphins. I'd suggest it even if just for the therapy and stress relief aspect of it.

Then, we just left society and had no contact. Sixteen months later the economy crashed; people lost their homes, their possessions, their livelihoods, and some, their lives—everything. Obama was elected president. The country went (back) to war (again). And we never even knew.

Awakening

Our story didn't begin with a bang. It was more like a whimper. One day I remember thinking: *Even though we were born into it, maybe we don't need to continue as sheep, moving in herds together stuck in traffic going to and from work, standing in lines together at the grocery store conveyor belt feed troughs. Maybe it's possible to just stop.*

Society romances and encourages the idea to work and work until you're successful, rather than enjoy life now and be happy mentally. We decided that we didn't want that for our life. The thought grew, we'd talk about the possibilities, feasibility, and practicality of leaving it all. My wife, Lucia, is a chameleon. She can be the stay-at-home housewife or the business woman, the free spirit, or the world traveler. We had nothing to lose but our possessions, which, for some reason, we'd worked so hard to accumulate. We made the decision. We would quit our jobs, split from the herd, and leave friends, family, and the rest of humanity in our dust.

Getting back to the basics started with the book, *Back to Basics* published by Readers Digest in 1981, which Lucia picked up at a garage sale. The concept of becoming self-sufficient wasn't new, but at the time there wasn't much content on the subject. No websites, books, e-books, or YouTube DIY videos. I think a coworker had given me a binder of printouts and copies, collected from who knows where, on all kinds of self-reliance subjects. So, I thought we could manage, and we eventually did— but with five hundred times more mistakes, cost, and effort than needed.

Disconnecting

Our first steps in disconnecting began with our search for land. We made day trips across Texas, New Mexico, and Mexico, and spent long weekends and holidays searching for the perfect spot. We really didn't know what we needed, to be honest; we went by what we liked. We ended up loving West Texas, near Terlingua. The land was dirt cheap (two hundred acres for under twenty thousand dollars), and the realtor took us out in two Hummers, because "one usually got stuck," to view the properties. On the final day, the last property to explore bordered Big Bend National Park and Mexico. This was a problem because Lucia was in the process of getting her citizenship and couldn't cross the border checkpoint. I'd have to go alone. The property was gorgeous. It had a giant seasonal river, with a twenty-foot waterfall (one of two), thousand-foot mountains, cliffs, enormous rock formations, caves with native carvings, rock arches, extinct volcanoes, sand dunes, grasslands, boulders, and tons of wildlife. There was no electricity, water, phone, or internet lines; no garbage, mail, or sewer services; no address, roads, neighbors, stores, or cell signal for a hundred miles. There wasn't even a road. It was perfect. We signed the next day.

Leaving the Matrix

It took some time, almost a year— a lot longer than we expected— to get our affairs in order: cancel insurances, close bank accounts, stop memberships, sell the houses, get rid of vehicles, boat, jet skis, and other toys. The rest, furniture, photo albums, laptops, stereo systems, TVs, phones—we burned to death! We even tossed wads of cash in in defiance of a system we now rejected.

With books in hand, we packed a truck and flatbed trailer with what we thought were the bare necessities, threw a cab-over camper on top, loaded the dog and cat (and a rabbit) in the cab, and headed west.

I had written "directions" on how to get back to the property:

> Trn off highway est, .37mls after marker 177. Go 4 x 4 17 then veer rt towrds [now thank my editors because this is my real writing] big mowntan [sure enough, there was a giant mountain]. At 5, pass through cool hill [no idea what that was now, but Lucia did say, "Wow this is a cool hill!" and we saw a bobcat]. When u hit dry [it had water] river, trn lft, 1.2, rt on rd [There was a piece of an old mining road]. When end keep strt for 7.8, look for rocks [I'd stacked some rocks] rt 50ft, then anothr rt 1 steel thing [this is actually a good description of some type of mining equipment]. Trn, go dwn very steep hill to flat [there was a flat area, the only one].

Even with my superb directions, we got turned around several times and ended up trying to navigate through the desert at night. You think navigating without road signs in the dark is difficult, try without roads. By the time we found the "flat area," it was pitch black, and we were exhausted. All we could do was jump in the camper and go to sleep. This was our first real taste that this journey wasn't going to be as easy as we'd thought.

Unplugged

The next morning was incredible. As soon as the sun breached the mountain tops, we were so excited to get outside, see our land, especially Lucia, since she'd purchased it, sight unseen. It was just as gorgeous as I remembered. It was cool: dew on the rocks, plants, cactus, flowers, birds, lizards, and jack rabbits (everywhere). She loved it. We had breakfast but really wanted to walk around. I showed her the waterfall, cliffs, and rock arches. That day, and the next few after that would be the happiest of us living there. Although there'd be more rewarding ones, those first days were euphoric and unreal, a once-in-a-lifetime event.

The following months didn't bring any sense of urgency. We had no expectations, no demands. We no longer needed to make money. We didn't have to worry about our power or water being shut off for not paying on time. Nobody was coming out here to reposess our vehicle. For the first time in our life, we had nowhere to be, and being nowhere felt great!

We enjoyed life, loved ourselves, each other, the animals, the land. Taking time to enjoy the smallest things is unbelievably more rewarding than the newest phone or making sure my car didn't get scratched. So that's what we did. Actually, that's not entirely true . . . we flew kites, swam, played cards, read, napped (lots of napping), hiked and rock climbed, found a waterfall, found arrowheads, found ourselves. We did a lot of sightseeing those months, not only of our land but the thousands of acres of mountains and desert around us. We even built a sign directing everyone to a tiki bar, one of two we'd made. I grew a long beard, and then I shaved it all off, then grew it again. We even made friends with a wild burro we'd named Luna. But basically nothing—for the first year or so. We'd still be doing it if Lucia didn't get sick of living in a pick-up truck bed.

Getting Ready

Surprisingly, it took a long time to really unplug from the matrix. For months you'd feel like you'd need to be somewhere or doing something. But eventually, we started thinking about and scouting the area for where we wanted to build the house. I wanted to locate the house atop the large waterfall, but the logistics would have been intricate to say the least. Eventually we found a great, central location with awesome 360° views that fit most of the other criteria for the perfect off-the-grid homestead. We took measurements, soil samples, photos, and video; made sketches over a four-day span; and then started designing the Octagon Cliff Cabin.

Several more trips to the nearest city (three and a half hours away) brought another dog, more rabbits, a couple more cats, ducks, chickens, a backhoe, front-end loader, and a shipping container for storage. We set up the camper at the bottom of the hill on which we'd be building, and then—we procrastinated some more. Living way out in the middle of nowhere, in paradise, well, it's hard, making oneself work. So, yeah, it was a slow start.

Gathering Supplies

The idea of building a home from one hundred percent recycled materials sounded very cool. We picked the top of an eighty-foot cliff for our home site, so the deck and swimming pool would cantilever over the drop off. It was finally time to get to work.

We built a (very long) driveway and, for a while, came to and left society, gathering materials and ordering stuff online in libraries and internet cafés. Neither the police nor fire department would come without an address, but Jerry, a sixty-eight-year-old UPS driver out of Odessa-Midland, drove hours and hours of rough dirt "road." We were three and a half hours from the nearest Walmart. It took one hour just to get off the property (eventually, we built a helicopter pad).

Anything and everything fit the bill, as long as it was free! Forty-foot utility poles, corrugated roofing, plywood, 2x Sheetrock skids, cee purlins, pipe, paint, plumbing, electrical, you name it. In the end, we had thousands of sheets of plywood, over a thousand pallets, hundreds of telephone poles, pipe, insulation, plastic, drums, buckets, blocks, bricks, load centers, appliances, torn bags of concrete, lumber, plugs and switches, wiring, lights, ceiling fans, windows, doors, and a wood burning stove. Eventually, we had enough to start construction on our dream home.

The Building Battle Begins

Building a house, in even the best conditions is a nightmare. Ask any general contractor. Everything, and I mean EVERYTHING goes wrong. We fought the elements, building challenges, even each other practically nonstop. Still, construction of our one bedroom, one bathroom home took only six months with two people working full-time using their bare hands (okay, to operate power tools with a generator), but we occupied the house within four months and finished from inside within the year. Beam by beam, column by column, metal sheet by . . . we built our cliff-side cabin, trying to enjoy the experience along the way, returning exhausted to our humble 4 x 8-foot truck mounted abode every night.

Lucia hated the camper, but I rather enjoyed living in the back of a pickup. Where else can you play Street Fighter (okay, I kept my Nintendo) and grab a cold beer from the fridge without ever leaving your bed? Quarters were cramped; we had to climb over each other to get out of bed. But on the positive side, being uncomfortable and cramped motivates you to get building.

The first few years in the house there were no walls, windows, or doors (by design). We created an open-air home to live with and in nature, watched the sun set and afternoon storms blow across the desert from our bed, and woke to torrential rains (and Luna the wild burro licking my face from the deck). Evenings in the desert offered cool breezes, which went right through the house. And the stars, oh, the stars from bed, they seemed to just go on forever. Life was good!

Life Outside the Matrix

A roof over your head is, it turns out, a very small part of living. There are many, many elements of life that we now had to provide for ourselves. So, we built a barn, a chicken house, a corral (which never really got used) for Luna, our wild (now mostly domesticated) burro, a bar, an indoor swimming pool, you know, the necessities. Life was good, but we needed to start thinking about long-term living and becoming fully self-sufficient.

The ducks and chickens were thriving, but one can't live on poultry and eggs alone. Next on the agenda was growing some greens. But in the desert, by someone who's never grown a potted plant, that turned out to be a lot more than we'd assumed. Contrary to what we were taught watching Saturday morning cartoons, you can't just throw a few seeds down, sprinkle with water, and grow food anywhere you want. In reality, when water makes contact with dry desert 110° dirt, there's a violent thermal and chemical reaction resulting in steam. Nothing grows, it only evaporates into dust.

After building a compost toilet, 9,000 gallon rain catchment system, a crude but working greywater system for the above-ground plants, and underground hydroponics for real production, we were finally able to grow our own produce to offset buying and gathering. Next on the menu, meat: javelina, rabbit, possum, skunk, turtle, porcupine, armadillo, fox, bobcat, deer, aoudad, antelope, snake, coyote, mountain sheep, quail, roadrunner, hawk, buzzard, dove, antelope, ring-tailed cat, bobcat, mountain lion, mice, rats, bats, ants, termites, crickets, frogs, worms, maggots, beetles—there were many sources, I just needed to manufacture some good traps!

We got a billy and a few nanny Nubian/Boer goats, some bees and Guineas (for alarms) and a rooster. Luna finally started pulling her weight, not literally of course, but she'd stand in as security and roam and graze with the herd. Everyone was free range (no fences, no cages) so they were free to roam (only being put up at night), so Luna did end up actually fighting off and defending the herd from several lions.

We added an aquaponics system to the hydroponics and ordered a hundred catfish and tilapia fingerlings. The ratio of store-bought (mostly canned) to home produced food finally flipped with the infusion of milk, honey, eggs, produce, and meat. So, we started focusing our attention on canning and preserving, making soap, pottery, dishware, glassware, tools, paper products (paper towel, toilet paper, paper), and candles plus solar water heater and other renewable energy systems in order to get off the generator completely.

We finally locked down most common comforts also, like building furniture (indoor and out), making rugs and pillows, fabricating a bathtub, and constructing automatic feed and watering systems incorporating some permaculture. With all materials and objects now coming from our stage one and two recycle bin system, there was no reason to buy or order anything anymore. We even repurposed and recycled an old concrete mixer into a washing machine so Lucia could stop using that old-timey washboard.

As time went on, we began experimenting with producing our own fuel in the forms of ethanol, biodiesel, SWO, methane, and some hydrogen. We weren't really leaving anymore, so only a few gallons a month were needed, mostly just for the heavy lifting and hauling.

Although we worked hard every day, we always managed to find plenty of time to lounge around with a cold home-brewed beer, wine, or frozen margarita made from homegrown strawberries and homemade ice without sight or sound of civilization. Now that's homesteading at its finest!

Our babies (animals) had babies who had babies, and eventually, we stopped leaving the homestead entirely. It wasn't because we set a date or anything like that. We didn't up and one day say, "That's it! No more contact with humans!" We just had no need (or desire) any longer. Durations between trips got longer and longer. It became a sort of *see how long we could last* thing that developed into a *have you realized we haven't been out in ten months?* to *how long has it been now? Four years?* No news, no TV, no internet (we had an internet dish, but I turned it into a solar stove).

Instead, for fun and entertainment, we:

- Read. I never read before and didn't know about Dean Koontz, Isaac Asimov, Von Däniken, Douglas Adams, James Redfield, or Charles Lutwidge Dodgson.
- Spent time with my family, animals, and myself.
- Played invented and learned games: football, basketball, frisbee, frisbee golf, catch, and stargazing.
- Flew kites, ran, mountain biked, swam, rock climbed, hiked, canoed the Rio Grande.
- Exercised our minds (thinking—what a strange thing to do for enjoyment).
- Practiced yoga and calisthenics in the sand and dry river beds.
- Made our own 18-hole golf course (and a miniature one as well).
- Collected rocks, meteorites, Native American artifacts, dinosaur bones and other fossils, shark's teeth, and shells.

For the next six years, eight years since we started, we wouldn't see another person. We eventually built, manufactured, and did everything we needed to survive, thrive, and have fun. One day, and even now looking back I don't remember when, but we just kinda stopped needing to go to town. We had become 100% self-sufficient, completely off the grid. We were living life (very comfortably, I might add) without mortgages, taxes, bills, expenses, income, bank accounts, or jobs of any kind. Self-sufficiency, self-reliance, or whatever you want to call it, was sweet!

No matter what life had to throw at us, we never needed or thought to seek outside help. Health, dentistry, food, emergencies, entertainment—we did it all, and we did it together. Not once did either of us ever think we needed to go back, or that we couldn't do it. As time went on, needing society or anything it had to offer completely ceased. Not only the need, but the thought itself. We forgot about society!

We, of course, had our mishaps— well, mostly me (broken arm, gnarly gash on my right arm, a few snake and insect bites). Our animals would get sick and have broken legs and cuts as well, and we'd make penicillin or take care of them in some other way. We had to, of course; there was no taking anyone to the hospital or a vet. It got cold, it got hot. It rained, it stormed violently, there was drought, there was flooding, there was fire, but we would prevail . . . just me and Lucia, together!

Is There a Downside?

Life wasn't all wonderful. Being totally on our own was a huge adjustment. There were a lot more downs than I foresaw, which should be expected when you have such incredible ups. The area was famous for people getting lost and outlaws hiding out. With no emergency services or hospitals (and no one even knowing we were out there), we couldn't receive help even if we wanted it. People did "disappear" out in the Badlands of Terlingua and Big Bend. We were all the medical and security we had. This meant we kept sidearms, modified shotguns, and rifles with night vision scopes, stocked enough ammunition to last (until we learned how to make gunpowder and reload), and practiced frequently. We trained our dogs to alert us of trouble and kept our own skills in hand-to-hand combat and medical training fresh.

Although winters barely dropped below freezing, summers could top 110° daily. Also, we failed at almost everything we did, at least once, which became disheartening and borderline depressing, so mental health was as important to monitor as physical health. Out there we relied 100% on each other! I was her (and she my) husband (wife), best friend, physician, dentist, fireman, father/mother, co-worker, psychologist, lover, butcher, chief, security, opponent, teammate, the list goes on.

I've been asked in interviews, "What would you have done differently?" My reply: "Everything." Everything can be done better, differently, more efficiently. There's always room for improvement. For example, I would never build with wood again. Not having to be the fireman (twice) would have been one less thing to worry about. When you eliminate enough of the problems, the inefficiencies, then you're working less and have less to fight against, and it changes the game.

It's really about what you want more. Do you want to worry about your house catching on fire and your animals freezing, or do you want the house or goat you saw on TV, regardless if it's actually the best or most efficient option? Likely, you don't have to think about any of this; someone else puts out the fire and raises and butchers your meat. Someone else makes your fuel and produces your energy, provides you your water, and deals with your waste. But when it's all up to you, terms like *best* and *most efficient* dramatically affect the outcome of those decisions and significantly outweigh terms like *want* and *dream.*

Although we were eventually successful, the homestead was a learning experience for sure. Finding the motivation to push through all the unexpected roadblocks and detours seemed impossible. Lucia had her God. I wish I had had some all-powerful father figure to talk to and give all those problems to fix. It would have helped a lot! Instead, I had to rely on myself and her, and cry when my strength failed me.

In the end, we learned some life lessons the hard way. In time we discovered tricks for getting around things and had a few eureka moments. The experience definitely made us grow individually. As a couple and as humans, we sometimes grew apart and sometimes grew together. We changed our lives forever for better and for worse. It was dramatic, often traumatic, sometimes romantic, but always heavenly. We sacrificed so much to live with so little and it was the best choice we'd ever made!

Why Go Off the Grid?

"Why would anyone want to live this way?" This is an easy one. We had no bills, debt, utility or fuel costs, mortgage, taxes, or expenses of any kind. No traffic, no lines, no waiting rooms. There wasn't any noise, TV, smart phones or stress of that nature. We didn't own any clocks; there were no alarms; calendars were a thing of the past. We didn't get sick. We didn't answer to anyone or meet any schedules. We ate when we were hungry, not because a meal time said we should. We went to bed when we were sleepy and woke up when we were rested. Build your dream house and dream life, with your dream wife (or dream person[s]). Maybe the better question is why would people choose *not* to live this way?

Then there's the "people" aspect of why we left. Many of you will understand and relate to this (it's a feeling shared by a lot of Americans), others will have no idea. I won't get too much into this other than to give a simple quote:

> He who knows humanity, prefers solitude.
> –Imam Ali

What to Expect

Physically—Obviously, strength, endurance, and, consequently, appetite and calorie intake increase with work. But what you may find interesting is that other muscles like eyesight, hearing, balance, taste, and smell grow more and are heightened with use as well.

Ringing ears (no kidding), nausea, dizziness, and headaches were the first symptoms of leaving society. It was explained to me once why the brain makes up noises and the other symptoms when there's a lack of it in a new environment. I'll try to explain.

Social environments, especially cities, are inhospitable for humans. The human body and its senses are constantly being bombarded with an overabundance of high levels of sensory input not present anywhere in nature, to a point that the senses no longer need to function at high sensitivity. In response to these pollutants, the brain automatically turns the senses down in order to protect them (and our sanity). If this continues for a long enough time, the body says, "Brain, since you're no longer using or needing this material here, I'll break it down (atrophy) and divert the cells, energy, and resources to other areas that do."

If this didn't occur, we'd suffer from daily pain, dizziness, nausea, and headaches. If, for example, you were in an environment where you heard babies crying twenty-four hours a day, eventually your brain would say this is a sensory overload and turn down the receivers for that vibration. Construction workers experience this as do soldiers and airplane mechanics. Now, I'm not talking about the destruction of hair cells at higher decibels. Just the "I didn't even notice" feeling when your alarm clock is going off.

We are accustomed to ambient noise levels of about thirty decibels, so when you leave the pollution and find yourself void of the car alarms, alarm clocks, honking, televisions, sirens, cell phones, motors running, bus brakes, cars, people, lights, moving images, smells of air pollution, car emissions, cleaning products, and people, your brain tries to compensate by actually generating sounds, smells, and visions to be processed and perceived. It's a very strange experience when sober and watching rocks move, or you see a waterfall off a cliff's face where one doesn't exist. The brain forces other senses to comply and even creates data to compensate for the lack of it. Try spinning in circles for a couple minutes, then stop and look around the room as your brain causes the room to rotate right before your eyes. We'd hear people over intercoms calling our names clear as day, cars driving by, and kids laughing. It starts from within a few days to a week, lasts several weeks, and can be quite disturbing, even painful.

Eventually, our bodies turned the volume and sensitivity back up to hear more, and stole material from other areas to regrow the senses. You'll feel like your ears, nose, and eyes are open; you're reborn, awake, and wondering how you had ever come to be asleep.

> Why do my eyes hurt? You've never used them before.
> –Morpheus

Psychologically—You'll feel the withdrawal symptoms of your other life along with boredom like you've never felt. Most feel bored after retirement and look for another job because they've never experienced free time. This is caused by a carved mindset, molded by work occupying so much of your day over so many years of your life. A dramatic change in this pattern creates a feeling of emptiness and loss of worth. The more years you work, the longer it takes to adapt. It was six months until I got into a new routine, and I had only worked ten years (from ages fifteen to twenty-five). Now I can literally sit and do nothing, just enjoy time, take in the air, the mountains, and the sea without feeling bored or that I need to do something. I always enjoy life!

Verbally—Talking isn't an efficient means of communication in groups of less than three. It all but ceases with two and, I assume, would desist when alone. Instead, you form a new, slower, lower offshoot of your former dialect, not needing to communicate things quickly, loudly or completely since everything is shared. Word and sentence ends get chopped because once the word and sentence's meaning are understood, there's no reason to finish. It's a waste of energy. Ever heard someone say they finish each other's sentences and thoughts? It's that tenfold when you spend every minute of every day together for eight years. Of course, spelling and the ability to write letters and sentences degrade since you don't use them. Meanings of words change, new words are formed, and thought patterns link up, creating the closest thing to ESP I've seen. It's understandable. This happened to you; it happened to me; we've handled it this way the last twenty-seven times; how should we handle it this time? Oh, right, the same way. It takes communication away via sound almost completely. Things get quiet around year two.

Conceptually—This was the hardest to adapt back to when returning. Out there, time slows relatively. I'm not referencing the space between the sun rising and setting, but the actual units of measurement themselves and how your body acts and reacts to them. "This will take me a few minutes," turns into a few days since simple steps, or even standing up, slow down. Flying into Dallas to do an interview with the Travel Channel, I couldn't get into the elevator. I know, those doors close on everyone, but I'd be still standing there having not even started walking when they closed. The time it took the data that the doors were open and I should proceed to reach my cerebrum, to the time I sent signals to my appendages to do so was too slow. Good luck with crosswalks. The red hand is much faster than the walking fellow.

Spiritually—Typically, religion becomes a social practice, difficult to practice alone. Leaving society, though, doesn't need to mean leaving your religion or faith. Prayer, worship, and connections can continue as you create the time and space. The personal relationship you have with your God (or Gods) and your beliefs aren't altered by the environment in which you find yourself or the people (or lack of) with whom you surround yourself. So, we built Lucia her own chapel for some one-on-one time with the Big Guy.

Metaphysically—After year five, you start expanding into your aura, freed from your physical body and worldly self. (I kid, but what's funny is that that's okay to tell you, but I can't tell you that you can do your own surgery.) Just like how our physical senses expanded, there was some type of, let's say, growth of sensations, perhaps what some would call premonitions or sixth sense. Maybe it's just heightened instincts or gut feelings, which are designed to keep you alive, combined with the time and silence to hear them, but we'd often know things. All types of things from small (It will storm tomorrow), to big (Something's wrong), to weird (I need to go to the barn), and those things were always right.

Time—As discussed above, time works differently out there, and I don't just mean telling what hour of the day it is. What I mean is that time is a construct made by society that has no relevance away from society. I mean time passes differently, slower. For example, a couple married for twenty years in society isn't the same as a couple married for the same amount of time out. If we use the in-society couple as our base and calculate the actual amount of time they spent together during that twenty year span and compare it to the time spent together for the couple that spends literally twenty-four hours a day together, you'd find out that the couple that spends twenty-four hours together is equivalent to a couple that's been married in society for like two hundred years. That's an enormous amount of time together. Coincidentally enough, when you spend more time apart than together, you naturally grow apart. When you spend more time together than apart, you'll naturally grow closer together.

And just like anything else, the more time you spend doing something, the better you get at it. Spend more time playing baseball than mountain biking, you'll be a better baseball player, and vice versa. Spend five minutes a day, or 1% of your day, being a father, you'll be 1% of the father that you would if you spent 100% of your day with your kids. Of course, there are other elements, but time is a great starting point.

The point is, there's a direct relationship between how good you become at something and how good that something is based on the amount of time you spend doing it. Living in society, when time is a highly sought and paid for commodity, versus living out of society, off the grid, where you spend twenty-four hours a day with your spouse and children, well, it's a completely different ball game!

Health—An interesting thing happens when you leave society—you stop getting sick, since there are no door handles or money to spread infectious germs. Before leaving, I'd get a cold or the flu, but after we left, neither of us got sick, not even the sniffles, not once. I'm not saying that everyone who has lived cut off from society escaped sickness. It doesn't work that way, but I would say the chances of getting the common cold are hundreds, possibly thousands, of times less.

The transition from society to solitary living wasn't as much of a shock as I had expected. The bigger shock was coming back. In 2010 we returned, and within three days I became deathly sick. Within twenty-four hours a simple cold developed into pneumonia that landed me in the ER. I woke up two days later confused and too weak to even lift an arm. I had no idea what happened.

Because you never get sick out there, there's nothing to boost your antibodies and immune system. Your body dissolves the white army, which means when and if you ever go back, catching a common cold could be lethal. Today I have to take HIV immune booster injections and AZ-Packs and wear an N99 mask and glasses on planes, and this was before COVID-19!

Personal grooming: out there, away from society, there's no need for hair styles or even haircuts, shaving (legs or beards), brand name clothes, or any other form of societally instilled notions of self-beatification. All notions of impressing or competing with anyone flow away. There is still a basic need for a bath now and again, and your spouse prefers you still brush your teeth daily!

Living Conditions: I get told a lot "I could do that no problem! I could survive on my own without anyone! I rough it all the time in the wild!" I don't know of anyone that would be able to survive "roughing it," out there, without help, at least not for very long. It's easy to say that you can survive without others, without comforts when you're healthy, eating well, and full of energy. If you're depressed or low (not at the top of your game health-wise and physically), you need comforts and support systems to bring you back around. It takes practice and know-how to really live off-grid.

You need to be prepared to live in different conditions: in freezing weather, in blistering heat, with torrential rain coming down on you while you're eighteen feet up on a ladder. Expect to have dirt everywhere all the time! Living constantly in construction means there's always dirt and mud everywhere; it always gets inside no matter how careful you are. Expect to be cut up all the time, with bumps and bruises (keep plenty of iodine). Expect to take cold showers for months or not have any running water at all. Expect that your bed may be on the ground (for a time), your clothing may be "cleaned" in a river, your toilet is the side of a mountain, and you will be doing all the cooking. Expect to be bored for days, even weeks on end, and then to be run ragged with non-stop work. Exhaustion, dehydration, fatigue, soreness, crying, arguing, these are your new pastimes.

The Aftermath

MSNBC was the first to break the story on what we'd done, followed by Yahoo News, CNN, *Esquire Men's magazine*, The Travel Channel, Coast to Coast AM, The Jim Marrs Show, *Men's Health*, *Men's Journal*, and many more (including a few Australian and Russian News agencies), all of which resulted in a book deal for my first book *Apocalypse: How to Survive a Global Crisis*, (of which we seem to be having plenty of lately), along with this book and my newest books, *The End* series.

In 2010, we formed a Mexican-based non-profit where we provided long-term self-sustaining second response relief in the form of renewable energy, alternative fuel, natural and sustainable building methods, and general self-reliance to countries hit by disasters (manmade and natural), as well as consulted for local and foreign governments. I did a lot of lectures, seminars, and even spoke at several universities and events on the subject. I consulted on a few TV shows and Hollywood movies and even started a few self-sufficient communities in Peru, Belize, and one right in in the US.

Cost

This is a bit of an oxymoron, but yes, you can afford to have free electricity, fuel, food, and a free home. It does take an upfront investment, though. The following is a breakdown of the initial expenses we incurred before even leaving. These costs were exceptionally higher than what they should have been. We wasted a lot on mistakes because we just didn't know. Let me make it clear that if you use this book, it will NOT cost you even half of what it cost us.

THE FIRST WAVE—GETTING THERE

Item	Cost
Land	$30,000
New (old) truck	$16,000
Trailer	$4,000
Tractor	$10,000
Camper	$3,000
Tools	$2,000
Taxes	$1,800
TOTAL:	$66,800

THE SECOND WAVE—GETTING SETTLED

Item	Cost	Item	Cost
Fuel	$3,400	Plants	$200
Generator	$500	Material	$2,000
Skid loader	$8,000	Hardware & misc.	$1,800
Propane	$720	Appliances	$800
Water tanks	$3,000	Livestock	$750
Food	$8,400	2nd generator	$600
Tools	$1,000	Renewable energy	$3,500
Portable carport (workshop)	$250	compost toilet	$1,500
Pumps	$250	2nd compost toilet	$30
		TOTAL:	$36,750
		GRAND TOTAL:	$103,550

Financing

To the naked eye it may seem like a lot, but you need to factor in the cost of expenses you would have generated if you had continued working. Before leaving, I calculated how much I spent per year.

NORMAL LIFE EXPENSES

Item	Cost	Item	Cost	Item	Cost
Food at home	$3,347	Clothing	$1,816	Personal care	$481
Food away from home	$2,434	Transportation purchase	$3,397	Reading	$130
Alcohol	$459	Transportation finance charge	$323	Education	$905
Housing shelter	$7,998	Transportation gas & oil	$1,598	Tobacco	$288
House utilities	$2,927	Transportation auto operations	$2,042	Misc.	$690
House operations & supplies	$1,547	Other transportation	$441	Gift & contributions	$1,408
House furnishing & equipment	$1,646	Health insurance	$1,332	Insurance	$390
Clothing	$1,816	Recreation & entertainment	$2,218	Pensions & SS	$4,433
				TOTAL:	$42,250

$42,250 x 6 years = $253,500. $103,650 - $253,500 = $149,850 net gain in the black.

That amount is almost half the cost of working every day; and that doesn't even include my time. This can be calculated as gains of worth to me (i.e., I have 1 extra hour of life) or monetary (I get paid $20/hour; ergo, that's how much my time is worth)

GAINS OF WORTH

Activity	Gain (Hrs./6yr) (lifetime)	Gain ($)
Commute	45 (5mo)	$900
Work	3,600 (17.3yrs)	$72,000
Lines	260 (2.3yrs)	$5,200
On hold	23 (1.6mo)	$380
Getting ready	150 (9mo)	$3,000
Clothing (buy/wash/iron)	80 (5.5mo)	$1,600
TOTAL:	34.5mo (121.1yrs)	$109,680

If calculated monetarily, the total gain is $259,530 x 2 (or more) people = $519,060. But there's no bank that's going to loan you money for leaving their system, even if that figure is in the black. You'll have to come up with the funds on your own.

Why We Came Back

We came back (at least partially back) for several reasons. The most important of which was to teach others to do what we did. After making a lot of money early on in my life, and then giving and getting rid of it all, I'm now a staunch believer that everything should be free and available to everyone. Things like copyrights, trade secrets, patents, capitalism, and materialism hinder humanity and development, despite what they told us about free and competitive markets. The fastest and healthiest way to advance is to share openly. If we know how someone else builds and does something, we can assist and improve on it. In fact, major corporations like Google, Apple, Facebook, GE, Procter & Gamble, BMW, Southwest, Sears, Chevron, MasterCard, Dell, AOL, Amazon, Toyota, Twitter, and even Microsoft (and of course Firefox, Linux, Android, WordPress, and Red Hat) are realizing and utilizing this mindset now.

So, we came back to help this movement and to help others. Unfortunately, though, if you're going to interact in a capitalistic society, you have to, at least somewhat, have something to do with money again. It's a paradox . . . It takes a lot of money to destroy money! But we learned a lot about ourselves, animals, and nature. Most importantly, we learned how to treat living things and how to live in balance and with respect toward everyone and everything on this planet. This go around is going to be much, much different!

Where we are now

We're back! Currently, besides traveling a lot, doing relief work, book signings, and speaking engagements, we're involved with several free-source, open-source, free-economy, and sharing-economy projects, including our Free Food Stores which combine grocery stores with an enormous indoor aquaponics in existing abandoned factories and warehouses in the US (currently Detroit) and abroad. Food, like water and air, grows everywhere, free, so, we're actually doing nothing at all—a complete 180° from doing everything ourselves!

I have probably the oddest profession now. I get paid nothing to show people what they need to do to not make money at all, because really, they have no idea how. We've been taught our entire life that money is so important. To date we've managed to bring self-sufficiency to people and communities all over the world, and we hope to continue.

Finally, we are working to help animals as a direct result of our love for Luna, our once wild and crazy burro. She was the first inhabitant of our homestead. She trained me on how to train (and love) animals. Luna got old and passed on shortly before we left, and we buried her in the exact place she stood the first time she saw us so many years before.. She was the one animal we never bought or adopted, but rather she adopted us. She lived on that land first as a wild burro. She opened her home and her heart to us, every one of us: me, my wife, the chickens, turkeys, ducks, dog and cats, the goats, guineas, rabbits, and the fish. Thanks, Luna, for all the love and tenderness and hope you gave us.

In honor of Luna, we've been spending most of our energy and time building a completely self-sufficient, off-grid, sustainable animal refuge in hopes of rescuing and helping animals that are currently being kept and caged in zoos, circuses, and as pets and private collections. We call it The Luna Foundation. We believe no living sentient being should be locked up. Everything living, every sentient being, including pets, should be free, as free as Luna. I'm glad she never used that stupid corral I built! Luna, please forgive us for being human. And rest in peace.

Chapter 2: Common Tools and Practices

In a world full of ways to make or acquire new and used stuff, there's no reason to work harder and more dangerously because you don't have the right tools or equipment. I've taught hundreds of workers, interns, volunteers, and workshop participants, and most have no clue of basic tool names, let alone how to use them properly, safely, and efficiently. For example, you didn't know that the most optimal angle for a shovel to obtain the most penetration for energy spent is 30%, or that it needs to be sharpened regularly, or even the best way to use a wheelbarrow.

You've lived watching people and TV showing improper, inefficient, and unsafe work habits and techniques. "Who cares?" If you're only using the tools for a couple hours a day, not you. But when laboring to build a futon, house, grey water system, or other major task, these minute bits of wasted energy and time, which we all know equals money, add up significantly and quickly, ultimately offsetting the savings of doing everything yourself, especially after thousands of holes or tens of miles of wheelbarrow pushing.

Know the least resistant work methods. They're critical so you save money and energy and don't injure or kill yourself or someone else. In the following pages, I'm going to review some basics that someone should have taught you a long time ago, starting with this:

With the exception of your power tools, don't buy brand name, especially not for disposables like saw blades, paint brushes, drill bits, and the like. Everything is made in China anyway, (yes, even German tools), and Harbor Freight has lifetime warranties just like everyone else. Besides, brand-name companies can and do choose when—or if—they'll honor their "lifetime" warranties.

Safety

With less hand tool use and more power, the greater the need for safety gear and safe practices. I'm not one for going overboard to the point where safety is hindering more than helping. But glasses, banded earplugs, and leather gloves have, at least for me, stopped bloodshed at least a dozen times each, specifically when used during those "this will only take a minute" moments.

If it's your first time with a specific type of machine, don't be afraid of it, but read the safety instructions. What not to do is in there.

Use common sense.

Dirt Work

Post holes: There are three types of tools you can use to dig post holes: clam shell post-hole digger, sharpshooter shovel, and auger. Use a hand or gas powered auger in soft soil for deep holes, a clam shell for anything up to 4 ft, and a sharp shooter for holes 1–2 ft deep. Use a rock bar to dislodge obstacles, and a cordless Sawzall with a pruning blade on roots.

Moving dirt: If you're moving dirt without a cart, for short distances, loft conglomerated clumps in an arced throw to create a pile, or spray dirt by fanning the shovel to evenly distribute it. For distance between a few feet and 10–20 ft, a wheelbarrow is best. For distances between 10–100 ft, use a cart or skid loader. 100 ft–1000 ft, use a skid loader. 1000 ft-plus, use a dump truck or dump trailer.

Hoeing: Hoeing doesn't take skill, just arm and back power. For bigger areas, use a metal rake, concrete mover, or bolt a ⅛ x 16-in piece of 4-in flat bar to any of the above. The wider the tool, the shallower the cut, whereas the narrower the tool, the deeper the cut.

Post Hole: auger

Post Hole:
clam shell post-hole digger

Moving dirt

Hoeing

Wheelbarrow: Wheelbarrows are energy hogs; if at all possible, for anything other than the smallest of distances, go with carts, Gorilla being the best. And always pull a cart, wheelbarrow, or dolly, leaving the pushing only for actual dumping. Just try pushing one over anything but flat terrain. What happens when you hit an obstacle? It stops abruptly, you topple over, everything dumps out, and everyone—but you—laughs. Now pull it and compare the difference in energy used.

Tamper: Tamping dirt is required before laying slabs for homes, driveways, walkways, sheds, etc. Tamping earth by hand is another energy hog though, causing back, arm, and neck fatigue. Use a gas-powered tamper whenever possible, leaving the hand tamper (page 65) for the smallest of tasks. Trust me, you'll wish you did after a couple hours of hand tamping.

Wheelbarrow

Tamper

Measuring and Leveling

Measuring tape: Get four or more cheap measuring tapes since they always go missing and rust or jam quickly. Another handy addition, especially for long distances or heights, is a laser distance meter. Basically, the laser version of a measuring tape.

Bubble level: Everything, and I mean everything in home constructions needs to be level or plumb. Do yourself a favor and skip bubble levels altogether, opting for more accurate laser levels. Otherwise, in a bubble level, the bubble needs to be not just inside the lines, but entirely in the middle. Ninety-nine percent of people get it inside the lines and say, "It's level!" On the same note, there's no such thing as "almost perfectly level" or "pretty level," it's level or it's not. It's not rocket science.

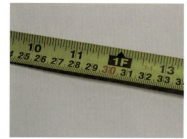
Measuring tape

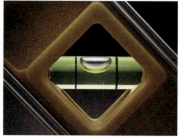
Bubble level

Laser level: You can't go wrong by investing in a few good laser levels. 360° rotary levels are best for doing land surveys and leveling slabs, countertops, rafters, walls, etc., whereas a self-leveling crossline laser is best for laying straight rows of brick or block, hanging sheetrock, doors, or anything that requires a vertical and horizontal line. Finally, whichever laser you choose, if you don't want to work in the dark, I highly recommend going with green lasers.

String: Measuring with string seems simple enough, but when you're running 1,000 ft through weeds, trees, and brush, a day of construction quickly turns into a day of untying knots and throwing string away. The key is to never turnaround or backtrack. Get a kite winding grip wheel or build a reel and spend the extra time to reroll before moving . . . it's a difference of minutes versus hours.

Water level: Laser, transit, and bubble levels are great for approximating and laying out sites, but for precision, nothing tops a water level.

String

Water level

Electrical and Plumbing

Circuits: With circuits, never exceed 75% of the fuse's or breaker's rated ability. For example, use 15-amp or less on a 20-amp circuit breaker. This entails installing 15-amp rated outlets and wiring for each 20-amp circuit.

Electrical boxes: For lath and plaster applications, locate electrical boxes ¾ in, or the plaster's thickness, beyond the wall plane so the plate sits flush.

Piping: For both electrical and plumbing pipes, avoid copper, steel, and PVC. Select low psi poly pipe, gray PVC or EMT conduit for electrical, with barbed fittings, and with clamps for water. They're easier, cheaper, quicker, and the least troublesome. And keep drain inclinations at ¼ in per ft or greater for lines with a diameter less than 3 in, ⅛ in per ft or greater for 3–6-in dia lines, and 1⁄16 in per ft or greater for 6-in dia and larger lines.

Electrical boxes

Piping

Drilling

Cordless drill: A cordless drill is a must, and the market is flooded, bringing prices down considerably. Go with a good, heavy-duty, 14v or larger, ⅜-in, compact, lightweight model. DeWalt is the best and is longer lasting.

> NOTE: For the price, though, you could buy 15 cheap drills that may last just as long, not to mention you'll have fifteen times the batteries and chargers and a lot more electronics to put in your stage two bins (page 25) when they're worn out! Welcome to the disposable age.

Corded drill: Cordless drills are great for small jobs (90% of a drill's work will be on small jobs). For larger jobs, a ½-in, heavy-duty drill is needed since torque drains batteries quickly.

Impact drivers: For drilling through masonry or compacted earth, impact drills are the only option, with rotary impacts being the best for chiseling and breaking.

Rotary hammer drills: Rotary hammers are a must anytime you're building or dealing with any form of masonry building material.

Drill press: Press drills are best for steel work or parts that need precise, straight holes where bending breaks bits.

Bits: Use the correct bit for the material: 118° for masonry, glass, tile, and soft metals; 135° for hard metals; 90° for hardwood; 60° for wood and plastic. Some types of bits are all purpose, brad point, Forstner, augers, spade, reamers, and unibits, some of which have special uses. To prevent dulling, use lower speeds for harder materials, and invest in a sharpener and a few ⅛–2-in unibits.

Cordless drill

Rotary hammer drills

Drill press

Bits

Cutting

Saw blades: There are as many saw blades as there are drill bits and a lot more saw types. Some are necessities; some just make the job easier. Again, match the saw and blade with the task and material.

Circular saw: Use a compact, cordless 5½-in circular saw for cutting or ripping smaller material like wood, plastic, metal, and masonry, and 7¼-in corded for larger.

Table saw: A table saw is a critical component for individual or repetitive work. Get the biggest available with a portable stand.

Miter saw: A miter saw is another critical addition to any construction project. Miter saws make quick work of lumber, PVC pipe, tubing, anything that requires a straight perpendicular cut. It also cuts in any degree up to 90°. Do yourself a favor, get a miter saw.

Jig and band saws: Jigsaws and band saws are used for odd shapes and versatility, and are able to cut curved cuts where other saws can't. If you're working with metals, a band saw is a necessity.

Saw blades

Circular saw

Table saw

Jig and band saws

Sawzalls or reciprocating saws: Sawzalls, also called reciprocating saws, are for hard-to-reach or limited-access areas. But they're also great in landscaping on branches and roots when used with an arbor blade.

Chainsaw: There are both gas and electric chainsaws. Either way, get a good brand like Stihl with multiple chains and an electric sharpener.

Sawzalls or reciprocating saws

Chainsaw

Angle grinder: Like a Sawzall, angle grinders are versatile and allow easy access, and they cut, grind, and sand numerous materials.

Chop saw: A chop saw is another must for cutting any amount of metal. Try hacking through 1-in Sch 80 steel pipe without one.

Blades: There are different blades for every tool and every material. TPI (teeth per inch) works the same for all of them though. For softwood, 6 TPI; hardwood, plastic, and PVC, 10 TPI; plastic, 20 TPI; soft metal, 10 TPI; medium steel, 14–18 TPI; hard steel less than ⅛ in thick, 18 TPI; hard steel more than ⅛ in–³⁄₁₆ in thick, 24 TPI; hard steel ¼ in thick, 32 TPI; and steel greater than ¼ in thick should be cut with a cutting wheel or cutting torch.

Cutting wheels: Cutting wheels that are attached to an angle grinder make a chop saw portable, giving us the ability to cut metal and concrete in the field. For concrete, use 40-grit silicon carbide, and for metal, 40-grit aluminum oxide.

Hand saws: I don't use or own any hand saws, and I don't think I've ever known someone that has, maybe my grandparents. I've never had the need for one. They've become like hand drills, outdated and obsolete, and will soon be sold in antique shops.

Axes and hatchets: Axes are another useless tool for the homesteader who's working efficiently. Build a hydraulic wood splitter instead. A machete, on the other hand, makes short work of branches, brush, and small trees.

Utility knife: Utility knives are the most used, versatile tools in your artillery. Get an offset grip with blade storage.

Angle grinder

Chop saw

Cutting wheels

Utility knife

Miscellaneous Tools

Ladders: Only use A-frame or extending ladders made of heavy-duty materials, aluminum for non-electrical, fiberglass for electrical.

Scaffolding: For scaffolding, set two A-frame ladders side-by-side with a 2 x 6–10-in cee purlin in between, or splurge and buy a nice set from a big box store. Another option would be to build your own.

Lifts: For larger homes, or when doing anything that requires carrying heavy or awkward material up a ladder or scaffold, scissor lifts, man lifts, and other lifts make sense.

Hoses: I don't use pneumatic tools like hand tools, air tools, hoses, and compressors. They're a thing of the past. Everything's gone to battery power. You will work a lot with garden hoses though. Do yourself a favor; if you listen to nothing else in this book, listen to this . . . save yourself a *lot* of headache and skip the "brass" (they're not brass) quick disconnect fittings you find in big box stores and go with ¾-in camlock fittings for twice the price and 100 times less headaches and leaks.

Ladders

Scaffolding

Lifts

Hoses

Chapter 3: Going Green

Going green has become a trendy term, used to impress, but it's the epitome of efficiency. Reusing, repurposing, and recycling, as well as conserving and using energy-efficient devices is critical to any level of self-reliance. Unlike most changes, adapting eco-friendliness only requires dedication to forming new routines. By unlearning learned concepts, breaking wasteful habits, and seeing from other angles, you modify your mind. It's *that* day when you can say, "I've gone green!"

Carbon Footprint

We'd like to leave a better place for our children, at least in theory. The quickest and easiest answer is to purchase carbon credits or offsets. The money goes towards the removal of carbons from the atmosphere, essentially paying for the carbons we generate. It's more crucial, beneficial, and rewarding, though, to take action yourself, locally and physically. But in reality, we really don't have time. The good news is you don't have to be an environmentalist to combat your own CO_2. All you need is a guide . . .

REPURPOSING

Being self-sufficient, we repurposed everything for need, regardless of whether we liked the planet or not. This book is packed with projects, objects, and ideas on the topic. Before recycling or trashing something, think, "Could this serve another purpose?" For example, consider those cheap plastic hangers that come with clothing . . . industrial strength chip-bag clips! Got cassette tapes? Miles of plastic line. Have crazy cords? Stuff them inside toilet paper rolls!

Through repurposing, we've been able to greatly reduce our personal waste footprint. Take a tire for example. We reuse it as much as possible, patching and plugging. When we can't patch it anymore, we cut it into pieces and make sandals, washers, grommets, or bushings, eventually shredding it into mulch, cooking it into charcoal to be used as fuel or biochar, or cooking it into tar as a fuel source. When you factor in the other 16,104 items the average American throws away annually, the possibilities are endless. It is too expensive for companies to consider, but free for us. Be careful, though, repurposing has become another one of those "trendy" time spenders, often ending in more time, effort, money, and CO_2 spent than what you're trying to save.

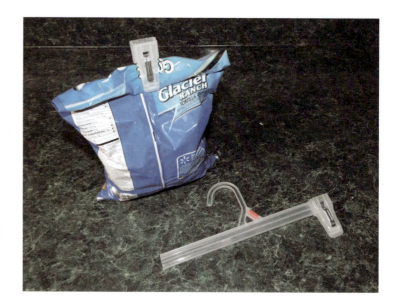

Glass to Aggregate

Glass in aggregate form is beautiful. If you've ever seen glass that's washed up on shore and has been tumbled in the sand, where all the edges are rounded and only the stone is left, you'll know what I'm talking about. Throughout the book, we use glass aggregate in many ways, everything from landscaping to fireplaces to simple decoration.

MATERIALS
(2–2.5) 5-gallon buckets of glass bottles, panes, vases, dishes, etc.
1½–2 gallons of water
½ in or larger chunks of scrap steel
2 charcoal briquettes
flat plastic bucket or mortar tray
2 x 3-ft piece of rabbit wire
weed barrier or tarp
rag

TOOLS
3½ ft³ concrete mixer
cart

WARNING: Never tumble glass dry; the dust is horrendous.

1. Add (2–2.5) 5-gallon buckets of glass bottles, panes, vases, dishes, etc., and 1½–2 gallons of water to a 3½ ft³ concrete mixer.

    NOTE: You can also dedicate an old front loader washing machine to tumble glass, which not only tumbles and washes everything in one step but is also a lot quieter.

2. Add a few ½ in or larger chunks of scrap steel and (optional) 2 charcoal briquettes as grit to prevent slip.

3. For pane or stained-glass windows, glass working, or forming glassware (page 53), let run for ½–1 hour. For bead work, landscaping or just general decorations, run for 2–4 hours, or longer if you're using a slush mill, which makes smaller and rounder pieces.

IMPORTANT: Make sure the mixer is almost level. You want it leaning as far forward as possible without everything coming out.

NOTE: To reduce noise, switch out the first bolt in each blade for ¼-in eyebolts, the eye out, with 2 nuts and washers, and use bungee cords to secure a piece of wood over the mouth to plug it.

4. Place a flat plastic bucket, like a mortar tray, underneath and dump the glass through a 2 x 3 ft piece of rabbit wire. A utility cart also works great and provides easy dumping.

5. Pull out necks, bottle caps, labels, etc., then wash the glass with a spray nozzle to separate powder. Or you can just let the rain rinse it all off.

6. Lay a weed barrier or tarp and spread the glass as landscape bedding or mulch, or use in concrete (page 62) or other aggregate applications. Pour wash through a rag, tie, and hang the dust and any cullet to dry for glass work ("Forming Glassware," page 53).

Tires to Mulch

Anytime we can recycle something that would otherwise end up in landfills is a good thing. Over one billion tires end up in landfills around the world annually.[2] Tire mulch can be used anywhere regular mulch can, the only difference being it'll last forever!

MATERIALS
tires
liquid dish soap

TOOLS
Sawzall with coarse (wood) and fine (metal) blades
micro hammer mill, woodchipper, or scrap metal shredder

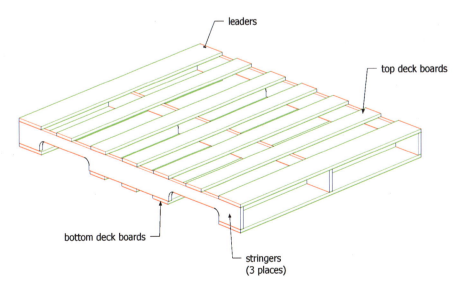

1. Cut tires into 1-in wide strips using the Sawzall and coarse blade, and using the dish soap as lube.

   NOTE: If you're using a lot of mulch, a scrap metal shredder will make quick work of it.

2. Remove the steel cable using the fine blade and feed the rubber strips through a micro hammer mill or, better, a Patriot chipper. Wash with dish soap and lay in the sun to dry.

Pallets to Lumber

Millions of pallets that are only used once are thrown away daily. Pallets, whether they be whole or in pieces, always come in handy. There are several sizes and types of pallets, ranging from 48 x 42 in to 42 x 42 in, 48 x 48 in, and everything in between, all broken down into either two-way or four-way loading based off of the number of sides a forklift can pick it up from. Some of the more common ones you'll see and are available to you for pick up are double-faced, double-winged, flush, four-way stringer, non-reversible, reversible, single faced, single-winged. You may even come across a few solid deck, skid, and block pallets, and maybe even some plastic pallets. The most common, of course, being the four-way stringer pallet, where the outside stringers are notched to allow forklift access.

What do we do with them? Anything and everything you can think of. There are a million free pallet project plans online. But before you can do anything with them, you need to know the anatomy of a pallet.

Basically, there are just four parts to a stringer pallet: top deck boards, bottom deck boards, lead boards, and stringers.

The cargo sits on the top deck boards, which measure around 3½ in wide, and the outer most boards, called lead boards, are slightly wider at 5¼ in and are usually slightly damaged from being hit with forks and run into things. Both top deck and lead boards get some wear from boxes and cargo shifting on top of them but are generally in the best condition for projects. I think the wear shows character!

Bottom deck boards, and even the bottom lead boards, are typically the same width as the top deck and lead boards but are always more damaged and worn since they're constantly sliding on the ground. Who knows in what chemicals, feces, and filth these slats have been sitting in. These slats, along with the stringers, get cut off, broken up and go into my firewood, charcoal, or wood gas bins.

Stringers are two-bys and are located on the sides and in the center, in between the top and bottom deck boards, and they create the space where the forks slide in. They're harder to work with due to the cutouts.

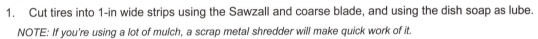
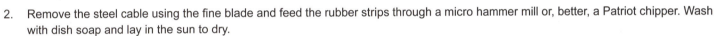

leaders

top deck boards

bottom deck boards

stringers (3 places)

Since slats are not all perfect, you'll need two to three times more pallets than calculated for your project to have a reasonable selection. If you'd like to know what your pallet has been used for, or what chemicals or pesticides it's been doused with, look up the two-line, ten-plus digit IPPC (International Plant Protection Code) label stamped on the side.

Where do you get pallets? You can collect free pallets from hardware or lumber stores, grocery stores, restaurants, and gas stations—basically any store. Companies typically don't care about their pallets and view them as garbage. Most companies have to pay the city to dispose of them, and many times they're more than happy to give them away. Just watch out for pallets painted "blue," which generally means that they need to be turned back into the warehouse for a deposit; you could get charged with theft for taking them. There are so many free pallets laying around, though, that there's really no need to mess with the returnable ones. But if in doubt, ask before you take.

Once you have your pallets, you'll want to break them down to harvest the slats without further damaging the pallet, which can be very tricky. Your first mindset will be to just attack the pallet with a crowbar and sledgehammer. Trust me, this doesn't work at all and will only serve to destroy the pallet—which if you're only wanting firewood, great—and it will damage you in the process since most pallets are made from a hardwood like oak and nailed together using annular nails that have threads rolled onto the shank, which are basically headless, permanent screws.

I've tried several methods to disassemble pallets using several types of tools to cut, pry, and beat these nails. Your most efficient option is to buy or build yourself a pallet pry bar, but you still have to deal with the nails.

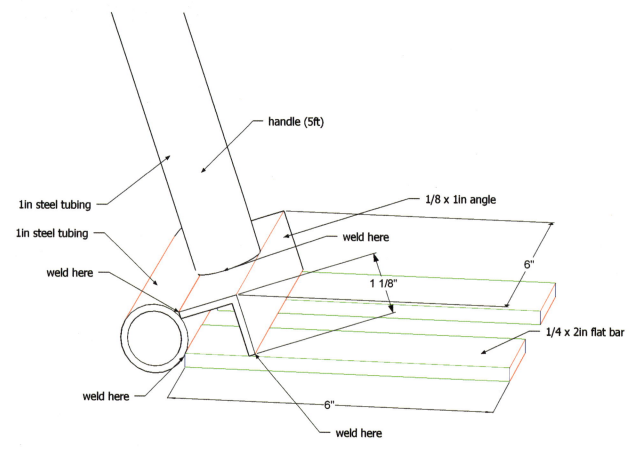

Otherwise, the simplest way, without buying or building any specialty tools, is to simply cut through the nail shanks from underneath each stringer and slat joint, using a Sawzall with a metal blade.

MATERIALS
pallets
cinderblocks

TOOLS
circular saw
prybar
framing hammer
miter saw
shop press

1. Flip the pallet upside down, and using a circular saw, cut all bottom deck boards even with the stringers, which will leave pieces of the bottom deck boards nailed to the stringers. After the boards are removed, pry the final pieces of the bottom deck boards off the stringers.
2. Flip the pallet right side up, place a cinderblock under either lead board, and hammer on the stringer. Repeat for all top deck boards.
3. Flip slats over and tap out nails. Trim split and chipped ends in a miter saw and separate the slats into piles based on width, length, color, and thickness. This will help greatly for storage or when it's time to pick slats for your project.
4. Clean up the bottom deck boards and stringers in the same manner, or using a shop press, break stringers and bottom deck boards into manageable sizes for a fireplace, wood burning stove, charcoal generator, or wood gas bins.

Stuff to Stuffing

Random items, stuffed animals, pillows, shipping and packaging materials, junk mail, and garbage from around the house can be used as filler for furniture, bedding, mattresses, pillows, paper making, or even home insulation. For home insulation, though, it's critical (and code) that we fireproof it first.

- For filler, cut open and extract polyester fill, down, feathers, wheat husks, kapok fibers, or other stuffing from couch cushions, bean bags, pillows, coats, extruded polystyrene, packing peanuts, and other stuffed goods. Place any extra in your stage two bins (page 25).
- Jeans are some of the strongest, longest lasting materials made, so it's a shame we discard them for having stains or a hole or broken zipper. Cut them up and use them as rags, or feed them through a micro scrap metal shredder or woodchipper to turn them into stuffing.
- Expanded and extruded polystyrene (page 28), also known as Styrofoam, can be processed into granules for reusing.
- Paper from phone books, textbooks, library books, mail, and any other paper products can be shredded for stuffing in a micro scrap metal shredder or woodchipper, or made into cellulose fiber (page 27) for paper, toilet paper, or paper towel making (page 37).

T-Shirts to Yarn

This is one of my favorite projects—well, anytime you make new things out of garbage is good times. Wherever you use yarn, you can substitute for T-shirt yarn . . . clothes, rugs, pot holders, blankets, you name it.

MATERIALS
T-shirts

TOOLS
fabric scissors

1. Flatten a T-shirt or similar shirt, and with a sharp pair of fabric scissors, cut a straight line across the chest, armpit to armpit.

   NOTE: If you're going to be doing several of these, I'd highly suggest getting rotary cutter and mat to keep your cuts straight.

2. Cut sleeves off, on both sides of the seam and at the hem, along with the neck and bottom seam.

3. Fold either side of the lower piece ¾ of the way over and, starting from fold, cut parallel to previous cuts, ½–¾ in away (½ in on thicker garments), leaving 1 in uncut on the opposite side.

4. Open shirt, then pull and center the uncut section on the right (if you're right-handed) with cut loops lying on the left. To start your yarn, starting from the very right side, cut from the outside up and in, angling towards the first loop.

5. Now just connect each loop, right to left, until you reach the end. Cut last loop up and out leaving you with one long cut of material.

IMPORTANT: It's critical that you keep the loops here separate. If you tangle them up in a big pile, you'll never get them unknotted. It helps to, after each cut, throw that loop over to the right-hand side, and as that pile grows, stretch it out straight on the floor, or have someone else completing the following step and rolling it into a ball at the same time.

6. Starting from either end, grab a small section and stretch it slightly (not much) until it curls over on each side equally, rolling in on itself. Repeat until you reach the end.

7. Repeat for the top section, folding it in half and cutting ¾ length strands until you reach the neck. Then open the entire thing up and cut every other loop until you're left with 1 long strand. Round corners, pull, stretch, and roll.

8. The sleeves are modified in the same fashion as the bottom section, since they're just smaller tubes.

9. Sew or tie all ends from every section together. (Knots can be hidden in knitting.) Knit as described in Chapter 4.

NOTE: I generally use non-organic clothes for yarn and other fabrics and cotton (socks, underwear, pants, shirts) for rags since cotton soaks liquids and is easier and better to clean with than plastics.

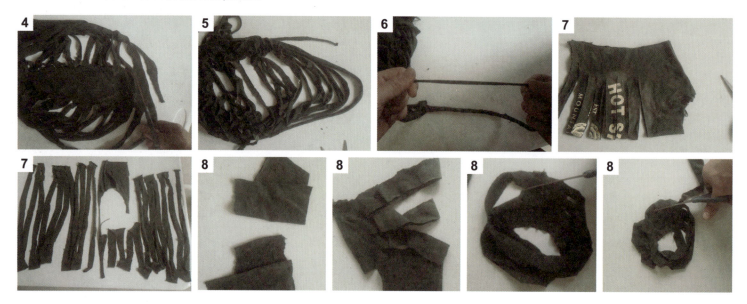

Cans to Pigments

We use cans and other metals for all kinds of things from inset and wall mounted light fixtures and lamp shades to 18-gauge sheet metal. To use cans for sheet metal, see Rocket Stove (page 156). But the smallest of pieces, along with other soft and hard metals, are placed in a chemical bath with oxygen and carbon dioxide injections to promote oxidation, or corrosion, turning them into base elements like oxides and carbonates, which are pigments for coloring. These pigments can then be mixed into fillers, binders, and preservatives for homemade paints (page 57).

For all colors, we need the three primaries and black and white:

Red

MATERIALS
iron or steel metal scraps
5-gal bucket
1 gallon water
4 c potassium hydroxide or acetic acid

TOOLS
burn pit (page 190) or UDS
pH meter
wooden or plastic stirrer
5-gal paint filter, coffee filter, or fine cloth
1-gal paint cans
Airtight container with a desiccant packet (page 248)

1. Fill a burn pit (page 190) or the bottom shelf of a UDS with iron or steel metal scraps and burn off any coatings, paints, and oils.

2. Fill a 5-gallon bucket with 1 gallon of water per 4 c of potassium hydroxide or acetic acid and add scraps.

NOTE: You can also use cuprous oxide if you want to get a red color. You can see the process in Homemade Solar Cells (page 139).

3. Check and annotate the pH, and recheck weekly, adding acids or alkalis as needed, mixing with a wooden or plastic stirrer. As material breaks down, add and stir in more.
4. To harvest, remove large metal pieces; mix and filter suspended sediment through a 5-gallon paint filter, coffee filter, or fine cloth.
5. Replace the iron oxide powder in the bucket, then dehydrate by cooking in an oven or in a solar dehydrator (page 137) for a couple hours, and repeat. Transfer the powder into a 1-gallon paint can. Sift the oxide and store in an airtight container with desiccant packet (page 248).

NOTE: A flat piece of sheet metal with 2 corners bent in, forming a funnel, works best for scooping the powder on one side and pouring it into the paint can through the other.

Blue Green

MATERIALS
5-gal bucket
2 gallons water
Copper
8 c sodium carbonate

TOOLS
burn pit (page 190) or UDS
pH meter
wooden or plastic stirrer
5-gal paint filter, coffee filter, or fine cloth
1-gal paint cans
airtight container with a desiccant packet (page 248)

1. Repeat the above steps, placing copper in the 5-gallon bucket with 2 gallons of water and 8 c of sodium carbonate (page 59) to make copper carbonate.

Yellow

MATERIALS
clay (page 59)

TOOLS
ball mill, industrial blender, or hammer
5-gal paint filter, coffee filter, or fine cloth
1-gal paint cans
airtight container with a desiccant packet (page 248)

1. For yellow, we just use clay (page 59), or loam if available. Pulverize the clay or loam in a ball mill, industrial blender, or with a hammer, then sift and store.

Black

MATERIALS
charcoal (page 61)

TOOLS
ball mill, industrial blender, or hammer
5-gal paint filter, coffee filter, or fine cloth
1-gal paint cans
airtight container with a desiccant packet (page 248)

1. Blend or mill charcoal.
2. And then, as described in Red, sift and store.

White

MATERIALS

gypsum

TOOLS

ball mill, industrial blender, or hammer
1-gal paint cans
airtight container with a desiccant packet (page 248)

1. Blend or mill gypsum. And then sift and store.

Secondaries

MATERIALS

colored pigments

TOOLS

5-gal bucket or 1-qt container
drill with painter mixer

1. For mixing larger quantities of pigments, use 5-gallon buckets and a paint mixer in a drill. Otherwise, for smaller batches, a 1-qt container will work perfectly.

   WARNING: It's important to always mix pigments in a sealed container and leave plenty of time for dust to settle. Inhaling or ingesting can cause pigment poisoning. Wear a NIOSH-approved toxic dust respirator when handling or applying pigment.

2. Experiment with colors, or mix red, yellow, blue, white, and black to get the following colors.
   - Brown 1:1:1:0:0
   - Green 0:3:2:6:4
   - Pink 1:0:0:1:0
   - Orange 2:4:0:7:0
   - Light purple 1:0:1:2:0
   - Tan 2:1:0:6:0
   - Dark grey 0:0:0:2:7
   - Light grey 0:0:0:2:1

3. Add the pigment ratio to a 1-qt butter or ice-cream container with a ¼-in hole in the lid. Place the eggbeater attachment of an electric hand mixer through the hole, replace the lid, and mix on low for 1 minute. Shake contents from the edges and repeat four times.

4. Using a funnel, fill PETE bottles, jars, or other clear containers. Replace the lids, mark the containers with a name or a letter and number to indicate the color or mix—for example, Becky's Beige or B2-7, which stands for batch 2, color #7—and document the mix ratio.

   NOTE: Keeping the exact formula for each color is important in case you run out or want to adjust the shade.

5. To use, you can mix the pigments into homemade paint (page 57). Or you can use them straight, but how depends on the size of the application. Touch-up paint guns work nicely for small applications; pneumatic or electrical paint guns for medium-large; and sand blasting guns for very large. You don't need much; a little pigment goes a long way.

RECYCLING

> *"Recycling a single aluminum can saves enough energy to power a TV for three hours!"*
> *–CT.gov[3]*

Recycling is just another method of repurposing. It's a preliminary step, where the object goes through an energy intensive process that breaks it into its smallest components to build new things that will be used for a little while before either being repurposed, recycled again, or thrown away. The process doesn't put a stop to waste, but it does drastically slow it. However, remember that no matter how environmentally low-impact it is to use recycled materials, if you don't already have them on-hand or on-site, the amount of gasoline used to acquire them nullifies any benefits.

Where to Recycle

Curbside pickup is obvious. If not available, local recycling centers accept and sometimes pay for your "garbage." Metal cans are accepted in almost every city, and scrap yards will purchase any metal, offering more if it is stripped down.

What to Recycle

- batteries
- toner cartridges
- metals
- organic material
- books
- nails/screws
- clothing
- wood
- furniture
- cooking oil
- drywall
- automotive oil
- wire
- electronics

Everything can be recycled. Don't accept that only "certain types of plastics" can or that chemicals or batteries can't. Companies say that and falsely label items as "non-recyclable" because certain things aren't profitable. Recycling companies aren't trying to save the environment; they're trying to make money. It's a lucrative business since it takes more money and energy to deconstruct or remanufacture products from old materials than to mine, transport, and manufacture from new.

Home Recycling

The only difference between recycling everything yourself and having someone else do it is money. The circle of life for an object goes from material mining, part manufacturing, component assembly, and retail shipping to consumer purchase and use, municipal shipping, and product disassembly. All of which cost money, even disassembly. However, there's still worth since recycling centers sell the materials back to manufacturers. They're not giving it to the manufacturers for free and the manufacturers aren't giving it to you for free. But you're just giving it to them for free. The point is you get more out of your purchase by recycling everything yourself instead of paying someone else do it. The key is learning what makes up each object. This requires a base knowledge of chemistry, electronics, and mechanics, but I've evolved my system into two stages simple enough that even children can do it.

STAGE ONE BINS

1. Choose a Stage One container. After a lot of trial and error, I settled with giant roll out garbage cans since I had a bunch left over from early fish farming endeavors and they're readily available, weatherproof, washable, and mobile, plus they hold liquids. 55-gallon drums also work. Otherwise, you can build simple 4-ft³ baskets from construction fencing. Start by cutting a 4-ft circle out of the fencing, and then wrap a 12-ft 6-in wall around the circumference, zip-tying the fencing to hold it in place, and flip it inside-out.

2. Designate an area or build a shed to keep the cans/baskets in and label each by content.

3. Familiarize yourself with the different forms, shapes, colors, sizes, textures that each material comes in or search online for easy sorting (see Metals, Alloys, and Organics below). And then place them in the corresponding bins.

   EXAMPLE: Soda cans are mostly aluminum. Wires and cords are mostly copper. Even though each have other compounds, they'd be placed in the aluminum and copper bins.

   IMPORTANT: Remove labels and stickers, and wash everything. Wash soup cans, jelly jars, used tinfoil, wire, disposable coffee cups, bones, electronics, and even car parts in the dishwasher, and fabrics in the washing machine. This keeps them from collecting bugs and readies them for repurposing later.

4. After stage one, components get broken down into their base elements, they are then separated into stage two bins (page 25). If the material is already in its most basic form, such as charcoal, sand, and silverware, it goes right into the stage two bins.

Metals

- **Sodium:** road, table, or sea salt
- **Potassium:** ash and banana, cantaloupe, orange, avocado, grapefruit, honeydew, guava, and kiwi peels and skins
- **Calcium:** bone, teeth, horn, hoof, nail, antler, hair, feathers, beak, lime, gypsum, which is in drywall and chalk.
- **Magnesium:** automotive blocks and wheels, golf clubs, electronics, water heater anodes
- **Titanium:** sporting goods; phone, automotive, or motorcycle parts; laptop components; medical devices
- **Chromium:** automotive, motorcycle, bicycle, boat parts, and shower and bathtub fittings and fixtures
- **Tungsten:** drill bits, saw blade tips, lathe cutters, milling cutters
- **Iron:** cast iron pots, pans, automotive parts, heaters, and bed frames, pig iron, wrought iron
- **Cobalt:** see Tungsten above
- **Nickel:** plumbing fixtures, rechargeable batteries, utensils
- **Platinum:** catalytic converter, spark plugs, hard disk drives
- **Copper:** wire, bronze, plumbing fittings, tubing, pipe, parts from electronics and appliances, pots, but not pennies
- **Silver:** some water purifiers, electronics, specifically RF (radio frequency) connectors, some audio wire connectors, small batteries like those found in hearing aids, some wind instruments
- **Gold:** parts typically in electronics connections, gold CDs
- **Zinc:** pennies, plumbing fittings, faucets, batteries, brass, hardware plating
- **Aluminum:** wire, cans, tinfoil, electronic parts, camera parts, automotive, motorcycle, boat, and bicycle parts, window and door frames, sporting goods, cooking utensils, electricity lines, CDs, heat sinks, musical instruments
- **Carbon:** charcoal, coke from charcoal, toner cartridges, batteries, filters, carbon paper
- **Lead:** bullets, weights, boat keels, roof vents/panels, batteries, electronics
- **Tin:** solder, tin cans and foil, foil plating, some dishware, tin ceiling panels, lithium-ion batteries
- **Silicon:** sand, glass jars, bottles, bulbs, furniture, and broken windows, fiberglass, fiber optics, pottery, ceramics, porcelain toilets and china, solar panels, silicon chips, semi-conductors, transistors, desiccant packets

NOTE: Throughout this book and your life, you'll come across things that require silica gel desiccant packets (page 248) to help preservation. To preserve the packets themselves, store them in an air-tight, moisture resistant container.

Alloys

- **Brass:** plumbing pieces, musical instruments, keys, bullet casings, bells
- **Bronze:** plumbing fittings, doorknobs
- **Steel:** hardware, wire, appliances, cold-rolled scraps, shavings, food, paint, and spray cans, pans, automotive, appliance, fans, and metal furniture parts

Organics

- **Petroleum:** Plastic bottles, jugs, bags, furniture, CDs and cases, disposable razors, toothbrushes, VHS/cassette tapes, toys, straws, lids, saran wrap, household products, product packaging, electronic parts, carpet, pipes, hose, tubing; polystyrene (Styrofoam®) molded packaging blocks, peanuts, fast food and coffee cups, to-go boxes, ice chests, crafts, beanbag filling, refrigerator insulation; textiles such as clothes, drapes, sheets, furniture coverings; stuffing, which is found in pillows, mattresses, furniture, padding; used oil such as motor oil, brake fluid, transmission fluid, power steering, hydraulic fluid, differential oil; paint; synthetic rubber, which is found in gaskets, O-rings, seals, and hoses

NOTE: Paints have short shelf lives, typically 6–12 months. A simple trick to extend this is to hold your breath, allowing your lungs to convert oxygen into carbon dioxide, open the lid, and exhale inside, then seal lid firmly with a grocery bag or saran wrap underneath. Oxygen causes paint to separate and dry faster, and since CO_2 is heavier, the CO_2 will remove the oxygen. Paints can also be used as an acrylic additive in mixes like concrete (page 62), or they can be mixed with other paints, just keep oil and latex, indoor and outdoor, and finish types separate.

NOTE: Knowing all the environmental damage that's caused to obtain the stuff, I'm amazed at how ill-treated oil is. People do an oil change and just discard it half-used like it's worthless. Just because your car has reached 3,000 miles or it's been a year since your last lube, that doesn't mean the oil's bad. There are so many other uses for oil (page 26) than the landfill.

- **Cotton:** textiles such as clothes, drapes, sheets, and furniture coverings; rope; stuffing from pillows, mattresses, furniture, stuffed animals, and padding; batting from furniture and car seats; dryer lint
- **Wood:** paper like newspaper, cardboard, telephone books, mail envelopes with adhesive and plastic windows removed, paper bags, wrapping; lumber and plywood scraps, branches that are thicker than 2 inches; furniture, sawdust, pencil shavings

STAGE TWO BINS

First, before we can dive into the wire, electrical wire, electronics, plastics, and other components already broken down in our stage one recycling bins, we need to construct our stage two bins and staging area.

1. Construct stage two bins from halved gallon buckets and hang them on the walls like we do in "Coops" (page 202). Alternatively, Harbor Freight sells less expensive parts racks. For larger components, use 55-gallon drums with the lids cut off, which are also used for plant pots (page 82), or even 30-gallon garbage cans work well.
2. Label each bin with the name of the recycled material, such as fabric, oil, EPS, iron oxide, and copper carbonate. And if needed, label them with the date they were recycled, and start recycling.

Wire and Scrap Metal (Iron)

For all metals painted or coated with or attached to plastic, such as wire, hand grips, sporting goods, circuit boards, and etc., cut the plastic, break it off, or burn it off in a burn pit, barrel, UDS, or gasifier, and separate the metal from the plastic before placing them in their respective stage two bins.

Electrical Wire (Copper and Aluminum)

Copper or aluminum electrical wire, bronze and brass knickknacks, and even some steel furniture all have a home in our stage two bins. Wire is so tedious to make, so whatever we have typically goes right into our stage two bins, then gets reused or re-spliced until the jacket falls off. The wire is usually then either recoated with new plastic, used as windings for coils and electric motors, or as pigments and nutrient supplements.

Knickknacks (Brass and Bronze)

Brass and bronze are difficult to separate into their basic elements, which are tin, copper, and zinc. Candlestick holders, bullet casings, knickknacks, and other brass and bronze items are more valuable around the homestead when cut into 1-in pieces, anyway. You can use them as sacrificial anodes (page 180). For the rest, chop them in a miter saw and melt into parts, tools, or ingots for later use.

Electronics and Appliances (Precious Metals and Electrical Components)

Electronics contain all kinds of components and materials from diodes, resistors, capacitors, switches, LEDs, and wires to gold and other precious metals to the circuit boards themselves, all important in other projects or in just building or fixing other electronic devices.

- **General electronics:** heat and melt solder points with an iron and pull all resistors, capacitors, diodes, switches, relays, and other parts. Place any wires in your wire stage one bin, and each additional component—resistors, capacitors, diodes, switches, relays—in separate stage two bins, labeling appropriately.

- **Embedded metals like gold, platinum, copper, silver, and other precious metals:** recover the metal through pyrolysis in a burn barrel (page 189) or pit (page 190), UDS, or gasifier, placing each metal in separate stage two bins, labeling appropriately.
- **Motor coils:** pull windings, burn off shellac with a torch or through pyrolysis like when recycling embedded metals, and pull magnets, bearings, and steel and carbon brushes. Place components in their respective stage two bins, labeling appropriately.

Windows, Bulbs, Dishware, and Bottles (Glass)

Recycled glass is great for decoration, mulch, landscaping, mosaics, aggregate for concrete, stained glass windows, and cullet for glass working.

1. Cut broken pane glass into smaller rectangles and squares to make panes for picture frames or windows. Store in respective stage two bins, labeling appropriately by thickness, such as ⅛ in, ³⁄₁₆ in, and ¼ in, or by type, such as tinted, annealed, and tempered.

    NOTE: For panes of glass, I like to use vertical racks built from ¾ in pipe flanges screwed into the floor with ¾-in pipes that are between 4 in to 1ft long screwed in. Cover the rack ¾-in pipe insulation or carpet for padding to protect the glass.

2. Tumble the rest in a concrete mixer until pieces are ¼–½ in ("Glass to Aggregate," page 16). Store in respective stage two bins, labeling appropriately by color, size, type, or use.

Pots, Dishware, Toilets, and Ceramics (Pottery, Terracotta, Ceramics)

Clay and terracotta pots, dishes, ceramic toilets and other trinkets and collectibles, when broken, can all be thrown into their own stage two bins to be later ground up and added to clay as grog when making pottery or added right into mosaics, crafts, walkways, etc. Label appropriately by type or use.

Motor Oil

Used motor oil, cooking oil, and other chemicals, don't really have a place in my stage two staging area. They kind of skip the entire process. I pour the fluids directly into recycled plastic containers taken from my stage two plastics bin, and they go straight back into my chemical storage cabinet.

According to the EPA, the clean burning of waste oil for the recovery of usable heat is a form of recycling. However, there are many other ways that old motor oil can be put to use:

- As a wood preservative
- For biodiesel
- To rustproof tools and hardware
- As a general lubricant
- To waterproof wood
- As a base for paint
- To waterproof concrete
- As a mold release
- As a binder for dirt roads
- As chain saw chain lubricant
- As drill bit cutting lube
- As raw fuel in a straight waste oil (SWO) modified vehicle

Cooking Oil

Producing oil for cooking in any significant quantities is an endeavor, whatever your medium: seed, nut, pig, vegetable. Extraction always reduces the final product to a mere percentage, so recycling it over and over and over isn't a nice thing to do for us—it's imperative. In fact, restaurants and fast-food joints reuse their oil over 300 times on average before throwing it out, and only then because it'll start smoking and taste different, not because it has actually gone bad.

Just like with paint, there are several tricks to preserve used cooking oil:

- **Reuse:** Keep oils separate since oil from meat spoils sooner than oil from produce. Oils that are used for, say, frying fish shouldn't be used to fry vegetables. This also will help to preserve flavors while cooking.
- **Filter:** To prevent organic solids in the oil from decomposing and going rancid, filter the oil before storing. Let the oil cool, then decant it through a coffee filter, cheesecloth, or several paper towels into a clean, sterile plastic container, filled to the top to slow bacteria growth ("Canning," page 245). Mark it with the type of oil and the date, and store it in a cupboard or fridge.

- **Preserve:** If you're not using oil daily, it'll stay good for years if kept in an airtight container in the cupboard. Freezing will keep it good for over 5 years and counting. Oil can never really "go bad," but it takes on a rancid smell and acidic taste due to light, air, and warmth causing oxidation and peroxide production, which are all halted in cold, airtight, dark spaces.
- **Repurpose:** Once you suspect your oil is getting rancid—the smell is unmistakable—repurposing becomes the final reuse. For cooking oils, the biodiesel straight waste oil (SWO) fuel tank is its last stand.

NOTE: Oil color doesn't determine if it can no longer be used. Cooking oil can be used until it's black without problem; the only noticeable difference is a burnt taste. In reality, as long as you filter it, you'll probably never witness it going rancid. Though after too many uses, the oil will lose its ability to cook because of excessive loss in hydrophobic properties, which results in smoke.

Candles (Wax)

When the missus used to do dumpster dive parties—there was a whole club of girls—she'd readily find candles where the wicks were burned all the way down, leaving a hollowed-out shell with over 50% of the wax still remaining.

1. If the candle is in a glass jar, heat the sides with a hairdryer, holding the candle upside down.
2. Otherwise, melt and reform the candle, per instructions in Pillar Candles on page 43.

Paper (Cellulose Fiber)

Building a home from cellulose turned into papercrete is the epitome of building with trash. Since there's no new hardware, it's built from 100% recycled material. But first, you have to turn paper back into cellulose fiber.

MATERIALS
5 gallons water
5 gallons lye or sulfuric acid
paper, cardboard, dry leaves, grass, brush, bark, soft wood mulch, wood chips, sawdust mulch, or other agricultural waste

TOOLS
large pot
slush mill, wringer-washer, pan mixer, industrial blender, or 600-qt wide blade dough mixer

1. Soak paper, cardboard, dry leaves, grass, brush, bark, soft wood mulch, wood chips, sawdust mulch, or other agricultural waste for over 2 days, or simmer while mixing regularly in 1:1 lye (page 59) or sulfuric acid and water until separation transpires, a process known as chemical pulping.
2. Shred the soaked material in a slush mill, wringer-washer with paddles, pan mixer, industrial blender, or a 600-qt wide blade dough mixer for 4 hours.
3. Dehydrate. And place in a stage two bin, labeling appropriately

IMPORTANT: If you're getting a lot of bubbles in the slurry, add a silicone-based antifoam agent.

Fiber

1. Soak, shred, and dry large ungulate manure, straw, cattail heads, hemp, jute, straw, kenaf, wheat, barley, and cane, in the same manner as Cellulose above.
2. Dehydrate. Place in a stage two bin, labeling appropriately

NOTE: For non-organic polyfiber, I run lumber store tie-down twine through a paper shredder, but any rope would work the same.

Plastic (Polyethylene, Polypropene, Polyvinyl Chloride, Polycarbonate)

By the time most plastics make it to stage two bins, they've been busted to pieces to remove other parts. Otherwise,

1. Separate plastics based on resin code, adding bins for nylon, PC, PVC, and ABS. Large pieces only need to be cleaned and stored, ready for fabrication.
2. For grocery bags, you can save space by rolling them lengthwise and flattening to 1 in, then rolling them from the bottom.
3. Insert the rolled bag through its own handles to lock it in place.
4. Or you can fold the flattened bag into triangles and tuck excess material into the fold.
5. Place them in their respective stage two bins, labeling appropriately by type.

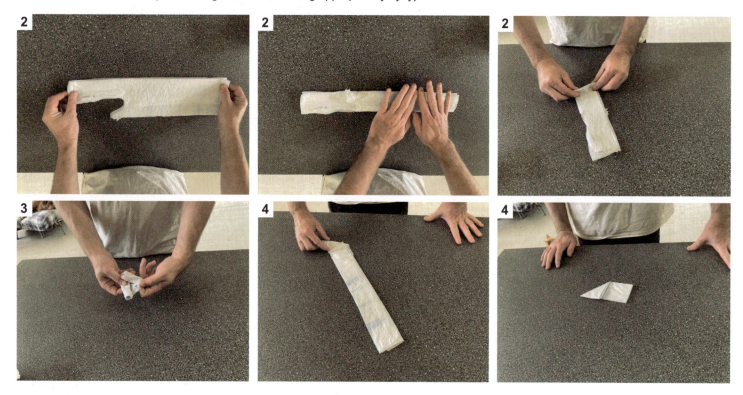

Extruded and Expanded Polystyrene (XPS, EPS)

Whenever anyone sees something that's white, light, and foam, they automatically think Styrofoam, or extruded polystyrene (XPS). Most of what they're seeing is actually expanded polystyrene (EPS), which is the jewel of the recycling world, at least in my point of view. Since it's only intended for temporary, one-time, super lightweight use, EPS is not constructed to last. It is therefore easy to take apart and doesn't release harmful agents in the process, which makes it the simplest material to recycle. Think Legos. Beads anywhere from 0.007 in to 0.25 in are lightly locked together and molded into blocks and shapes of various sizes at 96% air and 4% polystyrene.

Breaking the material down into singular beads can turn into a winter wonderland for the novice quickly. The static electricity in these things, especially when they're separated, is unlike anything you've ever seen. They'll get all over the floor, walls, ceiling. They'll stick to your fingers, eyelashes, the tip of your dog's nose, everything. The key is not to play their game. After a lot of different, and messy, attempts, I finally settled on a couple pretty clean methods using soap, water, and a blender or a mixer.

For some reason, the spinning motion of the paddle, accompanied by the water and soap, helps the beads let go of each other and removes their static electric properties in the process. The end result is a bucket full of clean beads, literally.

NOTE: For peanuts, coffee cups, and containers that have much smaller beads, use the small batch method or a vintage ice crusher with the same soap–water ratio.

Small Batches

MATERIALS

1000 mL water

laundry detergent (page 40)

TOOLS

blender

screen or mesh sieve

1. To granulate EPS, fill a blender with 1000 mL of water and a few drops of laundry detergent (page 40).

2. Break off a few pieces of EPS at a time and add them to the blender, set on high, until you get a thick consistency.
3. Pour the mixture over a screen, pick the big pieces out and throw them back in the blender, then spread the mixture out and let it dry.
4. Place in a stage two bin, labeling appropriately by type.

Large Batches

MATERIALS
2 T dish soap
2 gal water

TOOLS
5-gal bucket with lid
grout or mortar mixing paddle
Drill with ½-in hole saw

1. Break the EPS blocks up into hand sized pieces and fill a 5-gal bucket approximately half full. Place a grout or mortar mixing paddle inside the bucket.
2. Drill a ½-in hole in the center of the bucket's lid, feed the mixer's shaft through, secure the lid, and chuck the mixer into a heavy-duty drill.

    NOTE: I like using oil, soap, or paint bucket lids because they have that 1½-in plug on one side that makes the next step really simple.

3. Remove the lid's nozzle cap, or the entire lid if it doesn't have a plug, and fill the bucket with 2 T of dish soap and 2 gallons of water or until bubbles come out. Replace the cap and mix.
4. Place in a stage two bin, labeling appropriately by type.

Stuffing (Polyester Fill, Down, Feathers, Wheat Husks, Kapok Fibers, EPS and XPS Granules)

Stuffing comes in two forms, batting and loose, so you'll need two bins.

1. Remove stuffing from between the shell and filler of coats, jackets, furniture, mattresses, bedding, pillows, tablecloths, dishwashers, Christmas tree skirts, couch cushions, bean bags, coats, and other filled materials.
2. Place in respective stage two bins, labeling appropriately by material type.

Textiles (Cotton, Polyester, Silk)

We can get a lot of our larger fabric needs from old sheets and tableclothes and smaller from shirts and towels.

1. For fabric, separate based on material type. Remove stitching, zippers, buttons, and other decorations with a seam ripper or precision knife and lay flat. Using a large carpenter's square, or drywall T-square for sheets, draw and cut out the largest rectangles possible.
2. Place in stage two bins, labeling appropriately by material type.

CONSERVATION

You hear it all the time: "Conserve water, electricity, and heat!" But that's all you hear. You never get the details or effective methods.

Water

Want to save water? Don't let it run down the drain for no reason.

- Shower instead of bathing since baths use 4 times more water. Humans only need to shower twice a week. For those who "need" to shower 2–3 times a day, you're wasting 75 gallons.
- Use low-flow shower heads, which cut output by 50%, or place a piece of rubber with a ⅛-in hole inside. The water pressure won't change, but the volume will. If you don't like the results, make the hole bigger. If it's restricting too much, drill a second or third hole for 2 times or 3 times the flow.

NOTE: *If a family of four showers 10 minutes each day, they're using 700 gallons per week. Enough for one person to live on for 2 years!*

- Eliminate the 5 minutes of warming time, which wastes water and electricity, by locating water heaters centrally or install point-of-use heaters.
- 40% of your water bill is flushed down the toilet. Replace commodes with low-flow models or place plastic bottles filled with water or sand in the tank. You'll displace over 1 gallon per flush, 3,000–6,000 gallons per year, saving hundreds.

NOTE: *Make sure bottles aren't touching the mechanisms, which would result in an open flapper and a loss of over 1500 gallons per day.*

- Compost toilets (page 185) don't use any water. They're not only carbon neutral, but also carbon efficient. By turning your waste into compost rather than flushing it, you're offsetting your CO_2, eliminating your own footprint.
- Stop lawn watering. If your grass requires more than what precipitation provides, you have the wrong grass, and if the blades spring back after being flattened, it doesn't need water. Otherwise, pull it and xeriscape.
- Use water from cooking and washing on houseplants.
- Install a rainwater catchment system (page 169). A roof area of 25 m² receives 20 in a year, which would offset your bill by $3,300, enough for a family of four to drink, cook, bathe, and wash with for two months.
- Turning faucet handles a quarter turn provides more than enough water, and when you're not physically using water, turn them off. For some reason, Americans blast the faucet. At 90 psi and 5 gpm, that's a lot of water loss.
- Keep pipes in good repair. A leaky faucet that drips at the rate of one drip per second can waste more than 3,000 gallons per year.[4]
- Toilet tank leaks lose 200 gallons per day. Detect the leak by adding food coloring to the tank and fix it by adjusting the chain, bending the float up, or replacing the flapper or bottom seal.

Homemade rubber piece for a low-flow showerhead

Filled plastic bottles to displace water in the toilet tank as you flush

Homemade compost toilet (page 185)

Drought-tolerant and low-maintenance xeriscape yard

Electricity

There's no environmentally friendly method of generating electricity. Solar cell production is a dirty process. Hydro turbine dams disrupt natural food cycles and wildlife. Nuclear, hydrogen, and wind power are better, but the stigma attached to them hinders any real advancements. And of course, the pollutants of coal, coke, and petroleum are well known. By using electricity, we are not green, we're the opposite, directly contributing to global problems and ecological destruction. Though, getting rid of your smart phone, TV, laptop, lights, and AC probably isn't going to happen. One option is to buy green electricity—electricity produced by low- or even zero-pollution facilities. It's cheaper and you're buying carbon credits by paying your bill.

Lights

If you've managed to finally switch out those horribly inefficient, incandescent ceiling heaters for CFLs (compact fluorescent lamps), good job. Now, switch those for LEDs! If you're one of the 71% still using incandescents, you should know that they generate over 90% heat and less than 10% light. CFLs are 20% heat and 80% light, and LEDs are 10% heat and 90% light at equal luminosity, using 70% less energy, 90% for incandescents. And in my experience, they last 10 times longer, 100 times for incandescents.

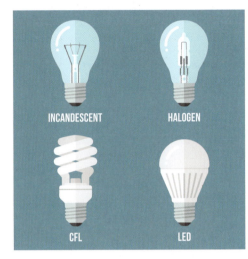

Refrigerator

Do you gaze into the depths of your multi-dimensional fridge, half lost in indecision, half in thoughts of life? Keep the door shut until you know what you want and what goes with it since opening and closing your fridge one time raises the internal temperatures by 25° or more, making the motor work harder to maintain the temperature—and you work harder to pay for it. You could even unplug it, and all your appliances, at night like we do since it's just a big ice chest. Also, if you haven't upgraded to an Energy Star labeled unit, now may be the time to do so. Old refrigerators can use 50% more electricity; you could be saving money by spending some.

> NOTE: Once a year, clean the door gasket and condenser coils to maintain a proper seal.

Freezer

Cold doesn't kill bacteria; it merely slows breeding. How much depends on the temperature. 0–5°F for the freezer is a good starting point, 36–38°F for fridges. If food goes bad, adjust to fit your culinary lifestyle, or stop buying extra food.

> NOTE: Don't store hot food in your fridge because it will make your fridge work harder, which is completely counterproductive. On the same note, don't locate your fridge in a warm area—near a heater vent or in direct sunlight.

Stove/Oven

Electric conventional ovens are a thing of the past. The technology is called Heat Coil Technology ("Off-Grid Applications," page 144) and is the same as incandescent bulbs. Gas ovens are even less efficient since less than 20% of the flame actually makes contact. You're not only wasting money but heating your kitchen and house (and fridge). This, like the fridge, makes the AC work harder, which means even more electricity and money wasted. Convection stoves and ovens are better, induction better still, and even better than all that are pressure cookers, crockpots, and microwaves, focusing energy into food directly. Barbecue grills are good even though they're energy hogs, since when you're using them, you're not paying to air-condition your stove. But the best, with zero carbons spent and energy used, are solar stoves and ovens (page 136). I just haven't found out how to incorporate them inside the kitchen yet.

- When using an oven, like the fridge, don't open the door to gaze.
- Glass pots and pans facilitate heat transfer more efficiently, heating up faster and lasting longer, and allow you to look inside without raising the lid. I would also suggest eating from glass since it heats while you eat.
- Ever wonder why two burners are smaller? Your vessel should be sized to the burner. If you're using a small pot on the larger burner, you're wasting energy.
- Preheating isn't necessary. Wiring in old homes was smaller, so cooking times were longer. Now ovens are 240V, 50A or more on 8 awg wire, so heat transfer is instant. Conversely, turn the oven off 15 minutes early, as it will retain enough heat to finish the job. Otherwise, you're cooking air.
- Turn off the stove when a boil is reached. If your recipe calls for boiled water, it only requires water at that temperature. Anything more and you're wasting energy (and water). Also, adding salt doesn't lower the boiling point. If anything, it raises it since solutions require more heat. To speed up a boil, put the lid on.

Water Heater

The typical home water heater accounts for 20% of electricity usage.

- Flip the circuit breaker when not in use. This alone will save over 95% of energy usually spent on cycling.
- Jacket it. The white metal you see is a jacket encapsulating the water heater in 1in of insulation. That's not enough. Wrap it at least 3 times with foil insulation to reduce your bill by over 10%.
- Repurpose the tank. Install point-of-use units as mentioned, which remain off for 5 days (since you're only showering twice a week, right?).
- Solar. Again, no energy, no CO_2.
- Adjust temperature. 110–112°F is high enough to compensate for travel loss without causing second degree burns, which occur at 115°F. If you're not getting over 105°F, insulate your pipes better.

NOTE: If you wash dishes or take hot showers to kill bacteria, you'll be disappointed, and wasting electricity. You'd need over 212°F, which is the boiling point, to kill germs. Being 70% water, your insides would boil first. Before that, at around 200°F, your skin would melt. Water doesn't need to be hot since it only acts as a ferrying medium for matter separated by soap.

- Keep the unit maintained. Hard water deposits cover components causing more electricity to be consumed than necessary. Eventually the tank fills with scale, often reducing it to 2 gallons. The unit will not only not heat when on, it will remain on 24 hours. Replace the sacrificial anode, and drain 5 gallons twice a year. If you have an older heater that's never been flushed, you own a very large, very good source of calcium carbonate (Chapter 2). Cut with an angle grinder to harvest and store in your respective stage two bin.

NOTE: Thermostats are the other culprits that cause identical problems. When malfunctioning, they'll signal to continue heating, even though actual temps are hotter than the thermostat setting.

Dishwashers

This is the first year we've used a dishwasher, not because we're against them (as I said, technology helps people be self-reliant), but when everything's battery powered, you tend to want to do many chores manually.

- When hand cleaning, soak or rinse lightly soiled items (glasses and silverware) first, then heavier dishes and plates, and soak pots and pans last. In this fashion, you'll always wash in cleaner water. Machine wash full loads on cold with no drying.
- Use 1 glass per person for 1–2 days. Or fill an entire new glass every time you need a drink and collect 13 half full glasses at the end of every day. Don't worry about it being "dirty"; bacteria takes over 48 hours to achieve harmful levels of reproduction, longer in water or an acid like orange or lemon juice).

Washer and Dryer

This is also the first year we've used a washing machine, but we've never owned a dryer since it's so wasteful, and that works pretty well for us. Washing and then hanging clothes to dry is just as effective and a lot more efficient.

- Use your washer with full loads and cold water, despite what the label reads. Again, unless boiling your clothes, you're not killing any bacteria. Soak saturated material.

IMPORTANT: Bacteria actually thrives and multiplies faster in hot environments (like an incubator).

Batteries

In the last year, you've purchased (and thrown away) approximately 100 disposable batteries. Four alkaline batteries costing $2.74 have a capacity of 0.0171 kwh, which means you're paying $160.23 per kwh! In contrast, residential electricity costs $0.06 per kwh on average, so batteries are 267,000 times more expensive! That's a lot of inefficiency and not being green! And I bet you didn't know you could recharge them.

- Standard, "non-rechargeable" batteries can be recharged a couple dozen times with a cheap, special charger available online (U.S. Patent #5,543,702).
- For rechargeable batteries, take care of them to get the longest life ("Harnessing of Renewable Energy" <x>).

Everything Else

Get rid of it (Chapter 14). Other than massive energy hogs that you can't live without, you simply don't need all the little gadgets, devices, contraptions and other junk!

Before electricity entered every home, the concept of doing everything electrically was absurd. Not because electricity wasn't understood, it was just unnecessary. Games, toys, appliances, and tools were all manually and mechanically operated, with few moving parts and fewer things to break. Items lasted, not days or months as now, but generations. And when things did break, they could be fixed. Parts were accessible and easy to repair. Now we live in an electronic dependent age, where you're irrelevant if you don't own the newest device and where manufacturers design products to force replacement. Proving point: 10 times more smart phones are discarded because they're outdated, not because they're broken. This is the ultimate form of waste, the complete opposite of conservation and efficiency. The good news is that companies still make mechanical, hand versions of all appliances and tools, and, of course, we can make our own tools (page 64).

Finally, flip the main breaker when on vacation. Not only will this save considerable energy and money, but it will drastically extend the life of your electronics and prevent fires. Also, the IRS, as well as many utility companies, offer tax breaks and rebates for energy-efficient upgrades.

Heating and Cooling

- Ever notice that switch on ceiling fans? That's an efficiency performance switch (EPS) with a reverse air flow function for seasonal settings . . . a backwards switch. During the warmer summer months, set the switch down, which rotates the blades counterclockwise, to circulate the "cooler" air located in the lower half of the room, while keeping the warmer air stagnated in the ceiling. In the winter, flip the switch so that the blades spin in the opposite direction, sucking that "cooler" air out of the lower half of the room up into the stagnated warmer air trapped in the ceiling, blowing it out, around and back down into the lower half of the room.
- Unless you live in a high humidity area, close vents in unused rooms and shut off the heater or air conditioner when not at home. With newer, larger wiring and more efficient climate control systems, it takes minutes to warm or cool a house. Even in freezing conditions, there's no reason to heat an empty house, since your pipes should now be protected, just like you don't leave your car heater running when you're at work. By using programmable thermostats, schedule your system to kick on minutes before arrival, saving $200 a year.
- Upgrade your unit. New, high-efficiency, 13 seasonal energy efficiency ratio (SEER) ACs run on 50% of what 15-year-old units use.
- Use evaporative coolers. Not only do they use a fraction of the electricity, but with global drought rising with climate change, they work almost everywhere.
- Use washable filters in your HVAC unit. Cleaning monthly and spraying coils and condenser fins with foam cleaner annually can save $1000 a year.
- For the hardcore environmentalists, get rid of temperature control units completely and construct natural or passive systems.
- Maintaining a good home envelope will prevent heating or cooling your backyards. Ask your utility company for a free home energy audit to locate leaks and areas of improvement.

Chapter 4: Home Production of Products

Anyone and everyone can do anything and everything that everyone else does, just as good or better!

    One of the easiest ways to save money and limit waste is to make your own products and gifts. Not only do you avoid buying into capitalism and consumerism, but you are also able to personalize your own products. It's effective, it's efficient, and it's a simple step toward self-reliance.

    Once you've learned the how to make stuff, or if you don't have the workspace or tools at home, or if you just need help on designs, tool use, or just extra manpower, head on over to a makerspace or makers collectives like TechShop, NextFab, and TaskRabbit for labor and work, and mfg.com for manufacturing. For selling your products be sure to check out Shopify and Volusion. For design SketchUp, AutoCAD and Autodesk, 123D Design, Blender, Tinkercad for 3D design, and Shapeways for 3D printing services. If you're in Texas or Portland areas, feel free to come by my free makerspace and tool sharing locations . . . We're always willing to lend a helping hand, share experience and skills, and provide ideas!

PAPER PRODUCTS

Making your own stuff is like printing your own money, so what better start than making paper itself!

Mold and Deckle

For most paper products, you'll need to make a two-piece assembly called a mold and deckle.

MATERIALS

1 window screen
2 thin sheets of plastic

TOOLS

measuring tape
Sharpie or pencil
square
utility knife
hot glue gun

1. Cut a window screen and 2 paper-thin plastic rectangles to 10½ x 13 in. Make an 8½ x 11 in cut-out in the plastic rectangles, centered, for a frame.

    NOTE: For regular thickness paper, a kid's plastic folder works well. For thicker paper, use thicker plastic. For larger paper sheets, use larger plastic and screen, and cut the center hole to desired size.

2. Hot glue the screen to one frame, which will be the mold, and place the other frame, the deckle, on top.

1

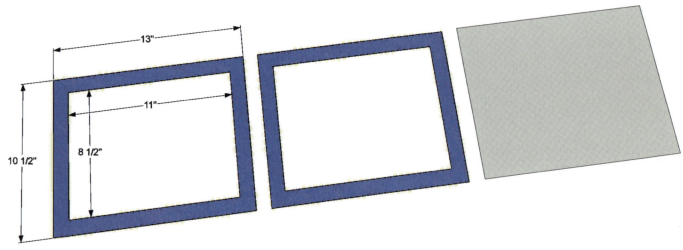

2

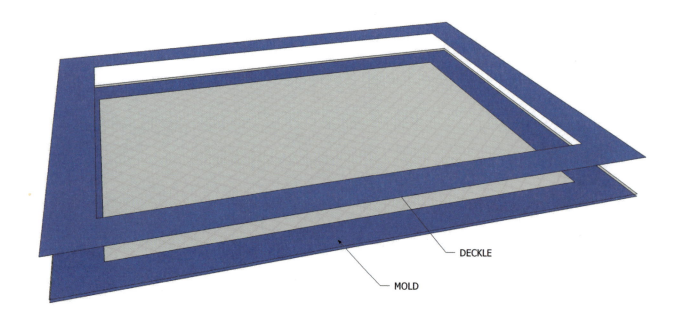

DECKLE

MOLD

Paper

MATERIALS
mold and deckle (see above)
green plaster
1 gal water
2¾-in slats of porcelain or glazed stoneware
2 felt sheets

TOOLS
vise or weights (3-L soda bottles, 5-gal buckets of water, etc.)
drying rack or towel

1. Mix up some green plaster without cement and 1 gal of water in a concrete mixing tub.
2. Place the mold and deckle in the bottom of your kitchen sink, add plaster, and slowly raise one side to 45°, slowly tilt back, level, and let it drain. Then clean off edges.
3. Place mold and deckle on a rack to drip-dry, and construct a paper press with two ¾ x 10½ x 13-in slats of porcelain or glazed stoneware.
4. Replace the deckle with a felt sheet of the same dimensions. Place entire assembly upside down on one slat, remove the mold, cover with an 8½ x 11-in piece of rag, then place the second slat on top.
5. Press, then remove and wring out the rag, and repeat. Exchange the rag for another felt sheet and add weights or clamp the press in a vise to remove any lingering water.

    NOTE: If your vise doesn't have rubber pads, use scrap wood to protect the slats.

6. Remove weights once dripping stops and place the paper on a drying rack or towel.

    NOTE: If you'd like properly-sized paper with sharp edges, run through a paper trimmer. Make multiple sheets for mass production by modifying the deckle, mold, and press by adding vertical and horizontal muntin bars at desired measurements. For smooth or semi-gloss paper, add kaolinite, also known as china clay, to the plaster mix at a 4:1 ratio.

Napkins and Paper Towels

Making paper towels employs the same steps as making paper, except we want a softer, thinner paper.

MATERIALS
green plaster
1 gal water
1 c bleach or lye (page 59)
1 c tannin
vinegar (page 232)
¼ T oil

TOOLS
18-mesh bucket sieve (page 64)
fine-woven rag (sheet, pillowcase, etc.) and rope
mold and deckle (page 36)
2 felt sheets
2 ¾-in slats of porcelain or glazed stoneware
vise or weights (3-L soda bottles, 5-gal buckets of water, etc.)
drying rack or towel
paper cutter

1. Mix up some green plaster without cement and 1 gallon of water in a concrete mixing tub. Add 1 c bleach or lye (page 59) and 1 c tannin to the green plaster mix to coagulate the fibers. Run mixer on high until you get a milkshake-like consistency, then store in an airtight container for 2 weeks or more. The longer, the better.
2. Run this finer pulp through an 18-mesh bucket sieve (page 64) to get really fine fibers, then boil the mixture and remove suds (chemicals) with a skimmer. Neutralize the lye with vinegar.
3. Let cool, then separate the water by pouring it through a 16 in²-fine-woven rag (sheet, pillowcase, etc.) atop a large pot or other suitable container, tied in place with rope as a filter.
4. Remove cloth, fold corners in, twist, and tie a knot with rope and hang the sack for several days outside, allowing the water to drip out and the ball to dry.

    IMPORTANT: If anything other than clear water drips out after 30 minutes, the cloth pores are too large and you're losing mix.

5. Once firm, remove a chunk, and squeeze. If no water drips, you're good. Otherwise, leave for another day.
6. Add ¼ T oil and knead until a dough-like consistency is reached.

   NOTE: Oils will keep the paper soft and malleable.

7. Repeat steps 2–6 from "Paper" (page 37).
8. Cut and stack or fold into quartered napkins.

Toilet Paper

How much toilet paper do you use? The average American uses 20,000 sheets of toilet paper every year. Money flushed down the toilet. When you have to make your own, you realize you don't need five handfuls. The process is the same as paper towels, except here, we want it even softer.

MATERIALS
green plaster
1 gal water
1 c bleach or lye (page 59)
1 c tannin
vinegar
¼ T oil
1 T aloe
empty toilet paper holder

TOOLS
18-mesh bucket sieve (page 64)
airtight container
pasta hand roller
drying rack

1. Repeat steps 1–5 from Napkins and Paper Towels (page 37).
2. Add 1 T of aloe and knead until a dough-like consistency is reached.
3. Instead of using a mold and deckle, run the pulp through a pasta hand roller to make long runs. Snake the run through a clothes drying rack, cut, and repeat the process, then roll each run around an empty toilet paper holder.

   NOTE: You can always build a smaller mold and deckle at 4½ in² for precut sheets that can be stacked instead of rolled.

HOMEMADE SOAPS, SOLVENTS, AND DETERGENTS

Soap is merely the potassium or sodium salt from fat acid and alkali, which happens to make grunge soluble. Cleaning products accomplish the same thing by using compounds and, therefore, are classified as detergents. Straight acids and alkalis burn and corrode chemical compounds from substrate in the cleaning process, rather than separating them as soap does.

Depending on the material that needs cleaning, we can produce all of them.

Bar Soap

The process is two-fold: triglycerides, found in fats and oils, split and merge with alkalis like sodium or potassium hydroxide (lye) when in direct contact, a process called saponification, producing one glycerin and one salt molecule (soap). Here's the catch. The ratio, the fat to lye value, has to be the same. Otherwise, you're left with greasy or burning soap.

   IMPORTANT: Despite what many people will tell you, there is absolutely no lye, potassium hydroxide (KOH) or sodium hydroxide (NaOH), in wood ash. Therefore, you do not need to run water through ash in a hopper to make soap.

MATERIALS
lye (page 59)
836 g melted oil
2 t salt
8.5 oz water
essential oils, honey (page 220), or glycerin
parchment paper

soap form, cookie mold, baking sheet, loaf pan, or halved milk carton
bubble wrap envelope

1. To start, you'll need lye. You can make potassium hydroxide (page 59), or use a drain cleaner, like Red Devil or Borax.
2. Add 836 g of oil to a plastic or glass mixing bowl, then in a separate bowl, dissolve and mix 2 t salt (if using pot lye) and the corresponding amount of lye depending on oil type (Table 2.1) in 8.5 oz of water.

   WARNING: The mix will heat to 200°F and give off poisonous vapors. Do. Not. Inhale.

3. Let both liquids cool to 100–120°F, then decant lye solution into oil slowly, making sure no bubbles form.
4. Mix from the bottom, using a wood spatula or stick blender on low until you reach a thicker, pudding-like consistency and a trace, a trail of liquid sitting on top of liquid, forms when removing blender. This takes less than 5 minutes.

5. Quickly stir in a few drops of essential oils, 9 drops of honey (page 220), or 5 drops of glycerin and pour into a plastic or parchment lined soap form, cookie mold, baking sheet, loaf pan, halved milk carton, etc.
6. Place mold in insulated bubble wrap envelope or polystyrene ice chest and leave out overnight at room temperature to promote gel phase, which creates clear soap. It is best to put it on top of the fridge towards the back because it is the warmest place in the house, slightly above room temperature. To deter gel phase and make opaque soap, place the mold inside your fridge, uninsulated.

   NOTE: If left in cold air, solution will form a lye layer on top. Slowing cooling prevents it, otherwise it can be washed off later.

7. Remove and cut the soap into bar sized pieces to cure and let it harden for 4–6 weeks, then taste test with your tongue. If you get "zapped," it's not ready.

   NOTE: Soap dries within hours, but we've only put the molecules in contact with each other. It takes longer for the chemical bonding of saponification. If the mixture never thickens, more fat is needed. If it thickens, but has a top grease layer, more lye is needed.

   WARNING: Do not use the soap for over 3 weeks since the lye is still processing and will burn the skin.

Liquid Soap

Bar soap is a very modern commodity, becoming popular only when chemical and high temp manufacturing made vats of liquid soap obsolete. But liquid soap, which Lucia and I prefer, is making a comeback. We prefer it not just because we have an endless supply of free pot lye, but also because you don't waste time and energy working up a lather.

MATERIALS

lye (page 59)
glass mixing bowl
stick blender
836 g melted oil
2 t salt

8.5 oz water
essential oils, honey (page 220), or glycerin
cheesecloth
liquid soap dispenser

1. Follow steps 1–4 from "Bar Soap" (page 38), using pot lye without salt in step 2.
2. Once trace is obtained, pour through cheesecloth or other suitable material into another bowl.
3. Let cool overnight to a brown, jelly-like consistency. Pour into a liquid soap dispenser, dilute with water at a 1:1 ratio if desired, and let cure for at least 3 weeks.

   NOTE: Since I work with my hands a lot, I prefer watering the mix, where Lucia has separate dispensers of full-strength, concentrated soap with coloring for identification.

TABLE 2.1 LYE ADDITIONS

Type	NaOH/g	KOH/g
Lard	0.138	0.193
Beeswax	0.069	0.096
Castor	0.128	0.180
Goose Fat	0.136	0.191
Hemp Seed	0.134	0.188
Linseed	0.135	0.189
Peanut	0.136	0.190

Type	NaOH/g	KOH/g
Pumpkinseed	0.133	0.186
Soybean	0.135	0.189
Sunflower Seed	0.134	0.187
Tallow, beef	0.140	0.196
Tallow, deer	0.137	0.193
Tallow, goat/sheep	0.138	0.193

Laundry Detergents

Switching to all-organic, natural cleaning products doesn't have to mean an increase in price. Instead of buying organic laundry soap, Lucia uses 1 c of full-strength homemade liquid soap mixed with 5 drops of orange peel essential oil per load, which seems to be plenty.

Household Cleaners

Scrub Cleaner

MATERIALS
1 c baking soda
1 c vinegar
1 T powdered orange peel
squirt bottle

1. For a general scrubbing cleaner, mix baking soda and vinegar 1:1 to a paste-like consistency. Add 1 T powdered orange peel, and store in a plastic container with a wide, screw-off lid or squirt bottle.

Spray Cleaner

MATERIALS
3 c vinegar

1. For spray cleaners, fill an empty spray bottle with homemade vinegar. It disinfects, shines, and dissolves dirt and grime on contact.

Drain Cleaner

MATERIALS
1 c dried lye crystals

1. For clogged drains, dump in 1 c of dried lye crystals. It'll saponify the trapped grease and wash away like soap suds.

HYGIENE PRODUCTS

Shampoo

MATERIALS

½ c water
½ c coconut oil
1 c tea tree oil
1 c peppermint oil

1 cucumber
1 lemon
Shampoo bottle

TOOLS

large non-metallic mixing bowl
stick blender

small funnel

1. In a non-metallic bowl mix ¼–½ c water, ½ c coconut oil, 1 c tea tree oil, and 1 c peppermint oil with a stick blender for 2–3 minutes in 5-minute intervals. Blend for 30 minutes or until it reaches paste consistency.
2. De-seed and skin 1 cucumber and 1 lemon (or 2 limes). Blend on high for 1 minute, add to solution and mix for 1–2 minutes.
3. At this point, add any oils, scents, or additives that you want. Below are some mixtures that I use for hair and scalp health.
   - For oily hair: In a separate bowl, dissolve ½ c KOH in 1 c water, let cool, then mix into oils.
   - For dry hair: Mix in 2½ t of glycerin and ½ c aloe vera into solution.
   - For shine: Add 4½ T almond, 2 ¾ t vanilla and ¾ t lemon oils.
   - For dandruff: Add 10 T apple juice, 2–12 T apple cider vinegar and 6 t clove powder.
4. Using a small funnel, pour the contents into a shampoo bottle. Let sit for 1 week to mature.

   NOTE: Because the alkali KOH is a preservative, refrigeration isn't required. But if you aren't using KOH in your shampoo, refrigerate.

   WARNING: Because this shampoo's strength is stronger than normal, use half volume or dilute with 50% water. If your hair feels dry after it dries, use more cucumber; if oily, more lemon.

Conditioner

MATERIALS

3½ T apple cider vinegar
3½ c water

essential oils (optional)
conditioner bottle

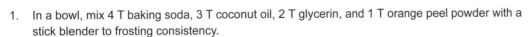

1. Add 3½ T apple cider vinegar and 3½ c water in conditioner bottle and shake. Then add oils, scents, or other additives as desired.
   - For oily hair: Add 6–8 drops of lavender, lemon, rosemary, or tea tree oils.
   - For dry hair or dandruff: Add 6–8 drops tea tree, peppermint, lemon, eucalyptus, or rosemary oils.

   IMPORTANT: Your hair and scalp—and skin—are acidic, around 4.5–5.5 pH. This is a natural body function to prevent germs from colonizing, as they cannot grow in an acidic environment. Therefore, never use an alkali-only based shampoo without acid additives or acidic conditioner. If you experience any discomfort, reduce acid or check pH.

Toothpaste

For toothpaste, baking soda is a must. It's a mild abrasive and a whitener, and, of course, it absorbs odors. I also like to add coconut oil or other antimicrobial, antibacterial agents, glycerin as an emulsifying agent to bind the substances and preserve moisture, and powdered orange peel as a natural whitener. My recipe is a simple 4:3:2:1 ratio.

MATERIALS

4 T baking soda
3 T coconut oil
2 T glycerin
1 T orange peel powder
pop top squeeze bottle

TOOLS

large mixing bowl
stick blender
small funnel

1. In a bowl, mix 4 T baking soda, 3 T coconut oil, 2 T glycerin, and 1 T orange peel powder with a stick blender to frosting consistency.

   NOTE: Baking soda is a salt, so your toothpaste will be salty rather than sweet like store-bought version. Add 5–10 drops orange, lime, spearmint, wintergreen, peppermint, essential oil, to compensate.

2. Using a small funnel, pour into a squeeze bottle with a pop-up top, like a travel shampoo bottle.

   NOTE: I add glycerin as an emulsifying agent since it's the only humectant available to us and it's a byproduct on the homestead.

Deodorant

Contrary to popular belief, deodorant doesn't actually mask the musk. It acts as a barrier, preventing the growth, reproduction, and colonization of beneficial bacteria that feed on the accumulated dead and decaying skin cells that are flushed out of pores during perspiration, a process that causes odor. Antiperspirant, on the other hand, affects the sweat glands themselves, preventing perspiration altogether. Preventing a natural body function? Never a good thing. But since the mindset adjustment to discontinue this social norm won't be made anytime soon . . .

MATERIALS

2 T baking soda

1 c starch

1 c coconut oil

½ c coconut butter

5 drops grapefruit oil

10 drops tea tree oil

deodorant container

TOOLS

2 large mixing bowls

stick blender

1. Mix 1–2 T baking soda with 1 c starch.

   NOTE: Starch acts as a liquid absorbent and baking soda as an odor absorbent.

2. In a separate bowl, melt 1 c coconut oil and ½ c coconut butter and mix with a blender stick, adding 5 drops grapefruit oil and 10 drops tea tree oil.

   NOTE: I add coconut oil and tea tree oil for their antifungal, antibacterial, and antimicrobial properties, and coconut butter to keep the oil solid at room temperature. Grapefruit is for vitamin C and aroma. More importantly, it replaces the acidic edge that was removed with the baking soda.

3. Decant oils into the dry content and mix to paste consistency.

4. Unwind an empty deodorant container so that the tray is at the bottom and fill the empty tube. Tap it against the counter to remove any air, replace cap, and place in a refrigerator to cool for 30 minutes.

Lotion

MATERIALS

2 oz beeswax

1 c olive oil

½ c coconut oil

lotion bottle

TOOLS

small mixing bowl

stirring stick

1. Melt 2 oz of beeswax, then mix in a small mixing bowl with 1 c olive oil and ½ c coconut oil, and let cool while stirring every 15 minutes.

2. Decant into lotion bottle.

MAKING CANDLES

The hardest part I've learned about making candles are the wicks, specifically fixing and priming them. I had no idea you couldn't just stick some string in melted wax and be done with it.

Wicks

You can buy candle string at stores like Hobby Lobby, otherwise we can make our own:

MATERIALS

4 T lye

2 T salt

½ c hot water

(4) 1-ft lengths of cotton string

laundry line

TOOLS

scissors

clothespins

1. Dissolve 4 T lye and 2 T salt in 1½ c hot water, then submerge (4) 1-ft sections of string, and let sit overnight.

   NOTE: The size of the flame (candle watts) and duration of the candle is directly related to the diameter of the wick. For more light, which means a faster burn, use cotton yarn, braided string, or multiple wicks.

2. Remove and cut into desired lengths, leaving 2–3 in extra, then attach a clothespin to the bottom and top and hang to dry for 2 days.

3. To preserve for later use, dip in melted wax.

   NOTE: For colorful, multifaceted flame, wind twist ties around the wick.

Pillar Candles

Candles don't have to be made from beeswax alone; make them out of paraffin, lard, or even petroleum jelly. There are many methods for melting wax from double boilers and crockpots to heat guns. I prefer using an electric drip coffee maker. The low heat is concentrated directly onto the carafe, which melts the wax at 135°F.

MATERIALS
wax (page 229)
candle holder

TOOLS
electric drip coffee maker
drill with ³⁄₁₆-in drill bit
wire

1. Fill carafe with wax (page 229) or recycled candles and turn on the coffee maker.

   NOTE: I usually set the timer to start 1 hour before I wake to make candles first thing.

2. Once liquid, decant wax into an empty candle holder or any container (plastic, cardboard, glass). For reusable molds, use 6-in Sdr 35 PVC pipe for 3-wick candles and 2-in Sch 40 pipe for singles. Just coat insides with vegetable or mineral oil before each use.

   IMPORTANT: Wax contracts when cooling, making a crater; add wax as needed.

3. Drill a ³⁄₁₆-in hole through the center and push wick through with a wire, leaving ¼ in at the top.

Emergency Candles

MATERIALS
cotton stuffing
petroleum jelly
tuna can
tinfoil

TOOLS
drill with ¼-in drill bit

1. Coat a wad of stuffing or cotton with petroleum jelly, resin, or tar, and place in a tuna can with an attached lid.

2. Drill a ¼-in hole in lid's center, close it, pull some fiber out of the hole and light it. It will burn for 30 minutes before you need to add another wad.

3. To store, fold wad inside tinfoil. When ready, cut an *X* in the tinfoil, pull out some fiber, and light.

MAKING ADHESIVES

Let's make our own adhesives. Because we can.

White Glue

This is your average, everyday glue that you can use on almost anything.

MATERIALS
1 c casein powder
½ t KOH or NaOH dissolved in water
10 drops tea tree oil
glue squeeze bottle

TOOLS
medium mixing bowl
small funnel

1. Mix 1 c casein powder with ½–1 t KOH or NaOH dissolved in water, adding casein by the teaspoon to the consistency of glue.

1. Let cool, and mix in 10 drops tea tree essential oil as an antimicrobial and preservative. Using a small funnel, fill an empty glue squeeze bottle.

Super Glue

Super glue can repair glass, ceramics, pottery, and anything else that needs something stronger than your typical glue.

MATERIALS
2 T vinegar (page 232)
1 t gelatin powder

TOOLS
plastic container
mixing stick

1. In a small plastic container, mix 2 T boiling vinegar (page 232) to 1 t gelatin powder, stirring rapidly until granules are dissolved.

NOTE: You can scale the recipe up; however, as with store-bought super glue, it only takes a drop. Any more and it won't cure.

HANDMADE LINE

Yarn

First, we must build a spinning wheel. There are more designs than imaginable. The following is by no means original. The original designer probably died thousands of years ago.

MATERIALS
hook screw
½-in dowel or cardboard from a hanger
hot glue
2 CDs
½-in rubber grommet or O-rings
batting (cotton, stuffing (page 29), wool (page 227), mohair, fleece, angora, silk (page 228), etc.)
toilet paper roll or other cardboard spool

TOOLS
utility knife
liquid soap (page 39)
5-gal bucket of hot water

1. Install a hook screw in the end of a ½-in wood dowel or the cardboard off a hanger with a little hot glue.
2. Place 2 CDs together and install a ½-in rubber grommet in the center. Then slide 2 in of the dowel's hook end through the grommet using liquid soap (page 39).

3. For a leader, tie the ends of a 4-ft length of yarn, cord, or twine together, loop through itself and slide a slip knot under the CDs. Wind above CDs ("whorl") several times, then through the hook.
4. Attach cotton (picked or stuffing), wool (page 227), mohair, fleece, angora, silk (page 228), etc. by drafting (pulling) 1-in batt material (a carded or combed grouping of inline fibers), inserting it through the end of the leader, through the loop, and back onto itself, then drafting another inch.

   WARNING: Don't pull past staple length of the material, an amount determined by the material's breaking point.

5. Hold the drafted end against the main fiber between 2 fingers of 1 hand so that the spindle drops ("drop spindle"). Give it a few spins clockwise to charge it, then catch and lock it in place between your knees.

   IMPORTANT: Always spin in the same direction. Otherwise, you'll unwind everything you've spun.

6. While holding the fiber in one hand, draft with your second hand then let the twists run up the fiber. Draft more, let the twists run more. Once your leader charge is depleted, spin to charge again, lock in place and repeat. By slowing drafting, you add more twists. By increasing drafting speed, you add fewer twists.

   NOTE: For Warp yarns (yarn that is placed in the longitudinal direction of the woven fabric) less than 35 is 4.75 threads per inch (TPI). Warp from 35–80, 4.50 TPI. Warp 80–110, 4.25 TPI. Filling yarns (medium numbers), 3.50 TPI.

7. Fiber tends to twist first in the narrowest areas, jumping fatter clumps of fiber completely. If this occurs, simply untwist that section, draft the clump out a little more without breaking it, then allow the twists to come back. Conversely, if you break the fiber, don't panic. Simply untwist 1–2 in of fiber, overlap 1 in or so, and retwist. This is also how you add more material when the material in your hand runs out.

8. Repeat spin and drafting sequence until you have a significant length of yarn or until the drafting becomes out of reach, then unhook the leader and unwind to just below the whorl, and wind yarn around the dowel, leaving over 6–10 in for the hook. Repeat.

NOTE: If your yarn breaks (from too many twists, loose fiber, or pulling on the fiber too much), lay spoon yarn over a pulled section and twist back together. This is also how you add new batts when low.

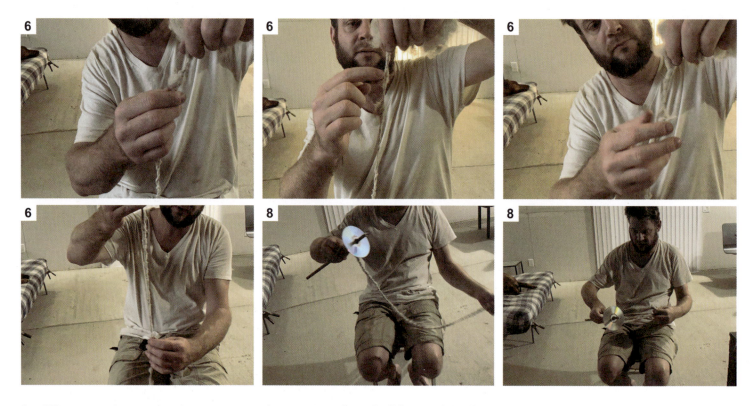

9. When you get as much yarn as you want, give an extra twist, pull off the remaining fiber, and transfer everything that's on your dowel onto an empty spool (another dowel or cardboard from a hanger works well), tuck the end in so it doesn't unwind, and repeat the above steps for a second spool.

10. To set to prevent unspinning, connect the ends of both spools of yarn to the end of the leader, in the same fashion you did with one, then spin the two together in the opposite direction (counterclockwise), keeping spools separate.

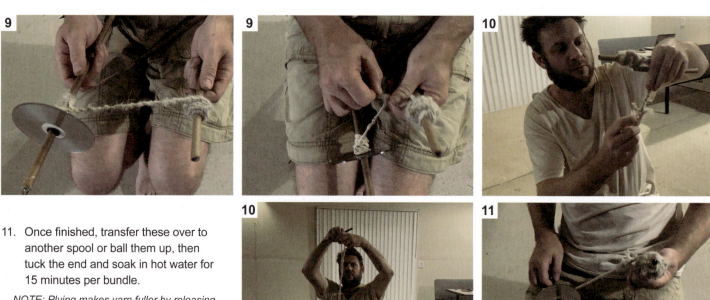

11. Once finished, transfer these over to another spool or ball them up, then tuck the end and soak in hot water for 15 minutes per bundle.

NOTE: Plying makes yarn fuller by releasing the torsion you previously set without loosening twists. Make your yarn ball as large or small as you'd like.

12. I don't comb my fiber ("wild spinning") or felt my yarn, because we spin for need, not looks. We don't like producing waste or exerting unnecessary energy. We, therefore, don't care about seeds, debris, or other particles. But if you want a store-bought look, comb your batt first and singe off loose fibers with a lighter after drying.

Twine

Follow the same process for spinning yarn, using rougher fibers like hemp, coco husk, coir, jute, henequen, straw, or sisal.

String

MATERIALS
thread

TOOLS
(7) 1½-in screws or hooks
2 worktables or sawhorses
wire hanger
drill

1. Install (3) 1½-in screws or hooks spaced 2 in on the edge of a worktable or sawhorse. Duplicate for a second set of screws on another stand, adding a fourth for your last anchor point. Set the sawhorses at desired string space, so that they're facing each other.

   NOTE: Expect a length reduction of 1 in per foot, so add accordingly.

2. Tie one end of thread onto the first of the 4 screws/hooks. Run out desired length, draping the end over the first screw on the opposite stand. Bring the thread back, loop around second hook, and so on. On the last (the fourth) screw, give it a few loops, then just drop the spool on the floor. No need to cut or tie.

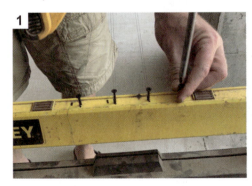  

3. Cut a 3-in long piece of wire hanger and bend the end into a hook and insert it into your drill.

   NOTE: For thicker twine or rope, use a thicker gauge hook, like a 16-d nail, for thinner thread, a paperclip works well.

HOME PRODUCTION OF PRODUCTS

47

4. Remove the loop of thread from the first of the 3 anchor loops, place it on the drill hook, and spin on high for 30 seconds for 15 ft of thread. Place loop back on screw.

   NOTE: Spin 2 or 3 loops together for thicker string.

5. Repeat for each loop of the 3-screw sawhorse, placing twisted loops back on anchor screw/hook. Then give any low hanging strands a few extra twists in drill until all are even.

6. Now place all 3 loops on the wire hook, reverse drill direction, and spin on high for 30 seconds for 15 ft.

   NOTE: 6 strands of 1/32 in thread in this configuration (double twist) makes ⅛-in string.

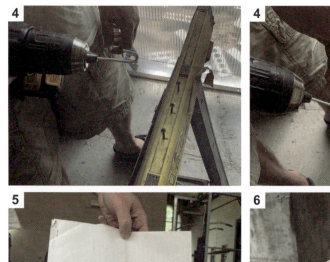

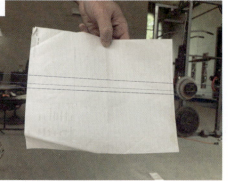

Cord

1. Follow the above steps to make string, then remove string from hook, tie a 1–2 in loop in the end and hook the loop onto something. Remove both anchor strings and both loops from opposite sawhorse, tie all 4 of these into a 1–2-in loop, and hook onto something, out of the way.

   NOTE: Adding 3 additional screws on each sawhorse helps to keep each string separated and twisted while you work.

2. Repeat the entire setup and above steps with attached spool (this is where not cutting the spool makes the process easier) an additional 2 more times, hooking each string out of the way.

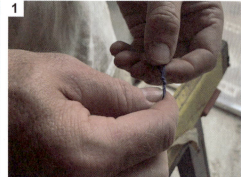

3. Now place the 3 spun strings back on the screws. Place the 3 loops of one horse on the hook and spin again in the opposite direction (now clockwise again) for the same duration of time.

   NOTE: In this fashion, 6 strands of ⅟32-in thread becomes ⅛-in string and the 3 strands of ⅛-in string become ¼-in twine and so on and so forth.

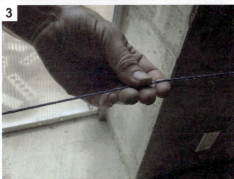

4. Cut off and melt ends with a lighter (synthetic materials) or cap with melted wax or wrap with electrical tape (natural materials), then ball or wrap on a spool.

Rope

The machine and methods I describe for making string (page 47) are exactly the same for making rope. 6 strands of ⅛-in string, twine, or yarn twisted in the same double twist configuration will make a ⅜-in rope, 12 strands will make a ½-in rope, etc. Expect a 12-ft:1-ft reduction. Burn loose fibers or leave rough, and don't forget to wrap, tape, wax, or melt the ends.

Plastic Bag Rope

Most of the rope we use around the homestead—be it for animals, rigging, straps, construction, etc.—we made from plastic grocery bags because they're 1) free, 2) strong, 3) waterproof, and 4) UV resistant, and 5) we had thousands in our stage one bin (page 23)! All reasons why they're horrible for the environment and why we "really" need to repurpose them.

MATERIALS
plastic grocery bags

TOOLS
scissors
(optional) string machine (page 47, step 1)

1. Pull a bottom corner and corresponding handle to flatten each side and fold lengthwise so handles overlap. Fold again lengthwise and cut off bottom and top handles, leaving 12 in of middle.
2. Fold widthwise, giving you 6 in, and make (6) 1-in cuts, cutting the last in half at the fold for 7 strips.
3. Daisy chain each of the 7 loops together and repeat with the other bags, balling or reeling as you progress, until you have the length you want. Repeat for 3 balls' worth.

   NOTE: 1 bag cut into 1-in strips and latched together will make 4 ft of 3-double-strand rope.

4. Place 3 equal lengths of plastic into your string machine (page 47, step 1) and twist as described, or braid together, daisy chaining more on as you go. Clamp the ends with a pair of needle nose vise grips, cut, and melt them together.

MAKE YOUR OWN SHOES

Who hasn't dreamt of having their own famous brand? Well, this is a real shoe-in.

Sandals

Shoes are the exception to "clothes lasting a lifetime" (see "Recycling" on page 22) since today they're built for quicker turnover. If we're going to build some, let's build a set that will last.

MATERIALS
car tire
liquid dish soap
¾-inch nylon strapping
¾-inch plastic buckle

TOOLS
Sawzall with coarse (wood) and fine (metal) blades
jigsaw with coarse (wood) blade
utility knife or cable cutters
crowbar
Sharpie or crayon
drill with ¼-inch drill bit
hammer and ½-inch wood chisel

1. Using a Sawzall with a coarse blade, cut a slot along the tire's diameter.
2. Once you hit the cables in the inside rib, switch to a fine-tooth blade or use cable cutters to cut them.

   Note: A crowbar greatly simplifies the process.

3. Repeat on the opposite side and again about a foot over, cutting a cross-section of car tire, equal to the length of your foot plus 3 inches.

   Important: Only use car tires. (Scraps can be collected from the highway.) Truck tires are too wide.

4. Cut both sides of the sidewalls 2 inches up from outside corners.

   Note: Narrower tires fit smaller feet better, and wider tires fit larger feet better.

5. Trace your foot outline wearing two socks (to account for spacing), then add five 1-inch (small) to 1¾-inch trapezoid flaps outside the widest and narrowest parts of your foot outline (one heel, two phalanges, two malleoli).

6. Drill ¼-in holes at the end of each inside corner for radiuses, then cut the pattern using a jigsaw or Sawzall with a coarse blade.

7. Using a utility knife, along the bottom of each trapezoid flap, make a wedge-shaped cutout into the outside face of the tire until you hit the 1-ply thickness of Kevlar webbing (about halfway through the thickness of the tire) to relieve tension, then bend all flaps up and in.

8. Chisel ½–1 inch strap slots in the trapezoid flaps vertically, two in the rear, one in the front. Run nylon strapping through tabs, add a simple buckle, and repeat for the opposite foot.

   Note: A decent tire is rated for 60,000 miles when loaded with over 2,000 pounds. The average person weighs 180 pounds and walks 1 mile per day, which equates to over 1,882 years.

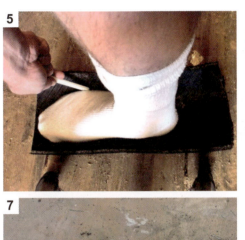

Flip-Flops

1. Trace feet on mud flap, door mat, or other thin rubber, thick plastic, or foam material, add ¾ inch to the sides and behind heel, and cut.

2. Now starting in the middle, cut down and around the heel along the inside line. Cut around and between big and second toes so that the cut-out creates a long flap.

3. Make a slot in the heel flap slightly shorter than the width of the toe flap, pull heel flap forward and slide toe flap into slot.

HANDMADE TOYS

Hasbro doesn't have a *monopoly* on toys, board games, or figurines.

Blocks

Got scrap dimensional lumber? There's no simpler way to make a toy than cutting and painting different-sized pyramids, cubes, bars, rectangles, flat blocks and prisms different colors (see "Paints" on page 57). Learning blocks is another version. Cut 2-in³ cubes and stencil, carve, paint, or burnish letters and numbers into each side.

Play Dough

If you use food coloring, the play dough will be edible. Safe for the environment and safe for your kids.

MATERIALS
1 c water
2 t blue die
2 t red die
2 t yellow die
1½ c salt
1 c oil
4 c flour

TOOLS
(6) 1-q plastic containers
stirring spoon
plastic wrap

1. Add 1 c water to (6) 1-q plastic containers, then 1 t blue dye or food coloring to the first, red to the second, and yellow to the third. Then for purple, add ½ t blue and ½ t red in the fourth. For orange, add yellow and red, and for green, add yellow and blue.
2. Mix in 1½ c salt (page 233) and stir until dissolved, then add 2 T oil and 4 c flour. Once thoroughly mixed, cover surface with a thin layer of oil. Remove and knead. Add oil as needed until it reaches play-dough-like texture. Cover with lid and store for 24 hours before use.

Dolls

MATERIALS
pattern
pins
stuffing
2-ft² fabric
string or elastic
yarn
hot glue sticks

TOOLS
measuring tape
sewing needle
thread
book
hot glue gun
pencil

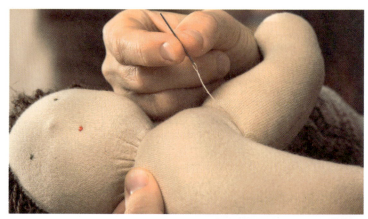

1. Cut rag doll paper pattern or find free patterns online. Fold body material in half and pin and cut body pattern.

   NOTE: The pattern has 2 arms and 2 legs, but if your daughter's into sci-fi, feel free to add more.

2. Sew body seam leaving a side hole, stuff with stuffing, then sew shut. Attach arms and legs, and sew elbow and knee lines in plane with body.
3. For the dress, choose flowers or other colorful print cloth. Place patterns, pin, and cut.
4. Place sleeve piece upside down on either dress piece so both radiuses align. Sew along radius.
5. Repeat for the other side and sleeve and back piece but before attaching all 4 together, fold collar over and in, and sew a ⅜-in seam.

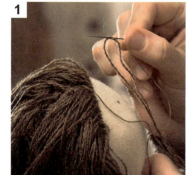

6. Run string or elastic through seam, pull and tie, leaving enough for head. Repeat for sleeve and bottom hems. Sew back piece with sleeve and flip inside-out.
7. For hair, rap yarn around a small book 30 times. Run a hot glue bead from top of head to the back and bottom, then open wrap in hands (double karate chop style) and place with strands to sides. Let cure then straight-stitch with similar colored thread.
8. Pull hair forward, and starting from top stitch, follow around each side to just below ears. Give her a haircut and draw face and shoes.

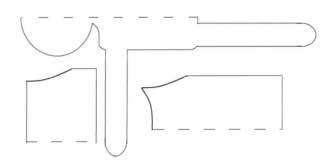

FORMING GLASSWARE

We can make most of our dinnerware from clay, which is easier (and safer), but there are a few niche objects that are superior with glass.

WARNING: Never look directly into your foundry. Always use heat protection in high radiant heat because of infrared and ultraviolet hazards, and, whenever looking into a foundry, always use a pair of American National Standard Institute (ANSI) certified goggles or a welding shield.

Drinking Glasses

MATERIALS
1 x 4 wood scrap
glass bottle
1 gal ice water
1 gal boiling water

TOOLS
C clamps
glass cutter
deep pot
bowl
400-grit sandpaper

WARNING: Wear leather gloves and safety glasses.

1. Build yourself a little cutting stand, with a couple scrap 1 x 4 cut into an L, or use (2) adjustable or rigid tri-square tools. Stack a couple blocks up and clamp or firmly hold a glass cutter perpendicular to and touching the bottle, just below the neck radius.
2. Oil the glass cutter blade with vegetable oil then place your bottle and have someone rotate the bottle while you hold the top in place (a ½-in drive extension on a ⅜-in socket helps), applying pressure to score around the outside.

3. Place upside down in boiling water for 5–10 seconds, remove and submerge in an ice bath for the same time. Repeat back and forth until you hear a pop, and then separate the neck from the bottle.

IMPORTANT: Only score the bottle once. If you hear a cutting sound, it means you're scoring twice. If you hear a crack rather than a pop, with no separation occurring, tap the inside, just forward of the crack, with the handle of a 5-gal bucket, letting the crack run around the circumference.

4. Smooth and flatten the rim of remaining bottle with a brick or sandpaper that's 400 grit or higher.

LEARN TO BUILD FURNITURE

The following projects are from early guides I wrote. In order to keep things simple for beginners, I don't use any rollers, hardware, tracks, or special joints, and the wood is recycled scraps and/or milled deadfall. That said, I wouldn't suggest making furniture out of wood because of fire and cleanliness concerns. But that's a whole other mindset changer!

IMPORTANT: Wash all cloth material to preshrink before sewing onto your furniture.

Box-Frame Bookcase

First know that you don't need your bed's box frame. There's nothing in it; it's just a spacer that you paid $300 for that you could have built for free. Second, the setup can also be used as an entertainment center, toy case, parts or tool rack, stage two shelves (page 25), display case, or anything else you can imagine.

MATERIALS
(2) 1 x 4-in x 8-ft boards

TOOLS
machine pliers
miter saw

1. Using pliers, remove the staples holding the fabric, batting, and cardboard to the frame, and place the loose material in your stage one bins (page 23).
2. Cut (4) 1 x 4s to 38 in long, or to box frame width from side to center divider, and place the lumber on top of each frame spacer set, including bottom and top.
3. Fill with material possessions.

Rugs

We can make doilies, pot holders, place mats, and even rugs and quilts by just braiding or crocheting with our own homemade yarn (or hemp, string, yarn, plastic rope, whatever)!

MATERIALS
T-shirt yarn (page 19) or yarn (page 44)
safety pins

TOOLS
scissors

1. Start by cutting up and making yarn out of your various old T-shirts ("T-Shirt Yarn", page 19).

   NOTE: 400–600 bags make a 3 x 3-ft mat, whereas 15 various T-shirts or 1 queen sheet makes a 30-in rug. Towels make incredible rag rugs, incredibly thick. Don't braid too tight, though; you'll have to work through it later.

2. Tie a 1–2-in loop knot in the end of 1 or 2 (2 for thicker mats) lengths of rag yarn, then perform 10–12, depending on yarn thickness, chain crochet stitches around the loop. Once you reach your starting point, continue on the outside of that loop, making a big spiral.
3. For braiding, tie a loop in the end of 3 or 4 lengths of rag yarn in the same fashion, and braid around the knot (it helps if someone holds the knot in place), running the inside strand through and around the knit during each braid. Once you reach the outside of your braided circle, continue making a big spiral.

   NOTE: Placing safety pins in the ends of all 4 strands helps when threading the yarn through the braid. Also, place all knots on the bottom of the mat.

4. When you reach the size you want, simply tie off the strands to the mat itself, cut off the excess, and you're done!

   NOTE: The great thing about these kinds of rugs is that if you run out or yarn or T-shirts, you can always tie it off for now, then untie the end knot and keep braiding later, making your rug bigger every year. For thicker rugs or quilts, braid using 2 yarns.

Futon

MATERIALS
(2) 2 x 8 in x 8 ft boards
(1) 1 x 4 in x 4 ft boards
(9) 1 x 4 in x 6 ft boards
(1) 2 x 4 in x 8 ft boards
(4) $\frac{5}{16}$ x 3½-in flat head bolts
(4) $\frac{5}{16}$ x 3½-in hex head bolts
(2) $\frac{5}{16}$ x 5-in hex head bolts

(20) $\frac{5}{16}$-in washers
(10) $\frac{5}{16}$-in nuts
1½-in coarse
  drywall screws
stain, paint, or
  varnish

TOOLS
angle finder
miter saw
measuring tape
Sharpie or pencil
drill with $\frac{5}{16}$-in and ⅛-in drill bits
band or skill saw with wood blades

paint brush or
  roller
palm sander with
  coarse and fine
  sandpaper

1. Take (1) 2 x 8 x 8 and cut 3 rear legs 2-ft 6-in long at 30° with a 1-in offset (alternate cuts).
2. Drill (3) $\frac{5}{16}$-in holes in the rear legs. Measuring from one edge and the 1-in offset, drill one hole 2 in from the edge and 3⅜ in from the end, the second 2 in from the edge and 9⅝ in from the end and the last 1¾ in from the edge and 1 ft 1½ in from the end.
3. Take the other 2 x 8 x 8 and cut (3) 2 ft 6-in long front legs, one end cut at a 97° angle and the other at a 30° angle with a 1-in offset.
4. Drill (2) $\frac{5}{16}$-in holes in the front legs. Measuring from one edge and the 30° end, drill the first 1¾ in from the edge and 9½ in from the end. Measuring from the same edge and the other end, drill the second hole 2 in from the edge and 4 in from the end.
5. From a 1 x 4, cut (2) 1-ft 4-in long arm rest supports (ARSs) and drill two $\frac{5}{16}$-in holes 1¾ in from each end. Round each corner to a 1¾-in radius.
6. From a 2 x 4, cut two arm rests (ARs) to 2 ft ½ in long, drill (2) $\frac{5}{16}$-in holes, 1¾ in from the edge and 5¾ in from each end and round corners with a band saw or skill saw.
7. From 2 x 4 scraps, cut (2) locks to 5½ in long. Drill (1) $\frac{5}{16}$-in hole 1¾ in from one end and edge, and round 1 corner on that end to a 3½-in radius.
8. Cut (4) 3½-in spacers from 2 x 4 scraps, drill a $\frac{5}{16}$-in hole 1¾ in from the end and edge, and round the corners.

8

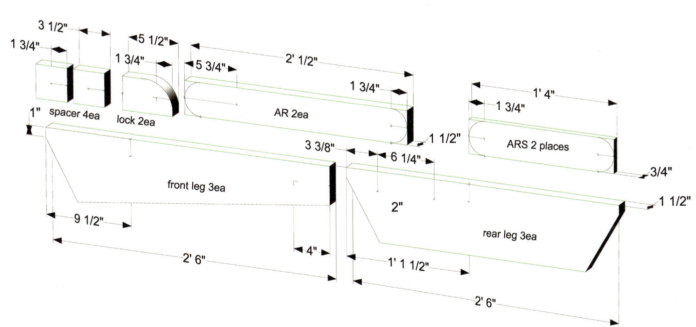

9. Hit all edges with a palm sander with coarse sandpaper, followed with fine.
10. Place 1 front leg on the outside of 1 rear leg, and repeat for the other two leg assemblies. Countersink holes on the two outside leg assemblies and install $\frac{5}{16}$ x 3½-in flat head bolts, washers, and nuts. Repeat countersinking and bolting for locks.

    IMPORTANT: Each lock's rounded corners must face the front legs.

11. Place armrests on the inside of the armrest supports, countersink and install $\frac{5}{16}$ x 3½-in bolts, washers, and nuts.
12. Place arm assembly on outside of leg assembly with a spacer in between, and install $\frac{5}{16}$ x 5-in bolts, washers, and nuts.
13. Place remaining leg assembly in the middle of the other two, 6 ft apart and square everything with a 24-in carpenters square.
14. For slats, cut (9) 1 x 4s to 6 ft long and drill ten sets of ⅛-in pilot holes ¾ in from ends on five planks, and drill eight sets 2¼ in from the ends for the remaining four.

12

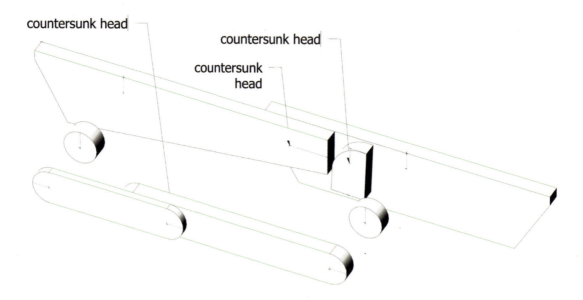

countersunk head

countersunk head

countersunk head

15. Starting from the front leg edges, install the set of 5 slats 2 in apart using 1½-in coarse drywall screws. On the opposite side, starting from the rear leg edges, install the set of (4) slats 3⁹⁄₁₆ in apart.
16. Drill 2 sets of ⅛-in pilot holes through slats above the middle leg assembly and attach with 1½-in screws.
17. (Optional) Stain, paint (page 57), varnish, or leave wood bare, and place a full mattress on the frame.
18. Operation: To lift the futon into sitting position, pull up and forward on the back while kneeling on the seat until locks engage (locks should swing freely). To lay it down, pull the back forward until the locks disengage, and then lower the back.

16

18

Table

For a table, sticking with the recycling motif, we went with a 6-ft cable spool, which is free at any utility company.

MATERIALS

6-ft cable spool
3-ft cable spool

1-gal polyurethane or 6 x 6-ft glass

TOOLS

pencil
measuring tape
string
jigsaw or Sawzall

¼-in drive rachet with ½-in socket
½-in wrench
bungee or rachet strap
drill with ⅜-in drill bit

1. Place the 6-ft spool on end, connecting bolt nuts up, heads down. Repeat for the 3-ft spool.
2. Wrap the center column of the spool with a bungee or rachet strap to keep slats from falling out, and remove nuts and connecting bolt nuts.

   NOTE: If the bolts begin to spin, you'll need to add a few 4 x 4 spacers underneath and have a helper hold a wrench on the bolt heads.

3. Once free, place and center the 6-ft spool side on top of the removed 3-ft spool side and drill each hole with a ½-in auger bit, using the existing hole as a guide.
4. Place the modified 3-ft spool side onto the 6-ft spool assembly and replace the nuts.

   NOTE: If you only have one spool, using a string and pencil centered on either 6-ft spool side, draw out a 1-ft 6-in radius circle on the bottom side and cut it into a smaller diameter circle using a jigsaw.

5. Cover with 8 layers of polyurethane or ¼-in glass.

   NOTE: For a less rustic version, make a 2-in x 6–8-ft wide circular form and pour, vibrate, sand, and finish an EPScrete tabletop. Place on top of the spool or fabricate a column in the same manner, 24 in wide x 26–28 in tall.

HOMEMADE PAINTS

There is no real category for coloring substrates, so I use the term "paints" simply to refer to the several processes, procedures and forms of adding or changing color.

Pigments

See "Cans to Pigments" on page 20.

Water-Based Paint

MATERIALS

pigments

filler: gypsum, clay (page 59), lime, calcium carbonate (page 57), talcum, cleaned ash, or silica

binding agent: flour, urobilin, dry egg yolk, honey (page 220), or casein

preservative: vinegar (page 232), rosemary extract, tea tree oil, salt, or creosote

TOOLS

blender

1 large mixing bowl

measuring cups

stirring spoon

1-gal paint can

paint strainer or nylon

drill

paint mixer

plastic bag

rubber mallet

NOTE: Scale each measurement as needed.

1. Blend 10 c of casein on high and store in a freezer until powder crystalizes, then pour it, along with 4¼ c ice water, into a large mixing bowl, adding 1 t of lye at a time while stirring until casein completely dissolves. Let sit for 15–20 minutes.

   NOTE: To use egg yolk instead of casein, separate egg whites from the yolk and dry the yolk by passing it between paper towels. Remove and discard sack, which will happen as it's being passed between paper towels, and mix the yoke directly with dry pigments using water to extend working time, or as an emulsion in 1 part water.

2. Mix 3 c pigment with 4¼ c water. Add the casein crystals and mix until paint consistency and solid color is achieved, adding pigment as needed.

3. Strain through a paint filter or nylon into a 1-gal paint can, mix in a preservative at 8 T per gallon.

4. If correctly done, the mixture should be thicker than what you'll want to paint with, so you'll need to dilute it by adding water 1 T at a time while mixing until you reach the desired consistency.

5. Label the can with the date. And then, to increase shelf life, add carbon dioxide, argon, or nitrogen, cover with grocery bag, and set the lid with a rubber mallet.

HOME-BREWED CHEMICAL COMPOUNDS

Chemicals and chemical compounds are the building blocks of nature. They comprise everything we know, build with, eat, and use. You need to understand not only the critical ingredients but how to harvest, convert, and work with these elements. Most are plentiful and available in everyday materials you probably already have. The rest can be surface-mined like salt, quartz, and clay (page 59) or subterraneously mined by sinking concrete caisson tunnels and wells.

Agricultural Lime (Calcium Carbonate)

Agricultural lime, also called Garden lime, is one of my favorites. It is widely used in the agricultural and garden industries as an insect repellent and to alter pH and promote healthy plant life, in livestock management as a disinfectant, as well as in the construction industry as an additive for concrete (page 62) and soil (page 73), and it is the most in-demand compound on any homestead. It's also widely available, and we don't have to do much to make it.

MATERIALS
limestone, water heater scale, eggshells, snail shells, or seashells

TOOLS
solar dehydrator (page 137), solar oven (page 136), or oven
heavy-duty blender
mechanical flour sifter
plastic container with lid
desiccant packets (page 248)

1. Break limestone, water heater scale, eggshells, snail shells, or seashells into ¼-in thick slices and dehydrate in a solar dehydrator (page 137) or oven (page 136).
2. Pulverize into a powder by filling a heavy-duty blender halfway with your dehydrated materials. Blend on low (chop), then medium, then fine or puree, until the shells are powder. Push contents down with a dowel through the plug hole. Let settle, pour into a mechanical flour can sifter over a clean plastic container, and sift. Dump remainder back into blender and repeat.
3. Store in an airtight container with a desiccant packet (page 248).

Potash (Potassium Carbonate)

Potassium Carbonate is a salt with many uses. Around the homestead I use it mostly in making soap, ceramics, glass, and bleaching. To make potash, you first need to make an ash hopper.

Ash Hopper

The ash hopper I currently use is a beta 7.2 version. I'm pretty satisfied with it for our requirements (which are higher than most).

MATERIALS
5-gal bucket with lid
½-in mpt plastic ball valve
6-in dia x 10-in Sdr 35 PE pipe

TOOLS
drill
½-in drill bit or unibit

1. Drill a ½-in hole on the bottom of one side of a 5-gal bucket, and install a ½-in male pipe thread plastic ball valve.
2. Cut a 6-in dia Sdr 35 PE pipe to 10 in, and drill ½-in holes every 2 in.
3. Center the pipe inside bucket.

Potash

MATERIALS
banana peels or hard wood ash
soft water

TOOLS
flat plastic container
(optional) solar dehydrator (page 137)
air-tight container
desiccant packet (page 248)

1. Fill sides with banana peels or hard wood ashes, then add soft water until full. Replace lid and let sit for several hours.
2. Place another plastic container underneath, fill the bucket again with water, open valve and let it drip, allowing the potassium carbonate (K_2CO_3) to leach out.

3. When dripping stops, dehydrate bronze liquid (potassium carbonate) in a solar dehydrator (page 137) or leave it in the sun. Repeat until water drips clear. Then dry the ash left in the bucket, add it to the stage one recycle bin (page 23) or compost pile (page 184), refill the hopper, and repeat.

   NOTE: If the solution is too deep, a glassy top layer will form, which will need to be broken and stirred or else further evaporation will be inhibited.

4. Scrape crystals into an airtight container with a desiccant packet (page 248).

WARNING: Although potash is not as corrosive as most chemicals, never use it with anything metallic and always wear a NIOSH-approved toxic dust respirator.

Lye (Sodium Hydroxide[NaOH])

Used in drain cleaner, soaps, water treatment, fertilizer, and making paper, and used as a detergent, lye is a great general, all-purpose chemical.

WARNING: Lye, aka caustic soda, is a notch up the corrosive ladder. Perform work in a vented workspace with acetic acid or another highly acidic acid to neutralize if chemical contacts skin.

MATERIALS
distilled or deionized water
calcium hydroxide
sodium carbonate

TOOLS
large, nonmetallic pot
wooden mixing spoon
coffee filter
air-tight container
desiccant packet (page 248)

1. In a large, nonmetallic pot, boil calcium hydroxide and sodium carbonate 1:1 in distilled or deionized water for 1 second while stirring with a wooden mixing spoon.
2. Pass NaOH solution through a coffee filter to remove calcium carbonate, then recycle the coffee filter and the calcium carbonate that is in it. What's left over will be the sodium hydroxide, or lye.
3. Dehydrate and store the lye in an air-tight container with a desiccant packet (page 248).

Clay (Hydrous Aluminum Phyllosilicates)

Purchase clay at any hobby store or dig it out of your own backyard for free. The southern United States is blessed with some of the most beautiful clays on the planet, only a couple feet from the surface. The color differs from region, depth, mineral content, and age, ranging from charcoal and light greys to oranges, reds, greens, blues, and even purple.

Clay is the most important material on our homestead. I use it to build terracotta roof shingles and floor tiles; ponds and natural swimming pools; and pots, plates, bowls, planters, and other pottery. In the garden, we use it in hydroponics (page 105), landscaping, and as a building medium. It can be used for anything from ceramic filters, coolers, porcelain toilets, and sinks to skeet for target practice.

MATERIALS
5 gal water
crushed pebbles, pottery, shell, bone, antler, teeth, glass aggregate (page 16), or sharp sand as temper

TOOLS
flat shovel
4 glass jars
5-gal water bottle
5-gal bucket
¾-in x 5-ft garden hose
3-ft rope
16-in² fine woven rag
air-tight container
2 x 2-in Sch 40 PVC pipe
billiard ball or other round object
cones 08–06
resealable plastic bag

1. Remove a 2 to 4-ft² section of sod and clear away the topsoil. Fill a glass jar or other transparent container half full of dirt, and then fill the rest with water. Mix and let settle. Mark "Test Site 1" and repeat in 3 other locations.

    NOTE: Dirt contains silt, sand, and clay, typically between 1:3:4 and 1:3:6. For pottery and smaller uses, this will work.

2. In a few moments, the sand will settle on the bottom, the silt will rise to the top, and the clay will be suspended in between. The test with the largest percent of clay is the area you want to dig in. Repeat the test process using a 5-gal water bottle or similar transparent container; place a second empty container, a 5-gal bucket, underneath; siphon and/or decant only the clay layer into the second container.

3. Let clay settle overnight, siphon off any water that's risen to the top, being careful not to disturb the clay. Affix a 16-in² fine woven rag (sheet, pillowcase, etc.) atop the first container with rope. Stir the clay, then pour it through the cloth.

4. Remove the cloth, fold the corners in, and twist. Tie a knot with the rope and hang the sack for several days outside, allowing the water to drip out and the ball to dry.

   IMPORTANT: If anything other than clear water drips out after 30 minutes, the cloth pores are too large and you're losing clay.

5. Once firm, remove a chunk and squeeze. If no water drips, you're good. Otherwise, leave for another day.

6. Once enough moisture has been removed and the clay isn't sticky when handled, seal it inside a large resealable plastic bag and inside an airtight container to cure for several months. Like cheese and wine, clay gets much better with age. The longer you let it sit, the more plastic it becomes.

   WARNING: Clay can never be stored in the open air; it will dry out. If it does, it cannot regain its moisture by simply adding water.

7. When larger quantities are needed, strip away the sod and sand to expose the clay, then dig until you hit the rock-hard clay. Harvest with a pick mattock and rock bar or with a bobcat or track hoe, breaking the dirt into clumps.

NOTE: If you can't find it in your backyard (or you don't need a swimming pool), try creek, river, or pond banks and beds or hills and mounds. After a rain, you'll see water seeping out from the sides; this means it's drained vertically through the porous material and has hit the clay.

8. Dry shards in the sun or in a dehydrator until brick hard, pulverize them, then add the clay to a 5-gal bucket filled with 3 gallons of water mixed with 1 cup vinegar.

   IMPORTANT: I know I said never let your clay dry out, but when clay has minuscule amounts of moisture, it actually prevents the absorption of more, which is why clay is waterproof only when wet. Water level, in relation to clay level, is also important. You don't want your clay to be too wet and runny or too dry. You need clay that can be instantly molded. This will take practice and trial and error.

9. Let soak for 4–7 days. Check your clay for plasticity by rolling a ½-in log and wrapping it around your finger. A good, moldable green clay won't crack, tear, or break. If it does, re-store it in the bucket of water and vinegar. If it's too soft and slimy, let it dry a little.

10. Before throwing the clay, add temper such as crushed pebbles, pottery, shell, bone, antler, teeth, glass aggregate (page 16), or sharp sand between granule-size and powder.

    NOTE: Why remove the impurities to just add them again? Impurities prevent warping, shrinkage, and thermal shock but will cause separation if there's too much and cracking if there's too little. There is no set formula for determining temper percentage. I just add the temper, fire the clay, and document the results.

11. To test how well it'll throw for pottery, cut a 2-in long piece of 2-in Sch 40 PVC pipe and pack it with clay. Push out the contents and flatten the clay into a mini tortilla. Repeat 4 times, making five tortillas, placing one to the side as a control.

12. Fill each of the four test tortillas with a temper. To fill, weigh the temper, then add 1/10th of it in each tortilla, working it in. Place one tortilla with the control, then repeat so that the second tortilla will have 2/10ths temper, the next 3/10ths, and so on, resulting in tortillas of 0%, 10%, 20%, 30%, and 40% temper.

13. On a billiard ball or other round object, shape each tortilla into a ¼-in thick bowl. Work any cracks with a dab of water. Let dry.

14. Once the bowls reach the consistency of sharp cheese, inspect them and document damage. Scratch a 0, 1, 2, 3, 4 in the bottoms, and fire to cones 08–06. Let cool, remove, inspect, document results, then fire to cone 5 and document. The bowl percentage with the best results is the percentage you use for that specific temper and clay.

    NOTE: For this reason, it's a good idea to use a temper and clay, locally found in abundance, for free.

Charcoal

Charcoal, forge or blacksmith coal, or charwood is a building block of many DIY projects from filters to soil amendments to gunpowder to terra preta to growing media, to barbecuing. Organic and non-organic waste materials are transformed into charcoal through a fireless, oxygen-free process called pyrolysis that releases methane and hydrogen, which we can also use ("Wood Gas Stove," page 157). In this method, cooking is self-regulating. You can build the reactor, start the burn, and walk away. It's a great way to use, recycle, and eliminate waste to produce products and fuels.

If you're only looking to make charcoal, not charcoal as a by-product of wood gas, you can build a simple charcoal production stove with 1-gal paint cans.

MATERIALS
wood scraps

TOOLS
drill with ⅛-in drill bit
(3) 1-gal metal paint cans with lids
rag

1. First build a fire in a fire pit, and while you're waiting, drill (3) ⅛-in holes in the center of the lids of a few metal 1-gal paint cans.
2. Fill the cans with wood scraps, hammer the lid on tight, and set them level in the fire.
3. After about 10 minutes or so, the wood will start smoking, followed by flaming as the heat ignites the gasses being released in the wood.

4. After this, jets of smoke will appear. Once the jets subside, toss a wet rag on top of the holes, or pull the cans from the fire to let cool.

Grout

Grout consists of cement and a very fine aggregate, typically sieved sand.

MATERIALS
cement
sand
(optional) plaster of paris
linseed oil, mineral spirits, or turpentine
water-acrylic solution
(optional) pigment (page 20) or dye

TOOLS
5-gal bucket or wheelbarrow
paddle mixer or drill

1. In a 5-gal bucket or wheelbarrow, dry mix cement and sand 1:2.
2. Add plaster of paris, whitening (optional), linseed oil, mineral spirits, or turpentine at 2:4:1:1.5–2.0, with water-acrylic solution (1:7) until frosting consistency, adding pigment (page 20) or dye as desired.

   NOTE: For voids less than a ¼ in, sift sand through a 550-micron sieve to get #30.

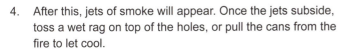

Mortar

Mortar is similar to grout in that it's a mixture of cement and fine aggregate, typically sand, but because it's used for structural strength, higher cement content is needed as well as coarser grout. Mortar is used for many tasks from plaster to brick walls to pavers, all with different strength and waterproofing criteria, and therefore, recipes vary depending on use:

- **Thin-set:** Water, cement, and #80 sand at 1:2.5:2.5.

NOTE: To get #80 sand, sift regular sand using a 165-micron sieve or a rotary sieve (page 64). Water should be combined with a 1:7 water–acrylic mix.

- **Tile:** Cement and #80 sand at 1:3. Add water until mud-like consistency
- **Wall masonry construction (CMUs and bricks):** Water, cement, and sand at 1:2:3–5.

NOTE: 1:2:3 makes 3000 psi mortar, which is good enough in most home constructions cases. If you're just doing a retaining wall, patio wall or anything for looks, adding up to 5 parts sand will bring you down closer to 1000 psi.

- **Pavers (non-waterproof):** Water, cement, and sand at 1.5:1:8.
- **Stucco:** Stucco consists of three different coats, first the scratch coat, second the brown coat, and last the finishing coat.
  Scratch and brown coats: Water, cement, and sand 1:1:3.
  Finishing coat: Water, cement, and sand at 1:2:4, plus 10% lime by weight and pigment stucco or mortar coloring of choice.
- **Rock:** Water, cement, and sand at 1:3:2.

NOTE: Because of the higher cement content, this mix will cure fast, so you'll want to add an admixture like sugar or lime plasticizer like in concrete (see below).

Concrete

Concrete is a mixture of water, cement, fine aggregate (sand), and coarse or large aggregate (rock, shell, etc.). Coarse aggregate, at less than 10 parts, doesn't affect tensile strength; it's just a filler. In fact, since rock is harder than cement, adding large aggregate actually strengthens concrete. It's also important to note that concrete isn't waterproof by nature, but when the psi is over 5,000, the incredible density makes it so. And if lime is added, it makes the concrete more elastic and smooth, and it prevents cracks and shrinking.

IMPORTANT: Water activates and provides transportation for cement, but it also weakens the concrete by creating micro tunnels and fissures once the water evaporates. Only use enough water to make the mix workable. To make concrete workable longer, add plasticizer admixtures like sugar at 1 t:120 lbs or hydrated lime (page 57) at 1:1.

Different jobs require different levels of workability, or "slump." For example, when using a concrete pump, you'd want a slump of 4 in whereas for building a rock wall you'd want a 1-in slump in order to be able to immediately hold the weight of a 100-lb boulder. The slump indicates how far the concrete will fall, or slump, once it stands on its own. The higher the slump, the more fluid the mix.

To test slump, fill a 12-in cone or a slump cone with concrete, in three stages. Tamp down each layer 25 times, and once the cone is full, strike off any excess to make the concrete flush. Lift the cone without disturbing the concrete and set it next to the concrete. Place a bar across the top and measure the distance between the cone height and the concrete height.

For integral coloring of any cement product, add 7–10 parts pigment per 100 parts concrete (weight). This will create pigment color undertone. Or add less pigment for concrete color undertone; that is, the grey will mix with and distort colors.

WARNING: Although 70% strength is reached in 28 days when concrete is moist-cured, full 98% strength isn't achieved until fully cured, which takes 1 year. Cover the concrete with plastic and leave the cover and forms as long as possible. Best hydration and strength occur when concrete is covered and has access to water for 1 year.

MATERIALS

cement

sand

¼-in to 1-in aggregate

water

TOOLS

concrete mixer, or wheelbarrow and shovel

- **3,000 psi:** Cement, sand, and aggregate at 1:3:3
- **4,000 psi:** Cement, sand, and aggregate at 1:2:3.
- **4,500 psi:** Cement, sand, and aggregate at 1:1.66:3
- **5,000 psi:** Cement, sand, and aggregate at 1:1.3:3

FABRICATING PARTS

I am often asked: "You purchase everything you need before leaving society, but what happens when something breaks and you have to replace it?" During my time away, we had a lot of equipment breakage—tools, tractors, vehicles, appliances, electronics, etc. Usually the part could be repaired before needing to be replaced, or we got by without it. There were items, however, that did require replacing, and I fabricated new ones. That's the easy way. You already have what you need. You just need to copy it. The hard way is designing and making pieces that don't yet exist.

There are basically 3 ways to make stuff: by hand, in a mold, or by mill or at least a lathe. Making items without a forge or machinery limits us to making smaller things like hinges, handles, some hardware and minor parts. With molds and machinery though, we can fabricate the entire object, a pulley, piston or housing. When making objects by hand, it's easier to work parts individually, then assemble them together. Pouring molds isn't reserved for just metals. We can form anything from plastics, clay, or cement. Combining the 3 approaches—that is, melting and forming plastics, clay, or cement into basic shapes to be turned, welded, and finished by hand—is the most efficient method.

Rubber Objects

You'd be surprised how many things have rubber parts (O-rings, gaskets, seals, washers), but nothing a jigsaw, wood punch, hole saw and/or utility knife can't carve out of a tire, mud flap or bike inner tube:

MATERIALS

rubber (bicycle inner tube, car tire, etc.)

TOOLS

white pencil or chalk

electric planer or belt sander

1. Trace the part you want to replicate on a piece of rubber.

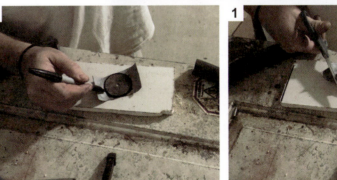

2. Using a utility knife, a punch (for O-rings), or scissors, cut the shape, then cut to desired thickness with an electric planer or belt sander. Compare and finish areas needed.

   NOTE: For larger and/or thicker pieces, use a jigsaw, belt saw, or Sawzall with a coarse blade or a pruning blade and water or oil to keep the blade cool, similar to the process of cutting tires in "Sandals" (page 50).

MAKING TOOLS

Bucket Sifter

Sifters, sieves, and trommels are a definite necessity when mining for, harvesting, breaking down and working with your own materials. It's the solid version of separating and decanting to purify. Use a bucket sifter for small jobs, a tripod or lean-to for larger jobs, and a rotary sieve when throwing dirt and stone all day.

MATERIALS
(1) 2-in x 2-in x 10-ft board
(1) 15¼-in² piece of rabbit wire

TOOLS
(8) #10 x 3-in screws
5-gal bucket

1. Cut (8) 2 x 2s to 13¾ in, lay (4) to form a 15¼-in² box, place a 15¼-in² piece of rabbit wire on top and sandwich with the remaining 2 x 2s, offsetting the seams, using #10 x 3-in screws to lock in place, 2 per side, 1 per corner.
2. Operation: Place assembly on a 5-gal bucket, wheelbarrow, or hand cart with desired screen size on top for the sieve. Pour 1 gallon or one shovel-full of material through the assembly and shake. Depending on which material you're wanting—larger (what's caught on top) or smaller (inside the bucket)—keep a second bucket to dump the contents in.

Rotary Sieve

This is another one of those projects that I went through many iterations of before settling on this one. Which, in the end, turned out to be the simplest design.

MATERIALS
old concrete mixer
1-ft x 6-ft rabbit wire or Metal screen
(22) #10 x ½-in button head screws
(22) #10 washers
(22) #10 lock nuts

TOOLS
drill
³⁄₁₆-in metal drill bit
⁵⁄₁₆-in wrench
Phillips screwdriver
cutting torch with size 1 tip

1. Using a cutting torch, cut (11) 6-in holes in a concrete mixer drum at least 1 in apart and 4-in OC from bolted seam. Repeat on opposite side of seam.
2. Drill (22) ³⁄₁₆-in holes along outside edges of holes on one side, repeat on the other, then install rabbit wire or metal screen (depending on desired sieve size) to inside of drums (covering holes completely) using #10 x ½-in screws, washers, and lock nuts.
3. Operation: Lock rotary sieve handle in the lowest horizontal setting possible, without material spilling out. Turn the unit on, place a wheelbarrow or cart underneath (if you want), and shovel in material. Once drum is full, back a second wheelbarrow or cart up and empty the sieve.

Hand Tamper

MATERIALS
1½ x 60-in Sch 40 pipe
½ x 8 x 8-in steel plate
6-in x 6-in ¼-in steel plate
glue sticks

TOOLS
stick welder with ⅛-in rods

1. Weld a 1½ x 60-in Sch 40 pipe to the center of a ½ x 8 x 8-in steel plate.
2. Cut four pieces from a ¼-in steel plate to 90° triangles and weld them to the pipe and steel plate as corner stiffeners.
3. Melt 2 glue sticks and coat the top 2 ft of the pipe for a hand grip.

2

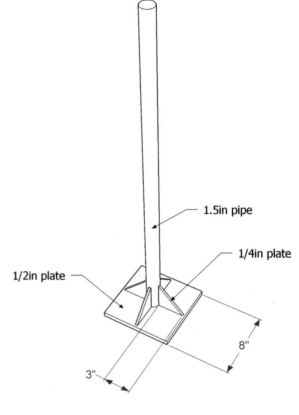

1.5in pipe

1/4in plate

1/2in plate

8"

3"

Chapter 5: Home Production of Produce

Have you ever heard the saying "money doesn't grow on trees"? It actually does in that you use money to buy food, and the more food you produce for free, the more money you have in your pocket. Growing your own produce is a staple DIY venture.

No matter your location or home size, you can produce significant quantities of food. That said, not all plants will grow everywhere, and getting one to grow doesn't mean it'll produce food. If you're not getting any production, you might as well grow a fern. You need to learn how to grow to produce (page 115).

Plants are just like humans. They eat, drink, feel, have families, babies, build communities, communicate, respire, perspire, overheat, freeze. Their bodies are like ours as well, but their heads are kept underground. Over time, I've learned what plants require not only to survive, but to thrive and bear fruit, enabling me to harvest and raise them productively, more efficiently, for free.

If you're dreaming of a giant greenhouse or housing an enormous commercial hydroponics or aquaponics system, it may be a while. I've been doing this for 10 years, full-time, and I'm still learning. Start small and work your way up. Study the content I've provided as well as material by others. Visit some amateur or commercial sites. It's a big commitment, multiplied by realizations, mindset breakers, mistakes, and accomplishments.

Take your time. Go slow. You'll get it. Everyone can!

WARNING: When searching for materials, try to use non-BPA, non-BPS plastics, as they tend to leach chemicals into your system. That said, most items, containers, straws, and bottles you use daily are made from BPA or BPS.

FORAGING AND GATHERING

At the most basic level of food acquisition, we have foraging and gathering. In the desert we had yucca, prickly pear, pitaya, mesquite beans, Texas desert sotol, cholla pencil cactus, and ocotillo. Make sure to pick up a field guide specific for your region and learn what's edible or medicinal around you. There is literally fresh free food growing around you all the time, even in your backyard, all you have to do is go out and pick it! There are too many edible plants and plant parts to list here, though you can see a short list in "Weeds" (page 103). Luckily, there are plenty of field guides listing them all.

NOTE: There are now apps that you can download to your phone that will take a picture of the plant and compare it to the edible/poisonous database to tell you if it's edible or not.

IMPORTANT: Even with a guide, identifying edible plants can be tricky to the novice. I've seen it time after time, people come out into the wild, misidentify a plant part or preparation method and become violently ill. If you're a beginner, it's important, even with a guide, to test wild plants and plant parts before consuming.

EDIBLE WILD PLANTS

You don't even have to plant plants to grow food. There are edible plants growing everywhere, all over this planet, at this very minute. In your neighborhood, in the park down the street, maybe even weeds (page 103) in your very own backyard.

I'm not going to devote an entire chapter to locating and identifying edible wild plants, not for a lack of knowledge on my part. On the contrary, there is such an overabundance of knowledge already out there, and there's just too much area-specific information that would need to be relayed and described in detail to do you any good. This, coupled with the facts that: (a) many edible wild plants share many similarities with poisonous plants of the same region, (b) some parts of a plant may be edible while other parts of the same plant are toxic, and (c) some plants or plant parts are only edible for certain periods of the year or when prepared in certain ways. You can see why there is no universal method for identifying all plants everywhere for everyone. I would highly suggest you purchase an in-depth, region-specific edible plant guide (or download the app) with detailed photographs, not drawings, of each plant and how to prepare them if you're interested in eating wild produce.

In the meantime, however, there is a basic test to determine if a plant or part of a plant is edible. Keep in mind this system only determines if a plant isn't extremely poisonous; it doesn't determine its nutrient values or if your body will agree with it. The following could take up to several day's testing for a single plant type, so it's important not to waste your time checking what's not readily available in your area. Also, remember that eating large portions of even common plants like beans, lettuce, strawberries, even bananas, can cause diarrhea, nausea, and cramps, so if you locate an edible plant, eat in moderation.

Lastly, in most cases, the test will leave you hungry and weak. Make sure not to attempt the test when you run out of food, but rather while you still have plenty in reserve to replenish your losses once complete.

1. Don't eat anything for 8 hours to ensure any effects felt come from the subject.
2. Don't pick or touch the plant before the 8 hours.
3. Pick the questionable plant and separate the flowers and leaves from the stem, and the stem from the root.
4. Rub a portion of each part of the plant against different spots on the inside of your wrists.
5. Remember, or mark with a pen, which areas on your wrist signify which part of the plant.
6. Wait 10–30 minutes for a reaction. If no stinging or burning occurs, apply one of the parts to your lips.
7. Wait 10–30 minutes for a reaction. If no stinging or burning occurs on your lips, apply the same part to your tongue. Do not chew or swallow, just rub.

8. Wait 10–30 minutes for a reaction. If no stinging or burning occurs on your tongue, perform the same tests with the other sections of the plant that didn't cause any adverse reactions on your wrist.
9. This concludes the first half of the test. If you experienced any reaction during any stage of the test, that section of the plant failed and is not safe for ingestion.
10. Boil any passed sections in water for 5–10 minutes then chew one section for 3 minutes. Do not swallow!
11. Wait 10–30 minutes for a reaction. If no nausea, stinging or burning occurs, chew the remaining pieces in that section in the same manner. Do not swallow!
12. Wait 10–30 minutes for a reaction. If no nausea, stinging or burning occurs, chew and swallow a piece of that section.
13. Wait 8 hours for a reaction. If you experience any discomfort, induce vomiting. If no reaction is felt, you may eat the remaining boiled pieces of that section.
14. Wait 8 hours for a reaction. If you experience any discomfort, induce vomiting. If no reaction is felt, repeat the above test for each section of the plant that passed the first half of the tests.
15. If no reaction is felt, the plant, or at least the 'passed' sections of that plant, are safe to eat in the future. If in doubt, don't eat it. It's better to be hungry than to poison yourself.

Grasses

The term *whole grain* only applies to the state of the grain when it's in its original or natural form. There are many, many different types of whole grains. Some of the most common that are grown and sold industrially are amaranth, einkorn, farro, oat, spelt, quinoa, barley, emmer, millet, rye, tiff and wheat. But what about the other thousand-plus wild grasses growing in yards, ditches, fields, and through cracks in the streets, which, to a lesser or greater degree, resemble wheat? Some really look like wheat, while others only resemble wheat because they have a cluster of seeds at the end of a long slender stalk. Can these grass seeds with a similar nutritional content to wheat be harvested, ground into flour, and eaten safely by humans as well?

In short, *all* seeds from *all* wild grasses are safe to eat and can be used as flour or cereal. Some, however, are better than others for nutrition.

Most grasses have tiny seeds, so grinding them loosely or pounding them with a mallet to break the shell, and then tossing and letting the wind or a fan separate the chaff from the seeds is the easiest way to process them. The chaff will not hurt you if it's ground finely and consumed; it is simply not always digestible and will pass through unchanged. In some grain species, the chaff is also a source of nutrition and is often actually better for you when left in. At the very least, it's a bulk substance, which will provide a feeling of fullness even when it doesn't provide nourishment, staving off the feeling of starvation.

And although humans don't have the enzymes to process the actual grass stock itself, it can be cut finely and added to bread, soup, or tea. Again, it is not usually digestible, but there is vitamin C and other nutrients in grass that will leach out into soup or tea. The same applies to most pine needles.

Even though they may not be digestible or nutritional, there are no poisonous grasses; just be sure it is actually a grass and that there's no fungus present. From a self-sufficiency and survival standpoint, however, the amount of energy gained from eating bread would barely exceed the amount of energy lost harvesting, milling, making, and baking it. Therefore, it's just not efficient!

First, you'll need to know when to harvest your wild grain. Wheat usually drops its seed, which is actually a fruit, twice per year, once in June or July and again in November or December, depending on location. The seed head has to be brownish tan in color. When you think the seed might be ready, remove the head from one stalk and grind it between the palms of your hands. If you get hard little seeds, then the grain is ready to harvest. This stage of maturity is called the hard dough stage, because when you try to chew the seeds, they are hard and will crunch when you bite into them.

MATERIALS
burlap sack or tarp
large storage totes

TOOLS
grain mill or stone mill

1. The simplest method of harvesting grain by hand without a grain harvester is for one person to walk down the rows of grass with a burlap sack or tarp, and another shaking out the tops where the seeds are kept into the bag.
2. As the bag fills up with seed pods, carefully empty them into a large storage tote or other suitable container.
3. When enough containers are filled, separate the chaff from seed by tossing them and letting the wind or a fan separate them, then grind the seeds into flour with a grain mill or by placing some seed onto a large flat rock, or concrete sidewalk, and rolling a long round rock on top of them. You're able to separate chaff from seed with the wind or a fan and mill in one step.

Trees and Bushes

Trees can be a major provider of not just shade, beauty, and fun, but food as well. Fruit and nut trees are the obvious choices, but trees that bear acorns, like oak, and seed pods, like mesquite, are great food additions as well. Mesquite is a leguminous tree that grows profusely throughout the Americas but especially all over the western United States. Its pea-like pods can also be dried and milled just like corn and acorn to make mesquite flour. Native Americans in the past, and even some of today's Hispanics, rely heavily on the mesquite plant as a source of food in dry regions that can't sustain corn, wheat, or rice.

Cacti

First off, true cactus fruit from any cactus is safe to eat, but some taste better than others. Also, the pads of most cactus, not just prickly pear, are edible as well. So much so that you'd have a really hard time finding a wild cactus that wasn't edible. Prickly pear, barrel, agave, cholla, Peruvian apple, dragon fruit, organ pipe, and pitaya cacti are all great edible additions to your back and front yard xeriscapes.

COST

You don't need a lot of, or any, money to grow food if you're repurposing materials you already have. The societal instilled notion of food costing money to grow is absurd. Fruits and vegetables, nuts and seeds, syrup, potatoes, bananas, apples, and everything else has been growing for millions of years, free of charge, before humans showed up. Even longer before the concept of selling plants and plant by-products for green pieces of paper, which are also plant by-products. What an incredible and simple idea, though: Let's take something that's all around us, has been free since the beginning, and is abundant and tell people they now have to pay us for it!

I don't have costs growing food (see my Free Food Factory on YouTube); I don't have costs doing anything myself. Now, sure, if you want me to harvest it for you, transport it to you, and put it in a bag so you can take it home, I'll charge you for my time, purchases, and transport expenses. Otherwise, if you're growing locally, naturally, and

organically and are accruing costs, you're doing it wrong! I've included many projects in this chapter to start you on your way. Just follow along with the methods I've used and choose which will best fit your needs.

METHODS

You don't need a ten-acre farm or even a garden to grow food. And it doesn't matter where you live; there's food growing this very second in cities, forests, deserts, jungles, up in the mountains, and even in the ocean! The following table shows different methods for efficiently growing just a fraction of the 200,000+ edible plant species currently growing all around earth, of which we consume less than 150. In fact, two-thirds of our daily food comes from just three of the tens of thousands of cereal crops known to man. There's so much food growing naturally on this planet, at no cost to anyone, someone should open a bunch of companies like my Free Food Factory and just give it away!

Before choosing what to plant, determine which food type is best for you and your location. You may learn that although you love almonds, you don't want to wait five years, or that, even though your diet calls for iceberg lettuce, romaine is easier to grow in your location. If you want to grow any plant any time of the year, make a grow room (page 96). I also suggest staying with perennials to save energy replanting after each harvest.

PRODUCE METHODS

Plant	Edible parts	Med	Type	Soil	Hydroponics method	Time to produce[3]
Asparagus	Young shoots	Y	Per	Potting/LAN/RB/ng	F&D	2–3 yr
Avocado	Seed/fruit	Y	Per	Potting/LAN/orchard/Mg	DRIP	3–4 yr
Banana	Fruit	Y	Per	Potting/LAN/orchard	DRIP	1–2 yr
Broccoli	Seed	Y	Per	Potting/Rb/LAN/Mg	F&D	10 wk
Cantaloupe	Fruit/oil/seed	Y	Ann	Potting/Rb/LAN/Mg	F&D	12–17 wk
Carrot	Seed	Y	Ann	Potting/Rb/LAN/Mg	F&D	1–13 mo
Cob Corn	Seed	Y	Per	Potting/LAN/Rb/Mg	DRIP	2–3 mo
Lettuce	Leaves/oil/seed	Y	Ann	Potting/LAN/Rb/Mg	floating bed	26 d
Potato	Root	Y	Per	Potting/LAN/Rb/Mg	F&D	25–4 mo
Soybean	Leaves/oil/seed/seedpod	Y	Ann	Potting/LAN/Rb/Mg	F&D	45–65 d
Strawberry	Fruit	Y	Per	Potting/LAN/Rb/Mg	F&D	3–4 mo
Sweet Brown Rice	Seed (cereal)	N	Per	Potting/LAN/Rb/Mg	F&D	120–150 d
Tomato	Fruit	Y	Per	Potting/LAN/Rb/Mg	DRIP	60–80 d

If you still can't decide, the following plants are some of my favorites, and I've included some tips and tricks for the most efficient ways to grow and eat them.
- In non-climate-controlled environments, plant lettuce and kale in late winter, heat-tolerant lettuce (Sampson, Nevada, etc.) and chard in early summer, and lettuce and kale again in early fall.
- Freeze Kale to turn its bitter taste to sweet.
- Watermeal is the smallest, simplest structured flowering plant known, at less than 1/16 in, which makes it a breeze to grow in almost any water environment. Nutrient levels are higher than most at around 40% protein, equivalent to soybean but with one-hundred times the production, harvest rate, and quantity.

- Duckweed (Lemna minor) grows wild, doubling almost weekly in any stagnant water body and is exceptionally tasty to us, fish, fowl and livestock. At almost 50% protein content, it's packed full of nutrients (4% fat, 8–10% fiber, vitamins A and B, lysine, iron and zinc). Puree the duckweed and add it to soups or stews, sauté it, or dehydrate it and add as a powder.
- Brambles, considered noxious weeds based on their "tendency to grow in neglected areas," are also chock-full of vitamins and antitoxins. The list includes blackberry, salmonberry, loganberry, tayberry, wineberry, youngberry, boysenberry, dewberry, raspberry, and thimbleberry, all of which are equally delicious and easy to grow (like a weed).
- Cattail tops are exceptional when prepared like corn on the cob. Rhizomes, like potatoes and pollen, can be powdered and added as a spice to other foods.
- There are three groups of sugar cane: chewing, which is the easiest to grow and very sweet; crystal, which is for making sugars; and syrup, which is for juices, syrups, and molasses. All are enormous sources of pure sugar when processed (see "Sugar," page 234).
- Strawberry seeds can take four weeks or more to germinate. But once they get established begin producing strawberries almost right away.
- Valencia oranges are better for juicing, navel for eating. Both grow fairly fast in warm regions.
- Finally, plants produce many by-products besides food, like pollen, fiber, oil, rubber, pigment, dye, cotton, sugar, syrup, molasses, starch, compost, glue, fuel, mulch, woodchips, timber, and much more.

NEEDS

Look up the root depth, spacing, pH, soil type, fertilizer type, light and temp requirements, RH (relative humidity), and percolation rate for each edible plant you're interested in growing, and make a Plant Needs table (see example below). Determine what each plant requires, which plants overlap in which areas, and therefore, which can be grown together.

EXAMPLE: We see that asparagus, broccoli, and potato could be grown together if the pH were kept at 6.5, temps between 60 and 65°, and RH at 70%. Thyme, tomato, and watermelon are another grouping if pH is kept between 6.0 and 6.5, temps at 70°, and RH above 50%.

PRODUCE METHODS

Plant	Soil	Depth (in)	Space (in)	Ph	N-P-K	Sun	Temp	RH (%)	Perc rate (in/hr)
Almond	Sandy clay/ sandy loam	24	240	7.0	2.5-.2-3	Full	86–95	20–65	0.31–0.75
Arugula	Sandy loam	12–18	1	6.0–7.0	2-1-3	Full, partial	50–65	50–70	0.60
Asparagus	Sandy loam/ loam/sandy clay	>48	15–18	6.5–7.5	10-20-10	Full, partial	60–70	60–70	0.31–0.75
Broccoli	Sandy clay/ clay loam	18–36	18–24	6.0–7.5	5-10-5	Full	60–65	70–85	0.25–0.31
Potato	Loam	18–24	10–12	5.0–6.5	5-10-5	None–full	50–65	60–85	0.54
Raspberry	Loam/sandy loam	24–36	12	5.5–6.2	10-10-10	Full	60–70	60–75	0.54–0.75
Thyme herb	Loam	14	12	4.5–8.0	5-10-10	Full, partial	70	10–80	0.54
Tomato	Clay loam/ sandy loam	48+	96+	5.5–6.5	5-10-10	Full	70–75	>45	0.25–0.75
Watermelon	Sandy loam	24–48	60–84	6.0–6.5	5-10-10	Full	65–75	>50	0.75

SOIL

Different plants like different soils, but most require a well-draining medium with proper amounts of minerals, nutrients and moisture-retaining material as reserves to access when dry. Amendments and conditioners allow us to rebuild poor soils or improve and maintain good soils to offset compaction, enhance cation exchange capacity (CEC) and water absorption and retention, colonize beneficial microorganisms (BMOs), and improve drainage. Perform jar, TDS, pH, and percolation (see Water) tests on your soil to determine its clay and sand content as well as its salinity, acidity, and alkalinity.

NOTE: Clay-rich soils require sand tilled in for aeration and permeability, while sand-rich soil requires clay to retain water.

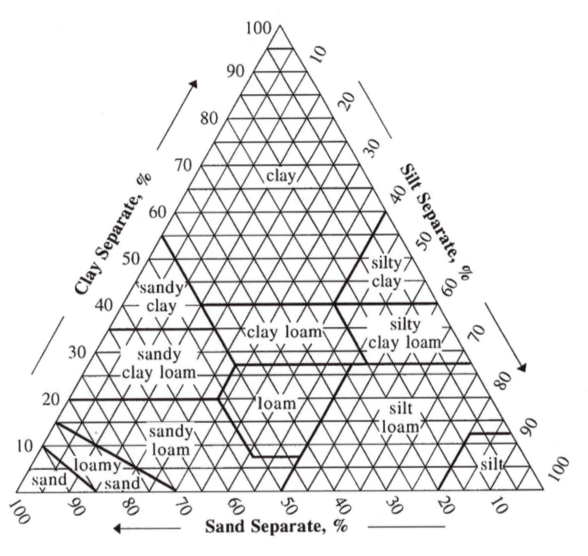

COMPARISON OF PARTICLE SIZE SCALES

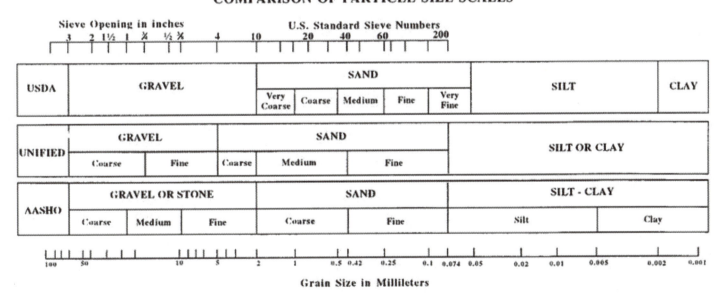

Beneficial Micro-organisms (BMOs)

Beneficial bacteria, fungi and other microorganisms are essential to oxygen, nutrient, air, and water intake. 1 t of this mixture contains over 4 billion BMOs, thousands of types of nematodes and protozoa, and more than 12 million fungi.

MATERIALS

3 c white rice or other starch
pantyhose
5-gal bucket
string
molasses
water
medium container with lid

TOOLS

aquarium bubbler

1. Bury 3 c of white rice or other starch in a tied pantyhose near a healthy tree's roots. After one month, remove and break up the contents, and hang it in a 5-gal bucket like a teabag.

   NOTE: For a full spectrum of microbes, plant several bags at different tree types.

2. In the bucket, add molasses and water at 1:3, insert an aquarium bubbler, stir, and let the mixture sit for 1 month at room temperature.

3. Remove the sacks of rice. Then pour the liquid into a container with a lid and dilute with water at 1:2, tea–water.

   IMPORTANT: Add BMOs to crops after tilling. Tilling soil exposes BMOs to lethal light, air and temperature fluctuations.

Biochar

Biochar creates a perfect environment for BMO colonization by protecting against diseases and retaining water and nutrients.

   Biochar is made from ground charcoal that is inoculated with organic nutrients and microbes and matured thermo-chemically to activate in compost. The process creates beneficial fungi filaments and larger microbes which draw in insects that leave frass. Biochar is under investigation as an approach to sequester carbon, so you'd be making your own carbon credits (page 15).

   Biochar is the most stable amendment known, lasting thousands of years since it's mostly carbon; other amendments like peat moss, hay, mulch and cocoa fiber break down quickly. Biochar is also able to absorb as much water as peat moss and is more productive than just soil and fertilizer.

   NOTE: During manufacturing, perform a slow pyrolysis keeping temperatures between 400–500°C to produce more char (≈ 35%).

Other Amendments and Conditioners

Match the amendment type listed in the table below with your plant needs. Reference your "Plant Needs" table (page 72). Add as much as needed to lessen or raise the specific traits of your soil.

AMENDMENTS AND CONDITIONERS

Amendment Type	Aeration	Light Weight	Permeability	Absorbent	Nutrient Source	Binder	pH
Gypsum	Y						Neutral
Coir		Y	Y	Y			Neutral
Peat Moss		Y	Y	Y			Alkaline
Algae		Y				Y	Neutral

Amendment Type	Aeration	Light Weight	Permeability	Absorbent	Nutrient Source	Binder	pH
Vermiculite		Y	Y	Y			Neutral
Perlite		Y		Y			Neutral
Activated Carbon		Y	Y	Y			Neutral
Wood Chips		Y		Y*			Alkaline
Sawdust	Y	Y		Y*			Neutral Alkaline
Sand			Y¹				Alkaline
Clay				Y			Alkaline
Top Soil	Y		Y	Y	Y	Y	Neutral
Lime		Y			Y		Alkaline
Compost		Y	Y	Y	Y		Neutral
Vermicastings		Y	Y		Y	Y	Neutral

* add with nitrogen

¹ only when mixed at high ratios

Soil Mixes

Add 1 T BMO per 1 ft³ to the following soil mixes:

- **Lightweight potting soil:** Lightweight absorbent material (such as perlite), sand, biochar, compost at 50:10:30:10. This soil mix is great for hanging pots, pots that are mobile, or just general potting needs.
- **Heavyweight potting soil:** Heavy absorbent material, sand, biochar, compost at 20:30:40:10. This soil mix is good for raised bed, garden, and orchard applications.
- **Humus:** Humus is mulch or other organic material, which you place around trees or spread to protect gardens.
- **Top soil:** Top soil can be decayed organic matter, compost, activated carbon or biochar, which is best used under sod, for edible landscaping, and for large outdoor crop applications.
- **Sub soil:** Sub soil is typically sand, which is an additive in the above applications, clay, or a mixture of the two
- **Parent:** Parent soil is typically rock or clay, which is an additive in the above applications.

LAYERS OF SOIL

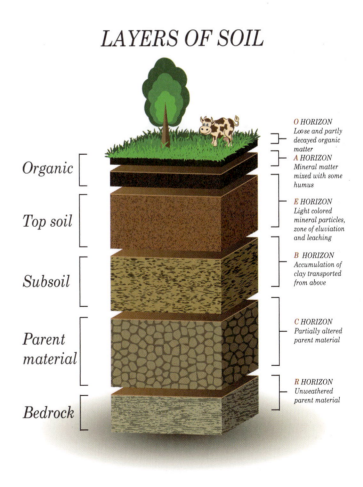

Organic

Top soil

Subsoil

Parent material

Bedrock

O HORIZON
Loose and partly decayed organic matter

A HORIZON
Mineral matter mixed with some humus

E HORIZON
Light colored mineral particles, zone of eluviation and leaching

B HORIZON
Accumulation of clay transported from above

C HORIZON
Partially altered parent material

R HORIZON
Unweathered parent material

NUTRIENTS, FERTILIZERS, AND NPK

There is no such thing as plant food. Plants don't consume nutrients like we do. They consume the minerals, chemicals, and other base components in the form of macro- and micronutrients and build their own food.

Store-bought fertilizer has a grade stamped in bold numbers, like 10-10-10. This is the percentage by weight of NPK (nitrogen, phosphorus and potassium), making it 10%-10%-10%. The remaining 70% simply consists of filler, usually clay dust, sand or granular limestone that you paid for and don't need. The ratios are recipes that work for specific plant groups to promote growth. Nitrogen (N) promotes leaf and stem development; phosphorus (P) promotes root development and reproduction, namely flowers and fruit; and potassium (K) covers most everything else, like metabolism, cell and tissue growth, movement, immune system, and more. If you're purchasing fertilizer, you can go one of two routes:

a) Buy only what the plant needs for what you want it to do. For example, if you're growing lettuce, you'll want it to grow as many green leaves as possible, and prevent it from going to seed and fruit as long as possible. For this you'll want about a 21-0-0.

b) Get a general fertilizer like 10-10-10, and let the plant figure it out. In this scenario, you're just dumping all nutrients on the plant equally and letting the plant eat whatever it wants. Walk-up, all-you-can-eat-buffet style. Plants, unlike humans, know which minerals they need and only eat that mineral and only as much as it needs. In this scenario I would suggest a 60-60-60, or the closest to 100-100-100 you can get. Just don't put too much or you will burn the plant, like I mention in "Backyard Garden" (page 97). What's not consumed is just washed away.

For trees, don't fertilize at all the first year, then add ½ lb of 21-21-21 for every inch of trunk diameter, up to 10 pounds per tree. And if you prune (page 91) or weed, don't remove the cuttings. Let the cut material decompose so that the nutrients go back into the soil. This goes for mowing your grass and picking fruit vegetables as well. What happens is NPK and other nutrients are removed from the soil by the tree, weeds, grass, and plants and put into branch, leaf, weed, grass, and fruit production, leaving the soil nutrient scarce. We then rob the plant of those nutrients by pruning, weeding, mowing our grass, and picking fruit, forcing us to then add additional nutrients so the plant can continue producing, and the cycle is never completed and never ends.

But if you want to make your own fertilizer specific to your needs, the entire world, including the air and oceans—and especially your stage two bins (page 25)—is filled with NPK and trace nutrients. You just need to know what you need and where to find it.

Compost (1-0.5-1.5)

1 yd³ of good, aerated compost contains the same NPK content as seven 40-lb bags of $27 fertilizer with most trace nutrients and BMOs. You can add seaweed or duckweed to round it out.

Manure (1-1-.5)

Different manures contain different amounts of NPK. Reference the list below and match it to your "Plant Needs" table (page 72) for the best growing results.

- **Bovine:** 1-0-0.5
- **Swine:** 0.5-0.5-0.5
- **Caprine/ovine:** 1-0.5-.1
- **Poultry:** 1.5-1-0.5
- **Equine:** 1-0.5-0.5
- **Canine:** 1.97-9.95-0.3
- **Rabbit:** 2.5-1.5-0.5
- **Bat:** 6-4.5-1
- **Crustacean:** 2.87-9.95-0

Bone Meal (3-15-0)

Bone meal provides a slow release of calcium, protein, phosphorus, magnesium, iron, zinc, and other trace nutrients. It can be made like any other meal (page 207).

NOTE: Finer particles will offer faster release.

Blood Meal (12-0-0)

Blood meal provides protein, nitrogen, and 30 trace nutrients, and can be produced like regular meal (page 207).

Compost Tea (1-1-1)

Compost tea from a well-functioning compost pile is high in nitrogen, phosphorous, and trace nutrients, making it the perfect organic fertilizer.

MATERIALS

T-shirt
water
1 gal finished compost or worm castings
(optional) ¼ c of liquid seaweed or kelp meal
 (page 78)

¼ c of molasses or unprocessed sugar
small aquarium air pump with hose and
 diffuser

TOOLS

scissors   ash hopper (page 58)

1. Cut a T-shirt along the seams, and lay it flat on top of the ash hopper (page 58). Dump 1 gallon of finished compost (page 183) or worm castings from your worm farm (page 208) on top. Tie the ends of the T-shirt together and place it inside the ash hopper like a tea bag. Add water at 1:4.
2. (Optional) Add a ¼ c of liquid seaweed or kelp meal (page 78).
3. Add a ¼ c of molasses or unprocessed sugar to activate the compost. Add a small aquarium air pump with diffuser. Aerate for 3 days, squishing the bag a few times per hour.
4. Dilute at 1:5 before using. Use the contents as hummus and repeat, leaving a ½ gallon of tea in the bucket to activate the next batch.

Worm Tea (1-1-1)

Like compost tea, worm tea is an all-in-one fertilizer, but the real benefits come from the incredible array of trace nutrients and BMOs present.

Urea (11-1-2.5)

Are you ready for another mindset breaker? We can use "pee" for all kinds of things!

Urea is pH neutral, highly soluble, odorless, and solid, and it is an extremely high, organic source of NPK when derived from mammal urine, including urine from a human.

Urine from a healthy person is clean and sterile. Asking livestock, or your wife and kids, to pee in a bucket, though, doesn't work. Your options are to urinate in a bucket or build a compost toilet (page 185) with urine collection.

MATERIALS

2.5-gal and 5-gal bucket   water
sodium bicarbonate or other pH neutralizer

1. Empty collection bucket daily into a mixing container with 1 t of sodium bicarbonate or another pH neutralizer, and clean the bucket before ammonia conversion.

   NOTE: For high pH soils, skip the sodium bicarbonate.

2. Dehydrate and store ("Potash (Potassium Carbonate)," page 58), or dilute with water.
3. Operation: Dilute with water 1:1 for lawns, trees, and bushes; 1:8 for produce. Apply generously around plant bases.

   IMPORTANT: Only use fresh, healthy urea that's less than a day old and is an amber color, or freeze it until you're ready.

Banana Peels (0-3.25-41.75)

Banana peels are packed full of potassium; they fall short in nitrogen and phosphorus, though.

Seaweed and Kelp Meal (1-0.2-2)

Kelp meal, or seaweed meal, has little NPK and micronutrients, but it is the one stop shop for trace nutrients.

Eggshells (5-1-0.5)

Eggshells are a rich source of calcium carbonate.

Ash

Ash typically has a low pH but is a good source of nitrogen and phosphorous with small amounts of trace nutrients (boron, copper, iron, manganese, and zinc).
    Wood/tree (0–2-6-15.65)
    Grapefruit peel ash (0–3.58-30.6)
    Orange peel ash (0–2.9-27)
    Potato skins ash (0–5.18-27.5)

Feathers (15.3-0-0)

Although feathers are not very soluble, even as meal, they are high in nitrogen.

Hair (12-16-0)

Hair provides significant amounts of nitrogen during decomposition. Not to mention we're limiting the amount of garbage we generate by reusing castoff hair, propelling ourselves closer to our goal of zero waste.

Coffee Grounds (2-0.3-0.7)

Coffee grounds are a medium-acidic source of nitrogen and potassium, magnesium, and copper.

Application

Applying the correct amount of each type of fertilizer is critical for producing. Too much nitrogen causes a tomato plant to bear leaves instead of tomatoes. Too much phosphorous makes a lettuce head produce flowers and fruit when we want more leaves.

- Use a high nitrogen ratio on young, growing plants.
- Use an NPK with a high potassium ratio just before winter.
- To help induce flowering and fruiting, use a fertilizer with a phosphorus NPK ratio, and just before fruiting plants, lower the nitrogen by 50%, and bump up the phosphorous and potassium by 2 times.
- For edible landscaping, use 1 lb of nitrogen-rich fertilizer per 1000ft² on all green, leafy plants
- For lawns, broadcast spread (hand spreader) a balanced blend (13-13-13) fertilizer over entire back and front yard grass areas, and new seed/sod 30 days after laying and again mid summer or twice a year.
- For trees in their second year, add 1 lb of balanced blend (13-13-13) for every inch of trunk diameter (up to 10 lb) per tree around base, at canopy outside edge. Then follow above NPK requirements for fruiting.

NOTE: Typically, outward horizontal root growth parallels canopy growth. In other words, however wide your tree's canopy is, the roots will more than likely reach just as far.

ROOTING COMPOUNDS

- **Honey:** Honey is a great root-starting compound and fungicide. Simply mix honey (page 220) and aloe at 2:1.
- **Banana peels:** Banana peels can be used as a nitrogen boost. Chop and meal (page 207) banana peels, then soak them in water to degrade and mineralize for 3 days. Strain the light pink water. Repeat until water's clear. Apply at 20:1 nitrogen boost–water.
- **Oranges:** Oranges can also be used to spur rooting when mixed with rice, honey, and brown sugar. Just chop and meal (page 207) 1 orange peel with 3 T rice, then add 4½ c water, 3 T honey (page 220) and 1 T brown sugar (page 235) and cook in medium frying pan on low, or in a solar oven (page 136) for 8 hours.

WATER

Plants are composed of 90% water; humans, 70%. Plants use water like we use muscle tissue, fat, and bone: to give our bodies form. Without our muscles and skeletons, we'd be a pile of skin and organs, and without water, plants would be a pile of skin and fibers.

Plants use water as a building block because it's simple. Rather than building complex carbohydrates and sugars like we do, they just grow skin and fill it like a balloon, regulating pressure for growth, light, movement, reproduction, cooling, security, disease, and more.

By providing or restricting water, you can activate actions like flowering, fruiting, oil production, and hibernation. For example, aromatic plants like mint and clove produce oil to conserve water during drought. Limit water and you'll get higher oil production. Also, restricting water during flowering spurs a faster fruiting and reproduction time as a response to linear preservation. Conversely, overly wet conditions cause leaves to grow fuller, larger and healthier, for obvious reasons. This is good for leafy green produce production and is why lettuce does so well in hydroponics.

Each species has its own preference for quantity and frequency of watering, along with rate of percolation or drainage. Knowing which plants need water, how much, for how long, and when becomes extremely confusing. Start by researching and documenting your plant's water amount, time of day, and percolation rate on your "Plant Needs" table (page 72). Then, when planting or potting your plant, to determine if the soil is right for your plant, perform a percolation test in the same manner as I describe below, adding sand (faster percolation) or clay (slower) or other water absorbing mediums found in soil (page 73).

Percolation Test

1. Dig a 1-ft deep hole in the area to be planted. Then saturate the soil by filling and draining several times.

Fill the hole and note the time. Let it drain and note the time again. Then convert to minutes per inch by dividing the minutes by 12.

Next, begin a water schedule based on groups of plants that require the same volume and frequency. For an example, see table below.

WATERING SCHEDULE

Group	Winter	Spring/Fall	Summer
A	Sat/Wed	Mon/Wed/Fri	Every day
B	Sat	Mon/Wed	Every day
C	Sat	Mon/Wed	Every day
D	Sat/Tues/Thurs	Mon/Wed/Fri/Sun	Every day
E	Sat/Tues	Mon/Wed/Fri	Every day
F	Sat	Mon/Wed	Every day

NOTE: Plants exposed to dry winds require additional water. Those in poor soils benefit by adding a wetting agent like liquid soap to water at a ratio of 1 t per gallon.

2. During vacations, use an automatic watering system or drip bottle.

OXYGEN

It's a myth that plants breathe in carbon dioxide and exhale oxygen, which is often confused with photosynthesis. All living things that we know of require oxygen for respiration. Usually, oxygen isn't an issue. It only becomes a factor when growing in greenhouses or grow rooms where access to fresh air is limited. Or lack of oxygen can be an issue when production is amplified to such an extent that the restricting element becomes oxygen.

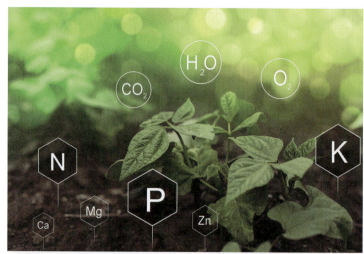

CO$_2$

Plants bring CO_2 in along with oxygen to build sugar and store energy, which releases excess oxygen. Lack of CO_2 can be a factor in greenhouses or grow rooms since fresh air is limited. That's why it's important to monitor both oxygen and CO_2 levels when growing inside.

LIGHT

Plants perform photosynthesis to convert light into energy, which occurs during daytime only. Fruiting is directly related to the amount of light received. As days grow longer, the plant takes this as a safe time to bear fruit, a stage that is called photoperiodism.

Shade

Shade is important for different reasons. Many plants can tolerate direct sunlight, but most need at least semi-protection from the sun's intense UV rays. Shade fabric, which is available in many types of materials, sizes, and configurations, accomplishes this by restricting incoming light.

A good shade cloth is a light color and is made from loosely-knit or woven polyester, with a light blocking rating from 5–95%. To get your shade cloth percentage requirements, you'll need to know the plant's light needs and the sun's intensity, in lumens, where you live. Reference your "Plant Needs" table (page 72) to find and/or document your plant's light needs.

If you aren't sure what intensity the sun is where you live, there are a few things you should know. At 12:00 p.m. on the equator, at either equinox, the sun puts out 11,803 lumens of visible light per square foot. At 0–23.5° Lat, it puts out approximately 90% of that; at 45° Lat, around 70%; and at the Arctic and Antarctic Circles, about 40%. At 10 a.m. and 2 p.m., those amounts decrease by an additional 25%. At 8 a.m. and 4 p.m., they decrease by 50%. So, between 9 a.m. to 3 p.m., you will have the maximum number of lumens at your location.

Follow the equations below to calculate your shade cloth requirements, which you can also document on your "Plant Needs" table:

Total Lumens x (Latitude % ÷ 100) = Lumens Available

Desired Lumens ÷ Lumens Available = Lumens Required x 100 = % of Lumens Required

100% - % of Lumens Required = % of Shade Cloth

For example, radishes require 7,000–7,500 lumens per square foot for at least 6 hours a day. This means that in order for radishes to thrive in, say, Key Largo, Florida (23.5° Lat and 90% total lumens), they'll require a 29–34% shade cloth to receive 7,000–7,500 lumens from 9 a.m. to 3 p.m. See the calculations below:

11,803 x (90 ÷ 100) = 10,622.70 Lumens Available

7,000 ÷ 10,622.70 = 0.66 x 100 = 66% of Lumens Required

7,500 ÷ 10,622.70 = 0.71 x 100 = 71% of Lumens Required

100% - 66% = 34% Shade Cloth

100% - 71% = 29% Shade Cloth

NOTE: Radishes, actually prefer plenty of sunlight. The longer the sunlight, the more the radish plant puts into root growth, which is essentially the production of actual radishes. So much so that I would suggest 12–14 hours of 7,000–7,500 lumens, which we know can only be achieved in grow rooms with artificial lighting. This is how I'm able to produce two times the production rate, two times the size of produce, and four times the quantity in a grow room (page 96). To learn more, make sure to check out my Free Food Factories.

Install your shade cloth perpendicular to the summer sun at solar noon for optimum penetration, or angle it for less.

IMPORTANT: This is one of the only times I'll say to stay out of your stage two bins (page 25). We don't want any materials for a shade cloth that are a) made from organic materials like jute, burlap, or cotton sheets, and b) aren't UV protected like most plastic tarps because they break down easily and rapidly in biological and photological conditions. Also, always protect young or newly transplanted plants from direct light for 1–2 weeks.

DARKNESS

The number of uninterrupted hours of darkness, it turns out, is actually more important than the hours of light because it is the determining factor of flower and fruit production. Without darkness there'd be no flowers since most plants grow according to circadian rhythms.

Plants are separated into three types based on these preferences: 1) short-day plants, which are usually fall–spring crops, that require over 12 hours of darkness, 2) long-day plants that bloom only when they receive less than 12 hours of darkness, and 3) day-neutral plants that don't care. By lengthening or shortening hours of light in your grow room (page 96), you can trigger or prevent flowering and fruiting. To trigger flowering, you would match your grow room lights to your plant's optimal light hours during its normal production season. To prevent it, you would match the light hours to your plant's off-season light hours. This is important in plants like lettuce, kale, and other leafy greens that we want to prevent from going to seed, and plants like strawberries, cucumbers, and other fruiting plants that we want to produce fruit, or go to seed, as often and as fast as possible.

COOLING AND HEATING

Temperatures work similar to light, triggering springtime plant growth when they rise. For example, you can extend flowering and fruiting stages by lowering temps toward the end of the fruiting phase to aid in ripening.

Most lettuces bolt in anything over 75°F (romaine, black seed Simpson, and Nevada at 87°F to 90°F), and apple doesn't even fruit until temps drop below 50°F. This means we can a) only grow plants for our region, b) construct separate greenhouses and grow rooms to divide plants into temperature groups, or c) use overlapping temperature zones as listed in your "Plant Needs" table (page 72), and accept the longer production times for plants growing in the upper and lower limits of their extreme temp ranges.

NOTE: Greenhouse vents, swamp coolers, and fans offer cooling while providing extra CO_2-enriched (currently 408.61ppm and rising) and O_2-enriched (209,000ppm and falling) air, while electric, gas, and wood stove heaters provide heat with or without the addition of CO_2.

WARNING: Plants are composed of so much water that, if allowed to freeze, expanding ice would rupture their bodies.

PH

Having the proper pH level per plant type is not only critical to the plant's health, but it also ensures the survival of BMOs (page 74), maximizes fertilizer effectivity, and unlocks nutrients that activate fruit production. Adding certain chemical compounds (page 57), alkalis or acids, allows us to adjust pH as desired. This can make soil growing in different regions and parts of the world tricky since some plants prefer more acidic conditions and others more alkaline. Again, my best advice is to grow plant types with common pH needs together, as listed in your "Plant Needs" table (page 72), so that they'll thrive more in your soil type, rather than raising and lowering the pH of your soil with amendments.

For example, forests, wooded areas, deforested farmlands, urban developments, areas that were once wooded, and humid regions tend to be more on the acidic side, while deserts tend to be more alkaline, with prairies and plains all over the chart. How do we have our cake and eat it, too, without twenty different pH zones? With potted plants, it's not that difficult. Otherwise, add high and low pH amendments (page 74), and just keep pH within the overlapping zones for each plant.

POTS

Fiber Pots

Fiber pots are great. Pots are like cages for plants. Imagine being stuck inside a 2-ft x 2-ft clay cylinder your entire life with no space to stretch your arms and legs. Fiber pots (and cardboard boxes) provide stability, soil, and water retention without restricting plant growth.

MATERIALS
cellulose fiber
pulverized manure and/or compost
sugar
vegetable oil

TOOLS
blender
2 clay pots
book

1

1. Mix cellulose fiber with pulverized manure (and/or compost) and sugar at 8:2:1 in a blender with enough water to make it clumpy.

    NOTE: Peat moss is also a suitable substitute.

2. Place a clay pot, small for smaller seeds and larger for larger seeds, upside down and spray it with vegetable oil. Then coat the outside surface of the pot with the mix to 2 times the clay pot's thickness or greater.

3. Spray more vegetable oil on the inside of a second pot and place it over the first, pressing firmly. Add a book and let the pots suck the moisture from the mix for 24 hours, then remove both the book and the pots and let the mix fully dry before filling the first pots with potting soil and seeds.

    NOTE: For starting large seeds like corn or watermelon, I use a lime or orange hand squeezer/juicer. To make cubes for smaller seeds like lettuce, pack ice trays, shot glasses, or other small forms. For very large plants, use doubled boxes (box inside a box).

Pellet made from a form to start small seeds.

4. When the plant's outgrown its pot, it's ready to go in the ground, pot, or box.

Small Pots

Pinch pots, bowls, or ceramic cups make great pots. For recycled pots, the sky's the limit. You can use anything from plastic cups and 1–2 L soda bottles with tops cut off (leave tops on for mini greenhouse effect) to 1-qt storage containers or even plastic grocery bags.

Medium Pots

For recycled, we have 1-gal used paint cans (wash well before use), 5-gal buckets, coffee cans, small waste bins, milk containers—basically, anything that can hold dirt. And if you're proficient in your pottery skills, give ceramics a try.

Hanging Pots

Convert any small to medium pot into a hanging pot instantly by simply drilling (4) equally spaced ³⁄₁₆-in holes around the container, ½ in down from top edge, removing cardboard tubes from 2 dry-cleaner hangers, and fish the hooks inside the tubes in each hole.

Large Pots

MATERIALS
35-gal plastic garbage can or 30-gal plastic drum

TOOLS
jig or skill saw with coarse blade
pencil
drill with ½-in drill bit

1. For larger pots, use a 35-gallon garbage can or cut the top 4 in off a plastic drum using a table saw, jigsaw, or skill saw.

   NOTE: I like using white semi-transparent drums because you can see the water level inside. Since only blue and black drums are UV resistant, you'll want to paint the clear ones white, leaving a 2-in vertical line for a site gauge.

2. Drill (6–8) ½-in equally spaced holes in the bottom of the drum, debur all edges, and place the drum right side up on a drip tray.

   NOTE: For garbage cans, flat lids without handles work best when placed underneath as drip trays. For drums, use an old water heater drip tray or cut the bottom 3 in off a 55-gal drum.

3. Make sure the bungs are installed tightly, flip it upside down, and place it near a window.

PESTS

We all hate pests; they really *bug* us, but not all bugs are pests! Plants need insects to pollinate, stimulate, and eliminate other destructive buggers. Lady bugs and honeybees are the obvious beneficial bugs of choice, but moths, flies, wasps, ants, butterflies, and beetles all pollinate plants. What plants don't need is pesticide.

Native plants have built up natural defense mechanisms towards native pests; it's only when we introduce foreign plants to native insects and vice versa that it becomes a problem. Otherwise, removing weak or rotting plants usually stops the attraction. And mixing cucumber, mint, bay, basil, garlic, pepper, clove, marigolds, and/or Thai lemon grass in gardens and around landscaping also works well as a repellant. Or finally, you could introduce pest-fighting bugs.

Beneficial Insects

There are ways to trap beneficial insects and transplant them in your garden or greenhouses, many of which I discuss in "Production of Proteins" (page 207); however, most beneficial insects are available from pet stores or online.

- **Ladybugs:** Ladybugs are attracted by daisies, and they consume aphids, mites, scale, and whiteflies.
- **Lacewings:** Lacewings, also known as hover flies, are attracted to composite flowers, and they eat aphids.
- **Nematodes:** Nematodes eat beetles, cutworms, and root weevil larvae.

Ladybugs *Lacewings* *Nematodes*

IMPORTANT: Nematodes can also hurt, and even kill, some plants. So you have to be careful which plants you put them on and which they have contact with.

- **Praying mantises:** Praying mantises eat almost all pests. But be careful, they'll eat beneficial bugs like lady bugs and lacewings too.
- **Wasps:** Wasps are attracted by caraway, carrots, celery, parsley, and Queen Anne's lace flowers. Wasps, especially mud daubers, eat leaf-eating caterpillars like braconids, chalcids, and Ichneumon, and they eat aphids and poisonous spiders like sphecidae and rabronidae.

NOTE: Wasps only become aggressive as a defense when you a) trespass in their yard, even if your home is in their yard, or b) swat them. If you find a wasp or bee in your home, feed it sugar water from a spoon and take it outside to your garden. To avoid swarms in the spring, cover pet bowls and compost piles, and don't leave soda cans and other sweets out in the Fall.

WARNING: Never kill or swat at a wasp, ant, or bee as, upon impact, pheromones are released onto you, sending an airborne message for others to "attack here."

- **Dragonflies:** Dragonfly is another insect that has a wide diet, munching on grasshoppers, midges, and even other dragonflies!

Praying Mantis

Wasps

Dragonfly

Sacrificial Crop

A sacrificial crop is a plant grown inside other plants for the sole purpose of drawing pests away from the main crops. These plants also provide a food source and habitat for beneficial insects.

- **Nettles and nasturtiums:** Nettles and nasturtiums attract aphids to the stem, whose honeydew attracts ants.
- **Chervil:** Chervil attracts slugs.
- **French marigolds:** French marigolds attract slugs, thrips, and nematodes.

Nettles and nasturtiums

Chervil

French marigolds

- **Radish, Chinese cabbage, and collards:** Radish, Chinese cabbage, and collard plants attract flea beetles and root flies.
- **Black oil sunflowers:** Black oil sunflowers attract leaf-footed bugs, stink bugs, and most importantly, birds that eat the seeds and the pests.

Radish

Chinese Cabbage

Collards

Black Oil Sunflowers

- **Blue Hubbard squash:** Blue Hubbard squash attract cucumber beetles, squash bugs, and squash vine borers.

NOTE: Plant the squash 2 weeks before your other crops.

- **Amaranth:** Amaranths attract cucumber beetles and stink bugs.
- **Buckwheat:** Buckwheat attract stink bugs.
- **Mustard and alfalfa:** Mustard and Alfalfa attract lygus bugs.

Blue Hubbard Squash

Amaranth

Mustard

Alfalfa

Homemade Pesticides

WARNING: Insecticides, homemade or not, will kill beneficial insects.

- **Deer:** The average Bambi consumes 5 lbs of greens per day, returning to the same plots. To mitigate the munching, mix liquid soap (page 39) with hot sauce at 2:1 in 1 gallon of water, and spray foliage 2–3 times a week. Or apply it directly after rain until the problem abates.
- **Grubs (Japanese beetle larvae):** In June or July, one time only, on soil, sprinkle bacteria-reproducing milky spore granules, which you can find online and propagate as you would in "Growing Mushrooms" (page 95).
- **Mites, earwigs, aphids, slugs, mealybugs:** Mix 4 T Canola oil with 1 t liquid soap and 1 gallon water. Spray the entire plant and surrounding dirt generously. This mixture will kill and ward off any soft-bodied bugs.
- **Water gnats:** Treat water gnats with BTI bacteria.
- **Waxy insects:** Boric acid strips the protective wax coating off most insects, but only use on soils with high pH. Otherwise, seaweed meal (page 207) and mulch (page 17) are safe alternatives.

NOTE: To prevent re-infestation, spray all plants with boric acid, even under leaf surfaces.

Deterrents

- **Floating row covers:** Protect crops aerially and terraneanly. Use a UV-resistant type material and cover your crops in late winter, 1 roll per row, anchoring all sides. Make sure it's large enough for adult plant growth.

Floating Row Covers

Diatomaceous

Volcanic Rock

- **Diatomaceous earth and volcanic rock:** Diatomaceous earth and volcanic rock are too sharp for slugs and other soft bodies to traverse.
- **Charcoal:** Charcoal (page 61) keeps away slugs and snails.
- **Scarecrows, pinwheels, and plastic grocery bags:** Shiny, large, and moving objects like scarecrows, pinwheels, and grocery bags, even balloons scare away birds and rodents.

Charcoal

Scarecrows

Pinwheels

Disease

- **Fungal diseases:** Mix a ½ c of baking soda, 4 T of vegetable oil, and 1 t of ivory soap with 1 gallon of water and apply to the foliage every 2 days.
- **Powdery mildew:** Mix milk and water 1:1 and apply to foliage once a week.
- **Disease-causing insects:** Suffocate disease-causing insects on fruit trees by spraying a mix of 1 qt of vegetable oil and a ½ c of liquid soap with 4 gallons of water on the trunk and branches during winter.

Powdery Mildew   *Fungal Diseases*

PROPAGATION

Since most produce we consume in our daily diet isn't native to our soil and climate, very few will actually survive direct sowing. Most require sprouting and pampering until they're strong and healthy enough to withstand the foreign conditions, pests, and microbiology of our backyards. This is why it's important to try to grow domestic crops, at least when growing outdoors. This of course isn't an issue when growing in grow rooms (see "Grow Rooms" on page 96). The good thing, though, is there's so much variety! There's literally edible food growing all around us, all the time, and it's all free for the picking, making purchasing plants for propagation pointless. Collect pollen and dropped seeds, cut clippings and cuttings, and even gather some types of leaves to plant! Also, check out free seed and cuttings on social media groups and websites.

Pollinating

Most plants exchange pollen from male to female via the wind, moths, flies, spiders, bees, and birds. Some exchange pollen by simply rubbing against each other. Some water plants like duckweed pollinate by bumping into each other, making pollination a simple matter of throwing a handful of duckweed into your pond and letting the currents and wind do the rest.

Direct Sowing

Seeds are an incredible design of nature. They come with enough food to feed the juvenile plant during its starting and partial seedling stage, without ever leaving its shell or setting a foot on soil.

There are many seeds that will grow if you simply poke a hole in good soil and drop it in. Some seeds, like corn and grains, can even be broadcasted across the surface of the dirt and still take root. But despite common knowledge, just planting even native plants in dirt and watering doesn't mean they'll grow. Some need to be artificially woken from dormancy, others helped out of or completely removed from their shells, and still others may grow but have been genetically altered to not produce fruit, requiring grafting or cloning. For those difficult plants, here are a few pointers I've picked up from the mistakes I've made along the way:

Avocado

Trees grown from store-bought avocado seeds will *not* produce fruit. Grafting (page 89) is the only means of propagation. Otherwise, if you're sowing from a homegrown avocado, follow the steps below.

Before you begin, decide on which avocado variety you would like. Cold-hardy Mexican avocado varieties include Joey (large black fruit); Opal (pear-shaped green fruit); Pryor (small, green, flavorful fruit); Wilma (cylindrical black fruit); Poncho (medium-large green fruit); Brogden (black, smooth-skinned fruit); black Wilma (pear-shaped green Opal).

NOTE: Like banana, cold hardy avocado are required for all regions north of 28° Lat if you want to grow them outside.

MATERIALS
toothpicks
non-store-bought avocado seeds

TOOLS
glass jar or plastic bottle

1. Place 3 toothpicks inside the seed and suspend it in a jar or plastic bottle filled to the top. Place the top side of the seed, whichever way it came out of the avocado, up.
2. After 2 weeks or 3 in of growth, plant in medium weight, medium perc soil (page 75), with the top flush with soil.
3. Fertilize every 3–4 weeks, March through October.

Garlic Greens

Break garlic bulbs into individual cloves and, with the peel intact, push the cloves 1 in into the soil with the pointy end up.

Peach and Plum

Remove seeds from the outer shell with a nutcracker and cold store for 3 months before planting.

Potato

Let a potato sit and sprout in a cabinet for 2 months. Then section the potato around each eye. Let cuts dry in a paper bag, seal well, and plant the pieces with the eyes, sprouts up.

Pumpkin

Some seeds won't, or will have a hard time sprouting in dirt and need to just break free from their shell a little before planting by wetting a paper towel (page 37) or other moisture-absorbing medium, placing and folding seeds inside, and placing towel inside a plastic bag or other plastic container until sprouts reach ½ in–1 in depending on the seed.

IMPORTANT: Stay away from sowing small plants inside a dampened paper towel, as roots burrow and attach to the paper, resulting in damaged roots during the extraction process.

Tomato

Seeds with delicate, intricate and winding root systems like tomato and pea should be sown in individual pods so their roots can't come into contact and get tangled, making transplanting a fruitless and even harmful endeavor. To achieve this:

MATERIALS
starter pods
plastic or Styrofoam egg carton
tomato seeds

1. Fill starter pods ¾ of the way full with lightweight, medium perc potting soil (see "Soil Mixes"), place individual seeds, and then top the pot off with soil. Water the plant and cover it with plastic.

   Note: Plastic egg cartons work great because they come with a plastic top that holds in humidity. If you use an egg carton, close the lid after watering.

2. When plants outgrow the container, relocate to a permanent large pot with trellis, a vertical garden, a raised bed (page 98), or a hydroponics system (page 105).

Pea

Pea is another sprout that quickly develops complex root systems, but pea plants differ slightly from tomato in that they, like kiwi and some of the others, should be sprouted first, before direct sowing.

MATERIALS
paper towel (page 37)
pea seeds

TOOLS
1-qt plastic storage container or ziplock bag

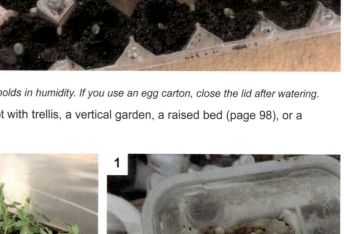

1. Simply place a soaked paper towel (page 37) inside a 1-qt plastic storage container or ziplock bag with the seeds.
2. After a few weeks, once the sprouts are visible, relocate to individual starter pods.

Lettuce

Even though lettuce is a direct-sow seed that can usually be sprinkled to sow, I thought to place a note here for it, and others like it that tend to have a less than 100% fertility rate. In which case I would suggest planting 2 or more seeds per hole, location, and pot, and then simply trimming back the less-developed sprouts once the plant is established.

Make sure, especially for lettuce, to cover with a piece of plastic to keep humidity in.

Pot Sowing

When temperatures are still too cold but you want to get a jump on the season, or the plant is expensive and, therefore, requires pampering, your best option is to sow seeds in plant pots (page 82) to later transplant.

The best pots for this are Jiffy pots or biodegradable fiber pots (page 82) made from materials like cellulose fiber, cardboard, jute, burlap, or cotton.

Fill pots 10% more than desired with lightweight, high perc soil (see "Soil Mixes"), plant seed as described in your "Plant Needs" table, water thoroughly (soil will drop 10%) and don't water again until soil is dry to the touch.

Grafting

Stem grafting is similar to cloning. Take a cutting, a scion, from an existing plant that's proven to be healthy and fruitful and splice it into the rootstalk of a developed, faster-growing, host plant:

MATERIALS
with parafilm or a plastic bag

TOOLS
grafting knife, sheers, and/or clips

1. In spring, find a top growing shoot that has an OD less than ¼ in and is at least 1 year old with active buds. Make sure the shoot has at least 1–2 in of straight, clean stem from a proven producing plant.

   NOTE: For root stalks or scions less than a year old, use grafting clips directly above the first true leaves.

2. Separate the shoot from the tree, and with a grafting knife, or better, grafting sheers, remove all leaves.

   NOTE: Grafting sheers makes this entire process effortless and dummy proof.

3. Sharpen the base, just below the lowest bud, into a 1-in wedge. To sharpen, make two cuts, and leave 1 side slightly longer than the other.

   IMPORTANT: If wedge cuts are not perfectly straight, the different tree tissues will not join.

4. Wrap the entire branch with parafilm or a plastic bag, leaving the cut tip uncovered.

5. Make a 1-in cleft incision over 6 in up and about a third of the way in on the rootstock.
6. Insert the wedge of your scion inside, longer side in.
7. Wrap the entire joint with parafilm or strips of plastic bag, overlapping to prevent water infiltration and cambial dehydration.
8. Keep plant protected away from wind and direct sunlight. Allow 3–4 weeks for buds to swell.
9. When the graft takes, bend over or cut back the host in steps of 1–3 in per week, to force budding, then pinch tips of buds out to stimulate branching.

   IMPORTANT: Never let anything grow below the host, but any existing, leave them for as long as possible to help growth.

Runners

Many plants such as strawberry, mint and spider plants reproduce on their own by extending runners into soil. To transplant, cut the connecting runners between parent and daughter plants, then remove and replant the daughter.

Roots

Raspberry, blackberry, rose, and a few other long stalk plants can be reproduced by removing, cutting, and replanting root sections.

MATERIALS
cotton string
peat moss, sawdust, vermiculite, sand

TOOLS
garden hand spade
pruning saw or pruning shears

1. Slightly unearth several inches of root near the stalk.

    NOTE: Roots of these plants grow very near to the surface, so it won't take much to unearth them.

2. Using a pruning saw or pruning shears, at a 45° angle, cut the root section of a long stalk plant close to the crown and 2–6 in down from that. For smaller plants, make your second cut 1–3 in from the first instead. Repeat for other root sections, cutting no more than 30% per plant.
3. With a cotton string, tie 6 cuttings in a bundle, 45° cuts together. Store for 2–4 weeks in moist peat moss, sawdust, vermiculite, sand, or a combination of all four, in your fridge's vegetable drawer. Keep it at 40°F.
4. Puncture a fiber pot (page 82), add clone gel or rooting compound (page 79) or honey (page 220), and plant each root cutting individually, 45° ends up.

Bulbs

Some plants like garlic greens (page 87) can be propagated by separating and planting the bulbs in the same manner as roots from long stem crops.

   The plants that can be reproduced using this method are shallot, leek, garlic, chive, onion, tulip, daffodil, hyacinth, crocus, canna, calla lily, gladiolus, lycoris, agapanthus, alstroemeria, bletilla orchid, crocosmia, oriental lily, Asiatic lily, and scallion.

Regrowing Food Scraps

After harvesting and consuming a plant, instead of sending it to be composted, consider re-growing. Many vegetables such as lettuce, carrots, celery, and onions can be regrown, at least partially, just by keeping them hydrated in shallow jar of water. Usually you won't get an entire head, but you'll get enough for a salad! On the other hand, an entire pineapple plant can be grown from just the top of an eaten pineapple by simply sticking the top down into a medium-weight potting soil.

Transplanting

Transplanting is never done in nature, but it gives people living in cold weather who experience shorter growing seasons a chance to get a leg up by skipping the seeding, sprouting, and growing stages, leaving the last stage, fruiting, to nature. Once youngling's roots have done all they can in confined quarters, it's time to transplant.

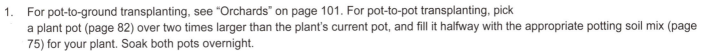

MATERIALS

potting soil (page 75)   plant pot (page 82)

1. For pot-to-ground transplanting, see "Orchards" on page 101. For pot-to-pot transplanting, pick a plant pot (page 82) over two times larger than the plant's current pot, and fill it halfway with the appropriate potting soil mix (page 75) for your plant. Soak both pots overnight.

   NOTE: Reference your "Plant Needs" table (page 72) to find and/or document any soil needs.

2. Lay the plant sideways and ease the root ball free by supporting, not pulling, the stalk in one hand. With your other hand, push on the sides and bottom of the pot if it's soft-sided. If the pot is hard, tap softly with a rubber mallet.

3. Massage the roots showing to activate growth. Cover roots with root growth hormone, also known as rooting compound (page 79), or honey (page 220), and dust new pot with little blood meal (page 77), bone meal (page 76), or kelp meal.

4. Center the root ball, making sure the plant stalk is plumb. Fill the sides with appropriate soil mix (page 75), and place the pot in partial light. Avoid watering for 5 days.

   NOTE: Don't be surprised or disappointed if your plant stops growing. It's feeling out—literally—its new house and establishing a new root zone. Once a substantial system has developed, the plant will begin redirecting energy upward.

Pruning

Plant tips release a suppressive growth hormone that lower branches to prevent growth (atypical dominance). By cutting the ends off top shoots, we nullify this process; allow lower branches to form for easier fruit picking and larger fruit; and limit growth in confined spaces typical to greenhouses, grow rooms, indoor gardens, and hydroponic growing. There are a few methods (LST, super crop, pinching, topping, FIM) to get the best production results.

IMPORTANT: Some trees require winter pruning, some spring. Check your plant's needs in your "Plant Needs" table (page 72)

1. If the tree already has side branches, which means it's 1 year or older, cut leader stem vertically to the nearest bud. Trim any branches to the nearest up-facing bud, and remove all branches under 30 in.

2. At 2 years, repeat upward-facing leader cuts and upward-facing bud pruning on all new branches, and remove any inward-facing shoots that are over 30 in long.

   NOTE: Like suckers, branches trapped in perpetual shade only suck energy from, and delay fruiting.

3. Repeat yearly, removing any crossed, touching, or inward-running branches at the nearest bud facing the desired direction to maintain a 24-in spacing.

TREE PRUNING

1. Water Shoots
2. Crossing Branches
3. Broken Branches
4. Dead Branches
5. Diseased Branches
6. Hanging Branches
7. Suckers

Terminal Bud
Internode
Lateral Branch
Bud Scar
Lateral Buds (Dormant Buds)
Node

45° Angle   Too Angular   Too Low   Too High

TRADITIONAL FARMING

With more than half of the world's population living in cities, I've personally never seen, owned, been to, or known anyone who has ever farmed in a traditional fashion. Traditional farming is extremely inefficient due to over 40% waste of harvest, energy and labor, environmental impact through fertilizer run-off and CO_2 pollution from tractors, and loss from droughts, freezes, diseases, varmints, insects, and the economy. Plus, even with machinery, it's really hard work. Planting, growing, and harvesting burns a lot of calories, for little—and sometimes no—return, not to mention the giant learning curve you'd experience having never farmed before, which, in the first years, would result in losses due to freezes, heat waves/under watering, flooding/over watering, under fertilizing, over fertilizing, insects, etc. In fact, a large percentage of the produce you buy from companies like Dole, Village Farms, Red Sun Farms, Vet Veggies, and Mirabel Boston isn't grown on traditional farms anymore; it's grown hydroponically in greenhouses.

Don't misunderstand; there's nothing wrong with soil growing for relaxation or as a hobby, but the calories spent to harvest food from dirt makes it impractical for self-reliance when there are more efficient methods.

CO-OP FARMING

Co-op farms are gaining traction, at least in California and Europe. Neighbors purchase stock in a local farm and draw monthly or quarterly dividends in real product. This method is not only more efficient, spreading a farm's large workload, but it saves consumers a trip to the supermarket and companies and truckers trips shipping food across the country and planet. There are still considerable losses and inefficiencies, but it's a step in a better direction.

COMMUNITY GARDENING

The hardest part of gardening is finding time to mine your investment. Co-op farms receive a percentage of the harvested crop, but community gardens own personal plots, sharing land and chores with multiple individuals to make it more efficient. Sharing chores provides an opportunity to save time while learning grow methods under the tutelage of experienced horticulturists, which minimizes losses.

MICRO GARDENING

Remember everything I said about growing to harvest, not just to grow? Forget it. We don't even have to grow a plant to maturity to consume it. Some young produce, sprouts, contain more flavor and over 30 times the enzymes, vitamins, minerals, phytochemicals, antioxidants, carbohydrates, fats, and protein per gram than their adult versions, making them great for weight loss since they're low in calories and rich in fiber and flavor (see "Produce Methods" table on page 71) and extremely efficient source of food production.

EXAMPLE:
Radish sprout, 100 g: 42 cal, 2.5 g fat, 2.5 g carbs, 2.5 g protein, Vitamin A 3%, Vitamin C 18%, fiber 0%, sugar 0%.
Radish, 100 g: 18cal, 0g fat, 4g carbs, 0g protein, Vitamin A 0%, Vitamin C 15%, 2g fiber, 2g sugar.

Seeds and Nuts

Growing up, we've all taken for granted the benefits of sunflower, pumpkin, and sesame seeds and pecan, pistachio and peanut nuts, never knowing there's an entire world of other seeds and nuts out there not carried in supermarkets.

There are many benefits to exploring the world of nuts and seeds not provided in stores. Not only are they the embryonic life of a tree, they are little capsules of energy, filled with protein and fats. Although nuts and seeds are plentiful in grocery markets, some items, such as the production of almonds, can be detrimental to the environment. Other nuts such as cashews, hazelnuts, and Brazil nuts are the best stand-ins for almonds. Therefore, it's important for generations to come that we approach this topic with a resourceful mind and with the goal to be as waste-free as possible. Finding alternatives to marketplace produce is a step in lowering the environmental footprints.

Nuts

- **Acorns:** Yes, nuts from regular oak trees, the one's squirrels fight for, are, despite what our mother told us, not only not poisonous but highly nutritious! Annual crops from oak trees in North America surpasses all other nut tree nuts combined, and yet no one knows about eating acorns. Roast, grind into meal (page 207) to make bread, cakes, etc., or boil or soak to eat plain.
- **Pine nuts:** We can eat nuts found inside regular pine cones. All pine trees produce nuts that are safe to eat. The difficulty is in the de-shelling, but once de-shelled, pine nuts can be used in desserts, salads, and most commonly, pesto sauce.
- **Chinquapins (chestnuts):** Chances of finding a nut bearing chestnut tree in North America is rare. Despite surviving forty million years, American chestnuts have become all but extinct within the last forty years. The reason is due to chestnut blight; introduced by man in 1904, the disease quickly spread, and by 1940, the chestnut species was destroyed. Today chestnuts are still surviving but only as sprouts from old roots, and although the sprouts try to reproduce, the disease often gets to them before they can mature enough. Although we will never have chestnuts like we did in 1900, the chestnut's close cousin, chinquapins, are still thriving and abundant. Once removed from their hard shells, they can be roasted and eaten, where they yield the taste of an era gone by.

NOTE: Water chestnuts, Chinese chestnuts, and sweet chestnuts are not native to America but are also alternatives to nuts that you find in the market.

- **Black walnuts:** Black walnuts are a native tree to the eastern half of America and can be harvested in early fall. Their trees are easily identifiable once the leaves start to fall and reveal 1½–2-in green globes, where the walnut is enclosed in its smooth, fleshy husk. The nut is difficult to crack but inside is a coveted flavor that can be used to complement baked goods. The hulls (outside coverings) of the walnut can also be used for medicinal purposes to treat parasitic worm infections, as a mouth gargle, and as a natural dye.
- **Hickory nuts:** There are over twenty species of hickory nuts in North America alone. The taste of the nut depends on what kind of species of hickory tree you harvest from. Some produce sweet nut, others produce meaty, earthy tasting nuts, and a few produce a bitter nut. Hickory nuts are usually eaten raw and straight out of the shell. Traditionally, they are cooked down into a porridge, or they can be pressed for oil that can be put in salads.

NOTE: If you're wondering where pecans are on this list, they are actually a hickory nut.

- **Hazelnuts:** About 75% of hazelnuts are cultivated in a small steep piece of land in Turkey, where local families produce and harvest these nuts for the majority of the world. However, the hazelnut tree, also known as filberts, is a tree that you can have in your own backyard, only taking 3–5 years to mature before its first harvest. They are relatively quick and easy to grow, don't require as much space as other nut trees, and produce sweet, tasty nuts during summers.
- **Brazil nuts:** Brazil nuts are rich and creamy nuts with a taste similar to a coconut's. These nuts are grown in the Amazon rainforests of Brazil, Colombia, Peru, Ecuador, and Venezuela. The flowers require a specific species of bees to pollinate and a small ground mammal called the agouti to spread the seeds.
- **Marcona almonds:** Unlike the more common California variety of almonds, the Spanish Marcona almonds are rounder and flatter in shape. The flavor is more buttery and earthy than the California almonds with a texture closer to macadamia nuts. It is highly sought after to make desserts like marzipan and a European nougat. It can also be roasted to eat as a snack, sprinkled over salads, or served with cheese.
- **Baru nuts:** Originating from the savannas of Brazil, these nut trees have an extremely low water footprint since they do not require an external source of water or heavy irrigation (unlike the almond industry in California). Not only are they environmentally friendly (unlike almonds), they are rich in nutrients (vitamin E, fiber, magnesium, zinc, potassium, etc). The flavor is a mix of peanuts and cashews with a harder texture.
- **Ginkgo nuts:** The ginkgo nuts are produced on the ginkgo tree, a very adaptable urban tree that can be found on the streets of Japan. These nuts must be cooked before eating, but once cooked they have a gummy and soft texture, and a taste close to that of chestnuts.

Seeds

- **Flaxseeds:** As one of the oldest crops in human history, flaxseeds are packed full of nutrients with a list of health benefits behind it. Ground flaxseeds are used in baking recipes and, when mixed with water, can be a substitute for eggs in vegan baking recipes. The flax plant is a fairly easy plant to grow in your backyard. In fact, you may have its wildflower cousins, the blue flax or the scarlet flax, already growing in your yard.

- **Chia seeds:** Chia seeds come from a member of the mint family that originated in Mexico, where its uses date back to Mayan and Aztec cultures. Growing the plant is extremely easy. Simply sprinkling the seeds on top of a wet bed of soil or even a wet piece of napkin can result in sprouts within days.
- **Psyllium seeds:** Originally from India, psyllium seeds are best known as a laxative used to treat constipation. Because it is odorless and flavorless, it can be incorporated into almost any culinary dish and baked goods.
- **Melon seeds:** The first thing people do when they cut open a watermelon is scoop out the seeds and toss them away. Little do they know, these seeds are not only edible, they contain an incredible source of magnesium and omega-6 fatty acids. These seeds can be eaten raw, or you can roast them like pumpkin seeds. They can also be ground into a creamy watermelon seed butter. Seeds from other melons such as cantaloupe, honeydew, and watermelon are also edible. (And no, if you swallow the watermelon seeds, they will not lead to a "plant growing inside your tummy.")
- **Jackfruit seeds:** The largest fruit in the world, jackfruits have been growing in popularity due to their sweetness and their use in vegan cuisine. Although one jackfruit can hold up to 500 nutritious seeds, they are usually thrown away. You can boil them, roast them, make them into curry, and much more.

NOTE: Other fruit seeds that you can consume instead of throwing away include mango seeds, papaya seeds, and apricot seeds (after extracting the seed from its hull).

- **Hemp seeds:** Hemp seeds have seen a rise in demand as the cannabis plant has become more and more accepted in today's society. It is nutrient dense, tasty, and can be used in a variety of ways. It can be pressed into an oil, ground into protein powder, roasted, mixed into dishes, etc.
- **Lotus seeds:** Used in many Asian dishes and medicine, the lotus seed is filled with fiber and calcium. It can be shelled and dried or used in baking, puddings, candies, curry, dumplings, and more.
- **Squash seeds:** Pepitas, or pumpkin seeds, are not the only edible squash seeds. All other squashes like butternut, spaghetti, acorn squash, and many more also yield tasty seeds that can be roasted and eaten.

Soaks, Sprouts, Microgreens

From seed to plant there are several stages of development: sprouts and soaks (soaked nuts), microgreens, and baby greens. If you enjoy seeds and vegetables, you'll love all of them.

Consuming sprouts, micro and baby greens are just consuming babies, infants, and adolescents, respectively. As in human development, the egg, or in this case, the seed, is packed full of everything needed, passed down from mother to child for the offspring to grow healthy and strong. As we age, those elements become deficient, and we must find additional sources of nutrients. More often than not, the younger the plant is, the higher its nutritional value.

I compare the difference between young and mature plants to fresh caviar and fast food fried fish. But not all plants are edible young. Some are either poisonous or, although edible and tasty, furnish better nutrient values in adulthood, not counting the energy loss through traditional farming—digging, planting, fertilizing, watering, protecting, and harvesting.

EXAMPLE:
Broccoli sprouts, 3 oz: 35 cal, 5 g carbs, 2 g protein, 4 g fiber.
Broccoli, 3 oz: 29 cal, 6g carb, 2.4 protein, 2.2 g fiber.

MATERIALS

jar with a lid   cheesecloth
bowl
rubber band
string or rubber band

TOOLS

scissors

1. For soaks, fill a glass, or plastic jar half full to full with seeds. (Loosely packed seeds will result in small soaks.) Rubber band a piece of cheesecloth over the opening, then fill it with water, shake it, and dump the water out.

   NOTE: Although the most popular sprouts are green leaf, herb, bean, and certain cereals, all edible nuts and seeds can be consumed at any growth stage.

2. Repeat four times, then refill the jar with water and soak for 30 minutes to 12 hours, depending on the type of nut or seed and their size, to activate germination. Once germination occurs, dump the water, and then store the jar upside down in a small bowl at 45° to drain. Keep it in partial light at room temperature.

1

2

3. Repeat the rinsing two to four times a day to promote growth, develop starch and fiber, and prevent souring.

4. For sprouts, spread the seeds or nuts out on half a paper towel (page 37), fold the other side over, soak with water, and place inside a plastic bag to store for several days.

   WARNING: Do not let seeds dry or sit in water.

5. Consume the sprouts and soaks with the seed before the first leaves (cotyledons) unfold and roots develop. Consume micros with roots after the first and second (true) leaves have unfolded and midway into the third leaves unfolding, or refrigerate them to halt growth.

   WARNING: Tomato, potato, paprika, aubergine, rhubarb, and other solanaceous species are poisonous when consumed before maturity. And more, bacteria especially love young plants.

5

Seed germination

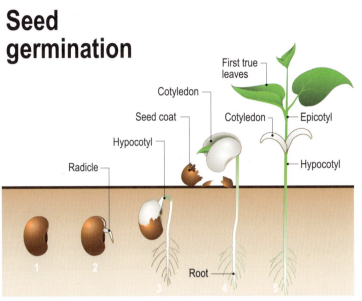

First true leaves
Cotyledon
Cotyledon
Seed coat
Epicotyl
Hypocotyl
Radicle
Hypocotyl
Root

Baby Greens

Baby greens are grown normally in sprouting trays, but they are harvested ½–1 in above root after the second leaves unfold but before full maturity.

Growing Mushrooms

Mushrooms are fat-free, low in calories, and filled with vitamins, antioxidants, and other nutrients. Unlike other plants, fungi don't possess chlorophyll. They obtain their energy through nutrients in their growing media: sawdust, grain, wooden plugs, straw, wood chips, cardboard, logs, compost, corncobs, cotton, cocoa seed hulls, and gypsum.

MATERIALS
¼ c water
fungi spores
paper
small plastic tote
large plastic tote
growing medium

TOOLS
small pot
measuring cups
50–100-cc syringe

1. In a small pot, boil a ¼ c of water; let cool. Add spores from a fruiting mushroom or a spore print and stir gently for a few seconds. Let hydrate for 3 days at room temp.

   NOTE: To obtain a spore print, when the cap is matured, outflowing and open like an umbrella, cut the cap off and place it gill side down on a piece of paper overnight. Store in air-tight container with a desiccant pack (page 248).

2. Fill 3 in of a sterile 6-in deep plastic storage tote with grow medium.

   NOTE: Larger fungi tend to prefer more coarse, arid substrates, while smaller prefer more compact substrates void of air. Depending on your fungi, I've found 3 growing mediums work well. Soaked wood chips, soaked straw (not hay), lightweight rich potting soil, pelletized ground straw, nutrient mix consisting of straw (brown rice, bird seed grains, wheat berry grain, etc.), and vermiculite and water at 1:3:1 with 1 T of gypsum per gallon.

3. Pelletize wood pulp to ⅜ x 1-in pellets ("Grass Clippings and Leaf Pellets," page 154). Stir water to suspend spores, dip/coat pellet and insert every inch or two vertically.

   NOTE: For straw simply pour pellets out over substrate. For nutrient mix substrate you can fill a 25–50-cc syringe and inoculate the mix by inserting the tip and pressing the plunger while slowly withdrawing. Do this every inch throughout the substrate.

4. Place tote inside a larger tote with lid and store at room temperature.
5. Check temp and RH (80°F, 100%) weekly, until white, threadlike roots colonize the entire container, which usually takes 3 to 4 weeks.
6. For center colonization, leave undisturbed for 1 week after colonization, then drop temps to 55–60°F (45°F for enoki mushrooms).
7. In 4 weeks, or when caps open, begin harvesting daily for 6 months by cutting, not pulling, stems.

   WARNING: Drafts or dry air are lethal to the mushrooms.

GROW ROOMS

Basements, spare rooms, garages, dens, and closets all provide a clean, protected, climate-regulated environment in which to grow plants—also known as a grow room. You can use indoor gardening methods (page 105) or even hydroponics (page 105).

There are a few key benefits of grow rooms that make them better than greenhouses and other grow mediums and that are worth annotating. In my Free Food Factory's giant grow methods, because of the amplified growing conditions, we've recorded two times the production rate; two times the size of fruit and produce; two times the sugar and nutrient contents; four times the quantity due to the indoor, year-round growing cycle; 99% less loss; and of course, due to the nature of hydroponics and aquaponics, 99% less effort, 99% less cost, and 99% less water when compared to current annual yield reports from industrial food production companies in the same zone. All without the heartache of bugs, pests, cold spells, heat spells, droughts, fertilizing, pesticides, or watering.

For example, leafing plants like lettuce, chard, and cabbage, should typically receive 8 to 12 hours of light each day. On the other hand, leafing and flowering plants usually require 14 to 18 hours of light per day to produce at the rates, sizes, and nutrient counts that I, and most grow room enthusiasts, are getting—something that's impossible in nature. Therefore, grow rooms allow us to achieve record-breaking production rates that would be impossible in your typical garden or greenhouse.

(Check out my YouTube channel *Dan Martin Does Everything* or other social medias for more about my Free Food Factory and other ventures and projects.)

PATIO GARDENS

My grandmother lived in a condo with a small patio that contained wall-to-wall pots. Pots on the ground; pots on tables, benches, and chairs; pots on the AC and makeshift stands; windowsill pots; pots hanging from hooks in eaves, door, and window frames; pots on the fence; pots on gnomes. She'd tell people, "Flowers die. Get someone you love a plant instead. They last forever." You'd be amazed how much food can be grown in a 10 x 20-ft condo patio by a child of the Depression, with a flair for "everything has its place."

Patio and porch gardens involve many methods: vertical gardens, overhead gardens, wall gardens, hanging gardens, raised bed gardens (page 98), and water gardens. Add plastic-covered storage shelves and you have a mini greenhouse.

NOTE: When positioning pots, keep the taller plants in back.

BACKYARD GARDEN

You may have thought picking up a book on "how to do everything" would have a massive chapter dedicated to gardening. A "grow enough food on a quarter acre to feed your entire family" book this is not. This book is more like, grow enough food in a spare bedroom. Gardening, like farming, for the same reasons, just isn't very efficient. And, like many of you, I don't really possess a green thumb. So, after moving my fair amount of soil around in circles, wasting money on fertilizers and dealing with insects, sweat and weather, I discarded the dream I'd picked up who-knows-where and ditched the ditch digging and pitch forking. So for now, we'll skip the traditional garden bed growing method. I do have plenty of mistakes, mishaps, and failures to pass on, though:

- **Animal bites:** To deter moles, rabbits and other beasts of Caerbannog from sinking their pointy teeth into your plants, spread blood meal (or holy hand grenades) around the crops. To deter deer, try scattering human hair (free from barber shops) on and around the plants. I get 50/50 results from hair, depending on precipitation.
- **Burn:** When too much fertilizer permeates the soil, especially nitrogen, the salts suck moisture from the plant itself after absorbing all the surrounding water, resulting in sunburn-like symptoms, root hair damage, and a lack of blooms or fruit. This results in leaf shedding, burning, and death.
- **Disease:** Plants get sick frequently since they're constantly being bombarded by fungi, bacteria, bugs, and other infectious organisms. Disease is usually manifested by a discolored spotting of the leaves and can be contagious, especially in tight quarters.
- **Dropping leaves:** Like human hair, leaves die and fall out naturally for many reasons. When healthy green leaves fall, which is more common in house plants, it's usually due to over-watering and/or shock from a change in routine.

Animal bites   *Burn*   *Disease*   *Dropping leaves*

- **Insect bites:** Little buggers munching on crops shouldn't be confused with disease. Holes are clean—not discolored—and omni-shaped, including the edges.
- **Nutrient deficiency:** If a nutrient deficiency first appears in discoloration or fading on newer, top leaves, add calcium (Ca), vanadium (V), chlorine (Cl), carbon (C), copper (Cu), iron (Fe), manganese (Mn), molybdenum (Mo), silicon (Si), and sulfur (S). If the deficiency is in the lower, older leaves, add nitrogen (N), phosphorus (P), magnesium (Mg), and zinc (Zn). If there is browning between veins, add potassium (K). If yellow, add Fe.

If there are dark green or grey blotches, add P. If the leaves turn yellow with brown spots but the veins stay green, add Mg. If the leaves turn brown with dark spots, then yellow and they curl up, add K. If darkness appears near the stem of leaves with yellow veins, add S. If there are torn stems, elongated leaves, and brown tips, add B. If the leaves stop growing and get smears of color, add Zn. If the leaves turn brown and fall off, add Cu, Mo, and trace elements like those found in fertilizers (page 76).

- **Overheating and sunburn (scorch):** 99% of a plant's water intake goes to photosynthesis and perspiration (transpiration) to prevent overheating. When a plant overheats, leaf wilting looks more like curling with burnt edges, and the eventual dropping of dry leaves. To prevent this, it's important to know which plants need how much sun, which you can find in your "Plant Needs" table (page 72). When you believe your plant has overheated, remove it from sun and water it.
- **Shock:** Plants suffer transplant shock during initial planting or moving, and it's pretty much unavoidable. Let's face it, plants aren't meant to be moving around the planet. Shock stunts growth, delaying production, and can cause leaf tissue to brown, similar to overheating. It can also cause vein darkening or yellowing along with wilting. To minimize shock, disturb roots as little as possible and water thoroughly after transplant with a sugar-water mix of 1½ c:1 gal.

Insect bites

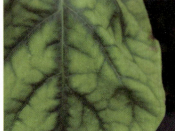
Nutrient deficiency

Overheating and sunburn

Shock

- **Wilting:** Plants wilt when not watered correctly. Visualize a plant's skeleton as a firehose. When there's water pressure, the plant—roots, stalks, leaves—is firm, strong, and full, like a firehose on full blast with the nozzle closed. When pressure's low (turgor), the plant is limp, dead, and droopy.
- **Overwatering:** To confuse things, overwatering will also cause wilt, usually accompanied by a lighter leaf color. This is because, like us, they need oxygen during cellular respiration (breathing) to break down carbs for energy (metabolism). So along with roots, they have lung-like feathery cells to absorb oxygen, which when underwater, suffocate and drown.

Since hydration can no longer occur without a working respiratory system, the plant begins conserving water (wilting), despite its roots being submerged. Unfortunately, we usually falsely interpret this to mean that the plant needs water and add more, which causes further trauma.

NOTE: If you're now thinking, "Oh, now I understand why my hibiscus . . . " pour in a couple cups of hydrogen peroxide (H_2O_2). It's like an oxygen mask on a drowning victim.

Wilting

Freezing

- **Freezing:** To confuse things even more, freezing conditions can also cause a plant to wilt for similar reasons to overwatering.

RAISED BED GARDENS

Why spend extra energy raising a garden bed? To keep moles, rabbits and other critters from eating plants and roots as well as provide some control over weeds and the plants' needs, which makes growing in dirt more efficient.

MATERIALS
weed barrier
bricks, blocks, CMUs, or with FCB or wood dimensional lumber
heavy potting soil
mulch (optional)

TOOLS
utility knife
measuring tape
4-ft level

torpedo level
3-lb dead blow hammer

1. Lay out and grade your garden area and lay weed barrier or pour a slab of concrete (page 62).
2. Construct 1 to 4 rectangular boxes with fiber cement boards or dimensional wood lumber (page 17) or by dry stacking bricks, blocks, or CMUs 6–24 in tall, depending on root depths, by no more than 3 ft wide and 8 ft long. The boxes can be as long as the available space, but they shouldn't be wider than double the length you can reach or work. If using multiple boxes, lay them out in rows east to west,

positioning shorter boxes up front, on the south end, and the tallest in the back, spaced 3 ft or more apart for cart access.

IMPORTANT: Use any non-biodegradable and non-photodegradable materials, but treated wood isn't recommended as it tends to leach chemicals into your garden.

3. Line the bottom with a 2-in drainage layer of gravel, then another layer of weed barrier to prevent roots from clogging the drainage layer.

NOTE: You could also line the walls with 6-mil plastic, sandwiching the top flap under the top course of bricks. The liner insures water soaks down to the bottom. Otherwise, it'll take the path of least resistance and travel out the sides. For poured or mortared walls, drill bottom or side weep holes instead of using plastic liner. And do yourself a favor and don't use rebar or wire mesh. It'll rust, expand, and blow out your masonry.

4. Then fill the box with heavy potting soil (page 75), 15% higher than desired.

NOTE: Because the boxes drain water and nutrients, I suggest pouring a slab, or at least adding weed barrier topped with sand on the floor between boxes. Otherwise, you'll quickly find forested aisle ways.

5. Plant your crops with adequate spacing (reference your "Plant Needs" table on page 72), with longer roots in deeper boxes.

NOTE: Plants with the shortest roots, like basil and relish, tend to cover the ground, where taller crops, like corn and sunflower, will have deeper shoots. By arranging in a raked auditorium-seating fashion, with the tallest crops in the back, no one's blocking anyone's sunlight. Another option is to build one box with stepped walls from 24 in to 6 in.

6. To naturally pack soil, water the garden with low-pressure spray until saturated. This will drop soil level roughly 15%, forming needed air pockets as water recesses. Top with 2 in of mulch (or other evaporation protection) if desired.

NOTE: Vines act as tall plants. Attach them to a lattice made from scraps along the back wall of the rear box.

GREENHOUSES

One of the reasons gardening and farming isn't as efficient as other methods is that in most locations, it's not year-round. Which by default, means you're already producing less than half of what year-round growers produce. By building one or several greenhouses over your garden, you'll get 2 to 3 times more production in just grow time alone. You'll also see larger production since plants don't have to spend energy growing deeper roots to stabilize in wind, heal themselves from pests and disease, or cool or heat themselves due to inclement weather. For more information on the benefits of greenhouses and grow rooms, check out my Free Food Factories.

The one problem I've run into with greenhouses, at least in hot regions, is they act like a solar oven, cooking the plants—especially lettuce. To prevent this, for your covering, incorporate a solar shielding or reflecting material like a shade cloth or multi-wall polycarbonate sheets, Aluminet shade cloth for desert locations. They harbor a tremendous R-value and offer 99.5% UV protection, while maintaining up to 80% light transmission.

MATERIALS
(2) 10-ft 1-in PVC electrical conduit or #6 rebar
(34) 10-ft ¾-in PVC electrical conduit
(15) ¾-in PVC crosses
(10) ¾-in PVC tees
PVC primer and glue
plastic paint

25 x 21-ft shade cloth, tarp, 12-mil greenhouse plastic, or shaded poly tarp
1 x 4-in x 20-ft metal stud or cee purlin
1½-in self-tapping stainless steel screws
garden hose or poly pipe

TOOLS
pipe cutter or miter saw
3-lb sledge hammer
string
measuring tape
pencil

hair dryer or heat gun
pull straps
plumb bob
utility knife
impact with apex adapter and #2 Phillips apex tips

1. Using a pipe cutter or miter saw, cut (10) 1-in x 2-ft PVC conduit or #6 x 3-ft rebar (20) ¾-in PVC electrical conduit, or 200 psi (thick wall) poly pipe to 5 ft and (60) to 4 ft. Prime the outside ends of all pipes along with the insides of (15) ¾-in crosses and (10) ¾-in tees.
2. Lay out and grade your greenhouse site, then stake (5) 1-in x 2-ft pipes or #6 x 3-ft rebar, 2 ft deep, in-line, spaced 4 ft 9⁄16 in OC, and another (5) in a parallel line, 12–16 ft over, depending on desired greenhouse height. 12 ft apart will result in an 8-ft tall greenhouse, and 16 ft apart a 6-ft tall greenhouse.

   NOTE: For large greenhouses, grade to ⅛ in per foot slope or more.

3. Slide a 4-ft piece of pipe vertically over each stake, and on top of each outside pipe, glue ¾-in tees, T stem pointed toward the pipes. Then on top of all inside pipes, glue cross fittings, legs left to right.
4. Complete the row by connecting the center fittings with (4) 5-ft horizontal pipes.
5. Then extend both lines vertically for another row on both sides.

6. Repeat for 5 rows total, two on the left side, three on the right with uncapped vertical pipes at the top.
7. The hardest pipes to connect will be the top verticals into the other side's fittings. Warm pipe insides with a hair dryer or heat gun at a rate of 1 in per 10 seconds, depending on temperature, letting gravity form your arch. Keep the pipes in place while the glue dries, using pull straps.

   NOTE: It's easier with 5 heat guns, one per pipe, working from the bottom up.

8. When finished, drop a plumb bob from each top cross to center, reheating and adjusting as needed.
9. With sandpaper, scour each fitting and any components, parts, and plant pots that aren't UV resistant, and paint (page 57). Then cover the structure with a 25 x 21-ft shade cloth, tarp, 12-mil greenhouse plastic, or shaded poly tarp, centering excess material on each side.

   NOTE: It's easier to cover the greenhouse on a windless day.

   IMPORTANT: Materials must be mildew proof, acid and tear resistant, and UV treated.

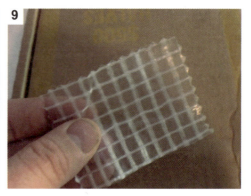

10. To tighten the plastic up, place a 1 x 4-in x 20-ft metal stud or cee purlin, legs down, flat on top of the excess flap on the ground, butted against the pipes outside of the greenhouse. With a person every 4 ft, grip and fold extra material on top of the stud or purlin, then roll it up horizontally, sandwiching plastic between the poles and tracks (purlin).
11. Attach poles to the track with (2) 1½-in self-tapping stainless steel screws from inside. On the other side, pull plastic tight and repeat.
12. Cut a garden hose or poly pipe scraps into (24) 1-in sections. Split the pipe, making a C, wrap the plastic around the pole and use pipe pieces as a clamp to hold the plastic in place.
13. Construct end walls using any material, medium, or frame with metal studs and tracks at the bottom.

    NOTE: Add a heat source in cold regions and a swamp cooler or vent and whole house fan in hot regions. And add a water source to keep RH at 60–80%.

EDIBLE LANDSCAPING

Edible landscaping is my favorite type of production. There's no cost or labor involved other than planting and harvesting. Plant delicious native trees, shrubs, ground cover, vines, flowers, weeds and let Mother Nature do the work. Or add pergolas, lattice, a water garden, and/or a picnic table garden, and treat your family and friends to a pick-while-you-eat salad bar at the next barbecue. You can't get fresher food than that! See your "Plant Needs" table (page 72) for plant options or contact your local county extension office.

Planting edible landscaping is no different from regular landscaping. I do have a few pointers, though:

Design and draw in-line with greywater systems.

Lay out, grade, excavate, and construct paths with piping covered by gravel or pavers before planting, that way you section off the yard so as not to trample produce when harvesting. Make the paths wide enough for carts.

Start small in an area you can monitor, and add on as you experience success.

If you desire an aesthetically pleasing motif rather than a wild food free-for-all, plant ground-huggers like kale and other salad greens geometrically around towering plants like blueberry or artichoke bushes, with herbs at the edges for borders.

Similarly, mix or accent your color pallet by intermingling onion or garlic with lavender, lilac, or violets; or red roses, violets, daisies, dandelions, and nasturtiums (yes, all edible), with red strawberries, rhubarb, and tomatoes.

No need to buy any seeds. Obtain cuttings or seeds from local or neighboring trees and plants to propagate (page 86).

Plan and plant per each plant's light and height requirements and percolation needs.

Locate shade and partial sun plants behind tall sun-thriving crops and/or around trees.

Keep areas around young plants weed-free until the plant is fully established and spread out.

Avoid highly desired foods like strawberries and lettuce unless you fence or cover the crops, or you'll have every critter within a mile radius scarfing down your groceries.

Never plant annuals. Having to replant the dead plants every year defeats the entire purpose of letting the landscape produce for you.

Stagger harvest times so you have fresh food year-round, and don't end up canning large harvests.

Position benches and gazebos in the center of your live salad bar as the intersection for all paths.

Consider dwarf trees for small yards, or dwarf them yourself by pruning (page 91).

Grow cattails and sugar cane along property lines and fences.

Work vine crops like potato, pea, bean, blackberry, raspberry and grape up and around trellises, lattices, walls, fence lines, and pergolas.

Plant mushrooms under large leaf species or in any other dark spots with heavy watering schedules (page 79).

Add composite flowers and daisies to attract beneficial insects (page 83).

Plant weeds—lots and lots of edible weeds. These are the easiest, least water consuming, and most productive plants you can possibly grow.

Balance everything with stones and boulders, bridges, water features, or brownscaping.

Give away as much food as possible. When you grow food wild, you'll have an abundance, and preserving loses a lot of flavor. Give it away to friends, family, co-workers, and, more importantly, strangers. Keep food free!

Orchards

Every back and front yard, if suitable, should be an orchard, even an orchard of one! With this method, I've never needed to side tie trees for support. Reference your "Plant Needs" table (page 72) for types and shading requirements depending on your location.

MATERIALS

weed barrier
compost (page 183)

washed rock, tumbled glass (page 16), other mulch (page 17),
 or charcoal (page 61)
(2) 18-wheeler or tractor tires

TOOLS

spade shovel

utility knife

1. Design, grade, and lay out the chosen area in a diagonal grid, spacing determined by the orchard's canopy size. Reference your "Plant Needs" table (page 72).

2. If transplanting, flood the tree's pot the night before. Then, where you're going to transplant the tree, dig a hole with a slight conical top 2 times wider than the pot and 1.5 times deeper, building an 8-ft circular berm with half the removed material.

IMPORTANT: Yearly, move the berm out to 2% beyond the canopy, following root expansion.

3. Check for proper drainage by performing a percolation test (page 79), excavating and tilling in proper amendments and conditioners (page 74) as needed.

4. Puncture the hole's walls with a metal rake or pitchfork so roots are encouraged to grow horizontally.

NOTE: Most tree roots only grow in the top 1 ft of soil. Smooth walls drive them downward where water and nutrients are more scarce.

IMPORTANT: If walls are hard, excavate and backfill the entire area to avoid root balling.

5. In the hole, mix compost to native dirt at 1:4, then remove most of it from the hole, leaving just a few inches in the bottom.

6. Remove the tree from its pot to transplant (page 91), and while one person slowly rotates it horizontally, lightly dust the root ball while rubbing and stimulating roots with your hand. You will also want to rub the hole walls with blood meal (page 77), bone meal (page 76), and fertilizer (page 76) and the root ball with BMOs (page 74) and root stimulator hormones, or mycorrhizae fungus and molasses, or honey (page 220).

7. Place the root ball in the center of the hole, the top of it 3–4 in above the grade. Add more soil mix if necessary, then backfill. Do not compact.

NOTE: If you have a mole problem, lay a sheet of galvanized chicken wire in the hole prior to transferring the tree.

8. Then cover the entire top of the root ball inside the berm with a bag of cow manure or compost (page 183).

9. Flood the berm with water, then lay weed barrier inside the berm, and cover with washed rock, tumbled glass (page 16), or other mulch, or charcoal (page 61).

NOTE: The practice of mulching is avidly argued between arborists, including myself. But mulching does occur in nature. Trees and branches die, fall and degrade, forming a layer of mulch over the soil, protecting the young from competing plants, herbivores and moisture loss while insulating from cold and heat. Eventually, the mulch breaks down adding soil and nutrients back to new trees. I don't mulch because it provides a habitat for weed growth. If you prefer to mulch, I wouldn't suggest killing or purchasing store-bought killed trees for wood chips and soaking them in colors and chemicals. Instead, invest in a woodchipper—Patriot being the best that I've found—and lay 2–4 in of chipped deadfall or pruned clippings.

10. Stack (2) 18-wheeler or tractor tires around the trunk at tree bases and fill the tires with water. (Optional) If you want to hide the tires, build a large berm using semi non-permeable material, at least 4 ft out and around tires, up to and covering the tires. Repeat for remaining trees.

    NOTE: The berm, along with the water-filled tire, acts as a thermal mass in the wintertime, and a water tank in the summer. The tires also act as independent composters and a food source for the trees.

11. Operation: Add 1 lb of food scraps inside the bottom tire weekly. 1 lb per week should equal a full tire in 54 weeks, the time it takes food to turn into compost in most locations. Otherwise, to test, fill a bucket up with food and wait until it breaks completely down. Add a little compost starter (anerobic bacteria), if desired, to jumpstart the process. Then divide the inside volume of the tire by 54 or 365 if you're adding scraps weekly. If you're having overfill food scraps, plant another tree or add overfill to the compost pile (page 183).

12. For the first few winters, place a third tire on top of the other two and cover it with plastic. After that, wrap the tire with livestock fencing, or (4) 8-ft stakes, and 6-mil clear plastic.

13. For cold regions, use lava rock or stone for mulch. The rock acts like a heat sink that, when combined with the water and tires, creates a thermal mass that absorbs the sunlight and heat from the day and releases it during the night while the water and plastic covering keeps a humid environment and acts like a greenhouse, preventing freezing. On excessively cold nights, heat 4–6-in stones in the fire and place them inside the plastic covering. Don't let them touch the tree trunks, plastic, or tires.

14. This setup will last the first five to ten years, when the tree needs these added benefits the most. Once the tree's canopy outgrows the tire's diameter, cut the tires off as described in steps 1–2 of "Sandals" (page 50).

15. With the tires now removed, with the first good storm, the inner edge of the berm will erode naturally and effortlessly inwards and outwards, enlarging itself by 1.5 to 2 times. This new berm will last your young tree another 5-plus years, at which point the tree's root system will be developed enough to not need assistance.

Weeds

First, unlearn that there are such things as "weeds." Mindset breaker: they don't exist!

All plants are edible for someone or something. It's just a matter of which are you going to spend your calories on helping to grow. Learn which weeds are edible in your region. If you have livestock, protect the weeds from them. Covering wanted "weeds" with metal cages and allowing goats to eat the unwanted ones works. In fact, the first thing they usually go for is the poison ivy and oak. They're a delicacy. If you resort to pulling and manhandling ill-mannered vegetation, at least Waterworld it by placing the cadavers in your compost pile so their nutrients can be recycled.

The following are a few typical edible "weeds" most likely growing in your yard at this very moment:

- **Three-leaf clover:** Clover isn't only edible, it's delicious when added to salads. Just keep an eye out for the four-leaf variety!
- **Chickweed:** All parts of the chickweed '"weed" are edible and it's one of the most common yard weeds.
- **Dandelions:** Of course dandelions makes the list. It's pretty much common knowledge!

NOTE: Older, more mature dandelion leaves can be a bit bitter; pick them when they're young.

Three-leaf clover

Chickweed

Dandelions

- **Dead-nettle:** Although not as common, dead-nettle leaves are one of my favorite because they have an almost mushroom-like taste.
- **Nettle:** That's right, stinging nettle, the scourge of the weed community, is edible. Because the needles are made from a crystal-like material, when boiled or blended on high, stinging nettle loses its sting and becomes a superfood high in protein, delicious, and packed with nutrition.
- **Dock:** Although not the best tasting, dock leaves can grow enormous and they don't taste bad. Just don't eat the roots.

Dead-nettle | Nettle | Dock

- **Henbit:** Henbit resides in the mint family, though it does not have a minty taste.
- **Pigweed and lamb's-quarter amaranth:** Hated by farmers and considered a noxious weed, pigweed and lamb's-quarter amaranth unfortunately bear the resemblance of spinach.
- **Plantains:** Very common around the U.S., both the seed stocks and leaves of plantains are delicious.
- **Thistle:** Thistles are another highly hated backyard resident and are highly edible and great tasting. Artichoke is another type of thistle.

Henbit | Pigweed and lamb's-quarter amaranth | Plantains | Thistle

- **Wild garlic and wild onion:** Growing up, I remember picking and eating both wild garlic and wild onion raw (yes, they taste just like garlic and onion and are members of the onion family). Both are highly widespread weeds in the U.S.
- **Ground ivy:** Ground ivy is probably the most prolific "weed" in your lawn. Lawnmowers often miss it due to the fact that it's super short.
- **Mushrooms:** Media and movies have really given wild mushrooms a bad rap. Contrary to popular belief, less than 1%–2% are actually poisonous. But here in the south and up in the northwest, they grow like, well, weeds. Hen-of-the-woods, oyster, and sulphur shelf top my list as some of the most prolific and delicious of the species.
- **Wildflowers:** Finally, most wildflowers are edible. Pick yourself up a foraging guide to determine which are best for your area.

Wild onion | Ground ivy | Mushrooms | Wild flowers

Mushrooms

Mushrooms can be a great addition to any edible yard. They grow fast in most locations, look magical, and per 100g, provide 22 calories and over 20% of the daily value of vitamin B See "Growing Mushrooms" on page 95 for planting and growing edible mushrooms.

INDOOR GARDENING

Supplement your house plants with edible versions like in the "Produce Methods" table (page 72), or grow an entire garden inside. Indoor gardens are often much better producers since they receive more attention than outdoor gardens, there are no pests, and they're climate controlled. All you need are pots, floors, and windows or lights to create your own grow room (page 96).

- Use the largest plant pot possible. Water is wasted at first, but unobstructed root growth will allow the plant to flourish, and repetitive transplant shock will be prevented.
- To facilitate regular plant relocation, use a lightweight soil mix (page 75) with 25–30% moisture-retaining media and construct or purchase a plant pot caddy.
- Use your watering schedule (page 79) or stick a moisture pH light meter 6 in into each pot, or each pot group on the same watering schedule.
- Don't add fertilizers for the first year; plants have enough nutrients in their seeds to get them through year one.
- Plants have different lighting and temperature requirements. Move plants as they react to their locations accordingly.

NOTE: If you're planning on keeping a considerable number of plants, design the south, east, and west walls of your house with plenty of windows.

- For growing mushrooms (page 95), keep a terrarium or wicker laundry basket covered, or reserve a closet or cabinet space.
- For plant pots, use recycled containers (coffee cans, buckets, paint cans, plastic jars, small waste bins, milk containers, 5-gallon buckets, small garbage cans, plastic totes). Basically, anything that can hold dirt. I'll even use doubled grocery bags.

NOTE: Plants don't care about what they're wearing, so there's no need to go overboard purchasing pots. Even better, make your own pots.

Lighting

In a process called photosynthesis, plants obtain energy from light and CO_2 and convert it into sugars to use for mass growth when it's dark, so lighting for inside plants is even more critical.

Different plants require different amounts of light and different intensities. For the most part, though, adhering to the package directions provides an adequate rule of thumb when growing in colder climates. For southern regions like south Texas and Arizona, "loves full sun" would fry anything but a cactus within hours, so dialing it back one to two levels tends to be more realistic in warm climates.

HYDROPONICS

The wonderful world of hydroponics allows us to grow large quantities of food without tractors, tillers, harvesters, gigantic irrigation systems, large plots of land, or even a backyard. There's no need for hardiness zones, adequate rainfall, or rich soil, making the setup great for small urban homes, city-dwelling apartments, and people with little growing experience and space. You can grow in a basement, attic, shed, spare bedroom, garage, or closet with the addition of grow lights and climate control!

Think of hydroponics in its simplest form. A hydroponic farm is merely a farm with automatic watering and fertilizing, and without the unpredictable weather, unnecessary costs, and energy- and time-consuming maintenance that traditional farms require. Plants only need water, nutrients, and light, which we can provide in a way that produces farm-level quantities in a fraction of the space and time. Hydroponics is much cheaper and easier than farming, and it offsets farming's environmental footprint since large crops can grow inside urban areas, eliminating the need to ship to cities, which reduces cost and CO_2 pollution.

After study, research, and years of failed growing attempts, I found that hydroponics are a more productive and efficient way to grow healthier and larger quantities of food for people like us—normal people who have no prior experience. According to our journals and logs, we're currently seeing two times the production rate, two times the size, two times the nutrient and sugar content, and four to ten times the quantity, with 99% less effort, 100% less cost, 98% less water, and 99% less loss when compared to annual yield reports from industrial food production companies of the same growing zone.

I've tested and modified most hydroponics systems and have even built new ones in an effort to discover the best. But there is no best, only better production when systems are built for specific plants. In the following section, I've laid out each system based on ease and congruent size of production, starting with beginner. The grow buckets and totes are meant to give you a taste of how the different systems work, how plants grow in nutrient solution, and how everything acts. For real production, graduate yourself up to grow towers, grow walls, and grow beds, leaving the commercial systems for expert growers.

For plumbing we can use a variable array of pipe types. For the pressure side, I typically go with thin-wall black poly pipe since I can bend it to will and since it doesn't require expensive fittings, which kill the price margin of hydroponic systems. Try to have your returns (the non-pressure side) be at least three to four times larger than your pressure side to prevent overflowing. For fittings, SharkBites work on any type of pipe, not just PVC and copper, depending on the color, with a gray collar being compatible with polybutylene pipe.

Before starting, though, use the "Produce Methods" table (page 71) to find the food type you wish to grow and to determine which system is best for your needs.

NOTE: Reference your "Plant Needs" table (page 72) for temperature, pH, and light requirements.

Grow Media

For the most part, I've only used grow media that I've harvested from our land, materials like volcanic rock, pumice, scoria, sand, shale, gravel, crushed rock. Or I've fabricated my own from blown clay, activated carbon, pottery shards, brick shards, glass shards, mulch, wood chips, coir, and rice and coconut husks. I have just recently worked with rock wool, foam, and expanded clay.

Some media, like lava rock and brick or pottery shards, have the ability to wick nutrient solution around to dry media where others can only absorb and hold the solution. Also, avoid uniform sizes and shapes in grow towers. Although visually appealing, they lack the ability to distribute nutrient solution. All media should be crushed to ½–¾-in diameters.

Whatever the material, make sure that it's inexpensive, and that it's a lightweight yet structural material that remains uncondensed yet oxygenated, doesn't fall apart when wet, and allows for free draining but still retains water. Make sure it's pH neutral and UV and bio resistant so that it doesn't breed algae, break down, or decompose. You can also mix media to compensate for poor qualities. However, before adding any media to your garden or plant pot, rinse the material, if not soak and boil it, to remove and kill any foreign contaminants.

Again, there's no media that's better than the others, but some work better in certain systems with certain plants, while other plants grow the same regardless of which system or media is used.

WARNING: Packing peanuts made from polystyrene are a possible human carcinogen according to the W.H.O. and may leach trace amounts of styrene into the plants and, therefore, into the produce consumed (even though you drink your coffee and eat food out of it every day).

Net Pots

Many systems use various sized net pots, plastic netted plant pots, with grow media, similar to the way they use regular pots. But since we've gotten rid of the rain, wind, hail, and other extreme weather, there's no need for major structural support. Consequently, I've found that in most cases, media and net pots are a waste of time, money, and energy and just cause a mess. Instead, you can use collars (see below) or at least make your own net pot out of recycled materials, sized to an adult plant stalk's OD times three.

Collars

Collars secure plants so that grow media isn't required. With wicks, we can sprout seeds directly inside collars, ensuring they're never transplanted, disturbed, or even touched until harvest, events that just slow production, and when added up, account for our extreme production rates. Both collars and wicks should be made from non-organic, non-biodegradable, UV-resistant materials like rubber, foam, PE, XPS, polyurethane, EPS, and moldable plastic.

Some good options for recycled materials are gym tiles, tire pieces, yoga mats, flip flops, carpet padding, open-cell Styrofoam, woven HVAC filter, molded packing, 4x8 sheets of rigid insulation, cups, and cup lids.

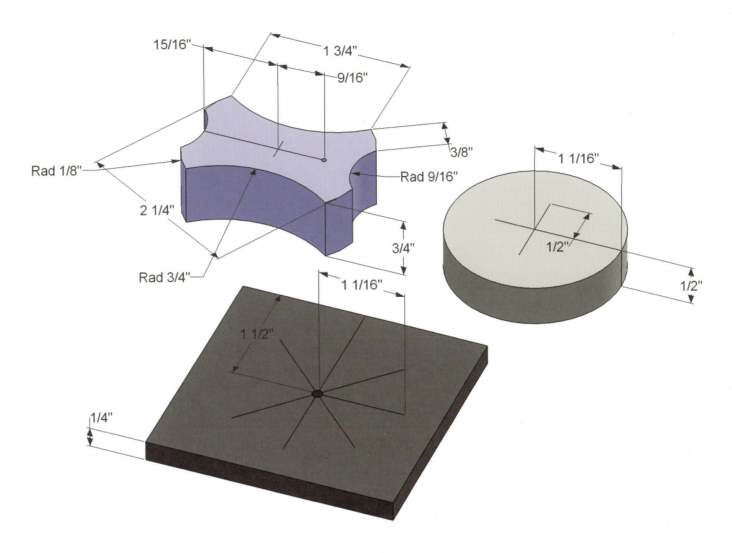

Hydroponic Wicks

For wicks, I cut a car shammy or the filaments of an old mop head into 5 in lengths. You can use anything with flat microfiber strips. Also, ask car washes for old curtain blades, which fall off occasionally and are thrown away.

Water pH

Minerals stay in a soluble state and are assimilated by plants at certain pH levels and become insoluble at others. When the pH drops below soluble levels, you'll get a nutrient deficiency for that particular chemical. As you can see from the following table, for hydroponics, the optimal range is 5.5–7.0 with deficiencies occurring above and below. It's better to balance toward 5.5 since pH tends to increase over time, and most additives will raise pH.

When adding chemical compounds (page 57), remember that adding acids lowers pH, while alkalis raise it:

ACIDS AND ALKALIS

Acids	pH	Alkalis	pH
Milk	6	Baking soda	8
Rainwater	5–5.5	Milk of magnesia	10
Vinegar	4	Ammonia/ washing soda	11
Acetic acid	3	Caustic Lye	12
Lemon or lime juice	2	Lye	13
Battery Acid	1		

Water and CO$_2$

You can experience a decrease in production due to a rise in production from a constant, uninterrupted supply of nutrients; your garden can become so efficient that production falters. This is because the plants become so healthy and, therefore, work harder and produce more. Their respiratory systems, as well as photosynthesis, accelerate and will often use up available CO$_2$ quickly. This isn't a problem when growing plants outside. However, in greenhouses and grow rooms, it's important to measure CO$_2$ with a carbon dioxide meter weekly. The outside ambient air content of CO$_2$ is only approximately 400 ppm, a drastic limiting factor. For commercial production, we bump up those levels to 1500 ppm and get an extra 30% increase in yields by adding a CO$_2$ generator. By providing additional CO$_2$, especially during photosynthesis, you not only avoid production slowing, but you can further enhance production by 10–30%.

NOTE: Between 500 and 1,000 ppm, production rises dramatically, around 30%, but not so much from 1000 to 1,500 ppm. It only increases by 1–5%, making raising CO$_2$ to anything over 1000 ppm not worth the energy loss for smaller growers.

Nutrient Solutions

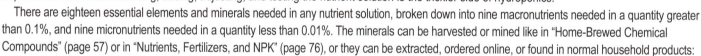

I reviewed nutrients earlier in the chapter, but hydro nutrients are different. Your N-P-K fertilizers don't hold water with hydroponics—literally. They need to be soluble, otherwise they'll just sink. Also, because the nutrients are being made available so quickly, if levels are off, it'll instantly affect the plants.

A nutrient solution consists of water and nutrients in the form of mostly dissolved solids. Regular tap water is the best option, since it usually contains chlorine, sodium, salts, zinc, sulfur, copper sulfate, calcium and other much needed metals. Test your water to see how much of what element is present so you'll know what to add. Otherwise, use reverse osmosis water since unlike water filters, it removes dissolved solids, and start from zero.

Natural soil-based nutrients are finite. If we don't fertilize when they're used up, the plants die. This is because many nutrients are either adsorbed first by larger plants, locked up in other minerals, or they wash away unused. Since there's no place for extra nutrients to "wash away" to, we can't just dump 10-10-10 NPK into our system and hope for the best. Understanding, adding, adjusting, and testing the nutrient solution is the trickier side of hydroponics.

There are eighteen essential elements and minerals needed in any nutrient solution, broken down into nine macronutrients needed in a quantity greater than 0.1%, and nine micronutrients needed in a quantity less than 0.01%. The minerals can be harvested or mined like in "Home-Brewed Chemical Compounds" (page 57) or in "Nutrients, Fertilizers, and NPK" (page 76), or they can be extracted, ordered online, or found in normal household products:

NUTRIENT ADDITIVES

Element	Forms	Source	(ppm x 1k)
Macronutrients			
Carbon (C)	CO$_2$	Air, CO$_2$ generator	450
Oxygen (O)	CO$_2$, O$_2$, H$_2$O$_2$	Air, water, O$_2$ generator, hydrogen peroxide	450
Hydrogen (H)	H$_2$O, H$_2$O$_2$	Water, hydrogen peroxide	NA
Nitrogen (N)	NO$_3^-$, NH$_4^+$, NO$_2^-$, N$_2$O, NH$_3$	Air, nitrogen sulfate (food additive), urea, nitrite, nitrate	5–60
Phosphorus (P)	H2PO4-, HPO$_4^{-2}$, KH$_2$PO$_4$	Food additive, fungicide, bone meal	1.5–5
Potassium (K)	K$^+$, KOH, KNO$_3$, K$_2$CO$_3$, K$_2$SO$_4$, KCl	Kelp meal, caustic lye, saltpeter, Spectracide stump remover, road salt	8–80
Calcium (Ca)	Ca^{+2}, Ca(OH)$_2$, CaCl$_2$, CaH$_4$P$_2$O$_8$, CaCO$_3$, Ca(NO3)2	Slaked lime, pool/road salt, leavening agent, agricultural lime	1–60
Sulfur (S)	SO$_4^{-2}$, H$_2$SO$_4$	Commercial cleaners, drain openers	1–15
Magnesium (Mg)	Mg^{+2}, MgSO$_4$	Epsom salt	0.5–10

Micronutrients			
Iron (Fe)	F^{+2}, Fe^{+2}, $FeSO_4$, FeDTPA	Pigments, coloring agents	0.2–0.6
Chlorine (Cl)	Cl-, NaCl,	Pool chlorine, bleach w/100% chlorine, sea water, road salt	0.01–80
Manganese (Mn)	Mn^{+2}	Liquid seaweed, manure, lime	0.01–0.6
Zinc (Zn)	Zn^{+2}	Manure, zinc salts	0.25–0.5
Copper (Cu)	Cu^+, Cu^{+2}, $CuSO_4$	Copper sulfate (dye mordant, etching solution, fungicide, root killer)	0.02–0.05
Boron (B)	BO_3^{-3}, H_3BO_3, BH_3O_3	Borax soap, boric acid (insecticide)	0.002–0.8
Molybdenum (Mo)	MoO_4^{-2}, Na_2MoO_4	Sodium molybdate (fertilizer)	0.001–0.01
Sodium (Na)	Na_2SiO_3, Na_2SO_4, NaCl, $NaHCO_3$, NaOH	Salt, lye	0–12
Nickel (Ni)	$NiSO_4$, $NiCO_3$		0.057–1.5
Silicone (Si)	K_2SiO_3, Na_2SiO_3, H_2SiO_3	Fly ash	0–140
Cobalt (Co)	$CoSO_4$, $Co(NO3)2$		0–0.1
Fluorine (F)	NaF	Tap water, dental products	0–1

* Most irons will remain soluble at low pH; otherwise, they require a chelating agent like pentetic acid.

NOTE: Because of all the phosphates and sulfates added, additions of phosphorous sulfides are seldom needed. Alternatively, nitrogen and potassium, being the most consumed, are often the most lacking.

Hydroponic Cooling and Heating

As mentioned, plants not only grow better in temperate environments, but they produce more. Temperature is also critical to prevent water-borne pathogens like water mold. Fortunately, with hydroponics we don't have to heat or cool all the ambient air, just the water, which is much easier and cheaper. In addition, by keeping water temperatures low, below 70°F, we maximize the amount of gas it can hold. Once the water gets to the mid-80s, you're looking at a 15% loss or 7.5ppm.

My number one suggestion for heating and cooling is to use solar energy (page 133). Alternatively, utilize a couple 500W aquarium heaters or chillers, or route insulated pressure lines through an in-line water heater or refrigerator water dispenser to keep temperatures between 65 and 68°F.

Grow Bucket (NC/DWC)

NC (non-circulating) DWC (deep water culture), or constant bottom feed, is a simple setup of suspending the lower water sucker roots in nutrient solution while leaving the air roots out to absorb nitrogen, CO_2, oxygen and other gasses in a humid environment. Because there are no moving parts, they're very basic in design, function, setup, cost, and use, with minimal monitoring required. Since they're passive (NC), there is zero possibility of failure from clogging, electricity, or component failure.

MATERIALS

1 c ground manure or compost tea

¼-in tubing

lightweight potting soil (page 75) or grow media (page 106)

fiber pot or hydroponic wick (page 107)

seeds or sprouts

TOOLS

5-gal bucket with lid

drill with ⅜-in drill bit and 2-in hole saw

5-lpm air pump with 2-in diffuser

2-in net pots

measuring tape

Sharpie

1. Select a solid color 5-gal bucket with a lid for the reservoir. Fill it with water to 4 in from the rim and mix in 1 c of ground dry manure (page 76) or compost tea (page 77) with 1 t kelp meal as the nutrient solution. Let sit overnight.

    IMPORTANT: If the bucket is semi-translucent, paint it white or algae will grow.

2. (Optional) Drill a ⅜-in hole in the lid, run ¼-in tubing through, insert a 2-in diffuser, and connect it to an air pump capable of providing 5 lpm.

3. With a hole saw, cut (1–4) equally spaced 2-in holes in the bucket's lid, and place 2-in fiber pots filled with lightweight potting soil in the holes long enough to sit in the nutrient solution and carry it to your seeds or sprouts.

    NOTE: Alternatively, you can simply use 2-in net pots with grow media and a wick.

4. Operation: Nutrient solution is pulled up from the fiber pot or wick, soaking the growing medium via capillary action until the roots grow long enough to reach the solution on their own. Because the water and nutrients in the reservoir are being absorbed by the plants but not automatically replenished, you'll need to add each periodically. Peas, okra, green beans, and leafy greens do well in buckets. I usually grow 2–3 plants per bucket, 4 for lettuce, and 1 for larger plants like kale, spinach, or cabbage.

Grow Tote (NC/DWC)

An NC/DWC grow tote is the same system as the NC/DWC Grow Bucket above, except we're able to grow many more plants with the same nutrient solution reservoir.

MATERIALS

medium storage tote

(2) ¼-in threaded plastic valves

¼-in clear tubing

net pots

grow media

wicks (page 42)

nutrient solution

TOOLS

drill with ½-in drill bit and 2-in hole saw

measuring tape

Sharpie

pH meter

1. In a plastic storage tote, drill a ½-in hole in the side just above the bottom radius, and install (2) ¼-in threaded plastic valves.

    IMPORTANT: To prevent algae growth, use a pigmented container or spray paint white.

    NOTE: For shallow-root plants like strawberry and lettuce, under-bed totes work well, but any container will do as long as you keep a 1:3–1:4 ratio of air to nutrient solution height and as long as the lid and walls can support the weight.

2. Point the leg of the first valve down and the second up. Then for a water level meter, attach enough clear ¼-in tubing to the second valve to reach the top of the tote.

    NOTE: You can skip the second valve and tubing and instead make a sight glass by painting a clear tote and leaving a ½-in wide, top to bottom, vertical strip clear to check the nutrient solution level. But be sure to cover the unpainted strip with electrical tape when not in use.

3. Level the tote, mark off inches on the water level meter, then cut 2-in holes in the lid, spaced per plants' requirements in your "Plant Needs" table (page 72). Place net pots, grow media, and wicks, and fill the tote with nutrient solution.

    IMPORTANT: The more plants the nutrient solution has to feed, the faster it'll be depleted.

4. Check pH and nutrient levels 2 times a week, regardless of water level, adjusting as required.

5. Operation: Water height provides roots access to nutrients, first via the wick, then ultimately, unaided. As the roots grow, the nutrient solution level must follow suit. Adjust the nutrient solution level via the valve. Normally, plants will extract the nutrients, leaving most of the water and showing false nutrient levels. The reverse is true in arid regions. To resolve and prevent nutrient deficiencies, remove the nutrient solution, adjust pH and nutrients in a separate container, and refill the tote periodically.

Tree Grow Barrel (Drip)

Since I don't know of anyone else growing hydroponic trees, this is the only practical setup I've been able to develop.

MATERIALS
5-gal bucket or 30-gal plastic drum
55-gal plastic drum
¾-in x 3-ft hose
5 gal nutrient solution
100-gph 12V bilge pump
activated carbon or other lightweight structural grow media
sapling
fiber pot, Jiffy pot, or starter wool plugs
1ft² semi-porous, non-organic cloth
(optional) (2) 1-in stainless steel hinges
 5 gal nutrient solution

TOOLS
drill with ¾-in bit or unibit
measuring tape
Sharpie
jigsaw with coarse blade

1. To create net pots for small or dwarf trees, remove the handle and drill ¾-in holes spaced 1½ in OC on all sides of a 5-gallon bucket. Or if you want to plant medium-large trees, drill 1in holes every 3 in OC in a 30-gallon barrel.

   NOTE: The inner container only needs to be as big as the full-grown tree's root ball. Therefore, a 30-gallon barrel can hold comfortably even the largest of trees.

2. With a jigsaw, cut an 11⅜-in hole in the bottom of a plastic 55-gallon drum for the reservoir, and slide the net pot into the drum. Cut an 18-in hole in the 55-gallon drum if you're using a 30-gallon barrel.

   IMPORTANT: Scour and paint clear or white drums to prevent algae growth.

3. (Optional) Cut a 1 x 1-ft hole just beneath the top of the reservoir, and add a stainless steel hinge to create a side door so you can monitor root growth and health.

4. Fill with 5 gallons of nutrient solution, drop a 100-gph 12V bilge pump inside, and route the ¾-in hose through one of the net pot holes so that it'll stick out the top.

5. Add activated carbon or other lightweight structural media and a sapling to a fiber pot, Jiffy pot, or starter wool plugs. Then cover the media with semi-porous, non-organic cloth like pants or thermals to help distribute nutrient solution evenly over the entire surface. Don't use organic fabrics since they deteriorate quickly and will clog up the system.

6. (Optional) Add a water level float and drain valve.

7. Operation: As the nutrient solution is pumped up from the bottom reservoir and distributed on top, it drips back down through the cloth, through the media, back down into the reservoir, allowing roots full and constant access for balanced and healthy growth.

Grow Wall (NFT)

If a DWC system is like a stagnant pond where plants can dip their toes in, the water of an NFT system is like a flowing river that the plants dip their feet in. The flowing nutrient solution in an NFT system overcomes the downfalls that riddle stagnant nutrient solution and DWC systems (e.g., low O_2 and CO_2 levels, nutrient drop offs, etc.). A grow wall is a very beginner friendly, easy-to-build-and-maintain NFT system, and there is no possibility of clogged misters or drippers.

NOTE: The system can be scaled to any size desired.

MATERIALS

(4) 4–6-in dia. 10-ft Sdr 35 PE or Sch 20 PVC pipe
(9) 1-ft pieces of pipe strap or L-bracket shelving supports
(6) 4–6-in 90° Sdr 35 PE or Sch 20 PVC elbows
(3) 4–6-in dia 10 ft Sdr 35 PE or Sch 20 PVC pipe
1½-in coarse drywall screws
zip ties
trash or recycle bin or a large storage tote or 30-gallon plastic drum
¾-in x 10-ft hose
¾-in barbed–¾-in mpt adapter
¾-in ball valve

2–3-in net pots
collars
hydroponic wicks (page 107)
seeds or sprouted plants

TOOLS

snap string
measuring tape
Sharpie
drill with 2–3-in hole saw, apex adapter and #2 Phillips apex tip

PVC primer and glue
miter saw with fine tooth blade
0.25-hp or 5-gph water pump

1. Mark a center line on (4) 4–6in dia. 10-ft Sdr 35 PE or Sch 20 PVC pipe, and cut 2–3-in holes every 6 in, or the distance of your plant spacing as listed in your "Plant Needs" table (page 72), stopping 6 in from each end.

   NOTE: For small-root plants like strawberry, a 4 in dia. pipe with 2-in holes, for 2-in net pots, spaced 6 in apart is satisfactory. Whereas tomatoes would require a 6-in dia. pipe for root space and would need 3-in holes for 3-in collars, spaced 4–6 ft apart. Never use net pots on tomato or other long-root plants.

1

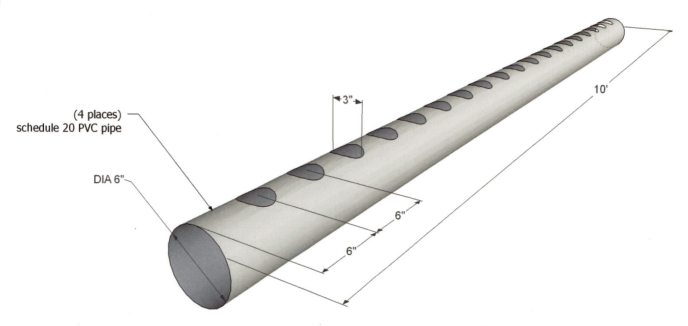

(4 places)
schedule 20 PVC pipe

DIA 6"

3"

6"

6"

10'

2. Pick a wall with good south-facing sun, and snap horizontal chalk lines at a ⅛ in per foot slope, in 10-ft long and 1ft 7½-in high increments. Increase increments for taller plants.
3. Along the center lines, starting 1 ft from each end, install 4 rows of pipe strap or L-bracket shelving supports, leg down, using 1½-in coarse drywall screws, Install them every 4 ft 9¾ in, skipping the first, sixth, and seventh when counting left to right, top to bottom, since these pipe sections will be supported by the pipe strap or L-brackets from the row below.
4. Install the (4) pipes in the straps or on the brackets and prime then glue (6) 4–6-in 90° elbows to the pipe ends, legs down and up, alternating rows. Glue 1-ft long vertical sections of pipe in between the elbows, including the bottom row, connecting each run.

3

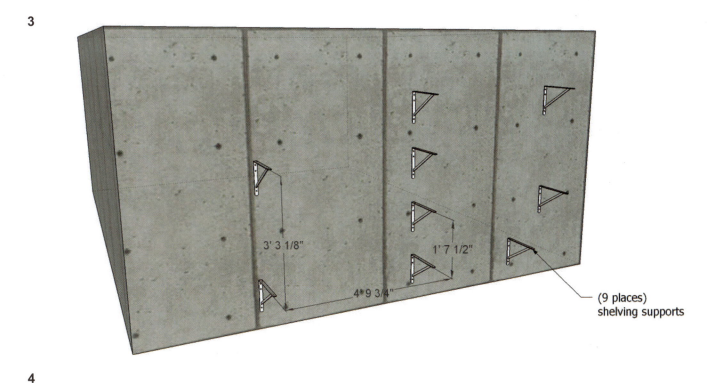

3' 3 1/8"

4' 9 3/4"

1' 7 1/2"

(9 places)
shelving supports

4

1'

1'

1'

1'

PVC cap

(3 places)
scedule 20
PVC pipe

5. To attach the pipes to supports if you're using brackets, zip tie them in place. For strapping, bring the strap up and around the pipe and screw it in place on top of the pipe.

4

5

6. For a reservoir, use a recycle bin or a large storage tote or cut a 4¼-in hole in the side of a 30-gal drum, the ¾-in bung up, and drop a pump capable of producing 0.25 hp or 5 gph with a ¾-in hose inside.

    NOTE: If your system sits near and above your nutrient solution reservoir, you can get away with just placing the return end over the reservoir.

7. Install a ¾-in barbed–¾-in mpt adapter along with a ¾-in ball valve on the end of the supply hose, slide the supply hose into the first net pot hole, place the remaining net pots or collars—with wicks and seeds or sprouted plants—inside the holes, fill the reservoir with nutrient solution, and adjust the flow rate through the valve to 3.25 gph.

NOTE: If you don't want to purchase net pots, plastic cups work great. Just fill them up with holes for root egress, using a long hole punch. Otherwise, like I said, use collars only.

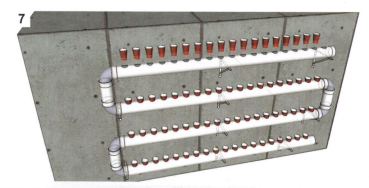

7

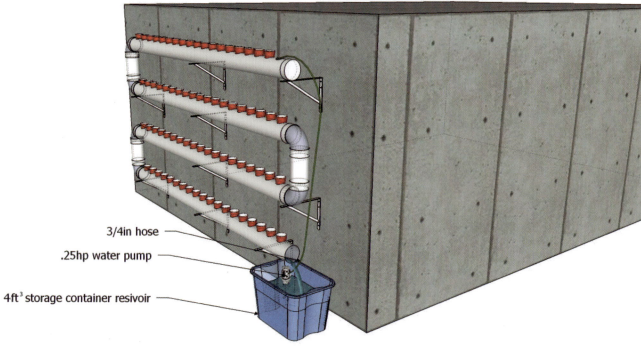

3/4in hose
.25hp water pump
4ft³ storage container resivoir

8. Operation: Plants are suspended above a continuously flowing stream of nutrient solution, typically ¾₄–⅛ in deep, stabilized in a net pot or a collar. In this fashion, the roots are allowed to dangle freely in nutrient solution. Pipes are best for shallow root plants like strawberry and lettuce since large root crops like tomato will quickly clog the channel, causing flooding upstream and die-off downstream.

AQUAPONICS

Connecting your fish farm to your hydroponics garden offsets most of the nutrient requirements via fish waste, and in exchange, plants and beneficial microorganisms filter and remove the fish toxins. By feeding your garden with water that has been used to cultivate fish, you don't have to pay for nutrients for your hydroponics garden or filter as much fish waste from your fish farm. You'll still have testing and mixing chores; however, the cut in cost and time is by far more rewarding.

8

PRODUCTION

Ready for your daily mindset breaker?

There's no such thing as vegetables. Everything that develops from the ovary—cucumber, eggplant, pepper, squash, tomato, pear, and apple—are all fruit. They're the offspring of the parent plants that have sex when conditions—darkness, temperature, nutrients, Marvin Gaye, and age—are right. The rest are just parts of the parent plant—stalk, root, and leaves.

Male plants have flowers with male genitalia, stamen, that spew out sperm in pollen all over your hands, butterflies, birds, bats, bees, moths, wasps, or just into the wind. Female plant flowers open their lady parts, stigma, which are wet and slimy inside. The sperm swims down through the style canal, penetrating the ovary where it inseminates and

fertilizes the egg. The egg then grows into a seed which houses a baby curled up in a little fetus-like ball. The ovary is the apple, pear, peach, plum, watermelon, cucumber, zucchini, or orange—the fruit that houses the seeds. Once we or something eats the ovary, or it decomposes, the baby is birthed and stretches its appendages in search of warmth, water, and nutrients. Some plants, hermaphrodites, have both male and female parts inside a single flower, which makes self-impregnation, and therefore, life, simpler.

Growing to Produce

There are three levels of growing: 1) growing plants, 2) growing plants and getting food; 3) growing and getting enormous amounts of food with the same or less effort, time, and energy. Level 3 is the goal, and in my experience, the most efficient growing is done in a growing room (page 96):

1. Germinate seeds as described in propagation (page 86) with 50% daylight or blue–red light at 1:9, adhering to an uninterrupted photoperiod cultivation schedule: 24 hours of light and 0 darkness (24/0) for 7–30 days, depending on plant type, at 80% humidity and 60–70°F.
2. Transplant (page 91) your sprouts into grow media or a collar if applicable, raise light racks to full height, 25% on dimmer, and feed your plant balanced nutrient solution with extra nitrogen at 9 ppm dissolved oxygen, and keep the pH (page 81 at 6.0–6.3 and the temperature at 67–72°F.
3. Step down the photoperiod to 18/6 in half an hour per day increments for 1–2 months. Provide plenty of CO_2 (page 80, 108), and drop RH to 65% throughout vegetative stage until fully developed.
4. To induce flowering, lower pH (page 81) to 5.7–5.9, switch off daylight lights or blue LEDs, and turn on warm white lights or red LEDs at 9:1 red–blue.
5. Raise phosphorous and potassium by 50% and calcium by 33% to raise the energy level and increase carbohydrate metabolism, and then lower nitrogen by 50% to halt vegetative production (NPK, page 76). Alkalinity from calcium needs to stay between 75 and 200 mg/L $CaCO_3$.
6. Step photoperiod down to your plant-specific dark cycle while lowering light racks 5% per day until reaching 50%. Increase the dimmer.
7. Crank the temp up to 80°F during lighting but stay at 67–72°F for dark. Trim back suckers and any shade producing branches and shoots.

    IMPORTANT: Do not induce flowering in anything other than fruiting plants. Prevent it!

8. Once pre-flowers emerge, continue pruning suckers. Step light back up to 18/6 while lowering racks to the lowest position, dimmer at 100%.
9. When flowers open, raise RH to 70–75%. Manually transfer pollen daily with Q-tips or pollen brush, using an electric shaver or toothbrush to loosen difficult anthers, or place bee boxes (page 216), a fly farm (page 214), a moth farm, or other mezzo protein farms (page 208) inside your greenhouse or grow room.

    NOTE: The more pollen that successfully fertilizes flowers, the more seeds the fruit will contain and the larger the fruit will be. We have our beehives installed directly in our outside walls. When the bees are finished pollinating, they go outside for food, allowing us to harvest honey (page 220) via Flow Frames from inside without opening boxes or ever encountering or bothering a bee.

10. Once fruit start developing, keep phosphorous and potassium going but ease back on nitrogen another 10%, and leave until ripe.
11. After harvest, gradually step back to vegetative nutrient solution, light type and intensity, photoperiod schedule, temp, and RH in steps 1 through 2, and repeat.

Harvesting

IMPORTANT: Only grow as much as you can pick; only pick as much as you can eat. Plants are living things, just like animals and us. And like slaughtering animals for food, there's no need to grow to kill for no reason.

- For leafy greens, including broccoli, cauliflower, beets, turnips, radishes, carrots, fennel, sweet potatoes, lettuce, spinach, collard greens, and chard, cut individual leaves at the stalk. Don't harvest the entire head; you'll most likely kill the entire plant.
- For tree fruit and nuts, wait until the first fruits fall to signal picking. Once you learn your plants' cycles and what to look for in ripe fruit, pick when fruits are still small. This will prevent any loss from spoilage as well as stimulate multiple harvests in the same cycle, actually providing a larger yield by weight in the end.

NOTE: Carrots can be picked at any stage and are sweeter when young.

- Pick in the mornings when plants, and fruit, are the most hydrated to prevent shock and preserve freshness.

IMPORTANT: As soon as you pick them, fruits and veggies begin losing flavor and hydration. It's best to only pick what you plan to eat that day.

- Most crops fall away easily or with slight twisting. If you have to break or cut it loose, it's probably not ready. Plus, any damage you cause only redirects the plant's energy from production to healing injuries. Remember, everything is about efficiency!
- To harvest cinnamon, cinnamon trees must be cut back at two-years-old to ground level, then covered with soil. Harvest shoots 1 year later and remove the bark.
- Non-tree fruit, and many "vegetables" will release a sweet scent when ready.
- When fruits, and again, most "vegetables," begin growing, they're rock hard, sour, and usually of a green tint. When ripe, they become soft, sweet and display deep, sometimes even intense colors.

Chapter 6: Harnessing of Renewable Energy

MECHANICAL ELECTRICAL GENERATION

Almost everything we have, use, and do today relies on electricity. Certainly, everything we need to sustain ourselves does. Power plants generate electricity by burning (or decaying) fuels or by harnessing existing elements (solar/wind/water). We can do the same.

Generators convert rotating mechanical motion into usable electricity, but not all motors produce. Those that produce rotational mechanical motion when electrically charged, when rotated mechanically, produce electricity. These are called *permanent magnet motors* (PMM or PMG). Generators that use permanent magnets are found in all types of recyclable broken electronics and equipment such as exercise equipment, old computers, washing machines, automobiles, aircrafts, starters, electric trains, trolleys, elevators, and traction vehicles like electric forklifts or scissor lifts.

Alternators that use permanent magnets (magneto or PMA) rather than field coils are also PMMs. Regular alternators will even work but need to be geared down to more than 40:1 ratio, require a 12V/2A amps supply (wired the same), and draw amperage that would otherwise go to charging. If you go this route, find self-exciting modules (one large red battery cable) from newer models, older tractors, or 80s GM vehicles with large engines like Mustangs and V-8 trucks. They start charging at 1000-700 rpm and produce anything from 50-200 amps. Otherwise, the table below provides a few PMM motor options.

PERMANENT MAGNET MOTORS

Model	Volt	amp	RPM	Model	Volt	amp	RPM
Fisher & Paykel washing machine				Stair stepper			
100S	50-100	8	720	GP0157H41H-1006A(B)	5.7	1	
100SP	50-100	56	960	57H41H-2006A(B)	2.8	2	
100P	50-100	112		GM12-15BY-30	5	0.5	80
80S	50-100	3	760	GP01	4.8	0.2	80
80SP	50-100	21	960	Aircraft ignition			
80P	50-100	42	800	ABB	3.7	0.3	23800
60S	50-100	3.5	520	ABB	3	3.2	19300
60SP	50-100	25	640	NdFeB 720	3.7	3.7	46000
60P	50-100	50	380	Air compressors			
Amatek PM tape drive				YJP280X-6	380	10526	1000
20	20	0.47	550	WH-1.5/30	380	48.68	790
30	30	0.15	325	Automobile "generators" (not alternators)			

Model	Volt	amp	RPM	Model	Volt	amp	RPM
37	37	0.35	2100	JFZ1711	14	65	
40	40	0.5	1050	Jft149F	14	107.14	
40	40	0.55	1600	Jft249F	28	35.71	
50	50	0.4	1200	Alternators w/built-in regulators			
50	50	0.6	1700	2C27	12	100	
50	50	0.1	1800	ES-1031-C		80	
50	50	0.6	2100	ONE WIRE 3G		150	
72	72	0.41	1800	Power-steering servo			
99	99	0.51	35	AMR800067A	48	18.75	
Delco PMA				YYL90S-2	240	6.5	
540	12	18	130	YYL6314	240	0.5	
440	12	15	150	Electric forklift			
420	12	25	275	7680zyt	12	6	1500
520	12	28	240	71-132 YC80A-2	240	3.7	2900
512	12	40	650	ML631-4	220	0.818	1360
500	12	120	1200	ML100L2-4	220	13.63	1420
10SI	12	63	1000	Electric golf cart			
Direct-drive				HN1240AF	230	25	30000
PMG1650-17	690	1450	17	PG36M555	24	0.625	2000
PMG3200-12	690	2900	12	RS-555244500	24	0.3	4500
PMG4250-16	690	3950	16	WRF-310CA-13350	6	0.15	5560
Treadmill				Electric scissor lift			
45ZYT05-3860	230	13.04	30000	YC series	380	10.52	2800
63ZYT10-8007T	230	13.04	30000	WTD2-P250-40	220	6	127
IBL-80ZYT	90	5.555	4000	Electric mobility scooter			
DC MOTOR	220	9.09	3000	TEC3650-2465	24	2	6500
Exercise bike				TEC3650-2440	24	2	4000
7D/CD	48	20.83	520	TEC-4260-0625	6	5.7	1700
DLYM02	60	20	490	TEC4260-1250	12	4300	3
SLT86BLF30	48	16.35	3500	TEC4260-2450	24	4300	3
IBL-100SW	48	25	10000				

When used as generators, motors have to be driven faster than their rated speed to produce anything near rated voltage. Most home DIYers need a motor rated for high DC voltage and current at low RPMs, so they avoid low voltage or current and high RPM motors. A motor rated at say 325 rpm at 30V when used as a generator, could be expected to produce over 12V at reasonably low RPM and much more at higher. Don't worry about the "much more," the controller will convert it to the correct charging voltage for your battery bank or BB. It is important though to keep the RPMs close to the original speed to prevent bearing failure and coil burnouts. An 18-24V cordless drill motor, available for $3 online or $10 at Harbor Freight is a good example. With a 36:1 gear ratio, 8-40 amps (no load – load) and 0-400 rpm (low) and 0-1400 rpm (high) drills are great options for smaller turbines. On the other side of the spectrum, because of their need for high RPM, alternators aren't ideal for low wind applications but do produce high current in higher winds.

Once you have your motor generator, perform a bench test using a drill attached to the motor's shaft under load with a multi-meter and a non-contact photo tachometer. You're seeking to learn the following: a) at what RPM do you reach your BB's charging voltage; b) what is the amperage at that RPM; c) what's the max RPM of the motor; d) what's the amperage/voltage at that RPM; and e) what's the amperage/voltage at the motor's recommended RPM?

Pedal Power

While you could build a hand operated charger by bending a ⅜-in rod into a hand-crank and chucking it in the drill, you'd get killer forceps, but not a whole lot of power. I've chosen a simple bicycle-powered, electric generation build to kick things off because:

- Wind, sun, rivers, and waves aren't prevalent everywhere.
- Although solar is currently popular, DIYers are sticklers for the classics.
- As the first project on the road to independence, it will give the novice reader an opportunity to work with PMMs and electricity while providing a boost of confidence in what may be a formidable subject.
- Pedaling for your power is a self-rewarding workout (that you're going to do anyway); why not put those calories to good use?
- A bicycle generator is an easy and quick build using household items.

MATERIALS

large plastic beverage cap
¼ x 3-in carriage bolt
¼-in fender washer
¼-in lock washers
¼-in nut

18V cordless drill
pipe strap
bicycle stand, milk crate, bicycle trainer stands, or CMUs
(2) 12 awg wires
(2) 12 awg x ⅜-in push-on female terminals

TOOLS

drill with ¼-in drill bit
⅜-in wrench

1. To make the sprocket gear, drill a ¼-in hole in the center of a large plastic beverage cap. I use the lid from a 59 fl oz Simply Orange container, but anything with ribs will work.
2. Insert a ¼ x 3-in carriage bolt, fender washer, lock washers, and nut. Then chuck into an 18V cordless drill.
3. Strap or clamp to the floor (sideways). Place rear forks on top of a metal stand, milk crate, bicycle trainer stands, or CMUs so the rear tire rests gently on the gear.
4. Pull the battery and connect 2 wires with ⅜-in push-on female terminals from battery tabs to BB (see respective sections).

As the driving gear (attached to the motor shaft, or wheel in this case) spins at a low RPM driven by the motor (you pedaling), it drives the driven gear (attached to the load shaft—plastic cap) at a higher RPM, causing the PMM to generate electricity. The exact ratio can be determined with the formula Gear Ratio = T2/T1, where T1 = number of gear teeth of gear 1 or the drive gear (which on most mountain bike tire tread, tends to be around 1 knob per 1 inch of tread) and T2 = number of teeth on the second or driven gear (again, in the case of the Simply Orange cap, is about 1 spine per 1 inch of circumference). The 26-in tire having a circumference of 81 in, and the cap with a 9-in circumference, when plugged into our formula: 9 / 81 = .1 or .1:1. This means the sprocket (Simply Orange lid) will rotate 1 time for every 10% or .1 times the wheel rotates, or 10 times for every 1 time, or 10:1.

By attaching a bike tachometer ($10 online) or timing RPMs of the drive gear, we can learn the driven gear's RPM using the formula $S1 \times T1 = S2 \times T2$ (S=rotational speed). For example, if peddling and your back wheel is spinning at an average of 15 rpm, you get:

15 x 81 = S2 x 9

1215 ÷ 9 = S2

135 rpm

This figure is further multiplied each time you switch gears. For example, a 21-speed bike with a gear 48-tooth chainring with a 24-tooth sprocket has a ratio of 4:1. On the smallest sprocket (12-tooth), I'm getting 4:1, which means for every 1 time my legs complete a rotation, my back wheel completes 4, for 540 rpm.

With the addition of a cycling computer, determine how many calories you've burned and how much money you've saved not going to the gym and not paying for 1 hour electricity.

Essentially, we're constructing a bottle, or sidewall, dynamo ($50 e-bay). The same setup can be installed on a broken stair stepper, rower, treadmill (given enough slope and the right gearing), or something as simple as a Gazelle, for an entire workout room.

Water Power: Micro Water Turbine

It's no coincidence that the world's largest generators are located at hydroelectric power plants like the Hoover Dam. Gravity produces uninterrupted electricity via rivers and lakes. Water turbines are as close to perpetual motion as we have. Since gravity is a constant, and we don't have to put in energy to get it, you have a constant, reliable, uninterrupted source of motion. Even when the sun goes down and the wind stops, water continues.

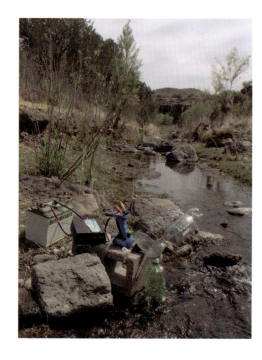

Similar to windmills, watermills catch the dense flowing medium in rotating cupped blades in either a vertical—VAWT or horizontal—HAWT axis configuration. How many RPMs they produce is determined by their size, gearing, and water flow. Power generated by moving water is a product of Net Head and Flow Volume through the wheel. Although the technology is cleaner and cheaper than most, and not as environmentally destructive as some, most homeowners don't live on waterways.

By adapting the peddle power setup slightly, we can make a decent little water turbine, capable of trickle charging our battery banks. Again, since the power is being produced 24 hours a day, it adds up.

MATERIALS

large plastic beverage cap
¼ x 3-in carriage bolt
¼-in fender washer
¼-in lock washers
¼-in nut

18V cordless drill
pipe strap
(2) 12 awg wires
(2) 12 awg x ⅜-in push-on female
 terminals

TOOLS

drill with ¼-in drill bit
⅜-in wrench

1. Construct the water turbine hub using the large cap and connect it to the 18V drill, as described in the Pedal Power steps.
2. Place (3) 2 L bottle caps, on the side of the hub, centered, equally spaced 120° apart, threads out. Drill (2) ⅛-in holes, and shoot (2) ⅛ in x ¼-in pop rivets in each cap.
3. For the paddles, screw the bottles into the caps and mark each in the same plane as the hub, then remove and wrap a sheet of printer paper widthwise around the bottle, lining up and centering the paper with the mark, fold the top flaps and trace and cut out the outline.
4. Use the cutout piece from the first bottle as a template for the remaining two.
5. Screw the bottles back into the hub caps, make sure all are facing the same direction (adjust as necessary), chuck in drill, and place in moving water horizontally so that paddles are at least halfway submerged. Strap the motor in place and wire to BB as described in "Peddle Power" (page 119).

NOTE: For higher RPMs, install 5 blades 72° or 6 blades 60° apart.

WIND POWER

Wind Turbine

There's a free source of clean fuel right above your head. It's not the sun, and you don't have to live in a coastal or plains region to tap it. Non-turbulent, dense air flows constantly 60 to 100 feet up and can produce energy/watts around the clock. Energy and power are often confused terms, power being measured in watts, whereas energy is measures in watt-hours, or in the case of wind turbines, kilowatt-hours or power times time.

Wind turbines mechanically convert wind into energy through generators. Home windmills run $169 to $431 for 300 to 1000w, and up to $5,000 for 4.5kW, or $0.50 to $1 per watt (comparable to solar). The cost is dropping fast as new companies flood the market. Aero, Aleko, Windmax, and Southwest all make great, affordable turbines with bearing swivel mounts, carbon fiber blades, smart controllers, and braking systems. Smaller units can be mounted directly to your roof while larger ones require a pole or tower. Both harness substantially more power (RPMs) than either man or beast can without needing feed or tiring out.

Don't let the kW rating fool you though. The max output in the highest winds before the brakes kick in and stop it completely is 4.5kW, which happens only about 5% to 25% of the time (depending on location). A 1kW unit can be expected to put out 100w or 876kWh *per annum* at a 11 mph average. An average 4-person American household, without electricity conservation, uses 876kWh *per month* or 10,650kWh per annum, meaning you'd need to install 10 to 12 1kW wind turbines, cut out 90% of your electricity usage (see chapter 1), or capture 10 times more wind force.

Wind force, and therefore generated power, isn't doubled by twice the wind speed though, it's actually cubed. So, 20-mph wind doesn't have 200% the force of 10-mph wind, it has 800% (2^3). On top of that, energy increases exponentially with speed, so a height with 12-mph winds can generate 70% more energy than a height with 10-mph winds. An increase of 30% more power can be achieved with a 100-ft tower than a 60-ft tower. This is also true with blade length and swept area in that a 10-ft blade has a 58% larger swept area than an 8-ft blade.

Some people express concerns over birds flying into mills or think that it will make too much noise. But home windmills won't kill birds or disturb neighbors. I've run 2 wind turbines for over 10 years and haven't seen even 1 carcass, and I only hear the mills when they're braking in high winds, in which case the wind is louder than the brake. With regards to sound intensity, a window AC is 180db. Most home turbines are under 45db and sit over 50 ft in the air. For comparison, a normal conversation is 60db.

System Design

There are two types of home turbines: horizontal (HAWT) and vertical axis (VAWT). These types are divided into three categories: micro (.05-.25kW) with a 2 to 4-ft rotor diameter, mini (.25-1.4kW) at 4 to 10-ft rotor diameter, and home (1.4-1.6kW) with 10–33 ft rotor diameter. The longer the blades, the broader the swept area (square footage of air intercepted). Although all are rated at a specific watt output, some are better made, longer lasting, and more efficient at lower heights.

Again, we can build our own simple, low output, mini HAWT by turning the blades of our 3-blade water turbine and u-bolting it to a pole. This small wind mill could charge a battery or run an outdoor light.

If you're going to purchase one, view the manufacturer's annual production and power curve (watts to wind speed) for various turbines beforehand. Compare the true output rating for the average wind speeds of your area at a specific height to determine your annual power production capability. If you're building your own, the only real design considerations are blades. There are a few key factors:

NOTE: I include a pre-designed, engineered blade pattern in Turbine Construction below for constructing your own turbine, but it's always good to understand the logic behind it to modify and make it your own.

- No matter the shape or length, it will never convert more than 59.3% of wind's available power (Betz's Law).

Low out-put mini HAWT

- Wider blades start spinning, or cut-in at low speeds (great for low towers), but cut-out, or stop spinning at high speeds (good for small generators). This is because their larger surface actually creates drag and acts like brakes.
- Thinner blades have trouble cutting-in at low speeds but won't cut-out in high speeds either (great for tall towers and large generators). This is because the smaller surface area requires more force, while more surface area requires less force.
- Similarly, for the same reason, more blades create more surface area to catch more air and, therefore, will cut-in in lower winds and cut-out in higher winds (great for low towers and small generators).
- Longer blades also provide more surface (swept) area. They cut-in with lower winds (good for low tower), but don't hinder or obstruct as much wind flow and, therefore, won't cut-out at high speeds (good for large generators).

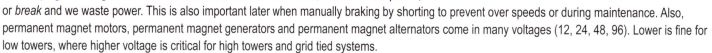

If the wind speeds at your turbine's location (height) are low, higher quantity, wider, or longer blades will spin faster and cut-in sooner. If wind speeds are high, then lower quantity, thinner blades will spin faster and cut-out later. If you have both low and high, use fewer thin, long blades that will cut-in with low wind and won't cut-out in high. And, so you get the most from your air and don't burn up a motor, for low winds use a small generator, for high winds use a large generator.

To give you an idea, 7 or more medium width, 24-in blades will cut-in at 8 mph (11 or more at 3 mph) but max out at 50 mph. Just 3 of the same size blades will cut-in at 12 mph and continue at wind speeds over 50 mph. I'd suggest starting with a longer/thinner, 3-blade configuration for tall towers, or you could use wider blades, test the system, thin, and retest as needed. I don't recommend surpassing 3-in width, or 100 times blade thickness in length.

For generators, if a motor is oversized to its blades, the blades will have a difficult time getting and keeping it running due to friction. If undersized, it'll either *brake*, and we waste power, or *break* and we waste power. This is also important later when manually braking by shorting to prevent over speeds or during maintenance. Also, permanent magnet motors, permanent magnet generators and permanent magnet alternators come in many voltages (12, 24, 48, 96). Lower is fine for low towers, where higher voltage is critical for high towers and grid tied systems.

A rough measurement of a homemade system sized to its maximum capability including tower, completely installed and wired, shouldn't cost more than $1 per watt (based on current costs). If it does, your generator is probably undersized for your tower or your cable is oversized for your generator. If it's less, your generator, cable, and/or tower are probably undersized.

NOTE: For VAWTs, there are many open-source blueprints (including several of mine) available online

Pole Tilt-Up Tower Construction

There are three home tower options which can be used with or without guy wires for small, medium, and large turbines: pole tilt-up, lattice, and freestanding monopole. Pole tilt-up towers are inexpensive and easy to construct and install with options for towers less than 100 feet. Lattice towers are generally used for towers under 200 feet, and monopole towers are used for towers over 200 feet. Since the tower is the most important part of the system, I'll describe pole tilt-up.

NOTE: Although not cost effective, a small turbine can be installed on a tall tower and vice versa as long as sweep is more than 10 ft from the ground. This would be applicable in high tree canopy (for small turbines) and oceanfront (for large) locations. Also, there is no limit to tower height. The higher the turbine, the more and more constant wind exposure you'll have, and the more power you'll generate.

1. Locate so turbine sits in debris-free, non-turbulent air or a minimum of 3 x height away and more than 10 feet above any obstructions.
2. Connect appropriately sized cables to turbine, and install turbine on pipe (see table for sizing).
3. At location, dig and lay conduit trench to BB and excavate a 8 (for 1.5 in) to 12 (for 4 in) x 48-in posthole (for under 30-ft tower).
4. For an anchor, set a 3 ft 4-in pipe, sized to your pole, centered inside hole with long sweep tee (sweep down and out towards and centered in trench) with a 2-ft pipe in sweep hole.
5. Connect a clean-out tee to the end of the horizontal pipe with a reducer bushing sized to your conduit (check free online conduit size calculators), run to your BB in horizontal port.
6. In the vertical port of the long sweep tee, connect a riser (to grade) and coupler. Repeat for the clean-out tee, adding a threaded plug.
7. Fill post hole with 2000 (1.5 in) to 5000 (4 in) psi concrete, and when cured, place turbine pole base at anchor coupler, install and connect wires to BB cables, and raise and screw in place.
8. Conduit acts as ground, so you only have to run and connect 2 cables through conduit from BB, to turbine cables.

2

2

3

3

4

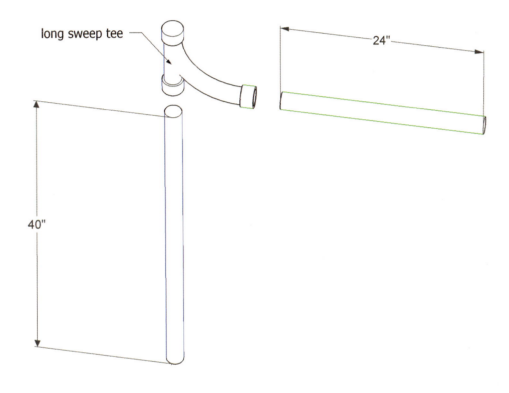

long sweep tee

24"

40"

5

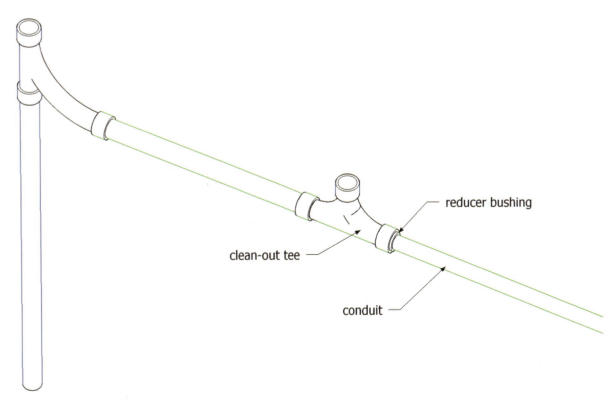

reducer bushing

clean-out tee

conduit

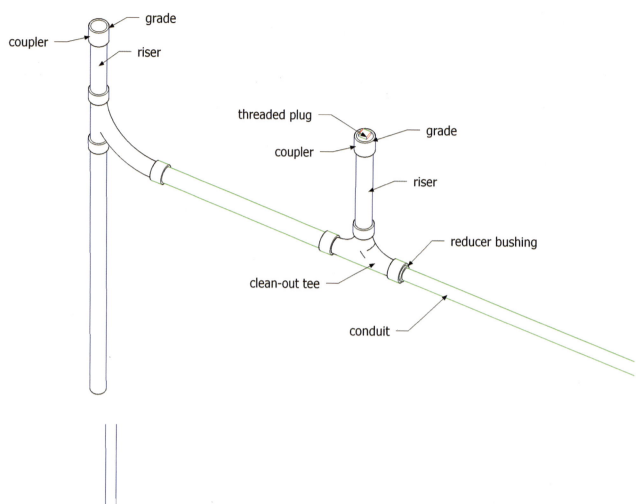

grade

coupler

riser

threaded plug

grade

coupler

riser

reducer bushing

clean-out tee

conduit

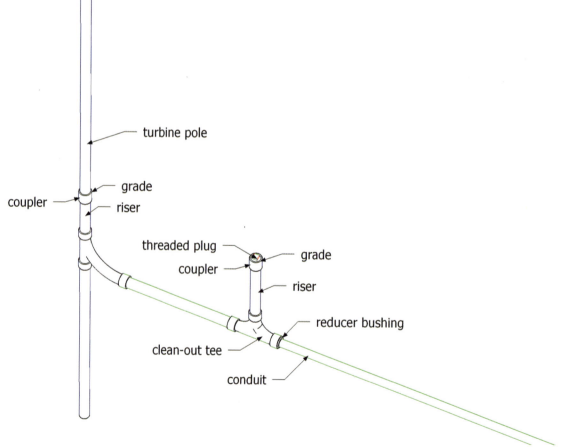

turbine pole

grade

coupler

riser

threaded plug

grade

coupler

riser

reducer bushing

clean-out tee

conduit

*CQ40 in high wind locations.

NOTE:all pipes require 1.5 x 5 in top stub pipe

9. For roof-mounted, cut appropriate OD hole (oval) in roof, ½ to 1 in from a rafter and joist. Install and plumb pipe (with boot), slide 1 to 2 in of rigid insulation between rafter and joist to limit vibration. Bolt using muffler clamps or U-bolts.

NOTE: If joists are finished, or if they don't align with rafter, use a pipe flange mounted to attic floor. If attic ceiling is finished, or you just don't want a pipe going through your roof, mount a pipe tripod onto roof, and attach to the rafter only.

WIND TURBINE POLE TYPES AND SIZES

Height (ft)²	<25ft	Guide wire	25-40ft	G.W. (dia/loc)	40-60ft	G.W. (dia/loc)	60-80ft	G.W. (dia/loc)	80-100ft	G.W. (dia/loc)
Pipe type	CQ20* or SCD40	N/A	CQ40 or SCD40	12g@30ft	SCD40	12g@30ft & 3/16@60ft	SCD80	3/16@20ft, 1/4@40ft & 3/8@60ft/75ft	SCD80	3/16@20ft/40ft, 1/4@60ft & 3/8@80ft/100ft
Length/dia (ft/in)	25/2 - 25/1.5		0-20/3, 20-40/2 - 0-20/2, 20-40/1.5		0-40/3, 40-60/2, 60-65/1.5		0-40/3, 40-60/2.5, 60-80/2		0-40/4, 40-60/3.5, 60-80/3, 80-100/2	
Energy Increase	20%			30%			40%		75%+	

Turbine Construction

MATERIALS

PMA
plastic spray paint
8 in x 40-in SCD80 (40 for blades under 32 in) PVC pipe
glue
construction paper
plywood scraps (any thickness)
¼ in x 32-in hose
drilling oil
³⁄₁₆ in x 7¼ in x 7¼-in steel plate
¼-in 24 x 1½-in zinc plated grade 6 bolts/head washers/nuts
10 in x 32 in 16 ga plate
(2) ⅛ x 1¾ x 33½-in flat bars
(2) ⅛ x 4 x 5⅞-in flat bar
SCD80, zinc plated steel pipe to match for sleeve bushings
(12) ¼ in x 1-in bolt/washer/nut
2¼ in x 7⅛ in 10-gauge exhaust pipe, fence post or .120-in tubing
citric acid
metal primer and exterior high gloss enamel paint
¾-in watertight nylon cord grip (cable gland)
SCD40 1½-in metal pipe
2-in 3 set-screw shaft collar
2-in SS washer
(2) Teflon washer
(2) SS washer
2-in (1¹⁵⁄₁₆-in bore) 3 set-screw shaft collar
PVC grease

cables or 3-phase wires
locking plug or trailer harness
⅝ x 1-in flanged (top hat or reducer) spanner bushing
⅝-in lock washer, nut and nylon or plastic hex nut dome or lug nut cover (optional)
Scotch tape

TOOLS

Allen wrench
saw table with fine tooth blad
hole saw
scissors
pencil
center punch
vice
drill with 1-in and 2-in hole saws
CNC router or jigsaw with coarse blade
4-in c-clamp
belt sander with coarse and fine grit sandpaper
calipers

measuring tape
drill press with ⅛-in and ¼-in drill bits and .125-.200 in, .200-.273 in, .273-300 in, .200-.373 in, .373-.400 in, .400-.450 in, .450-.500 inch stepping reamers
drilling oil
compass
hammer/nail
(2) ⅜ in wrenches
1-10 lbs torque wrench
arc or MIG welder
deburr tool

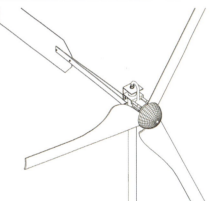

NOTE: For the turbine itself we'll use a PMA. There are many good units online, or you can rewire an alternator using permanent magnets.

NOTE: If your shaft doesn't have an Allen end, notch a ⅛-in slot with an angle grinder and cutting wheel, and use a screwdriver.

1. For the blades, cut an 8-in (8.625) SCD80 (SCD40 for blades under 32 in) PVC pipe lengthwise, 40 in long (48 in for higher/larger turbines or [2] 40-in or 48-in segments for 5 sets of blades) into 3 (6 for 5 blade setups) equal 9-in segments.

NOTE: You don't want to buy an entire length of 8-in pipe (unless you're doing 7-9 blades), especially when scraps are thrown away in construction dumpsters daily.

NOTE: If using plumbing PVC, either paint or replace every 5 years.

IMPORTANT: The leading edge is curved while the trailing is straight. Make sure your PMA turns clock-wise. Otherwise, flip the pattern.

2. Print pattern (to scale) and tape together aligning measurements. Glue onto construction paper, cut and place trailing edge flat against pipe edge. For shorter blades, reduce by 50%. For longer blades enlarge by 200% (for example) when printing.
3. Tape and trace, marking hole locations with a center punch. Flip and repeat, back-back.
4. Place pieces in vice. Cut wide radius with a 1-in hole saw and the rest with a jigsaw, just outside lines.

NOTE: This will provide you with (5) 5.9-in (2.6in at tail) wide blades and 1 spare.

1

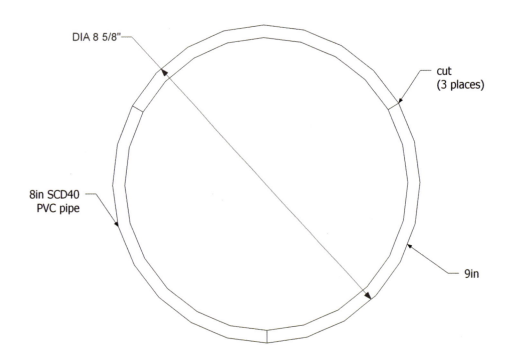

5. Stack and clamp blades then clean leading edges to line using a fine grit belt sander.
6. Cut LE (leading edge) jig out of scrap plywood. Using calipers, mark a line 1½ in back from blade leading edge. Sand profile individually, checking your work with jig as you go.

1

1

2

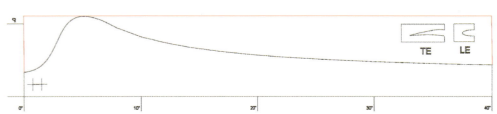

3

4

6

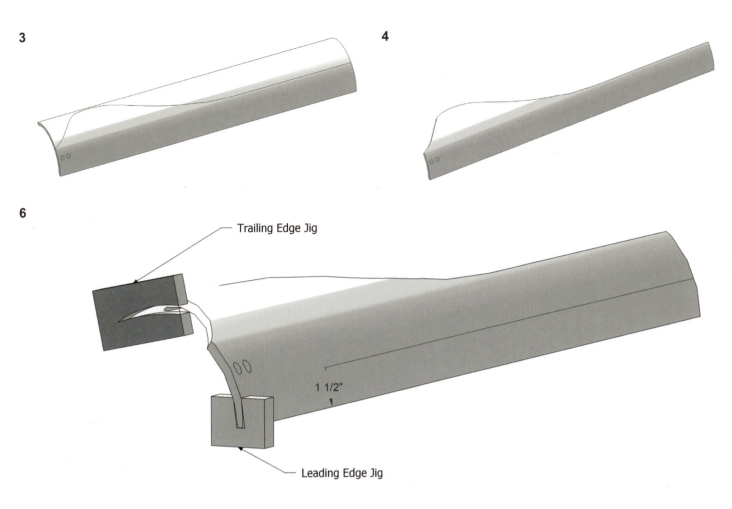

Trailing Edge Jig

Leading Edge Jig

1 1/2"

7. Repeat for the trailing edge using TE jig to form a deep high camber, low lift, medium speed wing airfoil using coarse paper; clean with fine sandpaper.

    NOTE: Sanding the L/TE adds minute increases/decreases in RPM/vibration and can be skipped.

    NOTE: For protection while working, it's a good idea to place a split (lengthwise) piece of ¼-in hose over trailing edge. Tape in place if needed.

8. Flatten outside (backside or inside pipe) surface around the bolt hole locations with coarse then fine sandpaper.

9. Place flat in a drill press. Pilot drill holes, step to .273 in with stepping reamers.

    NOTE: Without getting into aerodynamics and engineering, odd number of blades perform better than even.

9

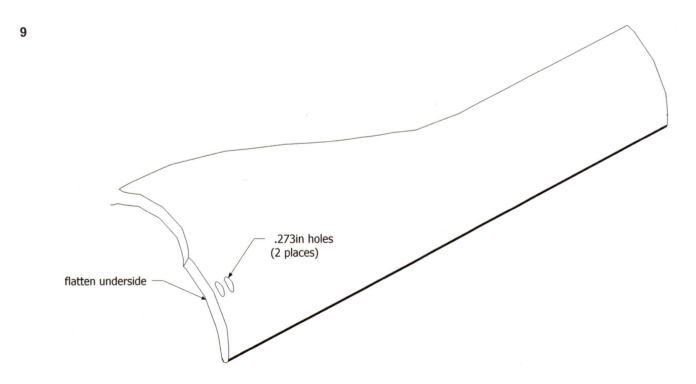

.273in holes
(2 places)

flatten underside

10. In a CNC router or with a jigsaw, cut your circular hub from ³⁄₁₆-in (¼-in for anything over 9 blades) steel plate, 7¼ in (10 in for more than 5 blades) wide. Divide and mark into 3 equal pie segments 120° apart (for 5 blade setups, divide into 5, 72° apart).

NOTE: Circular sawblades for hubs can be used for small blades.

IMPORTANT: If using a jigsaw, add about ¹⁄₁₆ in and trim to line later.

11. With a compass, scratch 3⅝-in and 3⅛-in radius circles into the hub; then center punch and drill (in a press) ⁷⁄₃₂-in holes stepping to .373 inches at cross points and center.

11

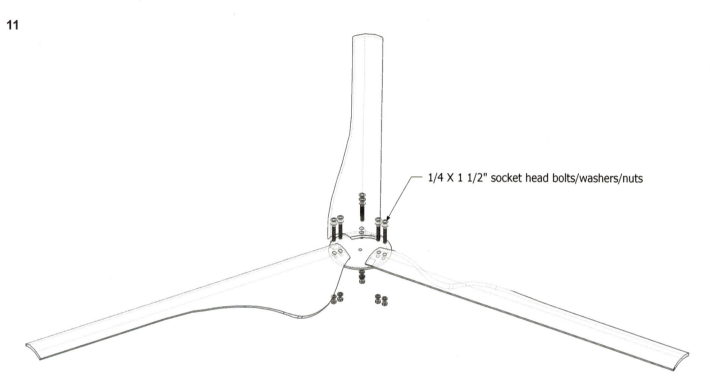

1/4 X 1 1/2" socket head bolts/washers/nuts

12. Nail hub to worktable and install blades using ¼ in-24 x 1½-in socket head bolts/head and nut washers/nuts.

IMPORTANT: Use zinc plated grade 6 hardware, lock nuts and locking compound for all hardware, and torque to 5 lbs.

NOTE: If using purchased carbon fiber blades, use existing hole pattern, and install ½-20 socket head screws.

12

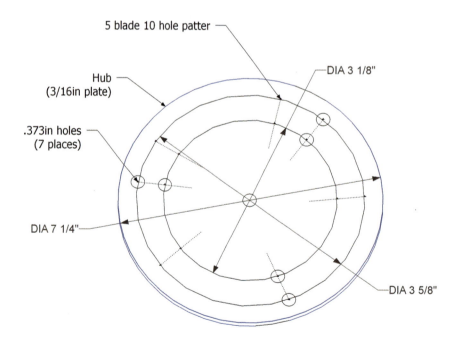

5 blade 10 hole patter

DIA 3 1/8"

Hub
(3/16in plate)

.373in holes
(7 places)

DIA 7 1/4"

DIA 3 5/8"

13. Measure/adjust tip-tip distance OC so all are equidistant, readjusting and tightening bolts as necessary.

NOTE: Hub/blade holes are reamed to fit tightly to limit play.

IMPORTANT: If not perfectly centered, hub will be out of alignment and balance, causing premature bearing failure.

13

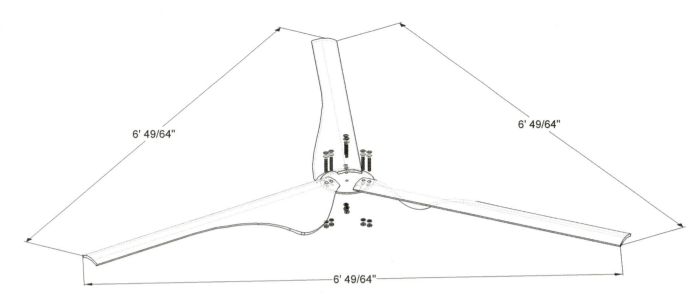

6' 49/64" 6' 49/64"

6' 49/64"

14. To test, remove blades, swap positions, reinstall, and re-measure.

16

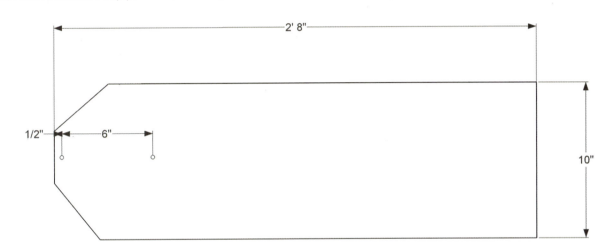

2' 8"

1/2" 6"

10"

15. If you didn't use a CNC, remove the blades, step pilot holes to ½ in and clean to the line.
16. For the tail, cut 10 in 16 ga plate or sheet metal to 32 inches (36 in for higher/larger) with 2 corners at 40° and (2) ¼-in holes through the middle (widthwise) 6 in apart, ½ in from edge.
17. For the tail leg, bend (2) ⅛ x 1¾ x 33½ in flat bars to 90°, 1½ inches in from either end and drill (2) ¼-in holes, ¾ in apart C.C. and (2) 6 in apart, ½ in from the other end.

17

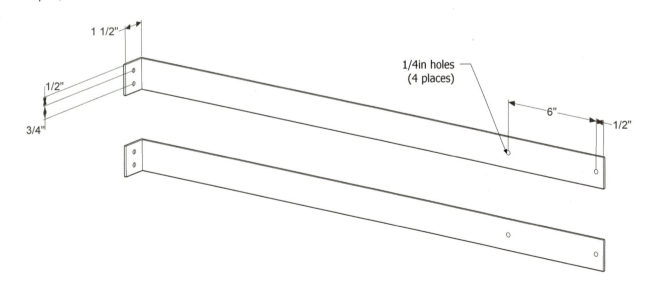

1 1/2"

1/2"

3/4"

1/4in holes
(4 places)

6" 1/2"

18. For a motor mounting bracket, in a table break or vise, bend one end of (2) ⅛ x 4 x 7 pieces of flat bar, lengthwise 90°, 1⅞ in from edge, and another one on the opposite side, 1⅛ in.

19. In the CNC (or with a hole saw), cut a 2¼ in (or your pole's OD) circle, 1⅜ in CC from first bend. In the big leg, transfer both tail leg hole patterns, and in the small, the hole pattern of each side of your PMA, centered.

   NOTE: *If your PMA has 4 mounting bolts, your bracket will have 2-holes/bracket. If your PMA only has 2 holes, you'll have 1-hole/bracket.*

19

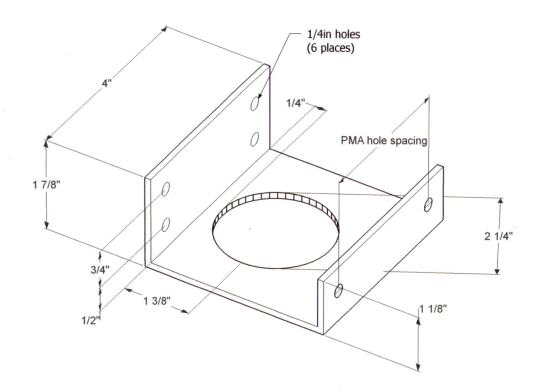

20. Measure from backside of each PMA mounting ear to housing back. Add ⅜ in for clearance, and cut 2-4 sections of SCD80, zinc plated steel ⅛-in – ¼-in pipe to match for sleeve bushings. Bolt to PMA to bracket using head washers and nuts.

   NOTE: *If you're using a larger PMA (with dual mounts) for higher applications, make the legs ¾ in, drill (2) ⅜-in holes in each, 1¹⁵⁄₁₆ in apart; and use ⅜-in bolts (usually x 8 in).*

21. Measure the inside distance between both brackets (7⅛ in for most). Cut and weld a piece of 2¼-in (2½-in SCD40 for higher/larger), 10 ga exhaust pipe (fence post or .120 tubing will also work) centered over holes.

21

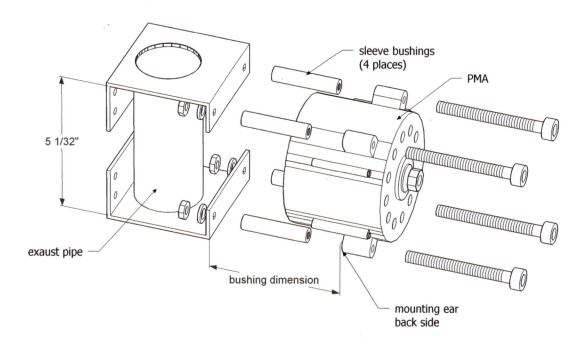

22. For a cable relief angle, bend a 8-in long piece of ⅛ x 4-in flat bar, in half 90°. Drill a ¹³⁄₁₆-in hole in either leg, centered, 1⅝ in from bend and install a 3-in watertight nylon cord grip (cable gland), then transfer hole pattern from top mounting bracket onto other leg and install using ¼ x ½-in bolts and lock washers.

23. Finally, install the tail arm and tail using ¼ x ½-in bolts and lock washers. Then take everything apart. Deburr all metal pieces. Clean with citric acid ("Home-Brewed Chemical Compounds," page 57), prime, paint (3 layers) of exterior high gloss enamel, and reassemble when dry. (Black paint is more visible to birds.)

24. Place a 4 ft SCD40 1½-in galvanized steel stub pole in a vice. Mount a 2-in (1¹⁵⁄₁₆-in bore) 3 set-screw shaft collar (such as found here—https://windandsolar.com/wind-turbine-tower-locking-collar/), 6in (or your bracket spacing plus 1in) from pipe end followed by a 2-in SS washer, Teflon washer, another SS washer for a yaw bearing, adding PVC grease between each, followed by the mount bracket.

NOTE: Make nylon washers from thin plastic cutting board. For larger, heavier turbines, I would highly suggest using a weight specific zinc plated wind turbine yaw bearing (such as found here https://windandsolar.com/yaw-bearing-for-1-1-2-inch-pipe/)

IMPORTANT: There must be at least a ³⁄₁₆-in gap between relief angle and pipe to prevent rubbing.

22

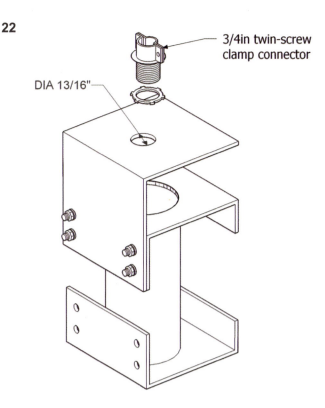

3/4in twin-screw clamp connector

DIA 13/16"

23

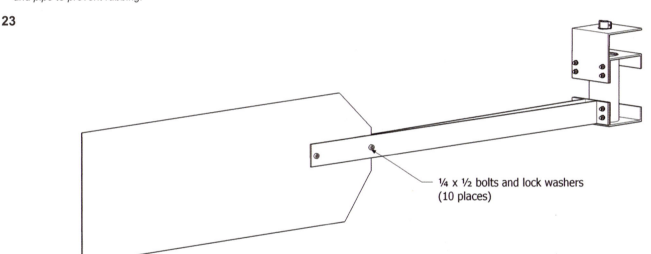

¼ x ½ bolts and lock washers (10 places)

24

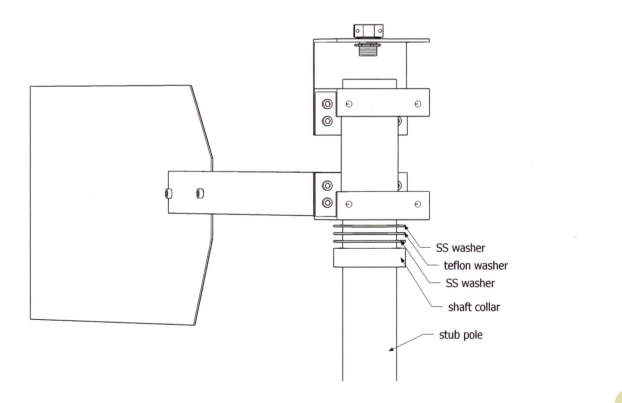

SS washer
teflon washer
SS washer
shaft collar
stub pole

25. Install PMA. Connect positive cable (12v) or 3-phase wire to hot terminal (grease) or wire harness. Run down inside of pole, tightening cord grip, leaving a couple inches slack coming out the top.

   NOTE: For this turbine, install a locking plug close to the base, accessible through the cleanout so the cable/s can be periodically disconnected and unwound (about twice a year). Use a trailer harness for 3-phase and a regular (properly sided) plug for cables.

25

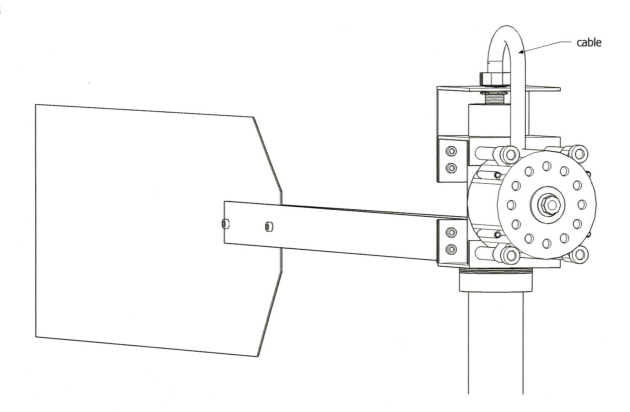

cable

26. Slide a ⅝ x 1-in (or shaft length minus HU) flanged (top hat or reducer) spanner bushing over PMA shaft followed by the blades hub and blades, lock washer, nut, and a nylon or plastic hex nut dome or lug nut cover if desired.

   IMPORTANT: If you have an imbalance, the heavier blade will fall. Sand off the back front face and recheck.

   NOTE: If your shaft isn't threaded, install a ⅝-in motor arbor to ⅝-in threaded shaft adapter/attachment.

26

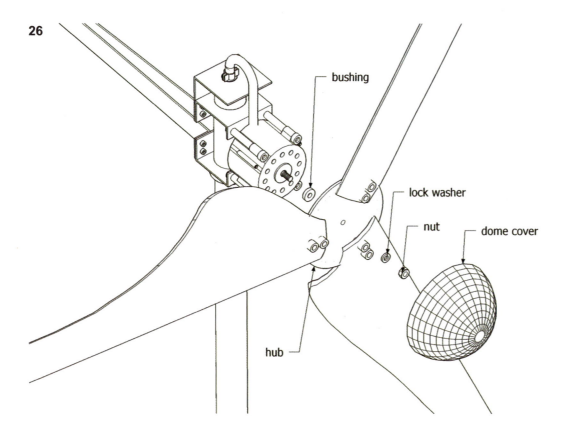

bushing

lock washer

nut

dome cover

hub

SOLAR POWER

Let's turn up the heat. The sun provides a spectrum of power options to fill our everyday consumption needs.

Solar Water Heater

There are basically, two types of solar water heaters: active, which requires a water pump to circulate the liquid, and passive or thermosiphon (TS), which relies on natural convection. The two systems are divided into two categories: direct (the home's water is circulated through both the collectors and storage tank), and indirect (a non-freezing liquid is circulated through collectors and tank, before giving up its heat to the home's water via a heat exchanger). Direct systems are better suited for mild climate locations where freezing is rare. Indirect is better for colder climates where freezing temperatures occur frequently. For now, though, we'll stay away from heat exchangers.

We can further break the two systems down based on efficiency, functionality, location, setup or configuration, and component complexity.

Warm Climates—passive. Passive systems are most efficient in high solar radiation areas since they function solely on natural convection. Water movement and heating begins and accelerates with higher temperatures. Because of this, the collection tank in a passive system must always be located above the solar collection array.

stripping down a water heater

Warm or Cold Climates—active. Active systems are well suited for both regions since pumps are the sole source of water movement, circulating the water through the solar collectors only when sunlight is prevalent. In locations where freezing is a factor, dumping (drain-down) or reverse siphoning warm water from the storage tank when temps dip below 32° is mandatory.

In either case, you'll need two basic components: a collector and a storage tank. Storage tanks are simple, any old hot water heater will work. I like using working hot water heaters (electric or gas) for storage tanks so that if you receive a few days of clouds, you have a backup. In hot regions where 300 days of sunshine isn't uncommon, and when temps rarely dip below 32°, a collector is a simple enough matter of just stripping down a second old water heater tank (gas or electric) and painting it black (or even leaving it dark rust colored). For mild climates that receive less than 200 to 300 days of sunshine, we can add a bit of insulation to a tank collector by building an insulated plexiglass box around it. Make sure to use a gas tank though since it allows hot air to flow through the middle, warming the water from both the outside and inside. For colder regions, you'll need a lot more surface area and a smaller cavity so the water heats up faster.

an old water heater as a storage tank

MATERIALS

refrigerator
(4) pieces of 2 x 4 plastic decking, vinyl, or CFBs
(8) 6-in L-brackets
(50) 1½-in SS screws
1⁄16 in x 36⅛ in x 72⅛-in sheet metal
¾-in aluminum backed rigid insulation
flat black high temp spray paint
double backed tape (measures about ⅛-in thick)

36⅛ in x 72⅛ in double paned, nitrogen-filled ½-in pane glass window insert
1-way reflective glazing
high temp RTV sealant
water heater
½-in PEX, poly pipe, PVC pipe, or other piping
⅜-in pipe insulation
circulating pump

TOOLS

wire cutters
⅜-in wrench
table saw with coarse blade
miter saw with coarse blade
router with 1-in straight router bit
square

drill with ⅛-in and ¾-in drill bits
pencil
measuring tape
impact drill with ¼-in socket adapter
½-in drive breaker bar with 1⅛-in or 1¼-in deep socket
pipe cutters

1. Remove the black condenser coil grid from the back of a refrigerator by snipping the copper tubing 3 inches from the steel-copper joint and extracting the ¼-in hex head screws. If you get it from anywhere other than a junk yard, evac the Freon before cutting (Freon is removed at junkyards).

   NOTE: You can also fabricate a collector using ½-in copper tubing, swaging the ends, adding flared couplers and painting it flat black with high temp paint.

   NOTE: The following measurements are based on a full 36-in unit. If yours is different, adjust accordingly.

2. Clean ends with a pipe cutter, de-dust, and flush with soapy water.
3. For the frame, cut (4) pieces of 2 x 4 plastic decking, vinyl, or fiber cement board: (2) pieces to 38-⅛ in, and (2) pieces to 74⅛ in, at 45° inverted angles on each end. Using a 1-in straight router bit, notch a 2¹⁵⁄₁₆-in wide, ½-in deep channel lengthwise, centered on inside (narrower) faces.

1

4. Assemble box (notch in). Square and install (8) 6-in L-brackets on inside corners using 1½-in SS screws (pilot drill each hole). Remove either (long) side piece and set aside for later installation.

4

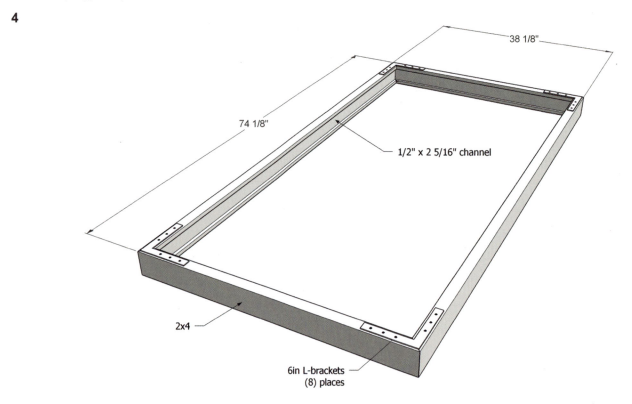

74 1/8"
38 1/8"
1/2" x 2 5/16" channel
2x4
6in L-brackets
(8) places

5. For a backing (also known as the collector), cut a sheet of ¹⁄₁₆-in sheet metal to 36⅛ in x 72⅛ in, place it on the bottom inside the frame, then cut a piece of ¾-in aluminum backed rigid insulation to the same dimensions, paint top flat black with high temp paint, and place it on top of the sheet metal.

NOTE: There are two schools of thought here. One maintains that using a reflective surface rather than a dull, flat, black surface bounces light back onto coils, while the glass restricts the egress of shorter light waves. This works because when light bounces, it fractures into smaller beams. I'd opt for this configuration, being a physics major, had I not gotten better results with dull, flat black collector surfaces. This second option also works in that dull, flat, dark colors absorb the most sunlight.

5

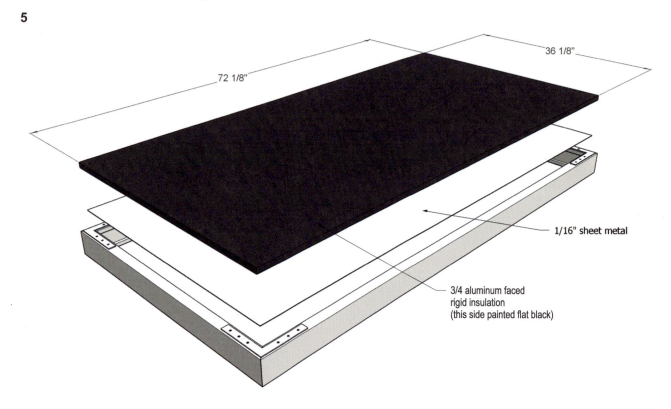

72 1/8"
36 1/8"
1/16" sheet metal
3/4 aluminum faced
rigid insulation
(this side painted flat black)

6. Place coil centered, mark, and drill (2) ¾-in holes where inlet and outlet couplers sit on frame. Place two layers of double backed tape every 1 ft and install coil to provide a ¼-in bottom gap. Repeat for top.

6

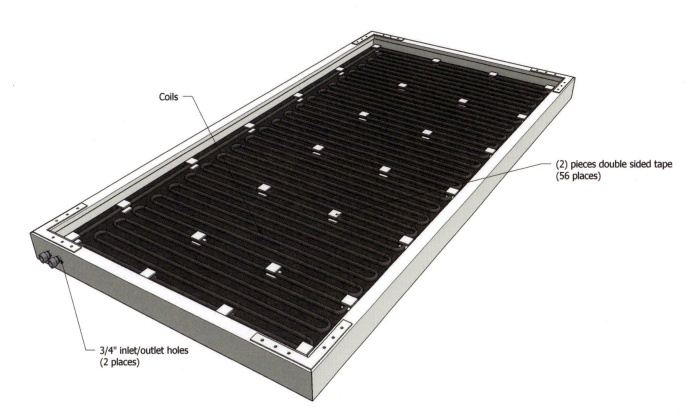

Coils

(2) pieces double sided tape
(56 places)

3/4" inlet/outlet holes
(2 places)

7. Fabricate or purchase and install a 36⅛ in x 72⅛ in double paned, nitrogen-filled (optional), ½-in pane glass window insert, with 1-way reflective glazing (facing inwards) using high temp RTV sealant (fill channel before sliding glass in).

7

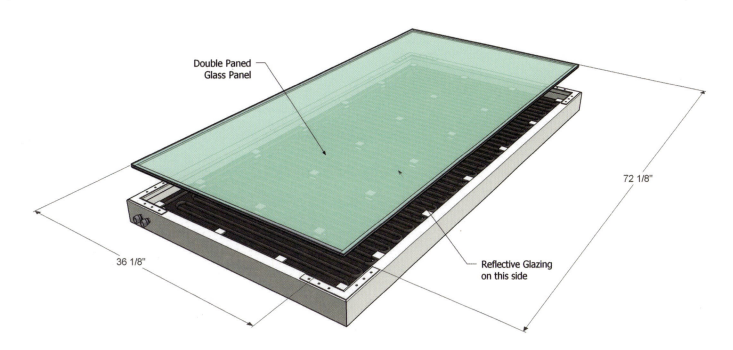

Double Paned
Glass Panel

72 1/8"

36 1/8"

Reflective Glazing
on this side

8. Replace frame side. Fill inlet and outlet holes with RTV, cleaning off any access.
9. Install on lower most edge of roof, with appropriate WAOI (Winter Angle of Insolation).
10. In the top of the storage tank (water heater), there are two additional ports with ¾-in MPT plugs (you may have to remove the round metal top piece and insulation to find them). Remove the plugs, add (2) ¾-in galvanized hot water heater (red/blue) nipples. The cold (blue) should come with plastic dip tube sized to your water heater height. Replace insulation and top cap and mark each solar hot and cold respectfully.
11. Install storage tank (above collector for passive, anywhere else for active), run ½-in PEX (or other) with ⅜-in pipe insulation from collector outlet (upper most coupler) to either solar hot water nipple, and from the solar cold nipple to the collector's inlet (lower most coupler).
12. Install a hot water capable, on-demand, circulating pump for active systems capable of maintaining your desired home GPM (typically 6 to 12 GPM depending on water needs, usage, and resident quantity) calculated to your head requirements ("Distribution," page 173) anywhere along the cold water line.

NOTE: It's a good idea to also install an expansion tank in the hot water line to absorb extra pressure during abnormally sunny or hot times of the day, to prevent the storage tank's pressure relief valve from activating and losing water.

13. Connect the storage tank's hot and cold water to the home's hot and cold water as you would normally. Fill collectors, tank, and expansion tank if used with water to purge air.

NOTE: The slower you run your water, the less your water heater storage tank will kick on, the longer it'll remain in the collector, the hotter it'll become. If you don't use hot water often, are experiencing extremely sunny days, or go on vacation, cover the collector and turn off your water heater.

NOTE: By installing in every room old cast-iron-radiator-style space heaters connected to the home's hot water lines, the solar water heater can become a home heater, replacing the need for a gas or electric furnace.

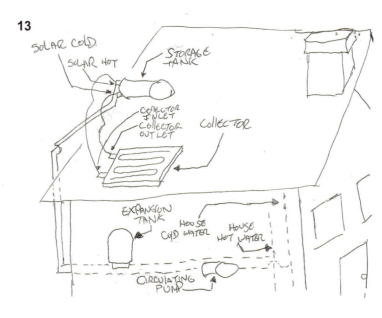

Solar Oven

MATERIALS
large cardboard box
insulation
medium cardboard box
aluminum duct tape
flat high-temp black spray paint
mirror, Mylar, or tinfoil
double paned, nitrogen-filled, ½-in pane glass window insert
1-way reflective glazing
black pot with glass top
(2) metal hangers
oven turkey thermometer

TOOLS
utility knife
straight edge
pencil
measuring tape

1. With a utility knife and straight edge, cut a large cardboard box 4 in out from any corner leaving the top pieces attached.
2. Repeat for opposite side. Connect fronts, then lay 2 in of insulation on bottom. Place a medium sized box (about 4 in smaller) inside. Transfer cuts ½ in lower and remove all pieces, including top (smaller box only).
3. Fill sides with insulation, tape exposed insulation cavity using aluminum duct tape (optional).
4. Paint bottom with flat high temp black paint inside, then glue mirror, Mylar, or tinfoil inside top flaps for reflectors.

NOTE: You can get Mylar (and a huge Fresnel lens) from old rear projection TVs.

5. Measure top outside diameter of oven and fabricate or purchase a double paned, nitrogen-filled (optional), ½-in pane glass window insert, with 1-way reflective glazing (facing inwards). Tape in place using aluminum duct tape.

NOTE: If you're using the oven for normal everyday cooking operations, I would suggest first, building the unit out of metal, and second, installing a high temp seal around the box/glass mating area along with (4) 3-in toggle clamps for easy installation and removal or incorporating a back sealed door in the back wall.

6. Remove tape and glass, place a black pot with glass top inside, and replace glass and tape.
7. Open reflectors. Stick (2) 2-ft pieces of hanger into box reflector sides, and adjust until you feel heat build at center of window. You can add a car solar shield to the front and double inside temperatures, reducing cooking time.
8. Add an oven thermometer inside or a turkey thermometer through the side and adjust when temps drop below 250° by rotating 1 to 2 times an hour. Keep equidistant side shade widths.
9. Operation: Stove will cook a whole defrosted chicken in 5 hours, a loaf of bread in 8 hours, pancakes in 1 hour, tortillas in 30 minutes, and will boil water in 1 hour.

Solar Chiller

1. Construct a solar oven as described, and place food or water inside a plastic bag instead of a pot.
2. Point stove into the deepest, darkest part of space at night, and let sit overnight. In the morning you'll have ice or frozen food.

NOTE: There should be no clouds, buildings, trees, or any other obstructions of any kind in direct line of sight with the chiller's AOI (angle of insolation—angle that captures the most exposure to the sun's rays). The principles that allow the stove to heat work the same for the chiller to remove that heat, heat is sucked out into the "heat sink" of the night sky, achieving cooling of about 40° to 60° below outside ambient air temperatures. Also, I would use polyethylene (plastic) instead of glass since it's nearly transparent to infrared radiation.

For an in-line water chiller, use the solar water heater in the same fashion. Just make sure to keep the water moving or it'll freeze and rupture the coils. If not in use, have a second, dedicated insulated hot water tank for cold water storage.

Solar Dehydrator

Everything dries in the sun, everywhere, even in cold/humid regions, it just takes longer.

MATERIALS
nylon window screen
(20) drapery hooks or metal hanger

TOOLS:
Sifter
(8) 6-in spring clamps
Staple gun with ½-in staples

1. Construct a large sifter ("Bucket Sifter," page 64) from scrap wood.
2. Starting from the back bottom of the sifter, using a staple gun with ½-in staples, attach nylon window screen stapling every 6 in around the entire frame, leaving the front flap loose.
3. Operation: Cut food slices ⅛ in to 3⁄16 in thin and hang food on drapery hooks or pieces of metal hanger, clamping front flap in places with spring clamps. Angle towards WAOI ("Photovoltaics," page 138).

Solar Still

A still is a type of filter for liquids, separating one type of liquid from another. This is carried out by turning the one liquid to gas, while keeping the other liquid/s in liquid state, which is especially beneficial for things like purifying drinking water, and even turning sea water into drinking water. We can do this because most liquids have higher vapor points (temperatures) than what water boils at. That said, there are some chemicals like ethanol with lower vapor points than water, but they aren't common in liquid form at room temperature or found in water supplies. Otherwise, some small solids are transferred via air current. The entire assembly being solar, just allows us to do it for free. A still isn't biased on what it separates. So, if you are continuously consuming distilled water, I strongly suggest adding sodium, potassium, calcium, magnesium, and other essentials ("Nutrient Solutions," page 108) to prevent deficiencies.

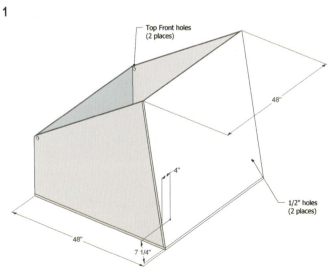

1. Construct (2) 48 x 48-in (height can be as tall as desired) solar ovens ("Solar Oven," page 136) using 1⁄16-in sheet metal or plywood (plywood shown). Seal all joints with acoustical sealant or Sta Put or SB-12 Metal Bond, and coat entire inside surface with elastomeric coating or heat resistance plastic liner.

2. Drill (2) ½-in holes in the back panel, 7¼ in OC up and 4 in OC in from each edge and install a float valve set at 6 in.

3. For a collection trough, drill (2) 1¼₆-in holes in the top front corners of each side panel, flush with front panel, then rip/cut a 47¾-in (or the ID of your box) cutout (centered) out of a 50-in section of ¾-in CPVC and slide through inside holes (cutout up) adding high temp RTV sealant. Seal along front of cutout where pipe meets front panel.

4. Tack weld a 24-in Lazy Susan (or install a solar tracking motor) to the bottom (centered) and install still on level location facing south ("Photovoltaics," page 138).

5. Acquire a 4 x 4-ft Fresnel lens ("Solar Oven," page 136), add high temp STV silicone around top edges of box, center lens and install #8 x ¾-in modified truss head screws every 3 inches OC.

WARNING: Wear shade-5 glasses when working with Fresnel lenses. To prevent fire, keep lenses covered until filled with water.

6. Cap off either end of trough pipe and connect the other end via ¾-in CPVC pipe to an old water heater (gas or electric) or other insulated tank for a collection tank, and an automatic high-pressure pump with one way check valve to home water or other desired source.

7. For the supply, connect both float valves in series, connected to the home (or other source) water supply. For larger clean water demands, connect multiple stills in series.

8. Operation: Turn on water and uncover when full and track sun ("Solar Oven," page 136). As the water boils, steam rises and condenses on lens, dripping down and into the collection trough. As the water level inside drops, the float valve opens keeping water surface in direct contact with the Fresnel lens's focal point. Routinely monitor water level.

WARNING: Temperature is well over 800° at focal point. If your lens isn't 48in², or if you change lens angle, the distance from center to water level must be 32 in (or focal point length).

2

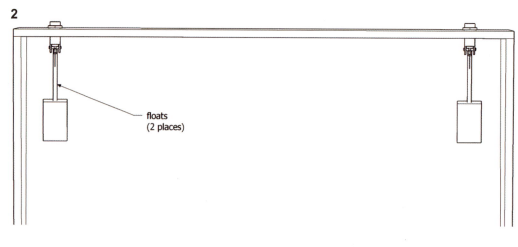

floats
(2 places)

3

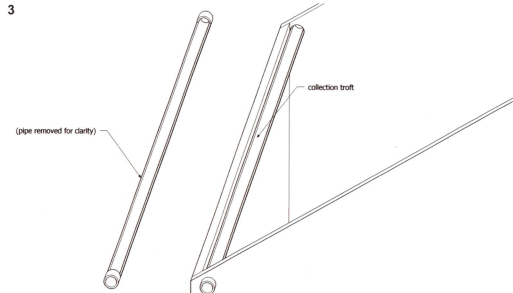

(pipe removed for clarity)

collection troft

5

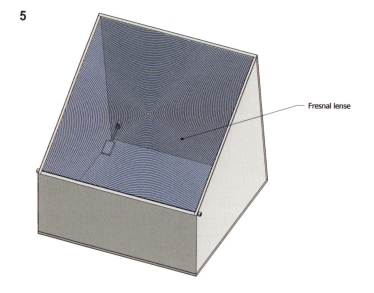

Fresnal lense

PHOTOVOLTAICS

Solar or PV panels have come down in price 75% in recent years. They come in many types, sizes and power ranges.

Monocrystalline (hexagon) are more efficient, but cost more than Poly. Otherwise, both are similar and are the most widely used. They are typically smaller (per watt) and weigh less, so they require less space and structural support over amorphous panels. Amorphous panels aren't as efficient but have slower and overall, less degradation. They're more durable, better performing in extreme conditions, and usually cheaper because it's faster to grow and harvest silicone amorphously than fully blooming crystals. Before building a solar panel, you should have an idea of how photovoltaics work, starting with connecting and constructing the smaller components.

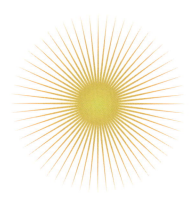

Homemade Solar cells

Solar or photovoltaic cells convert light into electricity (at an atomic level) by absorbing the sun's photons and releasing locked electrons via a material with special properties (known as the photoelectric effect). The electrons travel from one side of the cell through the circuit as usable electricity, only to get caught (and freed) again on the other side. It's simply a matter of retrieving and transferring these charged particles for our own use.

We'll start with building a single solar cell which you can then combine to build entire panels. Our single cell will measure 6 by 6 in and will produce about enough energy to power a single LED bulb.

MATERIALS

(2) copper foil or snail tape
(2) 36 gauge wires

2-L bottle
½ T gelatin

15% electrolyte to water solution

TOOLS

fine sandpaper
solder/soldering gun/flux
pencil

wire cutters
straight sheet metal snips
measuring tape

flat iron or flat panini press

1. For electrodes, cut (2) pieces of copper foil or snail tape ¾ x 6 in (pos) and 5⅞ x 6 in (neg).
2. For the neg electrode, heat either side directly on an electric stove on high for 30 min or 20 min after cupric oxide (black residue) appears or when it's thick enough to flake off. Let cool.
3. Gently wash off by hand with water, being careful not to bend or damage the cuprous oxide (red layer) beneath. Clean a corner of each electrode using fine sandpaper and solder (2) 36 ga wires as neg/pos leads.
4. Cut (2) 6½-in square clear plastic panes from a 2-L bottle. Make a batch of Knox Blocks sheets by mixing ½ T gelatin in ¼ c boiled 15% electrolyte solution until fully dissolved. Add ⅞ c 15% cold electrolyte solution. Apply thin layer to panes, and refrigerate.
5. Gently cut a ¼-in electrolyte free border. Place both electrodes onto either pane (leads on opposite sides) with a ¹⁄₁₆-in gap.
6. Place second pane. Weld the 2 borders together using a flat iron or flat panini press set to 175°–200°.

Homemade Solar Panels

Since a single solar cell can only generate minimum power, a number of them are needed, wired in series/parallel (i.e., a solar panel) to sustain any type of household needs. Cuprous oxide doesn't make a great semiconductor either (an 80W panel would measure 65m²), so we'll stick with silicone for the moment. You can, of course, grow your own, but bricks of blemished, chipped, or broken (A-C quality) 3 x 6 to 6 x 6-in mono-crystalline .5-.75V (3-10a) cells (available on eBay) are really cheap these days. And as long as the tabs are full length and undamaged, they'll perform as good as undamaged cells.

MATERIALS

(24) .75v A-B 6 x 6-in cells
tab ribbons
push-pins
(2) ⅛ x 1¼-in x 8-ft aluminum angle
⅛ x ¾-in x 1-ft angle
drill with ³⁄₁₆-in drill bit
clear Lexel sealant

³⁄₁₆-in x 1 ft 8⅜-in x 4 ft 2¹¹⁄₁₆-in archival or tempered glass, or ¼-in UV rated plexiglass
¾-in square 2-terminal block
14 gauge red and black wire
2-in painter's tape frame
1 pt clear polyurethane, epoxy resin, Flex Seal, elastomeric coating, or EVA film
(16) #10 x ¾-in pan head screws/nuts/washers

TOOLS

impact gun with apex tip adapter and #2 Philips apex tips
solder and 75w soldering iron and flux
pencil
steel straight edge
¹⁄₁₆-in tile spacers
wire cutters
miter saw
arc or MIG welder or rivets and rivet gun
drill with ³⁄₁₆-in drill bit

sawhorses or table
rag
citric acid
¾-in square 2-terminal block
Masslinn cloth
voltage/amperage meter or 500w bulb
4-in c-clamps
concrete vibrator
4-in paint brush

1. To build an 80W panel, apply flux to the 2 front lines of (24) .75V A-B 6 x 6-in cells.

   NOTE: (24) .75V cells soldered in series is 18V (for a 12V system). You'll need 48 (36V) for 24V batteries and 56 (42V) for 24V.

2. Using a pencil and steel straight edge, solder (2) .20mm x 1.5mm x 11-in tab ribbons by dragging a 75W+ iron from front to back, leaving a 5-in lead.

   NOTE: Cells are configured with the back 6 (2 rows of 3) tabs positive, and front negative.

3. Using ¹⁄₁₆-in tile spacers, place cells face down in 3 rows (leads up) outside rows pos-neg and middle neg-pos. Flux tabs and solder neg leads of the first to the second pos, second to the third, etc. It's easier to make a 3 column/row grid from pinned spacers at 6¹⁄₁₆-in centers.

4. Solder tab ribbon onto the 3 open positives. Push-pin (2) .20mm x 5 mm x 4½-in lengths of bus ribbon in front of either pos corner and the diagonal neg centered with a ⅛-in gap.

5. Repeat for the 2 adjoining pos-neg using (2) 10-⅝-in ribbons. Solder and clip extra.

6. For the frame, cut (2) ⅛ x 1-¼-in aluminum angle with opposing 45° angles to 1ft 8⅞ in and (2) at 4 ft 3³⁄₁₆ in. Then fillet weld (or rivet) (4) 1-in long pieces of ¾-in angle in each corner.

1–2

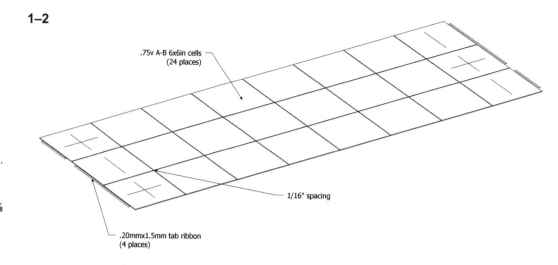

.75v A-B 6x6in cells
(24 places)

1/16" spacing

.20mmx1.5mm tab ribbon
(4 places)

6

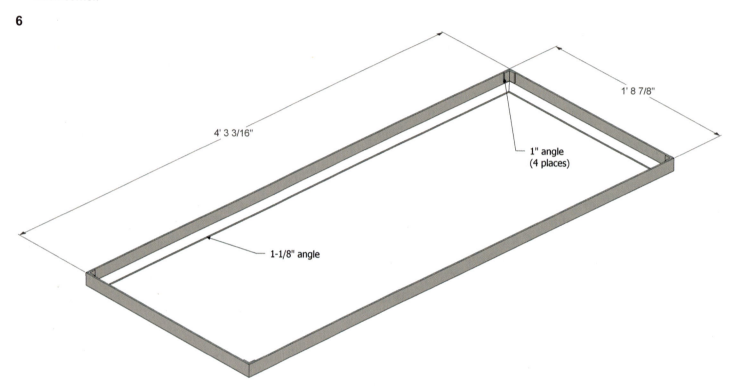

4' 3 3/16"

1' 8 7/8"

1" angle
(4 places)

1-1/8" angle

7. Cut (6) more 1-in pieces for retainers and drill ³⁄₁₆-in holes in either leg (centered) of each. Then drill (6) ³⁄₁₆-in holes ⅜ in down top legs of frame, equally spaced.

7

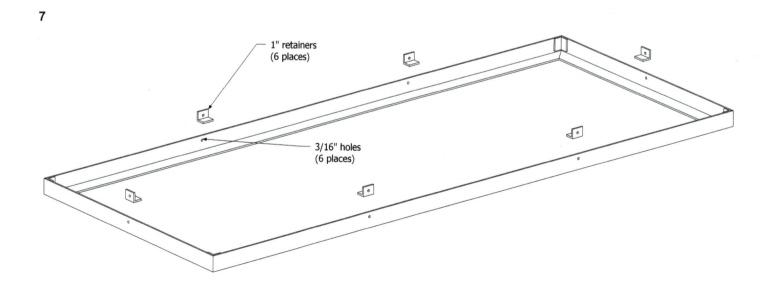

1" retainers
(6 places)

3/16" holes
(6 places)

8. Lay frame level on sawhorses or table, clean all pieces with citric acid, and apply a thick bead of clear Lexel along all horizontal frame legs. Let sit for 5 mins, then place (centered) a ³⁄₁₆ pane of 1 ft 8⅜ x 4 ft 2¹¹⁄₁₆-in archival (light reducing) or tempered (safety) glass, or ¼-in UV rated plexiglass, allowing for a ⅛-in gap on all sides.

8

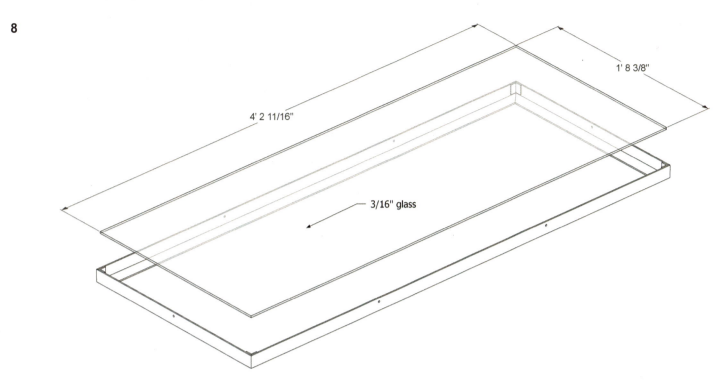

4' 2 11/16"

1' 8 3/8"

3/16" glass

9. Install a ¾-in² 2-terminal block in the positive ribbon corner. Clean glass with Masslinn cloth. Place and center your array and solder (2) 14 ga wires from your pos/neg ribbons, route inside ⅛-in frame gap and connect to block.

   NOTE: A blocking diode isn't needed since your controller or grid tie inverter will restrict reverse current.

10. Check solder points, voltage/amperage with a 500W bulb, replacing cells if necessary. Fill void with Lexus, pressing wires down with a pencil or flathead screwdriver. Install retainers with more sealant.

    IMPORTANT: Do not press glass. Retainer spacing allows for a ³⁄₃₂-in layer of sealant on both sides that, if pressed out, will leave pane loose.

11. To encapsulate (to prevent air exposure and slow degradation), tape frame in place and clamp a concrete vibrator to the sawhorses or table. Turn the vibrator on, then pour 1 pt clear polyurethane, epoxy resin, Flex Seal or elastomeric coating like Sylguard184 (or use EVA film) into cavity around array/frame, so all cells are covered. The vibrator works out the bubbles, but tends to move the array around.

12. Spread, thin, and flatten bowed cell edges with a paint brush. Let sit in the sun to dry for 1 week or until dry, then install retainers using #10 x ¾-in pan head screws/nuts/washers.

    NOTE: For additional protection, add ¾ x 1-in pieces of bicycle tire tubing between retainers and cells.

12

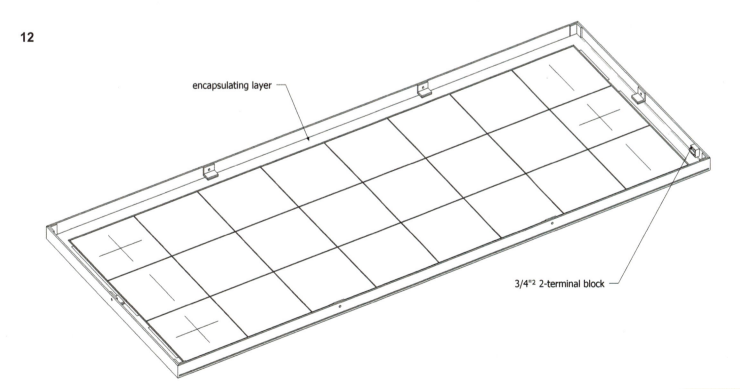

encapsulating layer

3/4"² 2-terminal block

Installation

For mounting, there are 3 options: roof, pole, and ground. In all 3 cases, frame stays are the same.

MATERIALS

14 ga x 1 in x 2-ft flat bar
(2) 14 ga 1½ x 4 in x 20-ft cee purlins
(2) 1½ x 4 in x 20-ft zee purlins.
⅛ x 1½ in x 6-ft flat bar
(22) ¼ x ½-in zinc plated bolts/washers/nuts
(6) ⅛ x 1½ in x 12-ft angle
(12) ¼-in butyl covered bolts (or anchors)
(12) ¼ x ½-in zinc plated bolts

TOOLS

arc or MIG welder
chop saw
drill with ¼-in drill bit
measuring tape
soap stick
bender
(2) ⅜-in wrench

1. Weld (2) 14 ga 1½ x 4-in cee purlins (1 cut at 20 ft, 1 at 14 ft 9½ in) together with (2) 1 x 6-in 14 ga doublers (outside, top, and bottom) to make a 34 ft 9½-in long top beam. Repeat for bottom beam using 1½ x 4-in zee purlins.
2. Drill a ¼-in retainer hole in top flange (centered) of the top beam, ¾ in OC from each end and every 6 ft 11⅛ in OC between.
3. For retainers, cut (22) 3¼-in pieces of ⅛ x 1½-in flat bar, bending either end to 90°, ½ inches in.

1–3

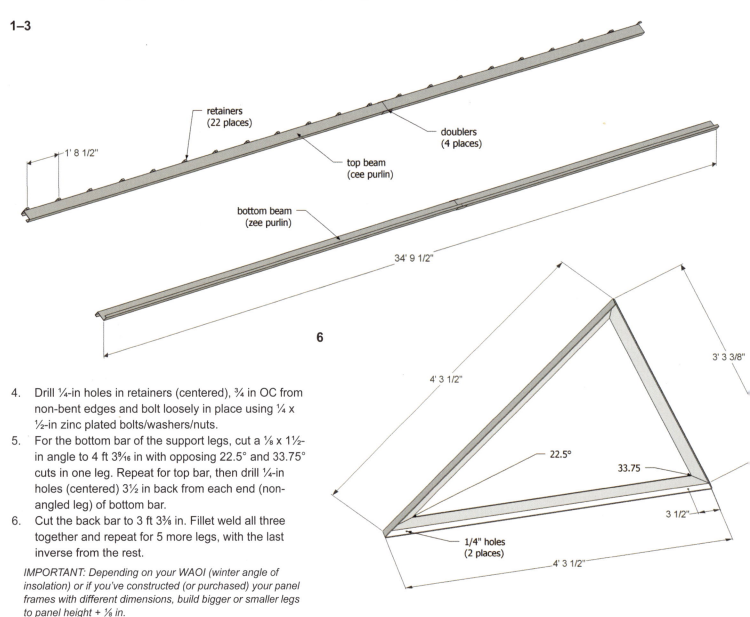

4. Drill ¼-in holes in retainers (centered), ¾ in OC from non-bent edges and bolt loosely in place using ¼ x ½-in zinc plated bolts/washers/nuts.
5. For the bottom bar of the support legs, cut a ⅛ x 1½-in angle to 4 ft 3⁹⁄₁₆ in with opposing 22.5° and 33.75° cuts in one leg. Repeat for top bar, then drill ¼-in holes (centered) 3½ in back from each end (non-angled leg) of bottom bar.
6. Cut the back bar to 3 ft 3⅜ in. Fillet weld all three together and repeat for 5 more legs, with the last inverse from the rest.

   IMPORTANT: Depending on your WAOI (winter angle of insolation) or if you've constructed (or purchased) your panel frames with different dimensions, build bigger or smaller legs to panel height + ⅛ in.

7. Mount legs to roof sheathing or concrete pads using ¼-in butyl covered bolts (or anchors) spaced 6 ft 11-⅛ in OC.
8. Install top and bottom beams (drilled flanges in) of legs using ¼ x ½-in zinc plated bolts, with the inverse leg located on the end (legs in).

8

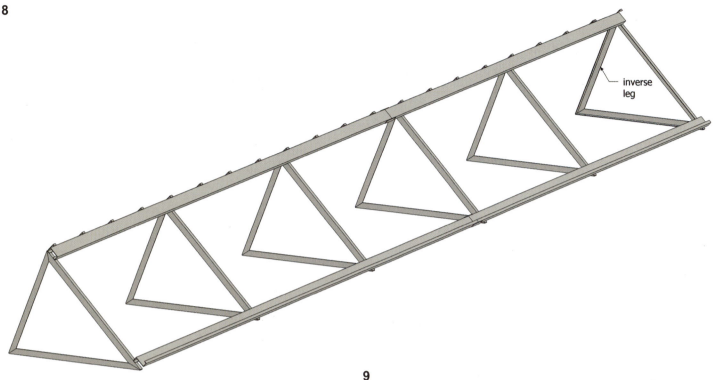

inverse
leg

9

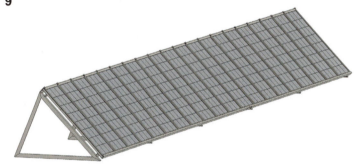

9. Slide panels in, starting at either end so that retainers sit in seam of two panels (move retainers away as needed). Snug down retainers.
10. Repeat for 3 more stays, leaving at least 4 ft between each of the remaining 60 panels.

NOTE: If cutting/welding isn't your thing, UNIRAC (https://unirac.com/solarmount/), or other rail system mounts are lightweight, strong, and easy to assemble in all 3 applications.

Orientation

To absorb as much light and prevent deflection (like skipping vs. dropping a stone), panels should be facing the sun at right angles. This is known as *insolation* and is a measure of solar radiation received on a given area in a given time, expressed as average irradiance in kWh/m²/day.

Obviously, some locations receive more radiation than others. However, even in extreme locales (especially with less radiation), in order to achieve total insolation, you'd have to constantly move panels, following the sun. Unless you're installing motors and light tracking diodes (ie. tracking systems), the best we can do is orientate towards the strongest source with the majority of light hours during winter. This is called the winter angle of insolation (WAOI).

NOTE: Free online calculators and worksheets are available to aid you.

Direction: Mount facing true (not magnetic) south (in the northern hemisphere) or north (southern) by adding (if positive) or subtracting (negative) your magnetic declination shown. San Francisco's magnetic declination, for example, is 15°.180° (magnetic south in San Francisco) + 15° puts true south at 195°.

Tilt: It's easiest to mount panels according to roof's pitch, but this usually skips the stone. A good rule of thumb is: latitude -15° (in summer), latitude (spring/fall) or latitude +15° (winter). We can achieve a more efficient tilt with some calculations:

Winter: If your latitude is 25-50°, multiply by 0.89 and add 24°. The result is the angle from horizontal that your panels should be tilted. These angles are ±5° steeper than what's recommended because in winter, most energy comes at midday, so panels should be pointed directly at noon sun. The third column shows how well this orientation compares to tracking.

By orientating panels to winter, when sunlight is shortest and people inside are using more electricity, you'll always have more than enough energy throughout the year when sunlight is longer and stronger and people are out more.

ANGLE OF TILT FOR A FEW LOCATIONS

Latitude	Angle	% of tracking
25° (Key West, Taipei)	46.3°	81%
30° (Houston, Cairo)	50.7°	82%
35° (Albuquerque, Tokyo)	55.15°	84%
40° (Denver, Madrid)	59.6°	85%
45° (Minneapolis, Milano)	64.1°	86%
50° (Winnipeg, Prague)	68.5°	88%

WINTER TILT

Latitude/Tilt: 30°/50.7°, 40°/59.6°, 50°/68.5°		
Season	Insolation (kWh/m²)	% of winter
Winter	5.6, 4.7, 3.4	100
Spring, Autumn	6.0, 5.8, 5.4	107, 123, 158
Summer	5.1, 5.1, 5.1	

If winter configuration isn't best because you have a summer cabin, are grid-connected, or have some other incentive, adjust tilt at least 4 times a year.

CALENDAR TILT OPTIONS

Winter	Oct 7	Lat x 0.89 + 24°
Spring	Mar 5	Lat x 0.98 - 2.3°
Summer	Apr 18	Lat x 0.92 - 24.3°
Autumn	Aug 24	Lat x 0.98 - 2.3°

Off-Grid Applications

Calculate, control, connect, convert, and tie each of the discussed RE systems (modules), individually or as a network (arrays/strings) of power production into a storage system for use.

IMPORTANT: Modules can be of different wattage/amperage, but must be the same voltage. The exception is that larger MPPT controllers can handle any DC voltage from 60-90A.

Configuration

In order to disconnect from the grid, you need to generate more electricity than you consume. Unless you just want to add modules until that's achieved, calculate the quantity needed. To do this, retrieve a typical winter electric bill. Divide total kWh by 30, giving you kWh/day consumption rate. Divide again by peak hours of sun (typically 8), giving kWh/hour. Multiply quotient by 1000 to convert kWh/h to Wh/h. Divide by module/s size to get total, then multiply by cost to fabricate (if any) and/or purchase (with shipping). Finally, add 5% buffer (for panels) since they lose 2-3% of rated power in the first years and .5% yearly after that.

EXAMPLE: Say your electric bill shows kWh is 1715 for the one month period. 1715 ÷ 30 = 57.16 kWh/d ÷ 5 = 11.43 kWh/h x 1000 = 11,430 Wh/h + 5% = 12,001.5 Wh/h ÷ 305W solar panels (for example) = 39.34 (40) panels x $275 = $11,000.00 or 25 with (2) 4.5 kW, $5000 turbines (for example) = about $16,875.

NOTE: There are free calculators online to help with the math (such as https:// sunwatts.com/solar-calculator/).

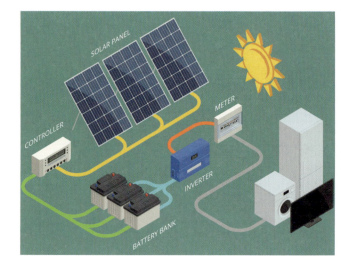

There's no difference in purchasing half the panels at twice the wattage or twice the panels at half, presuming the PPW is the same. However, there are pros and cons:
- If your system consists of (100) 50W panels, and a panel is damaged by a rock or hail, you're not down 200W and out the price of 4 panels when compared to a (25) 200W panel system.
- Often smaller panels are cheaper, but there's a limit: more panels mean longer, larger cables, structure, and installation costs.
- Logistically, if you lack the ground or roof space, there's no second option.

Cost

NOTE: If you're planning on selling electricity, doubling your system size won't bring in an additional source of income. Electric companies only compensate the difference between electricity used and electricity stored.

These figures don't cover inverters, cables, batteries, controllers, etc., so expect to pay $25-$50k (depending on quality of components), which is still pretty good to be 100% off the grid. If you were not doing it yourself and hired a company, they'd charge you 3 to 10 times that ("Building Without Killing," page 159). We could cut that figure in half with simple conservation and downright sacrifice.

The problem we Americans have is overindulgence. We eat too much, buy too much, work too much, want too much, use too much. Simple living, which most off-gridders embrace, is not about living without, but rather living with. Having a simpler life is determining what is important, or enough, and discarding the rest. The secret is to conserve and reduce use *and* reduce items. Now, I'm not asking you to burn all your worldly possessions (yet), but consider the enormous power suckers like coffee makers, toasters, irons, blow dryers, curling irons, clothes dryers, stoves, water heaters, incandescent bulbs, electric space heaters, and air conditioners. That's all.

These appliances are designed around what's called *heat coil technology*. It's like connecting a wire from your car battery pos-neg. You just made a *hot coil*, red hot! You're just shorting out the battery and converting electricity directly to heat, which is the fastest way to drain the stored energy. This is why your bill is so high. There're lots of efficient ways to make heat; electricity isn't one.

"How do you dry clothes, then?" or "I can't live without my coffee in the morning," I hear all the time. People really believe they can't live without something because they've been led from birth to think it. My simple answer: humans have lived without hair dryers, toasters, clothes dryers, and even doorbells for hundreds of thousands of years, and I don't believe even one person has ever actually died from lack of a doorbell. But solar retailers would never tell you this. More appliances means more modules and more cable! If I were a retailer, I'd give free toasters with every purchase, as banks used to. Take a look for yourself:

Once you're actually off the grid, you'll quickly find yourself conserving. Toss the garbage disposer, trash compactor, dishwasher, garage door opener, turn off TVs and lights and, of course, opt for the more efficient LED versions. (A 72 inch HD flat screen LED TV, with surround sound only sucks down 100W.)

Downgrade

Downgrade your use, not your system. Air conditioners and water heaters account for 90% of your bill. Rather than spending $10,000 on a system, you're spending $100,000. And before you say you can't live without them, again, humans have for hundreds of thousands of years. In fact, Freon-based ACs are a 20th century invention in lieu of natural and passive methods. I'm not asking you to get rid of them, just cut back. If sacrifice isn't for you, you'll find that by cutting module quantity by one-half, one-third, or one-fourth you'll still have a nice system, be partially off the grid, and reduce your bill by as much.

APPLIANCES AND WATT USAGE

Item	Wattage	Item	Wattage	Item	Wattage
AC	1500	Can opener	100	CD player	35
Blow dryer	1000	Coffee grinder	100	Cell phone	24
Ceiling fan	10–50	Dishwasher	1500	Printer	100
Central vacuum	750	Exhaust fans (3)	144	PC	150
Clothes washer	1450	Food dehydrator	600	Laptop	20-50
Dryer (gas)	300	Food processor	400	Radio phone	10
Garage door	350	Microwave	1400	Satellite system	45
Heater (portable)	1500	Mixer	120	Stereo	15
Iron	1500	Range	2100	TV 25"	130
Sewing machine	100	Light bulb(60W)	60	VCR	40
Table fan	10–25	Fluorescent light	16	Cable modem	50
Refrigerator	540	AC water pump	500	Circular saw	900
Blender	350	DC pump (6hrs/d)	50	Drill (½")	750

Voltage

Until now we've talked about wattage, but voltage defines the system. 12V modules are okay for small, start-up systems but prove cost prohibitive in larger systems due to massive wire size needed. As electricity travels, it loses performance through resistance, and more so with lower voltages. In order to reduce this loss to less than 5%, larger cables are required. Higher voltage experiences less resistance and loss, which equates to smaller wire and less cost. When we're talking about a few feet at $2.55/ft for 2/0 cable it's no big deal, but at 100 ft we're looking at $255.00 in savings. These savings ripple back through every system component.

Voltage is inversely proportional to current, which is directly proportional to resistance. Since current dictates wire size, by increasing module voltage from 12V to 24V or from 24V to 48V, amperage drops by 50%.

NOTE: If you already have 12V panels, wire them in a series for higher voltage vs. parallel for amperage. The power produced and stored (Wh) remains the same.

Controlling

Charge controller

The controller regulates several actions necessary to keep your system functioning smoothly including constantly monitoring and controlling battery state, preventing current reversal, preventing overdrawing (critical in batteries), and alerting for reverse polarity. The principle is simple: a circuit measures battery voltage, operating a switch that shorts, opens, or diverts power from or to the source, BB, and site when low or full to prevent overcharging or draining (damaging).

NOTE: If this is occurring, your bank is undersized and you're wasting electricity. Consider getting additional/larger batteries, or a diversion load. Conversely, if you're running out of power regularly, your modules are undersized or need supplementation.

Controllers come in 1-80A and 6-60V and are capable of handling up to 4kW. PWM controllers are rated and sized by array current or system voltage, are cheaper, but have significant loss (up to 60%). This may be okay for small systems, but for larger, or systems with different voltage (i.e., 48V array, 12V bank) your only option is Maximum Power Point Tracking (MPPT). They're rated by output amperage that they can handle, not the input current. They have minimal loss (2%), but are significantly more expensive.

In order to adequately size the controller to properly regulate, multiply module quantity by their wattage, and divide by BB voltage to get amperage. We'll also need a buffer (+25%) to handle light reflection and edge of cloud effect.

EXAMPLE: 42 panels x 305W ÷ 48V + 25% = 333A

IMPORTANT: Larger controllers or power stations only allow 48V input.

The largest controller is 80A. OutBack Power, Xantrex, Blue Sky Energy, Four Star Solar, Magnum Energy, MidNite Solar, Morningstar, and Schneider Electric (formerly Xantrex), are all good. You'd need 4 with 3 strings of 10 and 1 string of 12 panels wired in series and/or parallel to each. Then check controller's upper voltage limit, especially if you're wiring in series. String voltage cannot pass this limit; so give a 10% buffer for cold weather.

EXAMPLE: For the thinnest gauge wire, I'm going to connect 2 groups of 5 modules in parallel, in series for 96V. The open circuit voltage of 48V panels is 56V x 2 + 10% = 123.2, still within Outback's 150V limit. For larger, go with Xantrex's Xq 600V.

IMPORTANT: Unless your controller has a boost function, it won't charge a higher voltage bank. For example, if input is 25V, but your bank is at 25.5V, even though not full, power cannot flow. That's why you size combined module voltage larger. So, if you want a 12V bank, use a 24-96V solar or turbine string, 24V bank, 36-96V, etc.

Divide systems into subsystems. You never want your entire system, on just one component, because if it fails, you have zero electricity.

NOTE: If your string(s) are within the range of one controller but you're planning system (or family) enlargement or adding turbines, jump to an 80A controller now.

WARNING: Without controllers, you risk overcharging or evaporating electrolyte, exposing, warping, or growing plates, causing internal shorts, and igniting hydrogen.

Heat Sinks

There are times, especially during storms or summer (another reason we design for winter), that your modules will produce more energy than your batteries can hold. This isn't an issue for grid-tied systems, but, if not diverted, this will destroy batteries.

Heat sinks are just heat coils, dissipating excess electricity into the air or water. Most controllers come with heat sinks. As we're permaculture orientated, and because I don't enjoy waste, our excess is routed to pool, fish farm, and aquaponics water space heaters ("Hydroponic Heating and Cooling," page 109).

For homemade turbines, we can use them as dump load diverters as a means of braking during high winds to prevent damage.

Disconnects

Switches disconnect electricity from modules, the bank, or components when working on the system or replacing components without disconnecting anything.

Fuses/Circuit breakers

Fuses and circuit breakers (CB) protect your home in case of component failure.

Meters

Monitoring the component and module performance is important in knowing system health, but it's critical without a controller to monitor state of battery charge and prevent damage. If your controller doesn't have a display, or even if it does, meters can serve as a backup to monitor controller performance.

NOTE: Multi-function monitors like Tri-Metric 2020 or Xantrex ($150-200) measure battery voltage, state of charge, charge/discharge current, days since last full charge, and more. Which essentially provide advice as to adding modules or batteries. Use the following chart to convert your multi-meter reading to percentage of battery charge.

BATTERY STATE OF CHARGE

State	6V	12V	24V	48V	Spec grav/cell
100%	6.37	12.73	25.46	50.92	1.277
90%	6.31	12.62	25.24	50.48	1.258
80%	6.25	12.5	25	.50	1.238
70%	6.19	12.37	24.74	49.48	1.217
60%	6.12	12.24	24.48	48.96	1.195
50%	6.05	12.1	24.2	48.4	1.172
40%	5.98	11.96	23.92	47.84	1.148
30%	5.91	11.81	23.62	47.24	1.124
20%	5.83	11.66	23.32	46.64	1.098
10%	5.75	11.51	23.02	46.04	1.073

NOTE: Although called a 12V battery, its status of full/empty charge or discharge is anything but. Readings must be taken at least one hour after charging or discharging.

For even more monitoring, connect a solar irradiance meter on the array, a tachometer to turbine shafts, and an anemometer on the stub poles to compare module performance with charge rates.

Inverters

The inverter changes your DC BB to household current (110-240AC). Otherwise, you'd need to wire the home, lights, plugs, etc. with stranded wire and purchase DC refrigerators, blenders, TVs, etc., which is an option (there're a wide range of 12V appliances available for RVs). This is actually how we wired our first off-grid home.

There are basically 3 types of off-grid inverters (by wave type): square (least expensive/efficient), modified sine (most popular/economical producing between square and pure), and true sine (produces cleaner than grid power).

Most home inverters turn themselves off when not in use, powering up automatically when a draw is detected. Also, most appliances run more efficiently and therefore use less power with modified sine wave.

The inverter needs to be the same voltage as the BB with enough power to *continuously* supply your energy demands as well as handle the largest peak (surge) load and are sized accordingly.

Draw up a load worksheet schedule (see example) showing each electrical device, quantity, wattage, surge, and typical usage times. Highlight hours of simultaneous use. Add accumulative durations with the most overlap and/or highest watts. (If there's more than one, choose highest total). To determine wattage/surge, check back plate label, contact the manufacturer or test with multimeter (multiply watt by 1.5-2x (normal) or 2-3x (heavy machinery)) for surge.

LOAD WORKSHEET SCHEDULE

Item	Watts	Qty	Surge	11a	12a	1p	2p	3p	4p	5p	6p	7p	8p	9p	10p	11p	12p
Light	60	20	0								X	X	X	X	X		
Dishwasher	840	1	1200			X						X					
Fridge	720	1	2160	X	X	X	X	X	X	X	X	X	X	X	X	X	X
Stove	6000	1	0		X						X						
Microwave	960	1	0									X					
Computer	480	1	0							X	X	X	X	X			
LED TV	600	1	0								X	X	X	X	X		
Fan	360	4	0	X	X	X											
Window AC	1200	1	3600				X	X	X	X	X	X					
Furnace fan	720	1	1440							X	X	X	X	X	X	X	X
Blow dryer	1200	1	0														

In the example we see the load total at 6pm is 7620W and that the highest surge is 3600W. Most affordable inverters cap at 5000W and run $0.50-$0.75/W (MSW-TSW). But even if you can run everything through one, again, if that inverter fails, you're waiting weeks without power for a replacement. So either divide into subsystems per house circuit or floor sections or stack inverters.

NOTE: Adding surge loads aren't a concern since you won't be starting the microwave and dishwasher simultaneously.

Inverter stacking uses multiple compatible inverters in series (double voltage) or parallel (double amperage) controlled by a master device (computer, smartphone, tablet) via a rs485 port/cord. For the above load, (2) 4000W inverters in parallel will do; for electric stoves, dryers, water heaters, or shop outlets, 2 in series for 240V is the way to go.

NOTE: Some inverters or power centers come with integral controllers.

Storing

Even in a grid-tied system, or full-grid use, you should still keep a battery bank for backup when the power goes out, much like a generator, but cleaner. You can stack on garage shelves, lay on floors, or slide nicely into multi-shelf integrated battery racks, as long as they're kept at room temperature with plenty of ventilation. Batteries are the fuel tank of your system. Without them to store your energy, you would only have day-time power. Off-grid battery suitability determining factors are Ah (amp hours) quantity: performance capacity, amperage capacity, and cycle life.

Automotive batteries are composed of (6) 2V cells with thin lead plates in a solution of 33.53% sulfuric acid (98%) and 64.47% distilled water to produce 12V, and are rated ≈40Ah with a 5–10 year cycle life. That's 1a of 12V electricity for 40 hours, 2A for 20 hours, 4A for 10, etc. As previously determined, we need 22.5A (per Load Worksheet example) over a 13-hour period, which would require 7.3 (round up to 8) batteries. Add 5-10% buffer = 8.8 (now we are at 9).

Besides modules, batteries will be the most expensive component. A good residential battery will have 1, 2, or 3 thick 2V plates capable of holding several hundred times more Ahs. Designed to charge rapidly when the wind's roaring or the sun's blazing and discharge slowly when it's not. Golf cart batteries are the cheapest and most readily available that fit these criteria.* Lower voltage batteries conserve power better and have larger cells which provide higher current for longer periods of time.

BATTERY TYPES

Battery type	Voltage	Ah	Cycle life (yrs)	Price
RV	6, 12	60–232	4–8	50–200
Marine	6, 12	95–128	2–6	90–200
Mobility scooter (AGM)	6, 8, 12	4–200	4–8	150–500
Golf cart	6, 8, 12	150–245	2–8	125–250
Traction	24, 36, 48, 80,	300–840	10–30	500–2000
Gel	6, 12, 24	100–500	5–10	100–500
EV (Li-ion/Ni-Fe)	3.3*, 3.7*, 6, 12	38–200	10–30	40–400
Power station (LiFePO4)	3.2*	15–250	10–40	30–300
Automotive	12	40–90	5–10	40–200

NOTE: Battery technology is changing rapidly. By the time you read this, AGM and gel will be replaced by Li-ion, which will have started being phased out by NiMH, Lithium Sodium, Aluminum-Air, Li-air or something else. Aquion (salt water) is gaining footing and their prices are dropping. They're safer for the environment, non-flammable, non-hazardous, and non-explosive, unlike traditional batteries.

NiMh with its hydrogen-absorbing alloy for the anode are lighter, don't suffer from bottom memory effect, and have 2 to 3 x more capacity, compared to cadmium anode (NiCds). The downside is NiMh batteries have fewer cycles and a noticeable discharge drop towards the end of a charge. On the other hand, the new Lithium Ion Condenser batteries are very light, have a longer shelf life, increased life cycle, more rapid charge time, and don't suffer from any memory effects.

For indoor use, sealed are the only way to go. They need no maintenance, are more expensive and can't be refurbished, but don't off-gas, and, therefore, don't need venting. Gel is better than most and AGM is the best (higher quality and performance, longer lasting). Whichever you choose, make sure you have the right charger.

IMPORTANT: If not using a controller, DOD (depth of discharge) needs to be monitored. 50% is safe, whereas 20% is usually the limit. Either way, they'll last longer if you keep under 70% (shallow cycling). If your batteries never fully charge because your electrical output is greater than input, you need to supplement or enlarge your modules until you remain above the 90% nightly to prevent false memory formation.

For parallel connection, the most common method is for leads to be placed pos-pos and neg-neg with charging feeds placed on the last and main feeds on the first. The first and last batteries are used more since the last battery gets charged first while the first receives the least. When drawing, the same happens in reverse. In a 4 battery bank with a 100A draw, battery 4 provides 17.7%; battery 3, 20.3%; battery 2, 26.1%; and battery 1, 35.9%. Because the batteries aren't being treated equally, battery lifespans aren't equal, which means the entire bank fails sooner.

The same parallel configuration with opposing charging/main feeds means a more balanced drain and fill with battery 4 providing 26.6%, battery 3 providing 23.2%, battery 2 providing 23.1%, and battery 1 providing 26.6%. There are still discrepancies, but for low cost, small banks, it's negligible. For higher priced batteries, in order to get 25% performance across the board, each pos/neg lead needs to be of equal length, connected along with both charge and main leads to separate 1-post terminals. If you own, or are planning on converting an existing car to EV, it can also be used as a BB, saving half price on batteries.

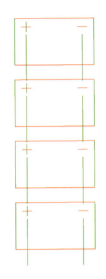 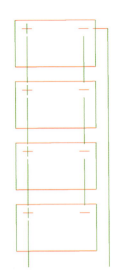

unequal or unbalanced draw   *more equal more balanced draw*

1. Construct your BB from high-strength materials able to handle 65 lbs per sq ft in a well vented (for vented batteries) space between 50°–80°.

   NOTE: FCBs on a steel rack makes an excellent spill proof structure.

   NOTE: Batteries no longer discharge when sitting on the ground, but cold, uninsulated floors can reduce charge state by 50%.

   IMPORTANT: Since hydrogen rises, just having an open window isn't enough. Vents must be located at the highest point to prevent pocketing. Do not locate near open flame source.

2. Place batteries with 2 in unobstructed clearance on all sides and 1ft 6 in vertical clearance, with terminals unidirectional.

Back-Up Generators

A backup source of power is always smart. A small generator can charge your bank during days of excess cloud coverage. A 50A producing charger ($50) only draws 310W. Or use (on alternative fuels of course) without batteries to provide electricity at night.

Wiring, or distribution, is the most important element of any system. Without it, you simply have a donkey walking in circles or a few roof-mounted, reflective art pieces.

NOTE: Cable diameter is determined by terminal-component spans. Also, DC current travels on the outside instead of the inside (AC). Therefore, small multi-strand cable (welding or automotive) is more efficient than solid or larger gauge stranded of the same OD.

IMPORTANT: Using a voltage drop table or calculator for the following wiring steps is critical.

1. Measure OC from terminal to terminal. Cut 1 each (black/red) length of quantity cable. Remove ½ in rubber jacket with a utility knife. Solder or crimp (soldering's better) ⅜ in (or terminal size) lugs. Cover with color coated cable heat shrink when cooled.

   NOTE: Purchase ready-made 2/0 cable online (@$3/ft), cut to your required lengths by the roll ($1/ft), or chop up old jumper cables.

2. Coat connections with conductive grease; connect in parallel/series as described with terminal covers.

   NOTE: For lower voltage cells (or if terminals are close together), use flexible terminal connectors on positives and braided strap (with covers) on negatives to save money and work.

3. Install a 2/4 exterior LC (load center) as a combiner or CB, with DC rated CBs (QO Square D breakers are UL listed for both AC (120/240V) and DC (12-24V) sized to array or turbine on structure's base, 4 ft from ground.

   NOTE: For multiple arrays or towers, install LC, slot count sized to system +4 (for add-ons) on a centrally located structure; route, underground, UF rated cables or non-UF through conduit, using MC extension cables as necessary.

4. Connect turbine or first panel's pos wire/s (for multiple string/turbine pos wires, connect each to its own CB) to a top mounted DC rated CB sized to load and the neg to the neutral bus bar, just as you would home wiring. Install a grounding rod, clamp, and wire connected to the neutral bus bar.

5. Connect a red cable with jumper leg to each main lug and a black to main neutral lug. Route underground to BB.

    NOTE: If system requires 2 (or more) controllers, set up 2 (or more) LCs dividing loads accordingly.

6. Attach controller(s) near BB and connect LC cables through DC amp/volt gauges (if not integrated) to controller's DC in terminals.

7. Install another 2/4 (3/6 for multiple controllers) LC (sized to controllers combined amperage) with CBs sized 1.25 x controller output.

8. Wire in the same manner . . . hot from controller's AC out terminal to CB (1/breaker) and neutral/ground to neutral bar.

9. Run a pos cable with leg jumper from each LC main lug and neg from neutral bus bar to BB. Connect the heat sink or load dump (if not integrated) to corresponding controller terminals, and mount underneath.

    IMPORTANT: If using homemade wind turbines, connect a manual 2-way wind-speed switch, sized to turbines maximum amp rating or above, before and bypassing combiner box/controller, connected directly to load dump.

10. Drill a ⅜-in hole in a winged buss type T-JJS DC fuse sized 25% larger than the biggest load, and install directly onto BB's pos terminal.

11. Install a 220V inverter (or stacked 110vs) and manual shut-off switch(es) (1/inverter sized to inverter) on the other side of the bank. Wire from DC in terminals to bank and back-up gen to AC in terminal.

    NOTE: Twist all cables from inverter to minimize magnetic field interference.

12. Call your electric company and cancel your power! When dead, disconnect the 2 main service wires and neutrals (if separate) from meter to prevent your system from charging the disconnected wires, and thereby, creating a *fallen live wire* situation (if you're staying on the grid or selling energy back to the grid, install a manual disconnect, sized to your amp load, so that you can disconnect power from the grid when charging, and connect, when drawing). They'll take a few days to shut power off, so don't touch anything until meter dials stop spinning (blank for digital) when light switches are on or the meter is removed.

    NOTE: The electric company will take their meter, leaving you with an empty box. If it's separate, pull and sell it on eBay. If connected, plug with plastic to keep insects/birds out.

13. Run 2 (or more) hot wires from each set of inverter AC-out terminals to home's LC main service lugs and neutral/ground to the common neutral bus bars main lug.

    NOTE: It may be necessary to wire in an auto transformer in stacked inverter configuration to throw one 180° out of line to achieve a 120/240 split phase output. For 110V only, wire a jumper (equivalent OD to hot wire) connecting both main terminals. Label panel "110V ONLY."

If you're not looking to get off the grid but want your system to reduce your bill or possibly sell surplus, a grid tie setup is for you.

First, is it financially feasible? This is called the *grid-parity*. It's cheaper to use power from the grid than alternative energy (based on system cost calculated over its lifespan). As of 2010, this was true by a factor of 5 (system cost/kWh was 5 times higher). The price of electricity is rising; however, as the cost of alternative energies continue to drop, the difference today is a factor of less than 0.05. These figures are for a complete turnkey system, though. Guess what happens when we design, purchase, and install it ourselves? We fall below the grid-parity to less than 0.25. As long as you're doing the labor, the answer is, yes. It is financially feasible. If you're not, wait 3 years. If the initial investment is out of your pocketbook range either way, a community shared system may be viable.

NEM or Net (what's left after use) energy metering is a billing policy that allows renewable energy system owners to slow down or stop meters when generating electricity, and even reverse current when producing to contributing surplus through a bi-directional meter. Like a BB, the balance can be used anytime. Credits called RECs are rolled over monthly or annually until a set expiration date, at which they're purchased retail or more often, wholesale (given away) or canceled.

NOTE: If you're able to make your meter stop (producing as much energy as you consume), you have a net-zero home (calculated on an annual basis). Similar to zero waste. You're not contributing any carbons and qualify for higher tax breaks and incentive programs. As part of the Energy Policy Act of 2005, under Sec. 1251, all public electric utilities are now required to make net metering available upon request.

If you want to sell excess, Feed-in Tariff (FIT) contracts don't use credits and generally pay for grid contributed power at a lower rate than what they sell you. This is a better option if you generate more electricity than you consume but worse if you generate less. There are 2 tariff levels: Generation tariff (you earn a fixed revenue/kWh generated, regardless if you use or export it) and Export tariff (you earn additional revenue/kWh put back into the grid).

Community shared systems (solar gardens or shared RE plants) are renewable energy power plants, communally owned, where local residents purchase shares or lease the equipment from a third party. In either case, the power is routed to surrounding homes via net-metering in the same manner. A few years back, I designed a community system that composed two neighborhoods (80 homes) with shared power plants in Las Vegas.

No special meter is needed for NEM since most units are already bi-directional, but a contributing meter may be needed for TIF. If you're also incorporating a BB, set up an anti-islanding device that stops your power from flowing into the grid (and cooking a lineman). There are many types of grid-tie inverters (all-in-one, plug-n-play, interactive, master/slave, charger/inverters, hybrid, smart). Most have anti-islanding devices along with power plant-grid inverters, LC inverters and grid-battery banks with controls that read and automatically switch between each as needed (ie. when the grid fails, batteries are low, producing access power, requiring energy). They usually also have UPS (automatic AC transfer), pure sine-wave grid phase matching, stackability, generator auto start/stop, and high pass through/surge capability.

WARNING: Never use a regular inverter.

NOTE: Hybrid or smart inverters also have built-in battery storage, and are web/Wi-Fi enabled, allowing access, monitoring, and controlling online from any device, anywhere. Also, interactive inverters require additional regular 12-120V inverters or slaves (usually 1/string, although micro inverters can be installed 1/panel) to control.

Non-controller Type Systems

1. Install your system as described without the controller (controllers aren't necessary since grid-tie inverters regulate power).

    NOTE: If installing tracking systems or double row ground mount structures, install panels with trunks/boxes facing each other, i.e., bottom panels upside down.

2. Mount a lockable main AC disconnect (off) rated to full inverter output, within 3 ft of meter/LC.

    IMPORTANT: Main disconnect must remain off until safety inspection is completed.

3. Connect switch to LC with conduit. Install a single high voltage grid-tie inverter (sized for the entire system) next to the switch in series (up to 600V) or micro inverters like Enphase or Aims, multiple parallel stacking 24-110/220V, sized to each group of 1, 2, or 4 panels inside the frame or corner of every or every other panel (bottom row only for double row installations) using self-drilling screws.

    IMPORTANT: Keep documentation of 5-year warranty for all equipment for field agent.

4. Snap the pos/neg trunks from every 2 or 4 (top/bottom 2 in 2 row configurations) panel(s) into the micro inverter and each inverter to the next in parallel, with the last routed to the LC underground.

    IMPORTANT: If installing more than 1 panel and inverter, make sure to get inverters with multiple inlet ports/trunks. For single row installations, I still recommend extra ports/trunks for future add-ons.

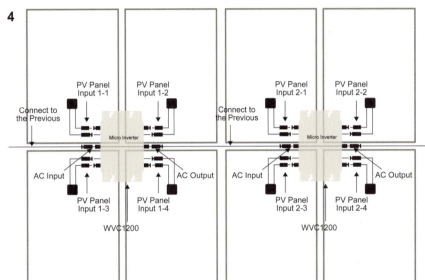

5. Install a sub panel combiner box with main disconnect (slots determined by string qty). Connect neutral/ground to neutral/ground bus bars.
6. Connect hot cables to DC rated 110 or 220V CBs sized to the max amperage of each string or turbine.
7. Connect a hot cable with jumper leg to both main service lugs routed through the switch to a top mounted (110/220V) DC rated CB sized to the entire system +25%.
8. Connect neutral/ground wires from combiner box's main neutral bus bar lug to LC's wires.
9. Request an inspection, and (if you don't already have one) get a dual registered meter. The agent will install it (at customers expense).
10. If you pass, all that's left is to sign the Interconnection Agreement. Of course, there are fees, permits, and other expenses, so expect to spend at least $2.00 a month to be grid-tied.

Chapter 7: Alternative Fuel Production

The greatest aspect of making your own fuels, is that you already own the materials to make them in and around your home. Remember, fuels aren't strictly reserved for automobile consumption. They can be used in furnaces, stoves, cutting torches, lanterns—you name it.

Biomass

Biomass is a type of fuel that takes what would normally be considered as trash and turns it into fuel. In our daily activities, we build up a lot of biomass by raking leaves, mowing lawn, cutting firewood, constructing and remodeling, and woodworking—and that doesn't even include the food and garbage waste we produce. These products are hauled to the curb and used as (bio)mass to fill a giant hole just outside town. They contain considerable amounts of stored energy. If separated by the methods in this chapter, they can be used as a direct fuel source in stoves, furnaces, water heaters, fireplaces, BBQ grills, and etc.

NOTE: All briquettes below can be further processed into charcoal, biochar, activated carbon, and coke ("Charcoal," page 61).

Fire starters

MATERIALS

1 qt wax
2 c sawdust
2 T granulated char
2 c dryer lint
toilet paper or paper towel tube

TOOLS

miter saw with fine blade
plastic container
mixing spoon
1-in dowel

1. Melt 1 qt wax ("Candles," page 27).
2. Mix 2 c sawdust, 2 T granulated char ("Charcoal," page 61) and 2 c dryer lint in a plastic container.
3. Slowly add the wax, stirring continuously. When mixing becomes futile, scoop the clumpy gook and deposit inside a toilet paper or paper towel tube, packing every ½ in with a 1 in dowel.
4. Let dry, then cut into preferred proportions: for dry, hardwood, 2 in sections are good; ½ in for dry softwood; and 1 in for damp wood.
5. When it's time to use, peel tube a little on one end, light peeled tube as a wick, placing logs on top.
6. OPERATION: Expect 15 to 45 minute burn time per starter, depending on section size. That's enough to dry and start even the wettest wood.

Wood Shaving Fuel Blocks

MATERIALS
5-gal bucket
1 gal wood shavings
1 to 1½ gal biodiesel, glycerin, WVO (waste vegetable oil)
milk or juice carton, or another sacrificial container

TOOLS
stapler

1. In a 5-gal bucket, hand mix 1 gal wood shavings with 1 to 1½ gal biodiesel, glycerin, WVO, or vegetable oil (see respective sections).
2. Unfold the top of a milk or other container and fill or pack with mix. Refold, staple, and store upright for use. Because the source here is the oil, with the shavings being an absorbent to give structure, we don't want loss from evaporation, hence the stapling.

Grass Clipping and Leaf Pellets

With an ash content of 1 to 6%, density greater than 600 kg/m, calorific value above 4.7 kWh/kg, chlorine or sulfur contents under 300 and 800 ppm respectively, and at 90% efficiency calorie output in a pellet stove or furnace, pellets are a phenomenal fuel.

Of course, any bio material, including straw, cocoa, rice husk, coconut husks, pine needles, wood chips or sawdust, char, shredded waste paper or cardboard, fine charcoal, dried manure (perfect moisture), coffee grounds, nut or seed shells, weeds, corn stocks, and other agricultural, industrial and municipal waste, can be made into pellets. A new or used pellet press can be purchased online.

Manure and Straw Fuel Patties

Most our harvested straw gets put to good use, and any soiled bedding quickly gets repurposed into fuel as cow dung patties. This is easy fuel, no presses, no stills. If you don't have access to straw or manure, farms always have field process residues and manure, and the ranch hands are always happy to have *you* haul it off.

MATERIALS	**TOOLS**
cellulose fiber	ball mill or concrete mixer with 5-in rocks
manure	earth tamper
fiber dust	

1. Dry mix 60:38:2 cellulose fiber (page 27) to manure to fiber dust (vol) in a ball mill (Chapter 2) or concrete mixer with 5-in rocks or steel ball bearings or billiard ball until pulverized into smaller than 1-in material.
2. Remove balls or rocks, add 5 to 15% water and mix to clay-like consistency (check moisture level with earth plaster test).
3. On anything other than masonry or earthen floors, pack into hand-sized balls, coat with sawdust, drop ball and press to the size of a pizza by hand (slapping) or with a lightweight hand tamper (page 65).

NOTE: For today's mindset changer: There are no hygiene or health issues in building, burning or cooking with remnant excrete, and there's no smell. It burns odorless at 92% efficiency (meaning almost no ash) with a caloric value near coal.

Junk Mail Fuel Briquettes

MATERIALS	**TOOLS**
junk mail, magazines, newspaper, cardboard, or other waste paper products	blender (see Tools)
	CEB (compressed earth block) mold
	shop press
	5-gal bucket

1. Pulp junk mail, magazines, newspaper, cardboard or other waste paper products in a blender or just soak in water overnight.
2. Place in CEB (compressed earth block) mold in shop press; and press with a bucket underneath (place any pulp caught in bucket in another block). Stack like adobe bricks in the sun to cure for 6 to 8 weeks.

Alcohol Stove

The next few projects provide ways to use biomass for cooking or other applications. All use recycled cans and are very efficient. These come in very handy if you are out in the wild and you are setting up your homestead and don't have a kitchen indoors just yet.

An alcohol stove burns odorless and smokeless, and if you spill the fuel all over your kitchen counter and floor while taking pictures for a book you're writing and Lucia yells at you, it won't smell like a gasoline pump or rotten eggs, and it will evaporate quickly. The stove makes a compact (fits in a back pocket with fuel) travel, camping, and back packing stove as well as a good Bunsen burner for various chemical compounds.

MATERIALS
3 to 4-in wide flat candy tin
clothes hanger
fiberglass insulation
5 to 6 T ethanol, alcohol, whiskey, or paint thinner
candle

TOOLS
thumb tack or drill with 1/16-in drill bit
wire cutters

1. With a thumbtack (or 1/16-in drill bit), punch holes 1/2 in apart through the lid or body of a round 3 to 4-in wide flat candy tin, halfway down top lid.

   IMPORTANT: Different fuels require different mix ratios (orifice sizes) for the most efficient flame pressure:
   Alcohol, 0.026 in (thumbtack or paper folded 4x)
   Gasoline, 0.014 in (2x)
   Kerosene, diesel, jet fuel, 0.011in
   Rubbing alcohol, 0.05in (1/16-drill bit)

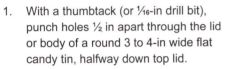

2. Straighten, then bend a hanger into 3 in tall M shapes and loop and tie in a circle creating a pot stand.

3. Remove lid and fill bottom with fiberglass insulation. Fill with 5 to 6 T ethanol, alcohol, whiskey, or paint thinner.

   NOTE: For traveling or camping, use a travel size hand sanitizer bottle, zippo fuel refill can, or other flat plastic container, small enough to fit inside the stove for fuel storage.

4. Close and adjust vents by rotating (mark side for lineup point), closing, and opening to facilitate fuel and air mix.

5. Place two more straight, 6-in long pieces of hanger through the crosses of the stand, place the stove on the stand with a lit candle underneath. Heating the stove from underneath vaporizes the fuel, creating sustainable jets (vapor pressure), and turning the can into an actual stove. Otherwise, there's the potential of burning liquid and flashback occurring.

6. Once you hear fuel venting, light the jets. If especially cold, or for higher elevations, flip pot holder upside-down, place hanger pieces across the 'M' indentations, and keep the candle underneath to warm.

7. Place pot on top.

   NOTE: If using rubbing alcohol, empty remaining water after each use.

   IMPORTANT: The flame should never pass the bottom of your pot. If flames overtake the pot, the vents need dialing back. When finished, or to dial back flames, extinguish flame with a wet cloth and shut off fuel (close vents).

Rocket Stove

A rocket stove uses sticks, twigs, leaves, or brush (anything that burns, wet or dry) and requires ⅛ the fuel typically required to cook a meal.

Materials

MATERIALS
(1) 46-oz can
(1) 1-gal paint or coffee can
(2) 14.5-oz can
(3) 1-in SS screws
insulation or ash
high temp silicone or water glass (optional)

TOOLS
Sharpie
measuring tape
drill with ⅜-in drill bit
metal snips
can opener

1. Place and trace a 46-oz can on the bottom of a 1-gal paint or coffee can. Measure and draw a second, ⅜-in smaller circle (centered) inside first circle.

2. Drill a ⅜-in center hole and with tin snips, cut inner circle out. Cut ¼-in wide tabs around circumference to inner line.

3. Place a 14.5-oz can lengthwise (perpendicular) on the side of the 1-gal can, 1 in from bottom. Trace, draw inner circle as in step 2 and cut circle and tabs.
4. Repeat on the side and bottom of the 46-oz can, then push inside paint can forming a pressure fit until side holes align.

5. Remove 14.5-oz can's bottom with a can opener, flip stove upside down, and press it through both holes.
6. Flip, remove paint can lid, and fill outer chamber with insulation or ash. Add high temp silicone or water glass (optional) and reinstall lid.
7. Remove the bottom of second 14.5-oz can, cut and flatten wall, then cut sheet metal into a 2-in T-like pattern lengthwise. Place inside the 14.5-oz can forming an upper platform (fuel feed) and lower (air inlet) chambers.
8. OPERATION: Feed twigs in side and drop lit paper in top. Continue feeding, keeping cooking pot off for full draft until you get coals. The taller and thicker the outer chamber, the more draft, the hotter and more efficient your fuel.

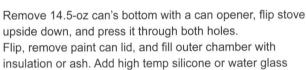
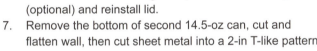
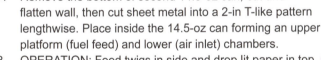
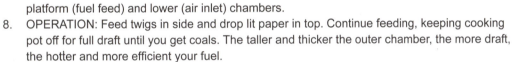

Wood Gas Stove

Also known as a hobo stove, Chinese stove, camp stove, and biogas stove, this stove recycles its own exhaust, burning it repeatedly. This is carried out by air entering the bottom and top. Bottom air is sucked up but blocked from entering the combustion chamber by the incoming upper air, and is forced, instead, out through and around the sidewalls, entering the combustion chamber through the side upper jets. Simultaneously, the upper air is sucked down into the combustion chamber, through the fire into the bottom where it's blocked from exiting by the incoming bottom air and therefore is also forced into the sidewalls. By now the sidewall air is superhot, pre-heating the burning wood causing gasification and release of stored combustible gases (otherwise lost in a normal fire). On the downward trip, upper air pulls these fuels along with it, exiting the upper jets under pressure, where it ignites, creating a recycled second fuel source. In other words, two forms of combustion from one fuel—very efficient.

MATERIALS
(1) 1-qt paint can
(1) 20-oz can or other short can with an outside diameter equal to paint can's inside diameter with lid removed
(1) tuna or 14-oz canned meat can (best) high temp RTV (silicone sealant) or water glass

TOOLS
drill with ¼ and ⅜-in drill bits
measuring tape
Sharpie
sheet metal snips
can opener

Materials

1. Drill ⅜-in inlet holes in the side or bottom of the paint can 1 in OC, ¼ in up.
2. Repeat for the 20-oz can, along with ¼ in jets around the side or top spaced 1 in OC and ½ in down.
3. Press 20-oz can inside paint can, add high temp RTV (silicone sealant) or water glass, then continue pressing until lips mate.
4. Drill ⅜-in holes around the top of the tuna or meat can, ½ in down, along with a 2 x 2 in square hole for a door. it's easier to drill the holes with the bottom intact as it gives the can stability and rigidity. Cut door out with snips. Remove bottom of can with a can opener. This can will serve as a wind shield, fuel feed, and pot holder.

5. OPERATION: Fill 20-oz can with wood chips, twigs, sticks, or other fuel and light. Once you see only jets on fire; place the pot holder on top, and add your pot to cook. As the wood burns down add more.
6. When finished, close all intakes to make charcoal and store as fuel for your next burn.

Chapter 8: Building Without Killing

IMPORTANT: The following content does not substitute for basic construction know-how. Local ordinances, laws, code regulations, and association rules and restrictions are not included.

Most American homes are built with cheap materials—namely wood. Anyone who's lived in a stick framed house knows the headaches that develop. And I don't mean cheap financially; to build the same size home out of concrete or metal would cost a fraction of the cost, and we're not killing anything in the process.

Unspoken detriments include the absence of thermal mass, need for additional insulation, carpenter ants, wood borers, powder post beetles, mice infestations, vulnerability to intruders and extreme heating and cooling requirements. Besides being famously unsafe and structurally weak due to little tensile or compression strength, harvesting wood constitutes the largest global, ecological, environmental, and economic impact by far by removing carbon scrubber sand displacing billions and trillions of animals annually.

According to *National Geographic*, the planet has lost around half of its forest cover to deforestation, and going by the data uncovered, the 100% mark will be nearly reached in our lifetime.[5]

In addition to the environmental impact, wood is the only building material created from killing another living thing. You're essentially stacking dead bodies, putting a bed in the middle, and calling it "home sweet home." I can't say I'm especially fond of living inside rotting carcasses, but that's just me.

There are plenty of other materials that are more weather resistant, structurally sound, long-lasting, and environmentally healthy. Some of which even come in premanufactured kits, delivered right to your door. By building with steel, stone, brick, cob, adobe, and other earthen materials, you will eliminate any detriment and create a home that lasts ten times longer. In fact, all of the home material types I discuss in this chapter are fireproof, termite proof, flood proof, and wet and dry rot proof.

When it comes to our homes, we fail to think. We simply do what everyone else does and build with wood, regardless of the consequences. It wasn't supposed to be like this. Widespread construction and use of stick homes was a "temporary" resolution during and directly after WWII as a method of bringing "cheap, quick housing" to a society recovering from a Great Depression. Now, as I mentioned, with most of the American forests harvested, lumber prices have skyrocketed. Today, we have to pay an arm and a leg to build with arms and legs. Very few countries (besides the U.S.) actually still use the stuff.

I, therefore, restrict the use of wood for anything other than temporary uses in lieu of converting back to non-living, more efficient home construction!

COST

Become mortgage free today! Is interest killing you? Is your mortgage spiraling out of control? Own your home outright and get rid of those pesky monthly payments! Act now and instantly qualify for a 60 month . . .

Sound good? Unlike the campaign above, this isn't some marketing ploy. The only practical way to have a mortgage-free home is not to get a mortgage in the first place. Home construction costs are composed of nine major parts, only two of which have to do with the home, and in reality, are free if done yourself (see pie chart to the right).

With a little know-how in different fields and the use of free materials usually found on the land, you eliminate the majority of these costs, and reduce the undertaking to a manageable, mortgage-free amount without wanting to kill anyone.

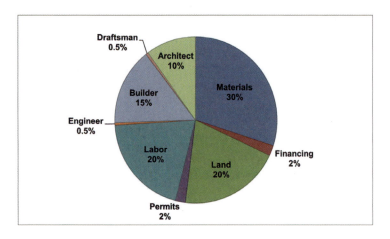

Pie chart:
- Draftsman 0.5%
- Architect 10%
- Materials 30%
- Builder 15%
- Engineer 0.5%
- Financing 2%
- Labor 20%
- Land 20%
- Permits 2%

LAND

The term "right land" is irrelevant. I've built homes in deserts, jungles, mountains, swamp lands, and even on a fifty-foot man-made floating island in the Indian Ocean. Some were easier to build on and some easier to live in; it's just about what's right for you.

Desert

Because rainfall and snow loads are minimal and building codes nonexistent in the middle of a desert, strength requirements are low, making options vast and design complexity minimal. Plus, dirt, sand, clay, lime, and rock are abundant, which makes building a home out of stone, earthbag, adobe, cob, concrete, rammed earth tire, sandstone, CEB, brick, or cinder block a great option.

Prairie

Rich soil, clay, sand, rock, and the addition of grasses make prairie regions optimal for cob, adobe, rammed earth tire, earth bag, sandstone, yurt (page 166), and brick homes that accent the landscape. And since there are no inclines, large boulders, or roots to fight with like there are in the mountains, hard soils like in the desert, or wet earth like in the woodlands, the plains are prime real estate for underground homes.

Forest

If you're building without killing, typically, there's not a lot of unoccupied soil in a forest. Riverstone, sand, caves, abandoned mines, and deadfall lumber are abundant, though, making stone, conversion (page 166), rammed earth tire, and earth bag homes doable if you can find a clearing.

Suburbs

In suburbs, everyone's always throwing out perfectly good construction materials: paper, glass, Styrofoam, concrete, paint, boards, and steel. These materials are good for building papercrete, EPScrete, concrete, metal stud framed (page 167), geodome (page 166), conversion (page 166), and modular homes (page 167). Or you could recycle an entire home by remodeling and renovating!

Jungle

The soils of various jungles around the world can vary dramatically. For the most part we're looking at high humidity, low air movement, and often, stagnant water, perfect conditions for concrete pier and beam foundations.

Mountains

Mountains are another location with a wide range of material options. Anything from rock, concrete, and steel to papercrete, EPScrete, metal stud, and even geodomes, conversion, and modular homes do great in mountainous settings.

Water

Ever wanted to live on the water? Minimal to non-existent laws and regulations, and anchor in international waters and you're your own country! For building, we're restricted to lightweight and waterproof materials, so conversion construction is key here. Convert sail boats, house boats, barges, and the like.

DESIGN

Designing your dream home is the most critical and, therefore, should be the most time-consuming aspect. Each element needs to be meticulously reviewed and reworked at least seventy-one times.

I'm often asked, "What's the best type of house to build?" Every expert earthship, cob, papercrete, or adobe builder will swear by their method. They'll cite facts and provide proof, showing that their material's superior. But, like land, it's just what feels right for you. The facts are out there. For example, there are a myriad reasons to favor underground homes: they're cheaper, easier to construct, safer, more energy efficient, and dirt is available everywhere for free. But I don't really want to live in an underground home. Weigh your Want/Don't-Want list, which we will create in our procedure (page 162), against the pros and cons, tripling all cost and time estimates.

Considerations

Most builders use wood to save time and money building cookie cutter replicas in tract housing developments since abnormal designs and heavier duty materials require more time, which eats into profit. By repeatedly using the same drawings, tools, workers, and hardware, there's no loss to learning curves and training.

And then you need to consider preferences, strength requirements, and aesthetic wants that add or reduce complexity:

- Two-story homes are harder to heat and cool and are more susceptible to wind loads and, therefore, require considerably more material and engineering.
- Roofs are the most expensive and complex component. By stacking floors and reducing the footprint of your home, you reduce the roof by 50%, and keep the same square footage at near half the cost.
- As we age, stairs become troublesome, making ranch-style and split-level architecture appealing.
- Wall thickness equals sound reduction. For example, 4 in of masonry or earth equals −15 dB.
- For stability, wall thickness should be 1/16 of the wall height or greater, with straight walls acting like dominoes and curved walls self-supporting.
- Roof slopes of 1:12 to 4:12 provide less wind resistance, with dome and hip roofs being more aerodynamic and therefore causing less uplift while oversized overhangs create more.
- Stronger sheathing eliminates structural roof members.

Building Codes

Your local building code provides free location-specific information such as loads, spans, building practices, soil qualities, and more, which engineers otherwise charge considerably for. In the North, that code is adopted from the National Building Code (NBC), where in the South it's the Standard Building Code (SBC); in the West, International Building Code (IBC); and internationally, International Residential Code (IRC); all available online. Use the prescriptive guidelines as a tool of reference. Even if code conformation isn't a requirement where you're building, adhering to it provides a good starting point of an acceptable level of safety to labor and affordability ratio.

It's also important to note that in most states, if you're following code, a structural engineer's stamp is not required on residential structural designs.

During this phase, you're the architect designing layouts based on owners' wants, the engineer calculating structural loads based on layout sketches, the draftsman drawing plans based on engineering data, and the interior and exterior designer determining aesthetics. And soon enough, you'll become the contractor supervisor, equipment operator, mason, builder, plumber, electrician, roofer, and gofer.

Take your time, make some rough sketches, share the experience with family and friends, do the job right, and *don't rush*; haste raises prices and delays projects.

And if you ever need a second opinion, engineering and architectural advice and plan proofing is available online, for free, in topic-specific forums or through REACH, or even hourly via JustAnswer.com, Upwork.com, and Fiverr.com.

IMPORTANT: If you're using wood, despite the restrictions I've implemented, at least mill your own dimensional lumber from deadfall. For structural requirements, determine the stress grade and type, and download a span table to calculate dimensions.

Procedure

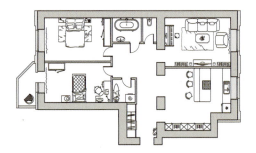

1. Decide the home's location and orientation:
   - If installing solar or wind power, plan for a clear southern view free from shade or trees.
   - Make sure the location isn't in a flood zone or dry riverbed.
   - Find a location that provides protection from storms yet is open to summer prevailing breezes.
   - (If applicable) Think about what will be required to bring in utilities and where you will place a road or driveway.
   - In cold climates, having a south-facing house is important to melt porch and walkway ice.

   NOTE: If you're going with a kit home, make sure the kit material is good for your location. For example, I wouldn't build a metal house on the beach.

2. Look up images of houses, bedrooms, furniture, flooring, and other house features with your family and write a Want/Don't-Want list that covers flooring type, room divisions, furniture and appliance locations, and anything else you can think of.

   NOTE: If you're building a kit home, make sure your ideas don't go outside the kit's limits.

3. Put those photos, concepts and sketches to digital paper using a free 2D or 3D architectural model design format or program like Sketchup, Blender, or Adobe Illustrator.

   NOTE: Many kit homes provide a free online drawing and concept tool for you to use.

4. Work in the room and building height, width, length, orientation, dimensions, and interior wall placement, and add service (wiring, plumbing, ducting, internet) locations and diagrams in multiple layers based on appliance (washer/dryer, water heater, oven), and also include shower, sink, toilet, and furniture locations.

   NOTE: A lot of kit homes have all of this already laid out in the kit, making your job a lot easier.

5. Walk the building site, removing and clearing any large visual and navigational obstacles (vehicles, tall grass, brush, etc). Then, at least 20 ft from the building site, install at least one level rod as a datum or base point. A 2-ft piece of ½-in rebar nailed into the ground and painted orange also works well as a reference point.

   NOTE: A level rod provides a unilateral connection between your drawings and the actual location, serving reference and starting point to transfer drawing foundation measurements from paper to ground. Without it you'd be guessing each corner's location, and the geometry of your foundation and forms wouldn't match up with the geometry of the terrain. If you'll be excavating for the foundation, you can get away with guessing, placing the foundations corners anywhere inside the excavated area.

6. Using grid (Alvin quadrille) paper or a computer program; a level rod, laser level, water level, or surveying rod; and theodolite for small, semi-flat areas or a total station theodolite for larger, steeper terrain or your phone's GPS and a mapping tool or app for really large projects, perform a leveling survey or land topographic survey of the building site, marking the elevation of every grid point (every 10 ft) both on paper and land surface using pin flags, taking note and labeling on paper any permanent landscaping features (boulders, trees, fence posts, etc). Then use that data to map the topographic geometry of the land into your home's drawings, adjusting the foundation to compensate for terrain elevation differences.

   NOTE: You can, and should, also use a theodolite to design your landscaping and yard drainage. If you don't have access to a theodolite, you can use a transit instead. Most of this stuff is available to rent at Home Depot or to purchase used on eBay.

7. Bring your design to life by physically drawing a 1:1 floorplan of the perimeter, doors, furniture, and even the direction doors will open with extra-large chalk on a basketball or tennis court or with paint on-site to get an idea of traffic flow, spacing, and efficiency. You'll find room for improvement and mistakes when actually walking through your design.

   NOTE: Doors should open in the direction of natural entry, against a blank wall, and should not be obstructed by other swinging doors. Doors should never be hinged to swing into a hallway.

8. (Optional) Finally, once all the bugs are worked out, workup the final design and shop drawings by transferring your topographic survey and home sketches to AutoCAD, Autodesk, Solidworks 3D, or another CAD program.

   NOTE: If you're not building your own kit building and purchasing one from a manufacturer, many kit building companies offer online tools that make accomplishing these steps a breeze.

LAYOUT

Once your drawings are ready, lay out the site according to your plans:

MATERIALS

brightly colored stakes (large nails, bolts, tent stakes, or
  scrap rebar)
(3) 2 x 2-in x 4-ft wood stakes
(8) 1 x 3-ft to 4 x 6-ft ledgers
wood screws
spray paint

TOOLS

measuring tape
plumb bob
hammer
laser level or water level
masonry line
screw gun with apex adapter and #2 apex tips
utility knife

1. Replace the four outside pin flags with brightly colored stakes (large nails, bolts, tent stakes, or scrap rebar) representing the four corners of the house. Check for square by measuring diagonally corner to corner using the formula $a^2 + b^2 = c^2$, making sure all measurements, including diagonal, are the same, all the way around, and check length and width, using a plumb bob to account for any unevenness.

    NOTE: If the terrain slope is greater than a few degrees, excavating (page 164) the area to level will greatly help and speed up the process.

2. For batter boards, hammer (3) 2 x 2-in x 4-ft wood stakes 5 ft apart, centered at least 4 ft out from each corner (10–20 ft for larger buildings sites to accommodate for ladders, equipment, machinery, materials, and scaffolding). Put them perpendicular to each other and perpendicular to each corner, leaving at least 12 in protruding up above ground.

     IMPORTANT: This is done so that when excavating, string can be removed and replaced to check measurements or give access to equipment, machinery, and materials without remeasuring or staking.

    NOTE: 2 x 2 x 4 ft treated drywall skid boards make great stakes and are free at lumber stores.

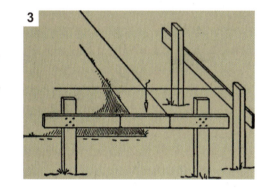

3

3. Install 1 x 3-ft to 4 x 6-ft ledgers between the stakes with screws, all level with each other, approximately 1 ft above ground level. Run masonry line taut over each corner stake, checking exact location with plumb bob. Then, with a utility knife, cut small kerfs in ledgers where each string lays, securing each string to the back of the ledger with screws. Mark each kerf "slab outside edge." Run another line inside the first, representing the slab's footing width, and cut kerfs and mark "footing inside edge." Then drop a plumb bob from each string every few feet, spray painting the string's location onto the ground.
4. Do the same for any interior load-bearing walls.

FOUNDATION

If the hat is the roof, the shoes are the foundation, which absorbs and distributes the home's weight onto the ground. Without a strong foundation, your home won't last, no matter how well it's built. Earthquakes, tornadoes, tsunamis, floods, and problematic soil would cause door misalignment, cracks, and warped floors and walls at least, and total collapse at worst.

The kit homes I describe below will come with plans and instructions for the shape, size, and thickness of your foundation, along with rebar or remesh placement, and anchor points. But there are still many foundation options. Choosing the best for your home and building site will save effort, time, and money. For example, although concrete is exceptional, it may be overkill. Conversely, brick may be strong enough, but not adequately suited to your environment. If you're going to use a material other than concrete, construct your foundation below frost lines, dress it with a 1–3-in layer of sand, and cover it with concrete or steel to provide a flat, level surface.

To ensure your safety and the safety of your home, use the local building code (page 161) and other resources to verify soil conditions and average bearing value.

- **Rammed earth:** In dry locations, earth can take heavier loads than concrete.
- **Stone:** Dressed or undressed, fieldstone is incredibly strong with the added benefit of being a heat sink.
- **Gravel:** 3 in of gravel is cheap, easy to work with, and self-packing.
- **Sand:** Sand alone is dangerous because of its tendency to shift. By filling and laying sandbags we lock it in place.

- **Brick:** Brick was highly popular in the 1900s, but use has since tapered off due to brick's vulnerability to moisture and tendency to flake and deteriorate, which is exacerbated since foundations are subgrade. Otherwise, in dry environments or where irrigation and groundwater systems are incorporated, it's beneficial and cost efficient when homemade.
- **Block:** Second only to poured concrete, CMU (concrete masonry unit) footings and columns or stem walls are the preferred method. They're strong, easy to transport and work with, quick, and long lasting.
- **CEB:** Like rammed earth, CEBs (compressed earth blocks) are able to take heavier loads and are easy to work with in dry locations. If you're pressing out earth blocks for walls, you might as well build a footing.
- **Recyclables:** Brick shards, broken concrete, reclaimed asphalt, demolished block, or other rubble is self-packing and usually free or cheap when recovered from demolished buildings, construction sites, roads, parking lots, and other sites.
- **Rammed earth tires:** Rammed earth tires are a great option when you have an overabundance of old tires. However, they do require wider excavation.

- **Concrete slab:** Concrete slabs, also called floating slab or monolithic slab, is going to be your strongest, most load-bearing foundation, meant for the heaviest of materials (concrete, brick, stone, adobe brick, CMU, cob, etc.). A monolithic slab is a very wide, thin footing that can also take on the role of subfloor or floor if finished off with polishing and a polyurethane or epoxy topcoat for an all-in-one floor. Footingless slabs are suitable on level terrain and in areas not prone to extreme meteorological events for lightweight superstructures.
- **Stem walls:** Stem walls prevent hydrostatic pressure from building under the slab, which causes uplift by water intrusion. Construct your stem wall 10in above the grade with concrete, stone, or CMUs using 5000psi concrete (page 62) or mortar (page 62).
- **Foundationless:** As mentioned, if the soil is hard enough or the superstructure light enough, a foundation isn't required with walls sitting directly on dirt. Of course, depending on your structure's material, the terrain incline, and meteorological conditions, a foundation may be better.

Excavation

1. Remove the strings from your batter boards, and using an excavator, a skid or track loader, or a backhoe or bulldozer, excavate and level the slab area to your slab thickness.
2. Using a compactor, compact the entire slab area first in one direction, then the opposite.

   NOTE: Since gravel larger than 1.5 in is self-compacting, you can also add a couple extra inches of gravel instead of compacting. This is especially beneficial for soft, sandy soils where sinking and cracking would occur, or hard clay pan soils where leveling to exactly 4-6 in is impossible.

3. Using your excavation machinery or a spade shovel, excavate the footing 12–16 in deep, 16 in for larger slabs.
4. Replace the strings and determine the location where each toilet flange will protrude up from the slab, mark it and the path it'll take back to the sewer main or septic tank cleanout with spray paint, and excavate with a ¼-in per 1-ft slope, 18 in deep and at least 4 in wide.

   NOTE: On larger slabs, it helps to erect batter boards for each location where something will protrude from the slab's surface. Do it in the same way you did for the slab edges itself, as noted in "Layout" (page 163).

5. Repeat for sink, shower, bathtub drains, and vents, routing to nearest sewer pipe, also with a ¼-in per 1-ft slope. Do the same for HVAC ducting, internet, electrical conduit, or anything else you'll be routing through the slab rather than through the attic.

   IMPORTANT: A P trap must be installed at the mouth of each shower and bathtub inlet, along with water pipe inlets and electrical conduit inlets, using your drawings.

KIT HOMES

When people talk about alternatively built homes, they're referring to the wall material and the method used. The materials for the foundation, floors, ceilings, roof, windows, doors, electrical, plumbing, and everything else is typically no different than a stick frame house. In my experience, with the exception of wood being extremely poor, I haven't found one material to be better than another. And it's not necessarily advantageous to keep one method throughout the entire home, anyway. For example, you may have enough reclaimed material for walls, but not the roof or floor. There are benefits and advantages to each, and by mixing, we take advantage of them all. Lastly, some materials and methods *are* better suited for one location over another. You can use any material in any region, but the cost and environmental impact will increase the farther it's removed from the climate for which it's suited. For example, adobe works in all regions, but it lasts longer in arid zones.

Then there's elements like size and ease of construction to keep in mind. Starting out, I wouldn't suggest you build an enormous underground dome home. The elements, know-how, and tooling that go into such a material and method are better suited to someone that's familiar with engineering and is experienced with working with steel, concrete, and earth.

Starting out, I would suggest small kit homes like metal arch buildings, tiny homes (page 165), yurts (page 166), Quonset huts (page 165), or simple conversion homes (page 166) made out of materials like shipping containers and metal silos, all of which are much cheaper, very easy to erect, require very little design, and require no engineering, almost no construction, and little tooling know-how.

Quonset Huts

Quonset home kits are perfect for the beginner DIYer who wants to build his or her own home with their own hands but knows nothing about construction and don't want to spend an arm and a leg. Even veteran experts love Quonsets (my latest build, The Water Castle, is a Quonset hut). There are no framing, studs, joists, rafters, or walls. This is why the military used them for so long, because they're cheap, go up in a day, require two wrenches, and anyone can build one. If you're willing to fabricate the arched ribs, installed every 4 ft, you can even run reclaimed roofing panels horizontally, bottoms up, or lath or cement, for a practically free Quonset house.

Tiny Houses

The tiny house phenomenon swept the nation a few years back, and they are still very sought after. Everyone loves tiny homes . . . but there's no secret behind building one. You can build it out of any material or medium you want. Brick, wood, cob, adobe, metal, concrete, a converted shed, a 20-ft shipping container, just, well, tiny. Unless you'll be traveling with it; in which case, I have some bad news for you . . . Tiny houses aren't new. They've been around for a very long time, over a hundred years, it turns out. They're called campers or travel trailers. In fact if you look at some of the original campers, they looked just like the tiny homes of today. Campers have been sought after and have been around so long, they've streamlined and made every element of the tiny house geometry and materials extremely lightweight and aerodynamic for efficiency, every single element from the obvious—doors, couches, toilets—to the not so obvious—door handles, insulation, faucets, and plumbing. Campers even have their own very tiny very lightweight versions of home appliances like tiny microwaves, tiny fridges, tiny washing machines, tiny TVs and tiny blenders. So yeah, sorry, not a new thing.

Again, if you're not looking to do the design work, manufacturing, and construction, you can opt for a tiny home kit with easy-to-read instructions, leaving you only with building the slab or wheels.

Campers and Travel Trailers

Although it may not seem like it, some campers and travel trailers are very livable, long-term. Retirees and snowbirds alike live most, if not many years, in their travel "homes." It comes with all the fixings; it's a ready-to-go home that requires zero construction. You just need a septic tank or city sewer hookup, water hose, and extension cord, and you're ready to go. Lucia and I spent the first two years off the grid living in an 8-ft x 12-ft cab-over-camper. Now *that's* a "tiny house!"

Yurts

Originally from Mongolia, yurts come in kits from manufacturers like Rainer, Pacific, California, and Yurtco in sizes from 10 ft in diameter to 40 ft, at around $10 k for a 30-ft model. I've personally installed several and can attest to their craftsmanship. However, when you're ready to begin designing the interior, remember that, like domes or G-domes, yurt floor plans are tricky because you're not dealing with straight walls on any axis. I would also sub all wood for metal.

Steel Barndominiums

Steel structures aren't traditionally associated with the term "home," but that's changing. A Barndominium is a combination of shop, stable, or garage with living quarters. A dual-purposed option for those of us who enjoy our hobbies. Kits like these and Quonsets (page 165) take the engineering out, bringing cost and construction time down dramatically. Of course, you can repurpose and remodel an existing barn for superior savings or go with an A-frame or Quonset.

Geodomes

Geodome is another build-your-own or get-a-kit type home, making construction, and even design, super simple. There are lots of material options, from small diameter beams (rebar, PVC pipe, conduit) for small structures like pens, sheds, aviaries, and greenhouses to large beams (oil well or irrigation pipe, cee purlin, steel tubing) for larger buildings like barns, shops, houses, and warehouses.

Construction is simple; a person who is inexperienced, out-of-shape, or has poor physical health could put a 30-ft structure together in hours. But wrapping your mind around part fabrication is another matter. The problem lays in design. Everything has to fit perfectly, like a puzzle. You'll need to be semifamiliar with solving deep spherical trigonometry problems, and you'll need to know how to work 5-place trig tables with ten-plus formulas in order to create 3-dimensional vectors and coordinate systems, which will determine chord factor and strut length and angle. Kits are much simpler since all of the math and fabrication has been done for you.

That said, there are free geodome calculators and formulas online if you want to throw your hat into the ring.

CONVERSION HOMES

I enjoy this method because the basic construction is complete. By taking advantage of people's tendency to discard and abandon perfectly good stuff, we can convert something from its original purpose into a home, prolonging its life.

Boxcars, shipping containers, abandoned missile and grain silos, mines, caves, water and fuel tanks, buses, planes, boats, culverts, construction dumpsters, and poly tanks really accumulate around the country, especially near major ports and agricultural areas. The waste piles up, becoming an eyesore, and is often sold or auctioned cheaply, given away, or paid to be hauled away. Imagine, not only getting a free home, but getting paid to take it!

Shipping Containers

Shipping containers run between $1000 and $4000 depending on steel prices and demand. Shipping containers also make great cellars (page 246) or storm shelters.

MODULAR HOMES

The last method I'll go over is modular. Until now I've discussed component-built homes, meaning all components are built on-site. This is great for dealing with unforeseen problems leading to design and construction changes—of which you'll have *many*—but it can create new problems during construction attributed to snow, cold, rain, dark, sleet, wind, mud, sun, heat, and other weather. Modular buildings only differ in that all components are built in a climate controlled, clean, weather protected, well-lit, flat warehouse or factory. This makes construction not only more fun, easier, and more comfortable, but multiple times cheaper, faster, and stronger since the homes are better built. Each section or module, which includes walls, trusses, flooring, and everything else, is then transported to and assembled at the site. I've just started constructing in this fashion for logistical reasons, but the benefits are enormous.

METAL-FRAME HOMES

If you *must* go with non-traditional stick frame house construction, at least go with metal studs, opting for aluminum siding, vinyl siding, or brick veneer. Metal studs are cheaper than wood, they last longer, and you'll have the only fireproof house on the block!

Chapter 9: Water Harvesting

Forget about electricity, fuel, rope, toilet paper, houses, and even proteins and produce. Without water, you're not going to get very far.

WATERWAYS

Rivers and Streams

Moving water can not only provide a source of electricity, food, water, minerals, and materials but can heat and cool as well, making water access a critical addition to any homestead. Connecting for home use or irrigation is a simple matter of excavating trenches for pipelines and adding submersible or spiral pumps.

Rainwater Catchment

"Is rainwater safe to drink?" This is the question I get asked most, and it's the one I asked when we first moved off the grid. I purchased a water tester kit and TDS meter, which tests for solids, chemicals, and minerals, and tested city tap water, bottled water, and our rainwater. The FDA states that up to 500 ppm is safe to drink.

San Antonio city water was around 250 ppm, which is not bad. Seattle, one of the cleanest cities tested, 220 ppm; Miami, 280 ppm; bottled water, 150 ppm. Our rainwater was 25 ppm, no chorine, fluoride, heavy metals, etc., which makes sense. Rain is the most efficient filtration and purification method known.

For catchment, storage, and distribution, we're looking at piping water from your existing roof or gutters into water tanks or constructing dams to form reservoirs for runoff.

Sizing

The average person uses 10 gallons of water a day drinking, cooking, cleaning, showering, bathing pets, watering household plants, and more, multiplied by 5 if they use water toilets times 365 days a year times persons in your family. That's 18,250 gallons per year for a family of three. We've found, with conservation, a family can live comfortably using 5 gallons a day with a compost toilet, or 25 gallons without.

Use the formula $w \div p \div 0.623 + 2\% = a$, or water usage per year in gallons ÷ annual precipitation amount in inches ÷ precipitation to gallons per square foot conversion ratio + safety factor of 2%, to determine minimum catch basin area. Or you can use it to determine the roof size needed to catch the water quantity needed.

Check your water bill to find your water usage and the national weather channels website for mean annual rainfall for your area. One inch of rain striking an area of 1,000 ft² of impermeable surface generates 623 gal, or 0.623 gal per 1 ft². And because of first-flush systems, droughts, global warming, and other unforeseen climate change elements, add a safety factor of 1–2%.

EXAMPLE: 18250 gal per year ÷ 32 (Central Texas) ÷ .623 + 2% = 933 ft² area needed. Which means a roof measuring 30 x 31 ft is enough to provide water for your entire family.

To reverse the calculations in order to determine how much water your catch basin provides, use the formula: a x p x 0.623 – 2% = gallons.

Gutters

Any roofing material will work to direct water flow, even shingles. Size and install gutters appropriately to minimize overflow. This means calculating the square footage of each drainage area for each drainage edge: For a flat roof, simply multiply width by length, which gives us the size of one gutter. For gable roofs (2 sides) it's two gutters, one on each side. For a hip roof, we have four planes to deal with, which means four gutters. Multi-faceted hips and valleys in different configurations and directions require dozens.

Once you have area, multiply it by the maximum volume of rain possible for your location, which is available at local permit office or "Appendix D," Table D1 of the UPC manual in gallons per hour per square foot, and compare with the table to determine gutter size and incline.

EXAMPLE: Using the roof example above, 31 x 30 ft = 930 ft² x .023 gal per min per ft² (Central Texas) = 1587 gal per min, we see a standard 6-in gutter with a 1/16-in pitch will work.

IMPORTANT: Upsize 1 size for each 50-ft length of drainage edge to maintain 1 downspout and cistern per drainage edge. Otherwise, add 1 cistern and downspout per 50 ft, and divide the tank size accordingly. Expansion joints should also be placed 50 ft or more from the ends.

GALLONS PER GUTTER INCLINATION AND PITCH

Volume (gal)	Gutter Inclination			
Size/Pitch (in)	1/16		¼	½
3	340	480	680	960
4	720	1,020	1,440	2,040
5	1,250	1,760	2,500	3,540
6	1,920	2,720	3,840	5,840
7	2,760	3,900	5,520	7,800
8	3,980	5,600	7,960	11,200

Cisterns

In most cases, rainwater is cleaner than tap or even filtered water based on ppm. If in doubt, get a water sample of your roof runoff. If you haven't coated the roof with elastomeric, though, you may want to now.

To catch the runoff, storage tanks can be anything from intermediate bulk containers (IBCs) and concrete to plastic, fiberglass, wood, and metal, as long as it's able to hold the specified gallons of water for a determined time period. In wet regions, generally one month is plenty, whereas nine months is common in arid. For 1520.8 gallons per month water usage, one 1500-gallon polyethylene tank would work where refill rate is often. In the desert, you'd need ten times that or four 3500-gallon tanks.

MATERIALS

3-in gravel
sand
tanks
(optional) first-flush diverter
silicone
(1 per tank) 1½-in bulkhead fitting
(1 per tank) 1½-in mpt–slp adapter
(1 per tank) 1½-in fpt tee
(2 per tank) 1½ x ½-in mpt reducers
(1 per tank) 1½-in ball valve
(1 per tank) 12 x 17-in meter box
epoxy
(1 per foot of tank height) #4 plastic rebar chairs
(1 per tank) ½-in mpt–barb adapter

½-in clear tubing
(1 per tank) 3-in bulkhead fitting
(1 per tank) 3-in mpt–slip adapter
Sdr 35 PVC pipe
(1 per tank) 3-in 90° slip elbow
(1 per tank) 3-in slip sanitary tee
plastic downspout
(1 per tank) gutter to 3-in slip pipe adapter to gutter tee
(2 per tank) 3-in slip 90° elbow
(1 per tank) 3-in sanitary tee
3-in PVC pipe
(optional) 4 x 8-ft sheets of 1-in insulation
(optional) backfill

TOOLS

excavator
flat shovel
hoe
level or laser level
measuring tape

string
drill with ¼-in drill bit and ¾-in hole saw
jigsaw with coarse blade
sandpaper
plastic paint

1. Excavate (page 164) or grade and mark out 6-ft 6-in circles, times as many cisterns as you'll be installing, 1 ft 9 in deep. Fill with 3-in gravel or compacted sand.
2. Place tanks side by side if you're routing to a central location, or place them at each roof corner or downspout.

3. For roofs with a lot of debris, install a first-flush diverter directly into the gutter's downspout connection.
4. Trace and, using a jigsaw, cut out the shape of your downspout onto the top of the tank below the lid. Repeat for each tank.
5. Connect downspouts to gutter (or first-flush diverter) and into the holes of each tank, or directly over open cisterns.

   NOTE: In the desert or locations away from smog, pollution, and leaves, there's absolutely no reason to divert rainwater. Placing a screen over or in each downspout to keep bugs and rodents out is usually enough. Otherwise, install a first flush diverter, rain head, or roof washer.

   IMPORTANT: Open tanks aren't a good idea in any location due to evaporation and accumulation of organic debris, which decay and create anaerobic bacteria.

6. To plumb the tank into the home, install a length of appropriately sized PVC pipe, teed either directly into your home's water main, or in your pressure tank brass tank tee ("Pressure," page 176).
7. To kill bacteria and pathogens, add colloidal silver at 100 ppb (NASA ISS dose rate). To prevent growth, add bleach at a ratio of 1 T per 500 gallons, or throw a sacrificial anode (page 180) inside. For city dwellers, see "Filtration" on page 176 for fabrication and installation instructions.

UNDERGROUND WATER

Wells, springs, and some rivers are supplied by underground rivers or aquifers, which exist under almost every inch of earth. There are two types: confined, which are trapped by gravity in layers of waterproof material, usually clay; and unconfined, which are only trapped on one side's clay layer.

Water in the unconfined aquifer is going to be easier to reach and harvest, requiring only tens of feet of digging and a simple bucket to extract. Although accessing water trapped in the confined aquifer is more difficult to access and harvest, requiring digging down hundreds of feet, dropping hundreds of feet of cable and electrical wire and a pump.

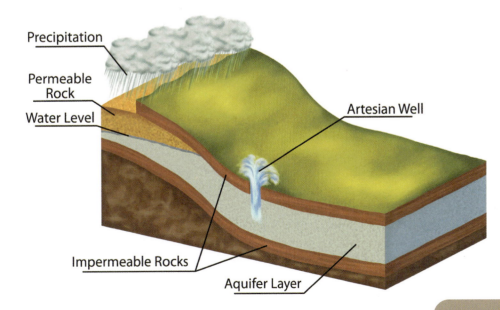

Precipitation

Permeable Rock

Water Level

Artesian Well

Impermeable Rocks

Aquifer Layer

Hand-Dug Well

Hand digging through a water table is impossible, even with a pump. And yet, we need to be as far into the table as possible to access water longer as the level fluctuates. So, start at the end of the dry season or during a drought, when the table is lowest.

MATERIALS
windless winch
8-gal buckets
bricks or solid CMUs
(optional) concrete well liners
¾-in hose

TOOLS
rope ascenders
¼-in rope
electrical pump
hard hat
extension ladders
harnesses
carabiners
trash pump
measuring tape
stakes
spade and flat shovels
pickaxe or mattock
plumb bob

1. Locate the lowest spot on your property, over 50 ft from septic fields and pens. Lay out and stake a 5-ft circle just above any flood plain on the house side. Dig as much as possible, using pick-mattock and shovel, using stakes and a plumb bob for reference and a 6-ft level, once inside.

    WARNING: Digging a well is dangerous. Never dig alone, egress at the first sign of collapse, and when not in work, cover with material that vehicles and animals can't break.

2. In all but the driest regions, digging down even just a few feet will cause water to infiltrate the well. You'll constantly be fighting mud and water, which makes everything harder and heavier. If you step away from the project for a couple days, or if it rains, pump and bucket out as much water as possible before continuing work.

3. When deeper than what can be thrown, install a windlass, 1-ft diameter pulley with rope ascender or friction knot, rope, and 8 gal buckets with screw-on lids; and don a hard hat.

    IMPORTANT: You don't want the handle that comes with the bucket; it breaks off easily. Remove the handle, and fabricate a new one from ⅛ x 1-in flat bar under and around the bucket ribs so the lid can be removed easily.

4. Check diameter and plumb frequently, having 1 assistant filling buckets and 2 up top removing them. Once deeper than an extension ladder's limits, chain multiple ladders together, tie a second rope every 10 ft, and use harnesses with rope ascenders on bucket line and carabiners for ladder.

5. Monitor your progress regularly as you pass through alternating layers of sand and clay. You'll be able to tell when you reach each layer by the presence of clay in the soil, typically after 10 ft.

6. When a good producing aquifer is reached, you'll notice that water infiltration speeds up significantly. Remove water using trash pump, and continue with as many workers, buckets, and ropes working on excavation that can fit.

7. Continue to the next clay layer, or to desired flow rate, then dry stack bricks lengthwise and perpendicular to the well wall. Or you can stack solid CMUs widthwise and parallel to the well wall, around the circumference of the well to 12 in above the water table, or for shallow wells, 35 in above grade. For deep wells, where cave-in may be a concern, install concrete well liners on top of brick or CMUs.

    NOTE: If excavation is mostly through rock, clay or other hard material, casing lining isn't necessary.

Photo credit: Lisaveya *Photo credit: Lisaveya* *Photo credit: Lisaveya*

8. Install bucket and windlass for an antique look or a modern electrical pump (page 174).

DISTRIBUTION

Now that we have all this water, what do we do with it? We have to move, filter, and pressurize it, if need be, and then we have to store it.
There are innumerable ways of doing this. Some fanatic, some fantastic, but unless bucket brigading is one, we're talking pumps.

Hand Pumps

- **Bucket (hand-dug well):** The simplest of pumps, the traditional windlass, lowers and raises a bucket into the well by reel.
- **Inertia pump (general use):** Install a handmade ball valve on the end of a long pipe and move it up and down inside casing. As the pipe descends, it fills with water, locking that water in place on the upstroke. Repeat the process and you get more vertical water movement until it breaches the top in surges.

  NOTE: For deeper wells, add a valve every 40 ft to distribute weight evenly. Otherwise, the weight will outweigh the applied downward force.

- **Hand crank (drum pump):** Living on a homestead where anything from rainwater to syrup, honey, and biodiesel is stored in 55-gallon drums, there's no escaping a good rotary hand crank, pump, or electrical drum pump for content extractions when filling up buckets, troughs, or vehicles. Most are built to screw right into the bung.
- **Yard hydrant (fire control):** A yard hydrant (page 181) is a great addition to any property, like a big spigot that allows quick access to clean, pressurized water without operating valves or pumping, and they can be installed anywhere, even in barns, feed stocks, front yards, and swimming pools, with or without a hose.
- **Pitcher pumps (well pump):** For wells shallower than 30 ft, you can get away with a pitcher or stand pump. They're easy to install and easy to work, with little chance of breaking. They even have a spout hook to hang a bucket.

Bucket   *Hand crank*   *Yard hydrant*

- **Flojak (well/emergency/general use):** Flojak is an easy to use, easy to install emergency back-up style hand pump that fits inside your existing well, given a large enough casing, supplying your home. The plastic construction makes it freeze proof but a little on the fragile side. It can also be used to pump out flooded areas, or pump water up from a creek or pond.
- **Bison (well pump):** Bison pumps are similar to pitcher pumps, but with a stainless steel construction and lift rods. They are a bit more technical to install, and more casing space is required to suit the 1½–3-in drop pipe, but they are able to pump at an astonishing 300 ft.
- **Simple (well pump):** Also installed as a backup or stand-alone, simple pumps are the top of the line hand pumps in cost, performance, material, and working depth, with a little more work than the others. They can even be connected to solar, wind, or bicycle power.

Pitcher pump

NOTE: When installing any of the deep well hand pumps, work the DP down around the torque arrestors to under 20 ft of the existing foot valve, which will take a little patience, but there's plenty of room. Also, there's a weep hole inside that leaks water to prevent freezing that should be plugged when used in non-freezing conditions. Otherwise, prime before each prolonged use and install a check valve before pressure tank to prevent back-draining your tank or house. Simple also makes a 1/5-hp 12V solar-powered motor that can be switched out for the arm.

- **Chain and piston (well pump):** A rope with flexible, or no, pistons, powered by hand, bicycle, animal, or electric motor for wells between 10 to 100 ft to 300 ft deep, 10–100 ft best operated by hand and 300 ft by dual handle, bicycle, or motor.

Electrical Pumps

Not all types of pumps are created equal. Electrical pumps have great pushing power but poor pulling. Jet pumps, though, employ a boosting design that assists in pulling by pushing water down a separate pipe. Some pumps are better for moving thick liquids like biodiesel; some can transfer partial solids, mud, and other garbage. For smaller, general pumps operated less than 24/7, brush motors are cheaper and heartier. For larger pumps running non-stop, brushless is more efficient, more powerful, and cooler.

Below are the most available, versatile, and reliable options that have worked well for me for different water moving applications:

ELECTRICAL PUMP APPLICATIONS AND ADVANTAGES

Type	Application	Type	Viscosity	Advantages
Centrifugal	All	Water	Medium	Best for thin liquids
Axial flow	Flood management, swamp cooler, and irrigation	Water	Medium	Best to for high flow rate at low head
Booster	Distribution, irrigation booster	Water	Medium	Allows pressure building for long distances and spraying at high pressure
Chopper	Where other pumps get plugged	Stringy material	Solid	Pumps liquids others can't
Circulator	Circulation	Water	Medium	In-line design
Drum	All	Corrosive	Thin, thick	used on drums
End suction	Transfer, circulation	Water	Medium	Lowest cost
Grinder	Black/grey water	Sewage	Thick	Accommodates smaller ID pipe
Jet	Well	Water		Lower cost than submersible
Multistage	Where higher pressure is needed	Water	Thin	Best high pressure, centrifugal option
Regenerative turbine	Gases	Vapor		Compact, for low flow and high head
Slurry	Mining, minerals processing, slurry transportation, dredging	Liquids, solids		Handles abrasive materials
Self-priming sump	Flood management	Water	Thin	Self-priming
Submersible	Flood management	Water	Thin	Submersible
Trash	Flood management, well drilling	Dirty water, mud, rocks, stone, and debris		Handles the largest of solids
Submersible well	Irrigation, potable water	Water	Thin	Silent, solar connectable
Positive displacement		Solids, fragile solids, shear sensitive	Thin, thick, solid	Best for higher viscosity, low flow, and high pressure
Concrete pump	Concrete work	Concrete, aggregate		For transferring and shotcrete applications
Diaphragm pumps		Corrosive	Solid	Seal-less, can run dry
Gear pumps		Oils and other viscous liquids	Thick	Few moving parts, simple construction
Plunger pumps	Pressure sprayer, reverse osmosis, wells	Water, detergents, crude oil	Thin	Best to achieve high pressures
Screw pumps	Fuel transfer, hydraulics	Oils, fuels, thick	Thick	Highest flow rate of positive displacement pumps

Well Pumps

The depth of your well will determine the type and size pump. Shallow well jet pumps can handle water flow up to 25 ft, whereas deep well or convertible jet pumps can move from 25ft to 100ft, and submersible well pumps, pumping water all the way up to 500 ft. A windmill-powered pump typically can pull water up to around 200 ft max.

Jet (25–150 ft at 1 hp): Single pipe convertible, a packer ejector, and horizontal well casing adapter is required to convert the casing itself into a pressure pipe. This is a better setup where you don't have a large enough casing to get 2 pipes inside. For open wells though, dropping two pipes is no problem:

MATERIALS

foot valve with strainer	poly pipe
(1–2) drop pipes	(2) stainless steel hose clamps
well seal	electrical caps
90 degree PVC fittings	circuit breaker
PVC pipe	wire

TOOLS

jet pump	various wrenches
PVC primer and cement	wire stripers
pipe cutters	

NOTE: Non open well deep well double pipe jet pumps require 3 to 4-in casings.

1. Install the barbed foot valve and strainer on the end of one PVC or poly drop pipe, or both, with stainless steel hose clamps and lower them down to 1 ft from bottom
2. Install the well seal (for closed wells), 90 degree fittings as needed, a length of horizontal rigid PVC pipe connected to the inlet (for shallow wells), and another length of pipe connected to the outlet (for deep wells).

   NOTE: If your foot valve doesn't come with a check valve in it, install one either above foot valve or at inlet.

3. Wire the pump to your circuit breaker panel on a dedicated breaker for the amperage of your pump.

Creek Pumps

Sometimes, the water you need is right in your backyard. Rather than digging your own well (page 172), all you need to do is install a pump that will pump water to your house from the nearest river or stream.

Water ram pump: Water flows via gravity into the module, typically a PVC pipe, which closes a flapper valve, causing it to fill with water. Once enough pressure builds inside, another flapper valve opens, allowing water to fill a sealed pressurized chamber. Water is then pushed out and up to the house or tank until an equalization between pressures (gravity-pump) is met, at which point water is rerouted to the pressure chamber, pressurizing under pneumatic pressure. Once a critical pressure limit is reached, the second flapper closes, forcing the pneumatic pressure to push the outlet water further up the pipe, 10–30 times higher than the original drop.

Siphon: Given the correct pipe size and slope using gravity alone, a siphon can move water long distances (miles, even traveling up and over terrain as long as the end is lower than the beginning. The siphon can be maintained with a manual or float shut-off valve at the bottom, shutting off when flow slows.

For example, if the water level of a rainwater catchment, tank, creek, pond, spring, or dam is already above the home's faucets, water can flow with gravity alone since there would be negative head.

NOTE: Just trench the pipes since hogs are known to chew through, especially in the desert.

Spiral pump: A waterwheel-looking contraption that causes positive displacement at low speeds. As long as the wheel turns from a stream, ocean, hand, or animal, there's output. This pump has low torque requirements, is low maintenance, with only 1 moving part. The Gravity Wheel converts river flow into water pressure through lift, creating head. It acts as a transformer, changing high volume–low pressure into low volume–high pressure.

PRESSURE

Water doesn't just come out of the ground pressurized, nor is it the pump's job. That task falls to gravity or a pressure tank.

Gravity: We're used to taking intense showers and rinsing dishes with a high-pressure spray; but gravity will distribute water just as well as your faucet. In fact, humans have always used gravity, like in New York storage tanks located on high rise roofs, or in town water towers. We can do the same by locating our storage tanks or cisterns (page 170) on hillsides, rooftops, or towers.

For every 1 ft we raise the water source we add 0.433 psi (static head pressure). For example, if our tank is sitting on a 10-ft stand, 17 ft up a hill, assuming a 7-ft shower head height and oversized pipes, we have 8.66 psi (10 ft + 17 ft - 7 ft = 20 ft x 0.433). At 50 ft, it's 21.65 psi.

Installing large diameter pipe, then reducing them at outlets will increase that pressure but will produce lower volume. For example, a 2-in pipe has a pressure potential of around 40 psi. Reducing the pipe to 1 in at faucet would increase pressure by about two times, giving 80 psi, which is typical city water pressure.

Pressure tank: Water pressure tanks run from 1 to 100 gallons or more. If you have three non-conservational people taking 30-minute showers simultaneously, you'll need a 100-gallon tank. A single conservative bather, or two at separate times, only need a 5–10-gallon tank. The tank has a rubber bladder inside filled with air at a set psi, typically 90 psi, which is easily adjustable.

1. For small tanks, install a ¾-in galvanized nipple and tee in the top of the tank with 1 leg routed through a 1-way shut-off valve to the pump and the other to the home's main.

    NOTE: If your pump's rated at 12 gpm, you'll need a tank large enough to give over 12 gpm draw down, or usable water, before pressure falls below the pump's pressure switch kick on level. If in doubt, go with a larger tank.

FILTRATION

Throughout the book, I discuss various filters like sifts, sieves, and screens. We use filters daily, not just for water but also fuel, grey and black water, pumps, air, dirt, food, and chemicals, depending on the size of contaminant or substance we wish to keep out.

Coffee, coffee strainers, vacuum bags, or jeans, all make good filters:

MICRON LIMITS AND CONTAMINANTS

Lower Micron Limit	Upper Micron Limit	Contaminant
0.3	0.4	Smoke, paint pigments
0.4	0.55	Bacteria
0.55	0.7	Lung damaging paint
0.7	1	Atmospheric dust
1	1.3	Molds
1.6	2.2	Flour mill dust
3	4	Cement dust
4	5.5	Pulverized coal
5.5	7	Commercial dust
7	10	Pollen
10	75	Silt
3	5	Clay
75	1000	Sand

MICRON MEASUREMENTS OF EVERYDAY MATERIALS

Material	Microns
Blue jeans	5
Cashmere	18
Coffee filter	20
Fine-grade wool	20
Flannels	28
Thick wool blanket	30
Nut milk bag	80
Nylon panty hose	100

Depending on size, a screen is excellent for removing hard particulates:
Mechanical sieves, micron cloth, and mesh filters also work for removing hard particulates, but they have different micron sizes and open areas:

SIEVE MESH SIZES FOR SIFTED MATERIAL

Sieve Mesh No.	Inches	Microns	Typical material
14	0.056	1400	Aquaponics
28	0.028	700	Beach sand
60	0.0098	250	Fine sand
100	0.0059	150	Biodiesel
200	0.003	74	Portland cement
325	0.0017	44	Silt
400	0.0015	37	Plant pollen

MESH SIZES

Mesh	Opening		Typical material
	Inches	Microns	
2	0.437	11100	76.40%
3	0.279	7087	70.10%
4	0.187	4750	56.00%
5	0.159	4039	63.20%
6	0.1318	3348	62.70%
7	0.108	2743	57.20%
8	0.0964	2449	60.20%
10	0.0742	1885	56.30%
11	0.073	1854	64.50%
12	0.0603	1532	51.80%
14	0.051	1295	51.00%
16	0.0445	1130	50.70%
18	0.0386	980	48.30%
20	0.034	864	46.20%
24	0.0277	704	44.20%
30	0.0203	516	37.10%
35	0.0176	447	37.90%
40	0.015	381	36.00%

Material filters are mechanical and chemical. They use the porous and absorbent nature of compounds like salt and charcoal for separation. But first, you will need a casing to hold the filter materials:

Casing

MATERIALS
¾-in bulkhead fitting
4-in PVC flat cap
18-in PVC pipe
4–4-in slp–mpt PVC adapter
4-in threaded PVC cap
¾ x ¾-in galvanized nipple
pressure gauge or pressure relief valve
(2) 4-in pipe or conduit clamps
x 16-in PVC pipe
(2) 3-in caps or plugs
¾-in galvanized nipple

TOOLS
drill
1⅝-in hole saw
measuring tape pencil
PVC primer and glue
1⁵⁄₁₆-in hole saw
¾-in fpt tap
2-in hole saw

1. For an outlet, drill a 1⅝-in hole, centered, and install a ¾-in bulkhead fitting (BHF) in a 4-in PVC flat cap.

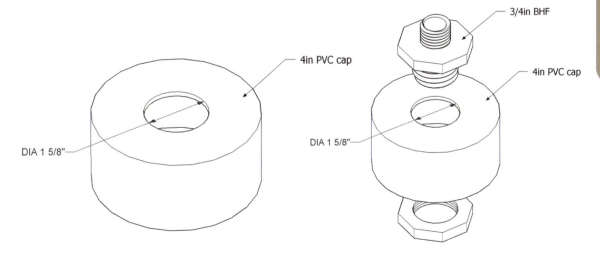

2 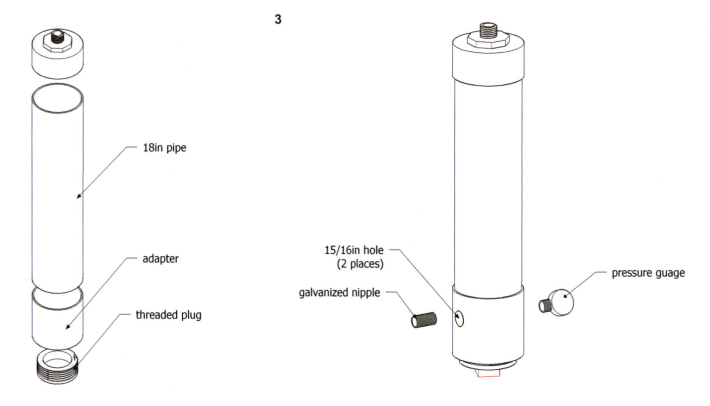 **3**

18in pipe

adapter

threaded plug

15/16in hole
(2 places)

galvanized nipple

pressure guage

2. Glue the cap onto an 18-in pipe and, on the other end, install a 4–4in slp–mpt adapter and threaded cap.

3. Drill (2) $^{15}/_{16}$-in holes in each side of the adapter wall through the pipe. Tap to ¾-in fpt and install a ¾ x ¾-in galvanized nipple as an inlet on one side and a pressure gauge or pressure relief valve in the other.

4. Mount upside down (plug up) on wall in system using (2) 4-in pipe or conduit clamps.

   NOTE: Build and connect as many parallel casings as desired to achieve faster filtration. Also, install shut-off valves on each side to remove and replace filters without losing water.

5. For the cartridge, drill, 2-in holes every 5 in around the circumference of a 3 x 16-in PVC pipe.

6. Glue 3-in caps or plugs (plugs have better clearance when inside casing) on top and bottom of cartridge, then drill, tap, and install a ¾-in galvanized nipple in the center of bottom cap.

7. Remove casing plug, insert cartridge inside casing, screwing cartridge inside the bulkhead fitting.

3

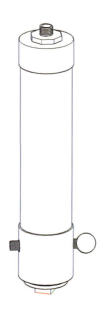

5

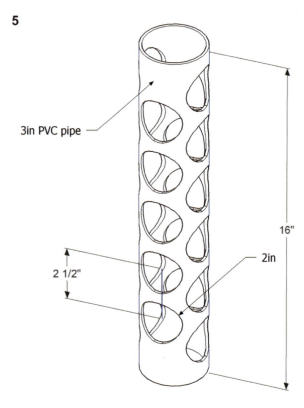

3in PVC pipe

16"

2in

2 1/2"

6

7

1

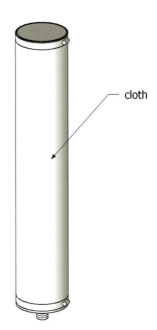

cloth

Screen Filter

Window screens are plentiful and cheap, but they don't filter out much more than large solids like sand, debris, organic material.

MATERIALS

9½ x 16-in   or woven wire
stainless   12 x 15-in stainless steel screen
steel rabbit   (2) stainless steel hose clamps

TOOLS

flat-head   screwdriver

1. Remove the cartridge from the casing canister. Wrap with 9½ x 16-in stainless steel rabbit or woven wire, followed by another layer of 12 x 15-in stainless steel screen, overlapping the edge by over 1 in. Secure with stainless steel hose clamps and return to canister.

    NOTE: Locate clamps at ends of cartridge to leave space for filter material.

Cloth Filter

Cloth filters a little more than screen, but not by much. Use cloth for removing water from materials and food stuffs.

MATERIALS

screen assembly
(1) sewn 4-in filter bag

1. Cover the above screen assembly with sewn 4-in filter bags.

1

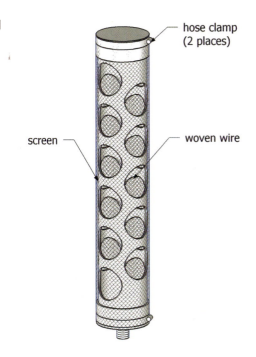

hose clamp
(2 places)

screen   woven wire

Biochar

Biochar is best suited for removing heavy metals, specifically zinc and copper.

1. Place a ¾-in faucet screen inside the bulkhead fitting (BHF). Then fill the casing cartridge with ground biochar. Replace woven wire, screen, and cloth filters.

    NOTE: You can also use regular activated virgin charcoal.

Carbon Scrubber

1. Fill the casing cartridge with pulverized 4–8 mm activated carbon, tap several dozen times to compact. Replace woven wire, screen and cloth filters.

    NOTE: Activated carbon from cedar, balsa or, coco shell is more porous and, therefore, works better for smaller contaminants under 20 Å where hard wood works better for larger contaminants over 50 Å.

Terracotta

Terracotta removes 95% of chlorine, pesticides, iron, aluminum, lead, and 99% of cryptosporidium, Guardia, and sediment. It does not remove fluoride.

Ceramic

Ceramic filters 99% of pathogenic bacteria including salmonella, cholera, and E. Coli, as well as cysts including cryptosporidium, sediment, organic chemicals, and lead. It will also reduce fluoride, heavy metals, nitrate, and arsenic.

Sacrificial Anodes

METAL ELECTRODE POTENTIAL AND VOLTAGE

Metal	Electrode potential E°, voltage
Gold	+0.42
Silver	+0.19
Stainless steel (AISI 304), passive state	+0.09
Copper	+0.02
Tin	-0.26
Stainless steel (AISI 304), active state	-0.29
Lead	-0.31
Steel	-0.46
Cadmium	-0.49
Aluminum	-0.51
Galvanized steel	-0.81
Zinc	-0.86
Magnesium	-1.36

When dissimilar metals come in contact, the less noble one becomes an anode and the more noble one a cathode, producing a galvanic cell, exchanging electrons, and releasing ions like a battery, which produces an electrical current, charging the water and distilling it through ionization. If you've ever drunk "ionized" water, you drank water that went through this process. Some metals are more noble or less than others. This electrode potential difference is specified in relation to one another in galvanic series. The electrode potential also changes depending on the fluid or electrolyte used. For example, the galvanic series of various metals in seawater is shown below:

Tin (-0.26 E°), lead (-0.31 E°), steel (-0.46 E°), aluminum (-0.51 E°), zinc (-0.86 E°), and magnesium, (-1.36 E°) when coupled with metals like gold (+0.42 E°), silver (+0.19 E°), stainless steel (+0.09 E°), and copper (+0.02 E°), all make great anodes

NOTE: The greater the voltage difference, the larger the plates, the stronger the current, and the cleaner the water.

Place the anode in pools, hot tubs, water heaters, swamp coolers, ponds, fish tanks, basically anywhere water is stagnant. Replace every three years.

STORAGE

There are hundreds of water storage options, from cisterns to septic tanks, to pools, ponds, and lakes, to vats and 5000-gallon poly tanks, and many more. Most are free or super cheap. You just have to be open-minded, creative, and willing to do some scrubbing:

- 35–50-gallon plastic garbage cans
- 65–95-gallon municipal roll-out garbage cans
- 30–55-gallon metal or plastic drums, which are free at most car washes
- Intermediate bulk containers, although not the best option, can be acquired anywhere
- Plastic kiddie pools: 3-ft pools hold 53 gallons; 4-ft, 94 gallons; 5-ft, 147 gallons
- 10,000-gallon vinyl above-ground pools, found in garage sales or curbside daily, or they are a few hundred bucks new
- Dumpsters: 2-yrd³ dumpsters hold 404 gallons; 4-yrd³, 808 gallons; 6-yrd³, 1,212 gallons; 8-yrd³, 1,616 gallons
- Construction dumpsters: 15-yrd³ dumpsters hold 3,030 gallons; 20-yrd³, 4,040 gallons; 30-yrd³, 6,060 gallons; 40-yrd³,12,120 gallons
- Old water, chemical, agricultural, or industrial storage tanks, standing or trailered
- 24-in PVC or concrete capped culverts. Concrete culverts are free since cities are converting to poly

- Fiberglass or concrete septic tanks
- Plastic or galvanized livestock stock tanks: 100-gallon, 169-gallon, 300-gallon, 390-gallon, 700-gallon
- Wood tank

NOTE: Bulkhead fittings are your best friend when piping into any tank. Familiarize yourself with their ID hole requirements and their inner styles (slip–slip, thread–thread, slp–thd, etc.). With the addition of containers, bulkhead fittings, and plumbing, you can build an array of permaculture systems from hydroponic media beds to fish farms, to water catchment systems, and much more. The versatility of creating your own rather than buying premade kits is endless, fascinating, and rewarding.

FIRE FIGHTING

Our homestead wasn't located "inside a 911 zone" nor did it have a physical address. When we did have problems, we were on our own. And if you weren't in the mood to be disturbed by a 2-person bucket brigade at 3am, you'd better have planned for some other means of handling the situation.

Yard Hydrants

Yard hydrants are basically quick-access, heavy-duty, full-flow spigots with a 2-in high flow discharge hose that, when paired with a high-pressure fire hose and carwash nozzle, can be permanently installed and easily unrolled in case of emergency.

Locate hydrants near crucial or hazard zones such as chemical lockers, battery banks, fuel stores, and, obviously, the house or barn. You can easily tap into any underground pressure pipe regardless of the source—pond, well, or cistern—with a simple tee. Anchor in place with a concrete column; there's going to be pulling involved. Once they're in place, use them fairly often to fill up buckets, stock tanks, test, wash your hands, or just for a refreshing drink. Anything to keep the seals working and the mechanisms from locking up when you need them the most.

Extinguishers

Similarly, locate portable extinguishers outside—not inside—utility rooms, kitchens, workshops, load centers, and other places a fire is likely to spring up. In the middle of a blaze, you don't want to be rushing into the middle of the fire to get to the extinguisher. And when choosing the extinguisher size, those 5-lb tanks are okay for the car, but keep the 20-lbers for the homestead.

IMPORTANT: Don't throw your extinguishers away. They can be repressurized, refilled, and repressurized again. Or emptied and pressurized with water.

Chapter 10: Waste Management

From hobbies, crafts, or construction scraps to packaging to human waste and food scraps and leftovers, to grass cuttings and construction materials, humans create a *lot* of waste. By converting the organic waste into compost and fertilizers; fixing, reusing, and repurposing materials and items to extend their life; recycling and upcycling everything we can into new materials and items; and turning the rest into fuel, we're able to achieve "zero waste." The good news is, everything degrades, biodegradable and non-biodegradable, if given enough time. We see this every day in nature, not so much in cities.

COMPOSTING

Whereas septic tanks and bio-digesters utilize anaerobic bacteria to break down organics into dark, rich fertilizer, composters use aerobic bacteria, along with fungi and other oxygen-loving microorganisms, which rapidly accelerate the decomposition process that would otherwise take years.

    The actual compost storage unit can be as basic as a pile right on the ground or a fifty-five–gallon plastic drum with holes or as complex as highly engineered bins. Whereas piles thrive allowing heat dissipation and liquid percolation, barrels keep animals from spreading contents and allows for easy mixing and rolling.

Kitchen Composter

A kitchen composter doesn't actually compost—at least it shouldn't—but it's needed, trust me (my wife). It is a bin meant to store food scraps inside your home, odorlessly. Otherwise, you'd be making trips outside five times a day. A large plastic container in the freezer works fine for daily storage, but a good five-gallon bucket can hold one to two weeks–worth of food scraps, depending on your household size.

    This is another one of those designs that I've had several iterations of, each one doing a little better job at keeping flies out and away from the food scraps. It wasn't until I visited a 94-year-old Hmong woman in North Carolina that I discovered the best, and probably oldest, method.

MATERIALS

5-gallon bucket

water

1. Fill a 5-gallon bucket half full of water.
2. Add food cuttings.
3. When full, decant water through a bucket sifter (see "Bucket Sifter" on page 64), placing scraps in compost pile.
4. That's it. And it's so simple and so obvious. It's exactly why modern toilets have water in them: it prevents the fly's from being attracted to and landing on our waste.

Pallet Compost Pile

A compost pile surrounded by four pallet walls is the easiest method of keeping compost localized and protected while maintaining the qualities of the pile itself.

MATERIALS
(7) plastic, or cedar, pallets
ranch wire or metal hangers

TOOLS
4-ft level
metal rake
hoe
spade shovel
wire cutters
4 ft x 8-ft tarp

1. Level a 3 x 8-ft area.
2. For the back and side walls, position 2 plastic or cedar pallets together widthwise, back to side, with the back inside and perpendicular to the side, with deck boards facing in. Repeat for the opposite side, mirrored.
3. Wrap and tie tops and bottoms of all touching pallets with wire hangers or wire. You can drill ¼-in holes through the vertical slats and thread wire through. Otherwise, just loop the wire around.

IMPORTANT: Don't use oak or pine pallets as they're biodegradable and will compost with the rest of the organics.

4. For front walls, position 2 pallets in front, leaving a 9-in (or 2 pallet's thickness) gap in the middle. Wrap and tie tops and bottoms of all touching pallets with hanger wire.
5. Slide 2 pallets back to back, perpendicularly into the gap as a divider, forming 2 chambers. Wrap and tie tops and bottoms of all touching pallets with hanger or wire.
6. Construct a carport-like cover or at the very least, cover the pallet composter with a tarp to keep the sun from overheating the pile and rainwater from leaching nutrients.

NOTE: If you live in an exceptionally dry and/or cold locale, line the inside with 12mil plastic, which will help trap in moisture and heat while preventing ventilation. Proper moisture and heat level is key. Too much moisture and anaerobes take over and odor develops; not enough and aerobes die of thirst. Too cold and aerobes can't function; too hot and they die of heat exhaustion.

2

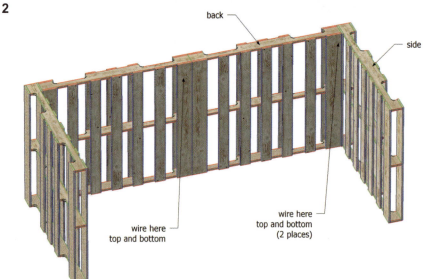

back
side
wire here top and bottom
wire here top and bottom (2 places)

4

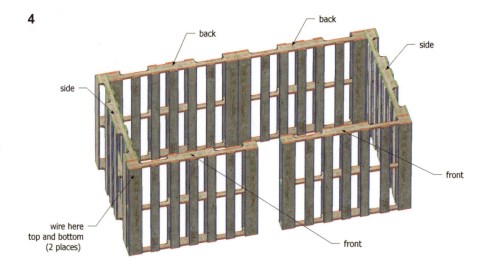

back
back
side
side
front
wire here top and bottom (2 places)
front

5

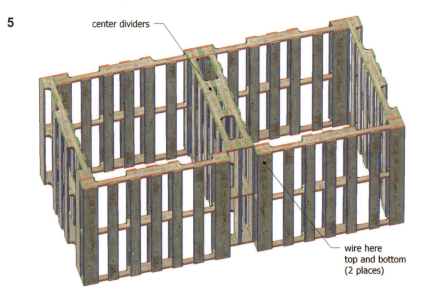

center dividers
wire here top and bottom (2 places)

7. Operation: Fill the bottom of the first chamber a few inches with branches and plant clippings to allow aeration, then fill at 1:2, brown–green items. Brown items are dry, carbon-rich items such as dead, dry lawn, plant clippings, leaves, wood branches, and pine needles. Green items are the wet, nitrogen-rich items such as plant and lawn clippings, leaves, food scraps, coffee grounds, tea bags. Add food scraps at 3:1 dry–wet, in between shovels of brown and green, alternating, adding 10% fiber in the form of paper, newspaper, paper bags, and cardboard (preferably shredded), or sawdust, wood shavings, straw, and hay.

    NOTE: Bacteria will break down meat and by-products, but since they attract pests, they're better suited for maggot farms or bio-digesters. And never introduce plants or weeds that have been treated with fungicides, herbicides, or pesticides.

    IMPORTANT: Compost piles should be at least 3 ft in diameter to generate enough heat for microbial reproduction, but no more than 6 ft high or pressure from the weight will prevent air from entering the bottom.

8. Try to maintain a proper balance of 40%–70% moisture. If contents are too wet or begin to smell, add more brown food scraps. If it's too dry or the composter fails to compost, add more green. Watering isn't necessary if the composter is covered unless contents are dry to the touch. Pierce the contents with rebar and mist it lightly with water, filling the punctures. To check interior moisture levels, stick rebar inside like an oil dipstick. Dry, rusty metal absorbs moisture well, so if upon removal the rod is damp, you're good.

9. Once full, open both doors (front pallets) by untying them from the dividers and, using a pitchfork, turn the contents by removing front pallets and flipping the pile into the empty chamber, placing the newest material on the bottom and the compost on top. Then begin filling the first chamber again. This not only mixes the contents in the second chamber but cools, aerates, spreads moisture, and oxygenates as well. For even better results, remove the middle divider and allow fowl access to the second chamber. Not only are the nutrients and bacteria they introduce highly beneficial but they also perform all the mixing work for you.

    IMPORTANT: As mentioned, odor indicates moisture levels and the need to turn. Interior temperatures also indicate turning times, with 140–160°F being normal and temperatures less than 130°F being a good indicator rotation is needed.

10. When the contents in the second chamber are cool and material is black and earthy smelling, composting is complete and you can remove and use the contents. The process can take two weeks in a moderate climate to four months in a cold one, and even years if the pile is abandoned. To test, fill a bucket with compost and water. Tightly cover the bucket with a lid and wait one week. When you remove the lid, there should be no smell if all the material has been composted since anaerobic bacteria will have nothing to eat. If there is an odor, something's wrong with your bin, causing the aerobic bacteria to die off. The problem most likely being not enough oxygen or too much heat, both resolved by turning the pile.

11. In theory, as you fill the contents in the first chamber, you're using the contents in the second so that, by the time you've filled the first chamber again, the second is completely empty (leaving a little compost on the bottom jump starts bacteria production) and ready for transfer. If this isn't the case and you're filling the first chamber faster than the second, you'll need to relocate the second chamber's contents for transfer. If, on the other hand, the second chamber's contents aren't finished composting in time for the transfer, add a second or even third filling chamber, making the pallet compost pile 3 or 4 (or more) chambers long.

12. Monitor both chambers and don't let the internal temps get above 160°F. To give you an idea, psychrophilic bacteria thrive in temps around 55°F. Mesophilic bacteria take over around 70°F to 100°F at which point thermophilic bacteria kick in, thriving between temps of 113°F and 160°F. If the temps higher than 160°F, bacteria will die off, slowing decomposition drastically.

Compost Toilet

Number two is the worst. We don't want to know about it or deal with it. Anyone who's had to access, maintain, or flush a septic tank can testify to its cruddyness. But unless someone is sick, the substance itself isn't actually dirty, diseased, or even contaminated with bacteria. It's what happens to the substance when stored that leads to putrefaction. By treating poop correctly, we eliminate the ugliness that *clings* to it.

Compost, or biological toilets break down bodily waste, commonly called humanure, into humus inside a self-contained system, completely disconnected from a sewer. Waste is deposited into a chamber which is rotated to ensure good air circulation and proper system health. The volume is reduced to 10% of original mass in three to twelve months, depending on the climate, waterlessly turning waste into want. Although compost toilets don't flush feces into a festering sewer system, they don't harbor germs, viruses, harmful bacteria or emit odor, making them, in most cases, more sanitary than current treatment methods.

Composting toilet pricing runs between $1000 to $2000. When moving off the grid, the first thing we did was purchase a top of the line unit. Before getting another style, I decided to do what I do best and design my own with recycled parts from my stage one and two bins. That was over ten years ago, and we still have the same one. That's longer than most people own conventional toilets. There's no moving parts or water to leak, so wear and tear is minimal.

MATERIALS

123-qt (36 x 13 x 13 in ID) or larger, Igloo ice chest
toilet seat
the Privy Kit Original 500 diverter or 3D printed urine diverter
PVC primer and cement
4-in slp–1in fpt PVC reducer adapter
1-in mpt–barb adapter
(2) 1-in Stainless Steel hose clamp
5 ft of 1-in hose
zip ties
(2) 1-in pipe brackets
(2) 3-in 45° Sch 40 elbows
silicone
3-in Sch 40 pipe

roofing butyl tape
3-in roof exhaust pipe boot
3-in exhaust pipe cap, wind turbine, or solar powered exhaust pipe
  air extractor
flat black spray paint
(4) 5-gallon buckets or square 27-lb kitty litter pails or equivalently
  sized containers
sawdust or peat moss
plastic scoop or cup
compost accelerator or 1 c compost
#10 x 1-in stainless steel countersunk screws
polyurethane or super glue
(4) ¼ x 3-in bolts (lag for wood, masonry anchors for concrete)

TOOLS

pencil
measuring tape
jigsaw with fine and coarse tooth blades
drill with ¼-in, ³⁄₁₆-in, ¼-in, and ¹⁵⁄₁₆-in drill bit
1-in and 3½-in hole saw

pliers
caulk gun
plumb bob
countersink
⅜-in wrench

1. For the container, I used an old Igloo ice chest, 123 qt or larger, or you can build a plastic box with an ID of 36 x 13 x 13 in, more or less.

2. Position the toilet seat in a comfortable location on either end of the ice chest lid so that it's sitting not too far forward or back and is centered, compensating for the ice chest's 1.5 in wall thickness. Lift the lid and mark position.

NOTE: The forward edge of the seat should sit flush with or slightly cantilevered to the forward outside wall of the ice chest.

3. Place and trace the location of the urine diverter flange. If your flange has an outside edge with a shape other than the inside flange contour, you'll need to cut it using a jigsaw with a fine tooth blade so that the two patterns are the same, leaving at least a 1-in border. This will help to facilitate cutting in the next step.

IMPORTANT: In order for the toilet to remain odorless, liquids must be kept separate. This is achieved with a urine diverter, the Privy Kit Original 500, which runs for $129 if ordered online at ecovita.net, so we printed ours using a 3D printer, imitating their design.

4. Draw the diverter's inside edge by subtracting 1 in (or your diverter's lip width), drill a ¼-in hole anywhere on the line, and cut using a jigsaw with a coarse blade. Place the diverter inside and check for proper fit, positioning, and flushness. Trim as needed.

NOTE: In this configuration, the toilet sticks out from the wall 2 to 3 times farther than conventional. If space is limited, turn the toilet seat and diverter diverter 90°.

5. Replace the toilet seat centered over the diverter and check that the alignment is still good. Mark hinge hole placement and drill (2) ⁵⁄₁₆-in holes and install ⁵⁄₁₆-in plastic bolts and nuts.

6. Remove and relocate hinges to the back of the ice chest if applicable.

7. If you're not replacing an existing toilet, skip to step 10. But if you're replacing an existing toilet, remove your old toilet, wax ring, and closet flange; then clean, prime, and glue a 4 in slp–1 in fpt PVC reducer adapter inside the closet flange, followed by a 1 in mpt–barb adapter.

8. Measure and mark the location of the barbed adapter onto the bottom of the body so that the compost toilet sits where you'd like it to, typically 13 in from the back outside wall, and drill a 1-in hole through body's bottom. Otherwise, if this is a new installation, drill the hole wherever you'd like the drain line to be located or use the existing ice chest drain hole.

9. Connect 5 ft of 1-in hose to the barbed adapter and the other end to the diverter with stainless steel hose clamps, then seat the cooler in position, pulling the hose through. Remove handles if necessary to achieve a flush fit.

NOTE: If you want to collect the urine to make urea (see "Urea" on page 77), add another 1 ft to the length of your cooler's ID, drill a 1 in hole in the lid of a 2.5-gallon bucket (or other equivalent plastic container). Place the bucket anywhere inside, inline, and route a hose to the bucket. Empty daily.

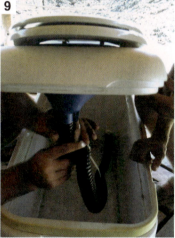

10. If you're not replacing an existing toilet, loop hose 8 in down from the diverter and secure it with zip ties for a water trap. (Optional) Secure hose to the underside of the body lid using 1-in pipe brackets.

11. Drill a 3½-in hole in the body (either side, or back) 2 ¾ in OC down and install (2) 3-in 45° Sch 40 elbows using silicone.

12. Drop a plumb bob from the ceiling to the center of the elbow and drill a 3½ in hole in your ceiling, repeating in your attic, if applicable, and roof.

13. Measure the distance from the elbow to the top of the roof, add 1 ft and cut a length of 3-in Sch 40 pipe to match. Install pipe using silicone and roofing butyl.

NOTE: Add 45° elbows as needed to circumnavigate rafters or other items.

14. On top of the roof, install a 3-in roof exhaust pipe boot and exhaust pipe cap. To help extract the off gases, paint the cap and pipe flat black or install a wind or solar powered exhaust pipe air extractor instead.

NOTE: Because dryness is critical, the venting system needs to be twice the size of the conventional 1½ in. Also stay away from 90° in lieu of 45°.

 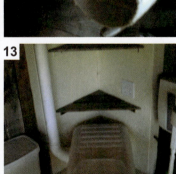  

15. Place (3) 5-gallon buckets or square 27-lb kitty litter pails or equivalently sized containers filled with halfway with sawdust or peat moss and 1 T compost accelerator or 1 c compost inside with the first directly below the diverter.

    NOTE: The diverter is contoured specifically to fit inside a 5-gallon buckets.

16. Close the cooler lid, make any final adjustments to the diverter, then drill ³⁄₁₆-in holes around the diverter lip, centered, every 1½–2 in. Countersink and install #10 x 1-in stainless steel screws. (Optional) Cap with polyurethane or super glue (see "Super Glue" on page 44) to help facilitate cleaning.

17. Secure the compost toilet to the floor by drilling (4) ¼ in holes on the inside bottom of the body, and install (4) ¼ x 3-in bolts. Lag for wood floors and masonry anchors for concrete.

18. It helps to keep a peat/sawdust container with a plastic scoop near for easy access. Place magazines in back to fill the space, and a footstool in front if needed.

IMPORTANT: Compost toilets don't break down paper well. Using regular toilet paper won't affect the breakdown process, but it will fill the buckets faster. I strongly suggest placing toilet paper in a plastic-bag-lined basket or use biodegradable paper. Also, sitting on a higher seat may feel weird at first, but it will pass and you'll find the extra height more comfortable. For children, add a plastic step.

19. Operation: Operate normally, minus flushing. Sprinkle ¼ in of peat moss or sawdust over feces after each use. Once the first bin becomes 7/8ths full, lift the lid, remove the last bin in the back, slide the front two back, and place last in front. When all are full, remove the last bin, slide the front two back, and spread the last's contents around your garden, bushes, trees, or plants, leaving a small amount of compost to seed and accelerate the next batch. Repeat.

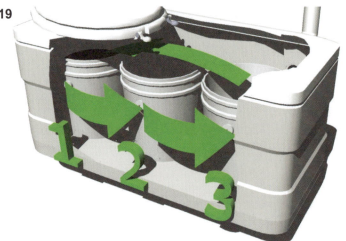

Tips and Trouble Shooting

There are Flies!

Air is pulled in through the toilet seat and passes over the bucket tops, pulling moisture from the media, drying out and decomposing solids in the buckets in the process. By design, there should never be flies or larvae. If there are, something's wrong, probably liquids mixing with solids, which is usually more of an issue for the ladies and is easily remedied with simple how-to-use instructions. If the problem persists, especially if you live in a humid climate, make sure the exhaust vent is screened. You can add scouring pads, scrubbing sponges, or a stainless-steel screen to the inside outlet, and remove the toilet seat feet so it sits flush.

The bins fill up in days!

A bin should fill in one month with two people using it full time, four part time, or ten seasonally.
If empty bins are filling faster, use only biodegradable toilet paper or don't use any paper at all, or add a second compost toilet in the house.

It's not composting!

When dumping your waste, you should notice several things proving that decomposition has taken place: the volume is less than 50%, there are no discernible shapes, and it has an earthy smell.

Air inside the unit becomes warm due to heat generated by the microbes, which naturally rises, drawing humid air up and out through the pipe, sucking fresh, dry air into the bins through the seat, which is why there's no smell. If outside or inside air is humid or too heavy to pull, air circulation stops, halting composting. Incorporate a roof fan or dehumidifier.

If contents still won't compost, it's okay, just place the bins in a covered area with a vented lid or screen for another month, replacing each with an empty bucket.

Compost Activator

Compost activator is just a food source for aerobic bacteria to consume and multiply. Adding 1 T sprinkled around compost assists and speeds up the decomposition period greatly.

MATERIALS
1 T BMO (page 74)

TOOLS
spray bottle with water

1. Mist manure lightly with water and sprinkle 1 T of a BMO (page 74). Otherwise, there's no better activator than the top 4-in of a proven compost pile.

   NOTE: Manure (page 76) is a perfect food for BMOs to flourish. If you haven't made any BMOs, you can use black, rich soil, not from a garden or lawn, at a 1:1 ratio with manure.

TRASH

Like "weeds," there's really no such thing as "trash." Everything, and I mean everything, can be used. There comes a point however, that the amount of work that goes into breaking down and reusing or recycling an object is more than what the object can provide back, which makes the process inefficient and not practical, leaving burning or burying, neither of which are extremely ecologically friendly. The question is, then, is it better for the environment to burn your trash or have it hauled off to the dump, where they bury it?

Burying trash, also known as carbon sequestering, what a strange mentality. Let's call a spade a spade here . . . We're sweeping our waste under the rug, literally a rug of sod—and probably some old rugs, too—to let someone else deal with later. The only difference between the two methods is the additional carbons released from transporting the garbage to its final resting spot. For the dump, that means the CO_2 I exhale dragging it to the curb; the CO_2, CO, PM, HC, NOx, SO_2, and greenhouse gases released by the garbage truck hauling it to the dump; and the same released at the dump by bulldozers. For burning, on the other hand, it's just the CO_2 we off-gas carrying the garbage to the burn barrel.

In both instances, the molecular bonds break, releasing gases. One, burning, does it violently and quickly through pyrolysis, and the other, carbon sequestering, does it slowly over time, photovoltaically or biologically. The same amount of compounds are going to be released from the trash into the atmosphere and environment whether it's during our time or our great, greatgrandchildren's. So, either way, the problem isn't how to dispose of garbage, it's how not to create it.

But for now, burning your trash is the easiest, most energy efficient, and most environmentally friendly method.

Burn Barrels

MATERIALS
55-gallon metal drum.

TOOLS
Cutting torch
Drill with ½in drill bit or a pickaxe

1. Using a cutting torch, cut out the lid of a 55-gallon metal drum.
2. Flip the drum upside down and drill ½ in holes every 1 ft or so around the sides and bottom.
3. Place the barrel away from flammable materials and dry leaves or grass.

Burn Pit

Burn barrels rust out fairly fast, in five years or so. A burn pit lasts forever. A burn pit can be as simple as digging a big hole in the ground. Once it fills up, cover it with dirt.

Burn Chamber

A burn chamber is good in areas where forest fires are prevalent or if you just want to keep dogs and other pests from pulling your garbage out of your pit and spreading it around the yard.

MATERIALS
(26) 8 x 8 x 16-in CMUs
(3) 8 x 8 x 8-in CMUs

1. Lay out and pour a 4 x 8 ft concrete pad (see "Concrete" on page 62) and stack dry CMUs (see "CMU Construction") on top, 6 along the back and 2.5 along the sides and middle, parallel with the sides. Leave the front open. Repeat for a second row, 5, 3, 3, 3, continuing 6-plus high.
2. Operation: At the end of the week, or when your trash cans are full, dump your trash into either cubby, burn, and repeat. Once one side is full, start using the other while you shovel out the ashes.

   NOTE: To cover the front, simply lay a sheet of 16ga diamond-cut steel mesh over when not in use.

Chapter 11: Homesteading Animals

Generations ago, families lived apart from society raising livestock to generate income. Even your grandfather may have butchered an occasional chicken, but those days are long gone. Today, farms and farmers auction their stock and buy groceries on the way home. But you can turn back the clock and create your own self-sufficient homestead by implementing a few elements of ancient animal husbandry. Understanding which animals are best for companions, security, pest control, and—yes of course food—as well as which do best in your region will help you have a successful homestead.

Roles

Pairing an animal with climate is the most important consideration. For example, since we shared a desert with mountain lions, we chose Rhodesian Ridgebacks (which hunt lions in Africa) as livestock dogs over typical border collies (which are from Northern Europe). Can you imagine a dog that's bred for maximum temperature of 80° chasing lions in 105°? Personal choice cannot outweigh health and comfort considerations. Even if that animal performs better at a specific task, that doesn't mean it's suitable for or will perform as well at your location.

After considering climate, you must determine your land and structure needs. Animals need open space to run (½ acre per burro or donkey, 250-300 ft² per chicken or duck, ¼ to ⅙ acre per goat or sheep, ⅒ acre per pig), clean dirt for bathing, clean drinking water, and water to keep cool. They need a structure or tree to get out of the sun, as well as abrasive surfaces to file down their hooves/nails. If natural surfaces like boulders, gravel, rocks, sand are not present, man-made surfaces such as concrete driveways, patios, pads, ramps, stone steps, faux boulders will need to be added.

I've categorized the following towards small homesteading families, as a bottom-line basis, to allow scaling and adding, based on ease of management, efficiency, behavioral traits, production or reproduction rates, and levels of comfort for average North American temperatures and terrain. Design your own, using your own criteria!

Work

Burro—the most dedicated work horse of the lot, they are always eager to lend a helping hoof.

Camels—in our neck of the woods (desert), horses don't last and require more water than nature provides. Their workload is better suited for camels or burros.

Goats—pound for pound, they carry more. And you won't find a better landscaper. Let them roam free gobbling grass, vacuuming leaves, clearing weeds and pruning trees, or stake in place to clear parcels. No more raking leaves or mowing lawns.

Chickens—for tilling, let your flock-o-fowl access the field and gardens after harvest to eat the waste and till, adding fertilizer before you replant.

Security

Dogs—they are obviously the first line of security. Humans have spent over 40,000 years genetically modifying dogs for security. Long before humans ever milked cows, raised chickens, or herded goats, even before farming or written language, they had dogs. From the Great Dane to the Chihuahua, once integrated into the family, dogs make great security systems. Again, the best dog for you depends on your climate. You could have the best security dog in the world (widely accepted to be the Akita), but if it's overheating, it can't think or function properly. Some other well-known breeds are Doberman Pinscher, German Shepherd, and Pit Bulls. My personal favorite, again because we're in hot climates, is the Rhodesian Ridgeback.

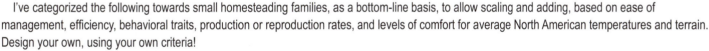

Guineas—they warn when predators encroach, signaling guard animals into action.

Pigs—when kept inside coops, they will keep small to medium predators at bay, especially at night when fowl won't flee.

Burros and Llamas—I was told to keep burros or llamas with my herd. Their level of job commitment wasn't fully realized until ours showed up with gashes in her face. I assumed she'd been attacked by a lion, but when I found a dead lion, I realized she was the aggressor. A burro's neck/jaw muscles can break bone. If the lion had attacked, our burro would have had rump and leg tears. Face damage suggests offensive wounds. I put 37 sutures in her mouth and face. What a badass!

Pest Control

Poultry—they consume seed, grass and insects, including spiders, scorpions, centipedes, and deter snakes, shuffling through brush. Include tick gobbling guineas to roam outer property limits, as chickens will only patrol the immediate vicinity.

Cats—they manage an onslaught of spiders, cockroaches, scorpions, mice, rats, and snakes (by killing and removing their food supply). I suggest Maine Coons, servals, and Savannahs, with the highest feline kill rate at 50%. In comparison, domestic cats have a 10% kill rate.

Bees—these keep stinging creatures away. Wasps are their natural enemy.

Bats and Purple Martins—common brown bats consume 7,000 mosquito-sized insects each night. To eradicate beetles, stinkbugs, grasshoppers, wasps, flies, dragonflies, and even fire ants, Purple Martins are your go-to-bird, scarfing down 1,200 insects a night.

Reptiles—we do encourage turtles, frogs, and even some snakes, since they displace venomous snakes by eating their food supply and them, and since they're also a food source for us.

Fish—control mosquito larvae (specifically mosquito fish and fathead minnows).

Anteater—my greatest discovery. They'll make their rounds from nest to hill, slurping up to 30,000 bugs a day. In Texas, they eat fire ants, termites, pine beetles, and other destructive creatures which are critical to tree decomposition but catastrophic to anyone using deadfall for lumber.

Bovines vs. Ovines

Texas is cowboy and cattle country, so probably the last thing you'd expect to read from a book about a Texas homestead is to never keep cows or horses. Why didn't I just jump on the bandwagon and buy some cows? Because I'm not a sheep. And goats are better in so many ways:

- Goat's milk is tastier. That's why higher-priced milk, cheese, cottage cheese, desserts, etc. are made from it.
- The lower sugar/higher butterfat content makes it easier to digest by those lactose intolerant.
- It contains less casein, smaller fat molecules, higher mineral and vitamin content, and 2% curd (vs. cow milk 10%), making it healthier.
- Virus and bacteria growth is more widespread in cow's milk because it causes an acidic reaction, rather than alkaline, as in goat (and human) milk. This is why cow's milk produced in a factory should be pasteurized while goat's milk can and should be consumed raw.
- Goat's milk doesn't need to be homogenized; it's already naturally homogenized.
- Goat's meat is healthier and leaner because they internalize their fat around organs; whereas cows externalize theirs around meat. This is why cabrito/lamb is used more in fine dining and health food stores and is priced higher.
- Goat meat is higher protein and lower in cholesterol than cow (or even skinned chicken).
- Goats are easier to handle and transport. They're not skittish in trailers and will even ride in a truck (or car, thanks Lucia!).
- They possess higher intelligence and can comprehend, learn, follow directions, and work more efficiently, and are often kept as pets over dogs for these same traits. My goats know how to come, get, go there, lead, pull a cart, pack, fetch, sit, stand, and "find your babies" (that's an important one).
- If a family of three butchered a cow, they'd have 750 lbs of meat to store! You would fill a large deep freezer hold and your fridge freezer, leaving no space for anything else. That's a 100% beef diet for the next six months at 2 lbs a day per person. If that doesn't kill you, and you survive the increase in your electric bill, I don't think you'll want to butcher another cow! On the other hand, bucklings weigh 30 lbs (200 lbs for bucks) which means you could fit two in a fridge freezer with space for other food.
- Goats' leather is stronger, more durable, and lasts longer; and the mohair/wool can be used or sold.
- Since goats have a varied diet, their manure contains a richer source of minerals and nutrients, won't burn plants, and is drier, lower in odor, and easier to use and store.
- Goats eat anything and therefore don't need to be fed. Cattle only eat specific expensive, water-hungry grasses. Imagine not feeding a herd of cattle or ever watering pastures. You'd have a herd of dead cows.
- Goats thrive in any terrain, consuming food inaccessible to cows. You don't need to decimate a forest, uproot foliage, and flatten landscaping to plant genetically modified crops.

- Due to their flex hoof and light weight, they don't stomp and crush food, killing it forever. Cows are grazers while goats are foragers. If cows are left in a field, they traverse from one end to the other, consuming every blade and kicking up every root, leaving a dustbowl and killing everything when it rains under their weight. Goats prefer dead or dry growth first, then tops, skipping plants between bites (foraging), giving plants time to drop seed and regrow. They've evolved from desert conditions where if they kill plants, they kill their lineage.
- Higher cost in fencing—for cattle you need at least 12 gauge wire but only 16 to18 gauge for goats.

Cows are farmed for bulk food to feed the masses and increase owner profit, which works. Distributing mass beef carcasses is highly profitable and the masses love them. However, in terms of taste, health, individual cost, ease of management, and environmental impact, cows just aren't as efficient as goats.

Horse vs. Mule vs. Burro vs. Donkey

Donkeys are shorter (3 to 4 ft) with shorter jaw bones, ears, legs, and longer hair. They came from England, excel in colder environments, and (should) live predominantly in the Northeast. Burros, entered with Spaniards. They're taller, with longer jaws and ears and short hair, and are therefore better suited to heat. Horses come in many breeds from many locales. Mules are usually sterile being the offspring of the three. Consider these comparisons:

- Although great transportation, since the average homestead is only a few acres, there's little need or space for horses.
- For labor, all work well, but burros possess more stamina and convert food to energy more efficiently. Horses naturally compete, making them harder to handle and break, whereas burros work together, hardly fight, and are easier and calmer to work with. They draw, load, and even ride softer (no posting).
- Burros are more intelligent, won't panic and run like horses when frightened but rather stop, study, and calculate. This is often misconstrued as stubbornness.
- Horses are standoffish and easily annoyed. Burros are just full of love (says Lucia).
- For security, burros' larger ears and eyes provide wider radar.
- Burros' hooves are smaller, harder, and have more spring, which is why they can climb and don't need to be shod.
- Like goats, burros consume a wider array of vegetation by foraging and grazing on food horses would never touch.
- Like cows, horses can't take heat as well as burros or goats. Even in normal environments, they need access to much more water.
- Burros are cheaper. You can purchase 10 for the price of 1 draft horse.
- Burros are less prone to disease and injury and have lifespans of 30-50 years vs 25-30 for horses.

There's a behavioral trait in burros that only intelligent mammals (higher primates, whales, dolphins) possess. They care for the safety and well-being of smaller living things. Dogs, cats, goats, turkeys, etc. will walk around or between their legs without the slightest stir. I've seen burros raise a hind leg to let a chicken by, or step over a tiny plant or flower to avoid crushing it.

Nutrients

Like growing to produce, we don't want to raise to sustain, we want to raise to produce. The following is the typical daily dietary nutrient intake requirements which must be made available through free ranging, food scraps, insects, supplements or feed (or other) to sustain and replenish product and bi-product production. Conversely, if the following aren't made available production of product and byproduct will plummet or cease, growth will be stunted, and disease could occur.

REQUIRED NUTRIENTS[6]

	Nutrient	unit//kg/ d	Animal				
			Cows	Swine	Birds	Goats	Fish
	DMI - Dry Matter Intake	kg	10.88	2.72	.113	1.36	.048
	Fiber	g	10	1.77	.75	1.65	1.5
	ME - Metabolizable Energy	MJ	76	36.91	.65	6	7
	CP - Crude Protein	g	.554	1.425	8	145	2
	Water	lt	.15–.26	.02–.03	0.2–0.6	.025–.04	0

	Nutrient	unit//kg/ d	Animal				
			Cows	Swine	Birds	Goats	Fish
Amino acids profile Major minerals	Lysine	g	.22	.091	.05	.35	.76
	Methionine	g	.044	.03	.3	.35	.022
			.044	.03	.3		.025
			.012	.011	.07		.005
	Cystine	g	.044	.03	.3	0	.022
	Tryptophan	g	.044	.03	.3	.11	.025
			.012	.011	.07		.005
	Threonine	g	.05	.038	.25	.5	.02
	Valine	g	.06	.04	.3	.57	.03
	Arginine	g	.031	.05	.37	1.15	.035
	Glycine/Serine	g	0	0	.27	.35	0
	Histidine	g	.033	.018	.09	.35	.015
	Isoleucine	g	.057	.033	.27	..46	.02
	Leucine	g	.088	.055	.4	.95	.035
	Methionine	g	0	0	.17	..17	0
	Phenylalanine	g	0	.03	.22	.6	0
	Phenylalanine	g	.083	.055	.44	.92	.046
			.083	.055	.44	.72	.046
			0	0	.55	1.12	
	Tyrosine	g	.083	.055	.44	.92	.046
	Linoleic	g	.083	.055	.44	.72	.046
			0	0	.55	1.12	
	N-3 fatty	g	0	0	0	0.305	0.025
	N-6 fatty	g	0	0	0	1.43	0.025
	Calcium	g	.054	.085	1.9	1.7	0.025
Major minerals Minor Minerals	Phosphorus	g	.04	.085	0.17	1.25	0.01
	Magnesium	g	.015	.05	0.025	.51	0.00
	Sulphur	g	.02	0	.035	0.16	0
	Sodium	g	.01	.02	0.082	0.23	0.015
	Chlorine	g	.012	.015	.03	0.25	0.02
	Potassium	g	.05	.04	0.082	0.45	0.015
	Copper	mg	.129	.15	0.44	10.45	0.005

	Nutrient	unit//kg/ d	Animal				
			Cows	Swine	Birds	Goats	Fish
Minor Minerals Vitamins	Iron	mg	.322	1.5	2.75	35	0.15
	Iodine	mg	.005	.002	0.015	.64	0.005
	Cobalt	mg	.001	.0005	.003	0.05	0
	Selenium	mg	.001	.002	0.005	0.14	0.0005
	Zinc	mg	.43	1.5	2.75	112	0.05
	Manganese	mg	.43	.36	1.65	35.74	0.033
	A	Iu	34.375	100	220	8690.73	6.4
Vitamins	D	Iu	3.437	15	27	663.255	6.15
	E	Iu	.206	.4	0.27	0.1	0.13
	K	mg	0	.04	0.025	0.35	0
	Riboflavin	mg	.04	.09	0.12	3.55	0.01
	Niacin	mg	.5	.5	.6	55.1	0.025
	Pantothenic acid	mg	.2	.3	0.12	9.35	0.05
	B	mg	.003	.0004	.0002	1.753	.0001
	Folic acid	mg	.03	.015	.007	.753	0
	Biotin	mg	.005	.002	0.005	0.045	0.005
	Choline	mg	2.3	5	3	666	2.55
	Pyridoxine	mg	.05	.137	.07	5.12	0
	B12	mg	.004	.01	0.005	11.5	2.5
	Folacin	mcg	.015	.022	0.01	1.2	.001
	Thiamin	mg	.04	.09	0.04	5.56	0.005
	Folate	mg	.003	.007	.003	1.2	0.005
	Vitamin B6	mcg	0	.001	0	0.6	0.005
	Myoinsitol	mg	0	.0003	.0001	0.45	.75
	C	mg	0	0	0	1.6	0.13

Supplements—Required nutrient amounts in table are given for non-working/non-stressed/non-producing, adult animals living in a temperate climate. Add 15% to the above numbers for young growing animals, pregnant animals, or those producing product or bi-product, as they will always have greater requirements. This is especially true for infants since as the animal grows, more energy is needed. In all animals of any stage or age, the biggest requirements are protein, calcium, and water since they're lost daily in production. The good news is that nature is filled with these. We know this is true because, again, birds and reptiles have been laying eggs, and mammals have been drinking milk for millions of years. That said, in a small (backyard) environment, you have no other choice but to supplement. Use "Required Nutrients" table and food source types listed in following tables to determine which nutrients are lacking, and therefore need to be supplemented. Then download a *nutrient content from common feeds chart* to determine which sources have which nutrients in what amounts (https://infonet-biovision.org/AnimalHealth/Animal-nutrition-and-feed-rations has a few good ones).

For example, you see that chickens need 16 g-CP, you don't have time (or desire) to grow meal worms and your grass only yard is CP low. By making protein (be it store bought or homemade) available throughout the day, they're receiving a balanced diet. On the other hand, if soybean (which is CP high) were cultivated or a bug-zapper installed, no protein, but still fiber, would need to be supplemented instead.

Needed supplements should be made available separately in bowls. Animals know when they need more iron, calcium, protein, etc., and eat only what's required, often leaving other bowls untouched. Otherwise, vitamin, calcium, and mineral lick blocks can also be made or bought and placed around.

Free-ranging

To the best of my knowledge, there are no true free-range (non-fed) animals. I ordered "100% Free-Range Laying Hens" from major breeders, and all stopped laying. After eliminating typical causes, I questioned their 100% free-range definition. To me, 100% of their dietary intake would come from the range, pasture, or prairie in which they traversed freely. But this isn't the case. According to the USDA, the term simply means the animal must have access to outdoors. That's it. There need not even be an edible substance out there. It could be a concrete parking lot.

In reality, my definition was the norm for thousands of years before terms like feed and supplements. In fact, the first records of the concept that you must feed your animals, coincidentally, emerges around the time radio and television advertising became popular. Suspect! In reality a true free-range chicken, one that has free access to open fields and pasture, produces a much higher quality produce.

Meat is leaner, has 4x Omega-3, 3x vitamins, 4x CLA (conjugated linoleic acid), 3x less fat and tastes better. Eggs are 4x lower in saturated fat, 3x less cholesterol and 7x beta carotene, 3–6x vitamins and 2x Omega-3. One acre will sustain the waste of 75–100 chickens, 2 ducks/geese (water acre), 8 goats or sheep or 2 cows before fertilizer burn kills everything.

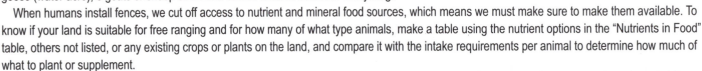

When humans install fences, we cut off access to nutrient and mineral food sources, which means we must make sure to make them available. To know if your land is suitable for free ranging and for how many of what type animals, make a table using the nutrient options in the "Nutrients in Food" table, others not listed, or any existing crops or plants on the land, and compare it with the intake requirements per animal to determine how much of what to plant or supplement.

Ecology—Don't introduce animals (pets or otherwise) until your structures are built and land and soils are ready. Trust me, you don't need any extra work or distractions when building your homestead. You MUST, and I can't stress this enough, MUST build up your ecology before introducing animals.

Build up your ecology for the animal type, say goats or cows, from the lowest levels (chemicals and nutrients), before adding said livestock. To do this, you have to build the soil's pH, nutrient levels, and permeability ("Soil," page 73) by adding materials, chemicals, and nutrients. Then and only then, can you plant, seed, or lay grass. At this point you still have to wait one complete season for the grass to drop seed and die off. Otherwise, if you were to add goats or cows, they'll graze it before it can go to seed, turning perennials into annuals. The only other way of rectifying this is to section off areas with fence, keeping livestock from grazing (for about a year) while the grass establishes itself.

For fish, ducks, geese, and other aquatic livestock, you have to do the same thing: add chemicals to your water to bring the pH into range, then add nutrients (mostly nitrogen), algae, and duckweed (minor and or major), letting them grow wide spread enough (one season) before adding feeder fish. Let the feeder fish establish themselves (about one season), before adding larger fish and or ducks or geese.

Otherwise, if say the algae or duckweed isn't given enough time to get a foothold in the pond before feeder fish are added, the feeder fish will consume all the algae or duckweed leaving nothing left to reproduce, and fish will starve. If larger fish are added before feeder fish are established, the same results. If you add ducks or geese before their food chains are established, they'll eat their food out of existence and starve themselves.

Food scraps— The average (American) family throws away 100 lbs a month. That's enough to feed 3000 maggots, 900 worms, 400 crickets, 50 tilapia, 20 chickens, 15 ducks, 10 geese or turkeys, or 2 goats or sheep or pigs, or 1 llama, alpaca, burro, or donkey for 1 week. The following shows nutrients from various foods.

IMPORTANT: Never feed by hand or bowl. It only creates dependency, which causes a mob mentality every time you step foot outside. Instead, scatter food stuffs at night. It doesn't take long to find, especially meat.

Automatic Feeders and Waterers

The most time-consuming chore on a homestead is feeding and watering cooped animals. It can take one person all day. This is why free-ranging, along with stagnant or moving water sources are such critical elements of any homestead. Otherwise, here are some great time-saving ways to feed and water cooped animals.

- **Float bowls:** Some of these come with their own bowl. Otherwise, clamp a box float connected to the end of a hose inside a 5-gal bucket or oil pan. Throw in a sacrificial anode (page 180) to stave off algae, bacteria, and larvae growth.
- **Ball point:** These are like the plastic version inside hamster cages. Screw on hose end or bottle tubes fit to 3-L bottles.
- **Bibb nipples:** Screw onto a bib. It takes a while for animals to learn how it works. You'll want to work with animals to be sure they are getting enough water.
- **Hog or goat nipples:** Again, bib or hose installed, mount to stable or shelter column or wall. The bowl collector hastens training.

IMPORTANT: Although automatic systems ease work load, it's still critical to clean, unclog, and inspect regularly. I recommend placing two at each location in case one malfunctions, and on rain water catchment systems (page 169), where storage and losses are critical, check often for leaks.

- **Pond:** Access to water bodies is the easiest, least troublesome method.

70-Pound Feeder

1. Cut circles in bottoms of a 5-gal bucket, 1½ in from outer edge, then drill (4) equally spaced ¼-in holes, ¾ in OC in and install ¼ x 1½-in bolts/washers/nuts.
2. Center bucket inside a 3½-gal hog pan or equivalent. Fill, place lid. Fill with deer corn, dog or cat food, chicken or bird feed and seed, etc. (Animals are homeostatic eaters and don't overeat. They stop when full.)
3. To hang, use 4 in bolts, attach pan and tie rope around top bucket rim.

NUTRIENTS IN FOOD

Nutrients	Source
Protein	meat, fish, eggs, beans, lentils, seeds, flour, fish, peanuts, soy
Calcium	bone, cereal milk, sesame seeds, dark leafy greens, beans, broccoli, eggshells
Phosphorus	pumpkin/squash seeds, fish (salmon, sardines, cod), Brazil nuts, beans, lentils
Vitamin D	fish liver oil, cold water fish, egg yolks, liver, oatmeal, sweet potatoes
Sodium	green leafy vegetables, roots, beans, blood, salt
Zinc	meat, bone, fish, barley, oats, soybean
Iron	clams, oysters, soybean, pumpkin seeds, heart, liver, kidneys, blood, white beans, lentils, blackstrap molasses, spinach, shrimp
Magnesium	beans, spinach, beet greens, papaya, beets, broccoli, raspberries

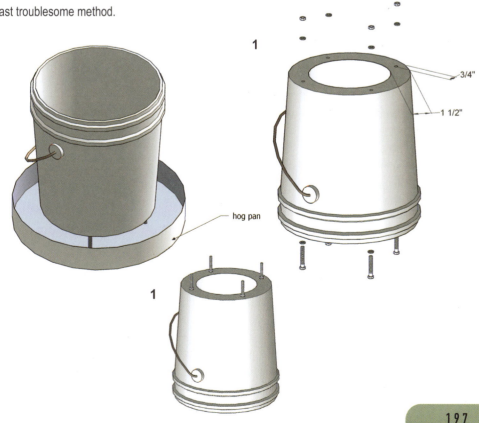

hog pan

3/4"
1 1/2"

50-lb feeder

1. Cut 6-in Sdr 35 PVC pipe 4 to 6 ft long. Prime and glue a 6-in Sdr 35 PVC tee to the bottom, followed by (2) 45° or 90° elbows in each leg.
2. Add a removable cap on top and strap or nail to a post, pipe, or tree with legs at animal height. Remove top cap and fill.

Bottle Feeding

Feed raw goats milk, replacer, or evaporated (goat) milk ("Milk," page 229) mixed at 1 tsp per 4 mL water, as often as the baby wants it, using an appropriately sized nipple on a .5 to 1-L PETE bottle or syringe (small mammals).

For kids, stand, lift chin mimicking the hanging udder in order to keep rumen door closed. To start kid sucking, squeeze some milk onto the nipple, let them smell it, then physically open the mouth (if necessary), insert, angle bottle down so nipple touches roof of mouth then angle back to vertical.

After a few moments, they'll begin ramming the bottle into your hand. They're not angry or frustrated, and you're not doing anything wrong. In fact, this means you're doing it right. It is how they stimulate milk to drop. Let kid wiggle, ram, hop, and kneel.

NOTE: Since milk only enters the abomasum stomach, you'll need to provide access to fiber (roughage) after 1 week, for healthy rumen development, reticulum and omasum, and the acquisition of microbes otherwise provided by mother's regurgitated cud.

50-lb feeder

Healthcare and Grooming

DISCLAIMER: I'm not a veterinarian, nor have I formally studied in the field of animal medicine. All knowledge is acquired during pre-med or general, medical, and surgical experience on the homestead and during relief efforts abroad. As long as you have an overall understanding of biology, you'll have no problem comprehending the subsequent content.

You will rarely have any reason to wash or clean any animal. As long as you adhere to the living conditions pointed out, animals (especially cats and chickens) are professional personal groomers. Chickens and guineas will even remove protein-packed ticks from larger animals.

Each has a special, scheduled regiment that's more efficient and healthier than anything we can do. Instead of washing (most grime and bacteria aren't water soluble), they take dust baths to soak up and scrub off in dirt, sand, or ash. Dirt also replaces vital microorganisms that continuously clean skin, feathers, and fur. Washing animals with soaps and chemicals removes or kills these organisms, removes fragile hair (naturally shed when needed), and strips waterproofing oils, undermining everything. Animals have been cleaning themselves for millions of years before humans.

NOTE: If you witness regular panting in any furry/feathery animal, to assist in shedding, you can brush lightly to remove access hair and wait a day; if panting continues, repeat.

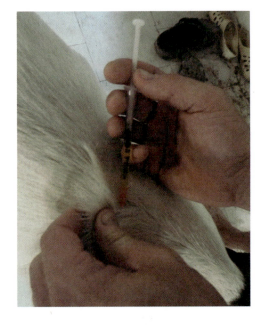

Trimming Hooves

Hooves are fingernails. If your animal is healthy, their nails will grow and be strong. They should never need trimming unless you didn't match animal with environment. In rockless pastures, farms, and yards, nails will grow long, split and fold over causing hoof scald or rot.

You have two options: trim nails yourself (impossible with an entire herd) or supply abrasives. If trimming, some, like Boer grow fast and need it almost monthly. After a few times, they don't seem to mind much; and you don't want them walking on overgrown nubs and suffering:

1. Wait for a good rain or soak for 15 min to soften. Lay animal, place in a stanchion, a cross tie, or have an assistant hold in place by the horns.
2. From a sitting or kneeling position, place the animal's ankle on your knee.
3. Clean nails by picking crevices between toe/s and nails with hoof pick, scrub with anti-bacterial soap using a hard bristle brush. Rinse and pat dry.

4. Examine for damage or disease, foreign objects and overgrown nails. Nails should never grow long enough to need nippers or sheers. If there's a lot of dirt extraction, excessive nail length is creating space for mud accumulation, and clippers would be required.

NOTE: Nail wall should protrude less than or equal to the toe sole height. Nail length differs since each species walks at a different angle. There is no correct, predetermined angle as different animals wear them down differently, like humans wear shoes down differently, so maintain original angle.

Overgrown nails

5. On goats, spread the toes, then starting from the tip, using a mandrill (sanding drum), or hoof trimmers or diagonal pliers, remove excess nail from left toe outside, inside, right tow outside, inside, and backs.

WARNING: Do not cut off too much. Nerve endings in fingers and toes in mammals are some of the most sensitive; so err on the side of caution. If you see pink, STOP!

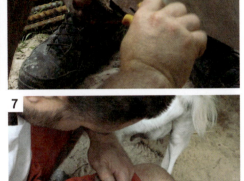

6. In ungulates, if sanding, follow with a rasp (file) or carpenter's plane, performing long, firm, forward (never side to side) strokes across entire wall surface to level, smooth, and even material.

WARNING: Never, ever file the sole. If you do, don't worry; he/she will quickly make you painfully aware of your mistake.

7. Check for evenness (wall thickness is congruent), angle, and nail level. Check length is level with or slightly above heel, without chips or rough edges.

Checkup

Bi-annually, whenever we acquire animals, and when needed, I'll perform a physical, checking for the following conditions:
- Stance/Motion: Stability (push side-side) of stance, strength of joints (lift up/push down), posture, open mouth breathing, swaying, head bobbing, twitching, and ability to walk/run without pain, limping, buckling or fatigue.
- Body Condition: Run your hands firmly over body. Check for: shiny or oily coat or skin (remember, animals clean themselves. If they're dirty, there's a reason. If it's not housing, it's health!); missing fur, feathers, or scales; skin for sores, lumps, or lacerations; joints, muscles, bones for sensitivity, pain, or discomfort; examine lymph nodes and ducts for heat, pain, and swelling; check around abdomen for swelling. (Reference opposite side for symmetry.) Laying birds should have swollen abdomens but shouldn't be accompanied by pain with pressure or diarrhea.
- Mouth: Check inside and outside for lacerations, sores, ulcers, tumors; excessive salivation or strenuous respiration; moist, slimy inner cheeks; soft, pink tongue; check for inflamed or infected, bleeding gums, good color, and capillary refill rate (under 2 sec); check for loose or missing teeth and tooth color, shape, and condition (teeth should be white(ish) and uniform with sharp K-9s (if applicable). Ground teeth can indicate too hard of (dry) food or inadequate access to raw meat in carnivores.
- Eyes: Check in a darkened examination room with a focused flashlight: compare symmetry of pupil diameter; inspect membrane for redness, discharge, inflammation or, swelling; for fowl, depress tear duct w/thumb to check for worms; left and right eye pupil response from 4 in (both pupils should respond simultaneously); corneas for smoothness, moistness,

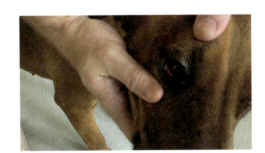

Healthy eye

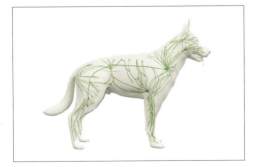

canine lymph node

opaqueness, ulcers, and any broken vessels. Check lid color (non-anemic animal will have pink to bright red inner eyelids—reference a FAMACHA card). Finally, check site by bringing an open hand in from the side of eyes. Look for blinking or flinching.

- Ears: Inspect inner cavity for: an absence of wax, presence of dirt, foreign objects; test hearing out of visual range with a bell or favorite squeaky toy, from far and low to near and higher volumes. Watch for reactions at each level. Remember animals have multiple times better hearing. What may seem inaudible to us, should be loud for them.
- Nose: Check for moistness, nasal discharge, congestion, foreign objects, and sense of smell (critical) by repeating hearing test using ammonia, vinegar, and/or a favorite food.
- Feet: Check for: hoof rot (nail and surrounding tissue should be free of foreign objects, infection, and bad aroma); hoof scald (should be able to walk without limping or holding hoof up); hoof abscesses (limping or hoof holding accompanied by heat); paws for pad or webbing lacerations, foreign objects and nail condition and length.
- Anus: Animals are much better than humans at cleaning their nether regions. Still, check under tail and around vent for: cleanliness, moisture, and softness, free of fecal matter, worms, or aroma; body mass (bony, hard tail base is underweight, soft, meaty base with firm tail is healthy, soft, meaty tail is overweight).
- Temperature (F): Insert thermometer at a slight downward angle, with lubricant, for 30 sec. Cat—101.5°, Dog—102°, Fowl—107.6°, Goat/Sheep—102.3°, Pig—102.5°.
- Heart rate/pulse (beats/min): Place ear or stethoscope over heart, measure rate and check for uninterrupted continuity: Goats/Sheep—70-80, Burro/Donkey—28-44, Cats—110-130, Puppies—70-120, Dogs—70-180, Toy breeds—70-220, Pig—60-80, Fowl—200-400.
- Lungs/respiratory rate (breath/min): Press ear or stethoscope over each lung, measure rate and listen for gurgling: Donkey/Burro—8-16, Goats/Sheep—12-20, Pig—8-18, Dog—10-30, Cat—20-30, Fowl—15-30.
- Digestion: Press ear or stethoscope half-way down and 1 to 3 in forward of flank. You should hear slow, regular, non-random, localized digestion sounds 1 to 2 minutes apart.
- Fecal matter: Collect waste and compare with previous droppings for: size, shape, dryness, non-cylindrical (in herbivores), non-spherical (in carnivores) with good, constant color; absence of undigested food, foreign objects or parasites; frequency; consistency/size (small/hard/packed indicates constipation, liquid or frequent may mean worms); perform fecal matter test:

1. Gather 1 tsp fresh feces in a pill bottle, mix 1 c of flotation solution (salt saturated water) and fill halfway.
2. Smash, add solution, then decant through a clean rag into cap with a microscope coverslip in contact with solution.
3. After 30 min, remove and place coverslip onto a microscope slide. Examine at 40x, 100x, and 400x if necessary for worm, eggs, and coccidia.

Parasites

You'll notice that free ranging animals don't contract parasites as much as backyard or indoor animals. The analogy is like grocery shopping vs. hunting: with the food trapped or easily accessible, bugs have easy pickings, jumping aisle to aisle, rather than having to search for their prey.

If you find any of the following, it's likely all are infested.

Fleas: Administer brewer's yeast ½ tsp per 10 lbs animal (for example, if your animal weighs 20 lbs give 1 tsp) or homemade yeast (page 208) 1 T per 10 lbs orally or sprinkle topically. Next, add garlic (an antibiotic/fungal/parasitic/platelet/cholesterol emic/tumor and vasodilator) to feed at ⅛ tsp per 10 lb of animal, ground to meal and dusted on or in pellets 1x per day for 2 weeks, then 2x per week to maintain.

Tick

Ticks: Rub vinegar or Tide under fur, around neck, down spine into tail and under leg pits once a day. Feed garlic: 1 tsp per 10 lbs of animal, ground to meal and dusted on or in pellets 1x per day for 2 weeks, then 2x per week to maintain.

Eye worms: Pussy eye discharge (ultimately sealing), excessive blinking or eye rubbing. For fowl, to kill all worms, give Valbazen ½ mL for 10 days (¼ mL for small birds) orally.

Ringworms: (contagious fungal infection) Ringworms look like pimples and later a protruding ⅜ to ½ in ring. Check area with a black light. If ringworm positive, affected area will glow neon green/yellow. Again, vinegar rubbed or soaked topically 4–5x day will alter pH enough to kill infection.

Tapeworms (including: giardia, roundworms, hookworms, whipworms): While sleeping, examine anus for yellowish, rice-like larvae. Orally administer a broad spectrum Benz imidazole anthelmintic like Fenbendazole at 1 mL/2.2 lb (add 1 mL/2.2 lb for animals over 140 lb).

Nasal bots (fly larvae): Extensive runny nose, snorting, head shaking or banging, nose rubbing, violent sneezing, front feet stomping. The condition usually isn't fatal, but would you want to live with maggots crawling around your nasal passages? Administer subcutaneously at 0.9 mg/ 10 lb (for non-milk producing) or orally macrocyclic lactone drench such as vomec (ivermectin), abamectin, or closantel.

To administer, fill lab flush, pump style liquid soap dispenser, flip-top or cone-top bottle, attach ¼ x 4-in rubber hose, grab top snout and pry open mouth. Insert tube in right side, behind teeth, into esophagus (not trachea). Pushing slightly against cheek, squeeze firmly and consistently. Gagging or coughing indicates liquid has traveled down the wrong pipe. Let animal recover and repeat.

Lung worms: Progressively growing cardiac/respiratory chronic breathing or coughing when exercising with possible weight loss. Administer macrocyclic lactone drench.

Barber's pole worms: Lack of eating, lethargic, extreme diarrhea, severe anemia. Administer any anthelmintic with moxidectin like Cydectin subcutaneously at 1 mL/ 20 lbs, 3 times a month and vitamin B at 1 cc/ 50 lbs 2x per day for diarrhea. If worms are prevalent in your area, drench (de-worm) 2x per year. If you feed, supplement with diatomaceous earth (dewormer) of 10% of feed weight for 90 days. then 5% feed weight per day (ongoing).

Banding

I stopped banding long ago, not for ethical reasons; but because they're consumed so young that taste and toughness aren't an issue. You may choose to castrate, though, for several reasons including: to preserve positive bloodline traits and characteristics, i.e. disease immunities and high milk or meat production, and reduce genetically inherited disabilities; to reduce problems of testosterone-fueled young males; for birth control; to reduce smell; and to produce leaner meat (if butchering adult).

Banding is the least painful method, but there's still suffering. After the procedure, the kid will lie on his side with his legs outstretched as if in shock. Leave be or get him up and moving. I find that by comforting and playing gently, the ordeal, pain, and memory seems to pass faster. Banding should be done as soon as balls drop. The younger they are, the easier it is on them.

1. Place band (sized for species) in grooves on plier tongs and have an assistant place the head between their legs and pick up animal back legs.

   WARNING: Never Use Old Bands! The last thing you want is the animal to suffer, only to have a band break and be left with an open scrotum wound.

2. Squeeze pliers, fully opening band; place band tongs-side toward testicles and pull sack through.
3. Make sure both testicles are completely through, that band is around the vein but not against the body, and nipples aren't caught before slowly releasing and removing pliers.
4. Check weekly for signs of sores. If present, administer 2.5 mL of tetanus antitoxin and clean with hydrogen peroxide.
5. OPERATION: As the band cuts off circulation to the testicles, veins/sack close causing the balls to die, dry up and fall off (this takes about 3 weeks). There's no blood, no sutures, no surgery, and the next day your now withered goat/sheep, will show no signs of trauma.

Tagging (ear piercing for animals)

Tagging is an inexpensive ($1/tag) method of identification to monitor health and maintain records. The process isn't extremely painful. No antibiotics or sedatives are needed, and there is no recovery time. In a few minutes, the animal won't remember what happened, and for the rest of its life won't notice its new bling.

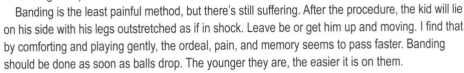

1. Place female side/receptacle in tagging tool clamp (lower side) and male with plastic needle (pin) in corresponding guide protruding from upper side.
2. If you look under the ear flap, you'll see 3 to 4 lines of cartilage. Target a centermost spot while avoiding lines. Clean both sides of ear with alcohol.
3. Have an assistant hold kid with kid's feet off the ground, place tool into position; and with a quick, strong motion, engage tool, releasing and removing ASAP.

Birth

Birth really has no place in a DIY book because there's nothing for you to do but watch (from afar). They don't need help, pain relief, or support. Usually, anyone (including family) in the vicinity, only heightens the likelihood of stress-induced complications. Some of our first-time mothers will walk miles to be alone. They do the same to die. Again, animals have been doing it just fine for millions of years before we came along.

Once born, it's important that the mother removes and eats the placenta. Mom and baby will remain inactive for several minutes. Baby will try to stand, and with help from mom, fall right on his/her face. On wobbly legs, it'll begin looking for nipples and drinking. If the mother doesn't immediately begin cleaning the face, suck fluids from nostrils and towel her/him off. If, after 30 minutes, the baby can't find the nipple and lies back down, guide the mouth. Within 30 minutes (or several days for carnivores) baby will try to jump and play, strengthening its legs and feet. Allow mother access to water while you babysit.

A few notes: If the cord is wrapped around baby's neck, reach in, adjust the baby (if cord is tight), and work it over the head. I've only seen it in movies. I don't think it's very common. Do *not* cut umbilical cords of any animal, including human. This process is for theatrical entertainment only, has no practical value and will only serve to harm! A baby's first milk, colostrum, is critical. It contains essential bacteria and antibodies, higher protein and needed fat, which encourages the first stool (meconium).

Fostering Fowl

Chickens—I've raised Rhode Island Reds forever. They lay large brown eggs. White Leghorns are the better white layers. Despite popular belief, there is no health or nutritional benefit of brown eggs over white. Brown eggs are just white eggs but brown.

Guinea—If you like dark meat similar to pheasant, guineas have larger breasts, less fat, and lighter bones (better weight-meat ratio), fewer calories, and 5% more meat (when dressed).

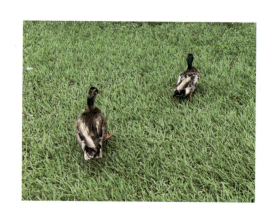

Ducks and Geese—Pekin, Aylesbury, Muscovy (best tasting), Ruel Kagua, and Sweden duck varieties for meat. Indian Runners are good layers, and Khaki Campbell are good eggs and meat. At 28 lbs a bird, geese have a better FCR (feed conversation rate), so they convert food to meat very efficiently.

Turkey, Peafowl, and Ostrich—The heavy weights: Peafowl have less than 1% fat, higher calcium, protein, and vitamins, turkey (the Broad Breasted Bronze for most locations or Giant White for the heat, and emu and ostrich produce a red meat with great flavor that is low in fat and cholesterol, similar to lean beef.

Other—You don't need to own land or even a backyard to raise fowl. My father-in-law had a few love birds in a small cage when we first met. Next time we saw him there were so many they wouldn't fit in the cage. I would opt for quail, though, specifically Japanese (Cortunix). They are as easy and almost as fast to propagate in a hutch as diamond doves but, of course, bulkier; and the eggs are tasty (considered a delicacy).

Coops

- Don't build on the ground. Every egg eater will find a way under, through, and inside.
- Don't build with wood or anything else that stores bacteria, fungi, spores, and other dangers.
- Build perches high. Most birds, including chickens, perch on tree branches at night. Their last instinct is to be trapped low in a box. If your birds don't feel secure and comfortable, egg production falters.
- Locate downwind or downhill from the house and water supply (applies to all animals).

1. For the cage, I used an old 3 x 4 ft dog kennel; but you can make one with 1-in conduit and chicken wire. Remove tray, flip cage and lay (4) 8 ft 1⅝-in galvanized chain-link fence line posts on top.
2. Install line post caps to ends with Lexel, locate 2 training wheel brackets on 2 poles so wheel centers align with cap tip. Drill and install ⅜ x 2-in carriage bolts and nuts (head on post side). Install on sides/back vertically, wheels up with (4) 4-6-in hose clamps, repeating for front.

1

2

2

3. At this setting, we'll get 2 to 3 inches (depending on wheel size) ground clearance. This is good for keeping birds in the cage, and moving the cage for feeding/ fertilizing. If you want the coop higher to negate predator access lower wheels as much as desired.

4. Cut the side and bottom from a 5-gal bucket, leaving 6-9 in on top, 3 in on opposite side; then bolt lid (glue to bucket with Liquid Nails) to any wall, level with a perch for laying boxes (1 per 3 hens).

5. For perches, cut 45° end notches (outward) in (2) ¾ in PVC conduits with a hacksaw; heat then bend inwards (notched side) ¾ in and hook and clip into horizontal bars, bow up, notches down, running cage width, at least 1 ft from top of cage. Chickens won't perch on anything less.

6. Cover with tarp during winter with floor panel on top for a roof.

7. OPERATION: There are 3 settings: ground, 4 ft, and 8 ft. Ground is only used with motherless chicks. Raise to 4 ft to teach chicks to fly and to 8 ft when chicks are grown. Move cage weekly to prevent burning. To round up chickens, shine a flashlight in their eyes at night and catch in a large net. For daylight, lay a 5-ft copper grounding wire with a 3-in hook with a ¾-in gap, by scooping the ankle.

Regardless of type, if you lock the coop up for any duration, you'll need at least 4 sq ft per bird floor space. Otherwise, the only limiting factor is perch space (10 in /bird). Feather-picking and cannibalism are caused by confinement, so having space and getting out is key for healthy, happy birds.

Here are some guidelines for other fowl:

- **Ducks:** Ducks ground nest, making them accessible to predators. This is easily resolved with a floating house or island.

- **Large birds:** Turkeys and peafowl roost higher, so I use 3 or 4 10 sq ft chain-link panels bolted together on 2 (3 panels) or 3 (4 panels) sides with a tarp on top and plastic cut to 2-in widths (seat belts work too) for chain-link weave to provide shade, and a 10 ft long, 3 in SCD40 galvanized pipe, 7 ft up for the perch.

- **Giant birds:** Emus and ostriches will use the same cage as large birds. Throw some plastic pallets in the corners with hay to allow waste to pass through, keeping bedding clean and dry. Move 1 ft each day.

- **Everyone else:** Don't waste your energy. If they don't join the rest, it's because they're happier sleeping outside (since you matched the animal with your environment). If, you have too many to fit in the 10 x 10 for large birds, build another or use a barn. We built a large barn for them and they wouldn't use it.

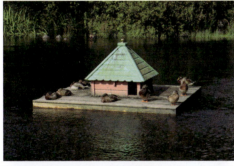

Bat House

In a world without insect repellent and insecticide lawn treatments, bats reign supreme. Bats are insectivores, (no, they don't bite) and have 1 pup a year. Invite them to your homestead with a bat house.

1. Cut (15) old ⅝ x 3 in cedar fence or pallet planks (page 17) to 18 in. Rip 2 length-wise in half widthwise and stack in pairs, 16½ in OC apart. Nail 5 perpendicularly on front and 6 on back, creating a 1¼ in gap (perfect for North American Brown Bats).

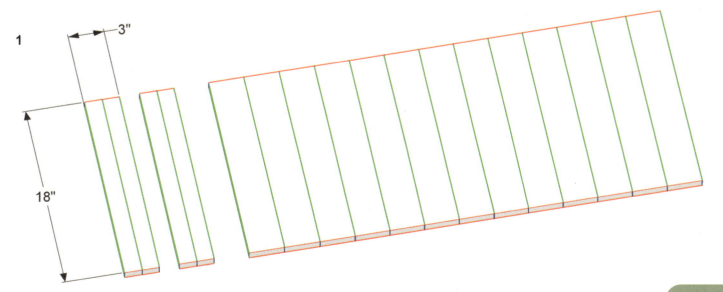

1

3"

18"

2. Nail 1 of remaining planks on top to shed rain and 1 on bottom, flush with back, as a landing platform (optional), both at 90°. Locate on pole near lights and water, at least 10 ft off ground (to prevent cats and other preditors).

1

2

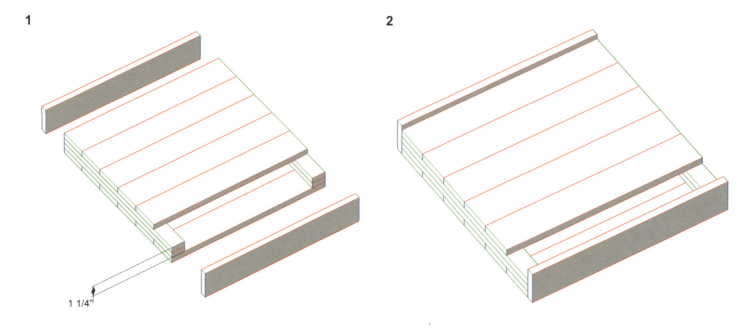

1 1/4"

Martin Houses

Purple martins are a close second to bats in insect control. They have 6 offspring a year.

1. Remove the skin of a 6 in or larger gourd, let dry, cut a round 2⅛ in side hole for a door, clean and let the inside dry. Drill (4) ⁵⁄₁₆ in vent holes in top and (6) drainage holes in bottom. Hang with door perpendicular to ground.
2. Mix ¼ lb copper sulfate ("Nutrient Additives table," page 108) with 1 gal water in a 2½ gal container, submerge gourd overnight. Let dry and paint white. Hang 10 to15 ft high using 2 ft of line threaded through vents. Repeat for 5 houses and space 1 to 2 ft apart.

Training Animals

Leading

Any animal can be trained to be a lead animal. In fact, in most packs/herds/schools/flocks, lead animals arise naturally with the others following naturally. All of my animals follow me wherever I go. So, if you can train your animals to follow also, leading isn't needed. Otherwise:

1. Begin placing lead ropes at 1 month. They'll think it's a toy to chew on, which is fine.
2. At 2 months begin leading. They'll think it's playtime. Some trainers will discourage this method. They want the animal to know it's serious. I'm not serious, and I'd rather it be a fun process.
3. Construct a lead harness by tying a loop in the end of a 6 ft ⅜-in cotton rope. Wrap around neck, just behind ears. Bring loop up to either side of jaw, double and feed another loop through. Place adjustable loop over/around snout and cinch snugly leaving a two-finger gap. Remember: never leave a lead, halter, saddle, or harness on an unattended animal.

IMPORTANT: Take routine breaks. Animals have shorter attention spans than humans, about 20–40 minutes. If a lesson goes beyond that, it doesn't matter what you do, they will NOT learn it.

4. To teach to follow on command, they need to learn to stand still. Give a short lead line or holding halter; pet or scratch neck (not face), armpits, and sides. Add slack and move onto the back, belly, and hind quarter, walk in front and around to the other side and repeat. Then stop on the left side and wait.

5. If they're being fussy and running around, try the process in a round pen while you stand in center. Once the animal realizes that walking around in circles isn't as fun as standing next to you and getting attention, they'll learn to stand still.

6. While standing, give a verbal cue to turn left. Begin walking while pulling gently on halter in that direction, repeating as many times as needed to get movement. When achieved, praise and scratch or give their favorite treats so they know they're understanding your messaging. Repeat.

7. If it seems like she's being stubborn, repeat cue, pull gently on harness again, and this time push back with your body gently on flank/ hip, using your body as a pivot point to encourage turning their butt around.

NOTE: Some trainers use a lead whip handle. I never found the need. Also, there's absolutely no reason to ever pull the rope. It should only be used as a form of communication. You shouldn't be tugging on her (or anyone), and she shouldn't be tugging on you either. Both behaviors need to stop now.

8. Walk to the other side and repeat, turning her in the opposite direction. To go forward, give your verbal cue, lower the line and start walking. If she doesn't follow, repeat until she does.

NOTE: They're not being stubborn by not moving, so don't get impatient. You're the one now standing by the door, telling her to open, and she's the one ignoring you. It's a language barrier (plus you're kinda boring).

9. To stop, give verbal cue, raise line up, remove slack (don't pull), and stop walking. Do the same to reverse. When packing in a caravan, leading is easier. Just wrap lead around saddle horn of another burro/goat (preferably, its mother) and go for a fun walk. Never tie to saddle horn, in case it needs to be released quickly. Never tie to a rigid object since this will cause panic and possible injury.

10. At first, they'll resist being pulled and will run to either side or ahead. This is fine. They'll quickly find a position (usually slightly back and to the side) that's most comfortable where the line is slacked.

11. If the animal fights the rope or panics, release and tie off to a movable object such as a sturdy branch above wither level several times a week, then several times a day. Once they realize they're ok, lead together again and again.

Packing

Since they're already familiar with wearing the lead, they should have no problem donning a halter. The pack saddle isn't much heavier but should still be introduced early without weight:

1. While holding lead, let her see (remember how they see objects) saddle blanket, towel, or padding until bored. Then begin routine of petting and scratching using blanket. Do 1 on side, place blanket into position, remove, and repeat for the other.

2. Eventually leave blanket and repeat with saddle. Remove saddle, and with an assistant holding lead, place girth band over with saddle centered on blanket with at least 2 in extending on all sides. Adjust, walk around; remove girth/lower, cinch girdle 2 fingers and take for a fun walk.

IMPORTANT: "Fun" walks in this context doesn't mean human walk. Human walks are the MOST boring walks ever! We don't stop to listen to critters, smell the roses—or the poop—or walk perpendicular to the path to stare at the scenery. We fail to nibble the delicious plants underfoot. We go too fast or too slow and too noisily. Boring.

3. After your walk, repeat the process in reverse. Repeat the preparation and walk daily. After a few weeks with blanket and saddle, signaling "We're going for a walk, and it's going to be a lot of fun." If she could, she'd literally help you put it on.

4. All that's left is to add weight. Start with 10 lbs and add 10 more each day up to animal's full load. Load front first then work toward the back. Always balance the load, and never load more than animals can comfortably bear. For a typical donkey, this is around 125 lbs. for a goat, 10% to 20% of their total body weight—around 25 to 50 lbs I've found to be pretty good. A 2000 lb mule can carry around 400 lbs. Follow with more fun walks.

Driving

Before your animal can pull (actually, they push) a cart, it needs to learn how to pull.

1. Connect (2) 10 to 12 ft ropes to each side of halter, stand behind (10-12 ft) with each rope resting on the hind legs to get them used to the feel.

2. Do this for several days, then load pack saddle (or cart saddle) and drive lines, and walk behind, giving cues while an assistant leads from the front of animal.

3. Keep lines taut and hold above waist, feel animal's movements, and let them know you're there by constantly making micro corrections. The animal will likely overcompensate and fish tail.

4. To stop fishtailing, give cue, pull slightly (and evenly) back, then give slack. To reverse, repeat, stop. To go, slacken lines and give "go" cue. Repeat several dozen times, taking scenic strolls until it becomes second nature. This is called long lining. Burros pick it up exceptionally fast. They're very intuitive. Horses, not so much.

5. Next eliminate lead and try a few dozen more times. Once ready, add the cart. Let her size it up: smell it, shake it, move it, and climb on it. It'll hasten the process if the cart is actually stored in her sleeping quarters.

6. To get her used to the cart approaching from behind, go for a walk, leading while another animal pulls a cart using the same cues. The next day, bring shafts over rump, but don't tie. Instead, give lots of love and attention, then remove everything and repeat the next day.

7. When ready, hitch shafts and walk a few steps, remove and repeat daily. Finally, get your assistant back with the lead, connect cart, and drive (don't forget your cues—use them, even if not needed). Finally, disconnect lead and go solo!

Once your animal knows how to pack and pull, they can learn to mill. For animals, milling is just pulling a cart around in circles. It's easy work to learn (if they're already pack and cart experienced) but extremely boring (no horrible smells, perpendicular side-tracking, etc.). Consider this when allotting work hours (especially in the heat) and supplement activities afterwards to compensate.

When you first introduce the animal to the mill's shaft, you'll receive a different reaction. Whereas a cart was chasing, the shaft seems to be following alongside. Burros, being more socially oriented, aren't bothered, but horses (and others) don't like the pole to get too close. Simulate the mill in a round corral and long lining from center (lunging).

Drafting

Drafting, for the animal, is simply pulling a really crappy cart.

Start younger burros by drilling (2) ½-in holes in the front corners of plywood, carpet, or plastic sled and connect breast plate extensions.

Practice cues and drive line directions with a load of 10 lbs, increasing 10 lbs an hr. Once you reach your body weight, remove that weight, take a rest, and then drive like a cart (no weight).

After a few days or weeks, attach swivel and a log or other odd shaped object, and drive a few rounds. Connect plow or other farming tool and practice for a few days before hitting the open field. Practice micro movements, as these will be the types of corrections you'll use most when plowing.

IMPORTANT: Again, plowing is boring, jeez is it boring. Pay attention to work hours, especially in the heat and compensate afterwards.

Photo credit: kaikups

Riding

Teaching a burro to take a rider is much easier than teaching a horse. If you've already taught it to stand, wear a saddle, and take a loaded pack, it's even easier. Still, there's a difference between placing an object on an animal, and climbing on its back (predators jump on animals' backs).

1. With halter on and lead in hand, start your loving routine, paying extra attention to areas around saddle. Pull saddle from side to side, several times on each side.
2. Place a foot in the stirrup and give a little weight, but always maintain an exit. They'll walk forward. Bring full circle and try again.

   NOTE: The animal is balancing what may be an unpleasant experience with what is turning into an unpleasant experience. So if it becomes frustrated (or if you do), stop, reward, and start again tomorrow.

3. Repeat for as long as it takes until the animal stops walking forward, effusively congratulate her, and take for a fun walk. The next day, repeat, placing a little more weight, then more, until you're able to get a leg over.
4. At this point, have an assistant take the lead, connect your reins and keep them in hand while mounting each time.
5. Fully mount and steady yourself, disembark, and again celebrate her achievement. Eventually, when you're both ready, have your assistant lead while you give light physical and verbal cues. Repeat several times; then disconnect lead. Once they realize you're not going to be on their back for the rest of their life, they don't mind so much.

   IMPORTANT: With each lesson learned, the animal must go on a fun walk, uninterrupted by your timeline. And lessons must always be a good experience for the animal. If it's a bad one, you're teaching the opposite! You're teaching them to never let a human get on their back.

Animals learn through observation, imitation, and repetition. For them (and all children), this is a fun game that gives them attention and time with you. They'll even train each other. The more you ride, the more comfortable they'll get. My outlook is, I had to carry them (well Lucia did) down the mountains a LOT when they were little; they can carry me a little!

All of the time you spend with your animal can be considered education. No, we're not teaching them geography or calculus (though I wouldn't mind), but they love learning. They need constant, new, visual, aromatic, auditory, and physical stimuli to build a healthy, strong mind, especially when young. Take them on field trips exploring around and outside the property, learning about leaves and sticks, still and moving liquids, sand, rocks, creatures, and yummy plants in a relaxed, fun way. Then quiz on everything learned.

Chapter 12: Production of Proteins

For most, 100% of meat consumption comes from store-bought food, of which, according to the Bureau of Labor Statistics, on average, over $1000 per year is spent on meat alone. Add that to the $3000 per year typically spent in restaurants, and that's over 10% of the average annual income. Imagine getting a 10% pay raise!

There are over 18 billion different types of proteins in plants alone. To avoid confusion, "proteins" in this chapter refers to the traditional definition: those from animal and animal by-products.

MICRO PROTEINS

Meals, emulsions, bacteria make up micro proteins, with blood and feather constituting the highest amounts.

MICRO-ORGANISM PROTEIN COUNT

blood meal	1 T = 12 g	fish meal	1 T = 9 g	kelp meal	2.1 g
feather meal	1 T = 12.75 g	protein meal	1 T = 8.55 g	algae	9.1 g
Yeast	1 T = 4 g	evaporated milk	1 T = 5.4 g		
powdered egg	1 T = 6.9 g	insect meal	1 T = 9.75 g		

How to Make Meal

Blood and bone meal are the obvious, but anything can be milled: fiber, feathers, and chemical compounds for fertilizer; evaporated milk, yeast, and powdered egg for recipes; rice, coconut husks, meat, insects, and starches for feed; spices, fruits, nuts, and salt crystals for flavoring. If you don't have access to blood or bone, ask your butcher. They'll be glad to give you as much as you want. Maybe pass off some meal as thanks.

MATERIALS
container desiccant packet

TOOLS
heavy-duty blender or slush mill or hammer mill or ball mill

¾-in wood dowel
mechanical flour can sifter

1. Dry ingredients either in an oven on medium with the door cracked or solar dehydrator to brittle. Don't blend hydrated materials.
2. Fill a heavy-duty blender halfway. I recommend keeping a separate blender—you don't want bone meal to mix with your morning smoothie. Blend on low (chop), then medium, then fine or puree until powder. For higher mass materials, run through slush mill or pulverize in a hammer mill (bone). For finer powder, pass through ball mill.
3. Push contents down with dowel through plug hole. Let settle, pour into a mechanical flour can sifter over a clean container, and sift. Dump remainder back into blender and repeat. Store with desiccant packet.

NOTE: When empty, place doweling through hole and mark just before it contacts the blades to keep from blending your dowel.

Growing Yeast

MATERIALS
jar w/ lid
raisins or other dehydrated fruit
rain or purified water
1 c flour

TOOLS
mill
strainer
mixer
frosting spreader

1. Fill a jar with 25% raisins or other dehydrated fruit (page 244) and 50% rain (or purified) water. Secure lid and shake 1x a day, removing lid for 5 minutes a day.
2. Continue for 8 days or when all fruit is floating or fizzing and the lid pops when opening (yeast is ready to propagate).
3. Strain, pour liquid back into jar, discard raisins, close and let sit for another week.
4. Mix in 1 c flour to paste consistency, replace lid and let sit.
5. After a few hours you should see the dough rise (mark jar if in doubt), spread onto a tray, let dehydrate, then break and mill (see "How to Make Meal" on page 207).

MEZZO PROTEINS

Outnumbering us by 200 million to 1 and by a combined weight by a factor of 1000, with over 97% of animals fitting into the category, insects are a massive protein source. Every single insect is edible. Some of the more common are beetles, caterpillars, ants, cicadas, locusts, crickets, grasshoppers, and dragonflies. So, if there are so many, why farm them? A lion is easier to find, catch, and kill than the weight of a lion in insects. When we breed our own in the thousands for meal, feed, or food, the mass is contained and easy to harvest. I've picked out a few of the easier to raise types for beginner farmers.

I've chosen five projects to get you started in farming mezzo proteins: worm farming is great for composting, silkworm for silk, black soldier fly larvae and beetles are good for feed, and for humans, crickets are my choice, but people can eat any of these.

Worm Farming (10.5% protein)

This is one of those store-bought products that I've tried (and I've tried them all—rotating bins, tiered towers, boxes, trays), and none (DIY or store-bought) functions very well. After working out the kinks, stealing the best traits of each design, I designed the unit below. It's a little more detailed than your typical worm farm, but it makes up in efficiency, ease of use, and absence of common, often catastrophic problems associated with these systems.

MATERIALS

(6.25 LF) ⅛ x 2-in flat bar	newspaper
(19.75 LF) ⅛ x 1-in flat bar	sand
(4 LF) ⅛ x ¾-in flat bar	peat moss
(3.25 LF) ⅛ x ¾-in angle	aged compost
cardboard	blue or red worms

TOOLS

chop saw	protractor
bar or rod bender	straight edge
string	vise
plastic 55-gal drum	jigsaw with plastic cutting blade
measuring tape	spray bottle
pencil or Sharpie	scale
welder	5-gal bucket or wheelbarrow

1. Cut and label (a–l) as noted for the following sifter parts: from ⅛ x 2 in-flat bar—(1) 2 in x 74¼ in (label a); from ⅛ x 1-in flat bar—(1) 30 in (label b), (1) 36 in (label c), (4) 2 in (label d), (2) 2¾ in (label e), (6) 21¹⁄₁₆ in (label f), (2) 9³⁄₁₆ in (label g), (1) 11⅛ in (label h); from ⅛ x ¾-in flat bar—(1) 3 ft 6 in (label i), (4) 1½ in (label j); and the rest from ⅛ x ¾-in angle—(2) 1 ft 10⅜ in (label k), (6) ¾ in (label l).
2. For the sifter frame, cut a 10½-in long, ¹¹⁄₁₆-in wide notch in the middle of part (a) with a chop saw and bend into a hoop in a bar or rod bender. Wrap around top lip of 55-gal drum (or use string), mark (trim if necessary), remove, and weld seam.
3. Weld both (k) pieces to bottom (cut out side) of hoop (a) (flanges in and down), 4⅛ in OC from center, parallel to cut-out (trim as needed).

2

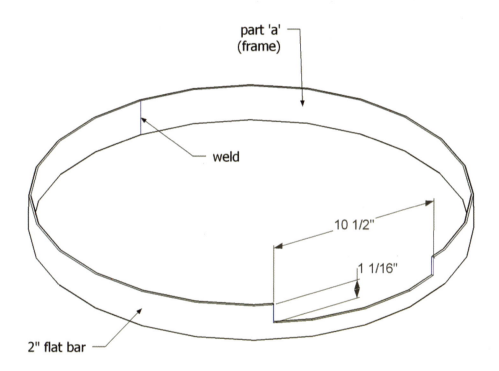

part 'a'
(frame)

weld

10 1/2"

1 1/16"

2" flat bar

4. Weld (2) (l) pieces onto hoop (a) (legs up), ⅝ in OC down from bottom lip, 4⅛ inch OC in from either (k). Weld the remaining (4) (l)

3

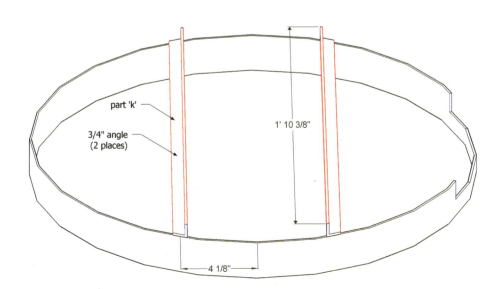

part 'k'

3/4" angle
(2 places)

1' 10 3/8"

4 1/8"

pieces onto hoop in the same fashion, equally spaced.
5.   Then flip frame right side up (cut out down), and weld (4) (j) pieces, 4¹⁄₁₆ in OC out from center of (k) pieces, with a 130°outward

4

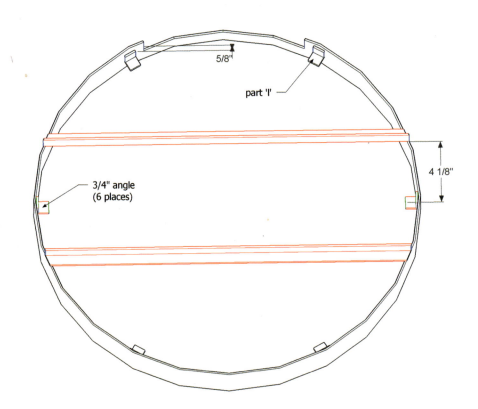

inclination for the center sifter guides.

5

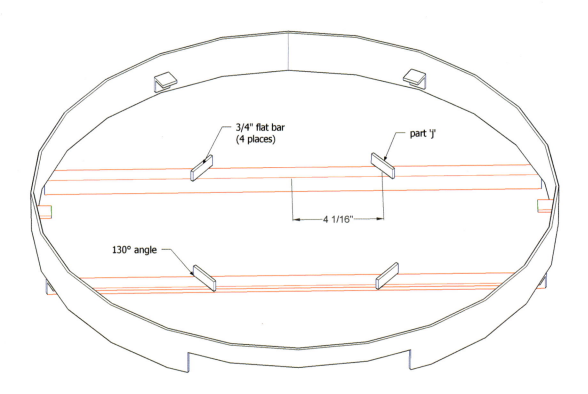

6. For legs, on piece (I), make a 100° bend with a 145° inclination ¾ in from either end, then a 260° bend with a 145° inclination 1 ft 6½ in OC over, another 260° bend with a 145° 1½ in from the last, and finally one more 100° bend with 145° inclination, leaving a ¾ in long foot (trim as necessary).

7. Duplicate for (2) more legs, flip frame, and weld the ¾ in feet to protruding flanges of pieces (I), leaving cutout clear.

8. Fabricate the sifter by bending piece (c) into an 11⅜-in circle in the bender and welding ends. Weld piece (h) in the middle and pieces (g) 21³⁄₁₆ in OC out on each side.

9. Rotate 90° and weld an (f) piece to pieces (h) and (g) (perpendicular), and (2) more 21³⁄₁₆ in OC. out on each side. Repeat for opposite side.

10. Finally, weld (2) (d) pieces and (1) (e), parallel to (f) pieces, on opposite side of piece (g). Repeat for opposite side so you have a symmetrical grid.

11. For the sifter handle, bend the middle of part (b) around a ¼ in bolt held in a vise with equal leg lengths. Bend ends out 195°, 5⅜ in in, and weld to sifter circle. Place sifter on and in frame on sifter guides with handle through cutout.

6

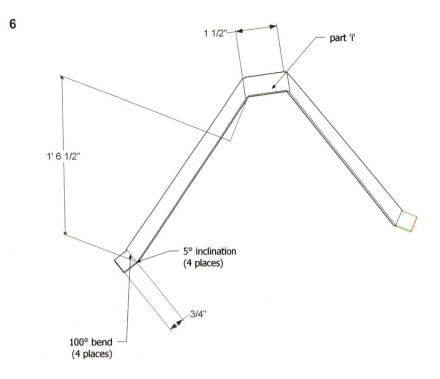

7

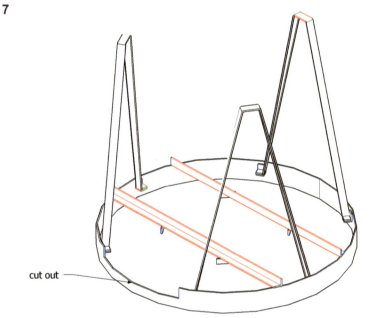

9–11

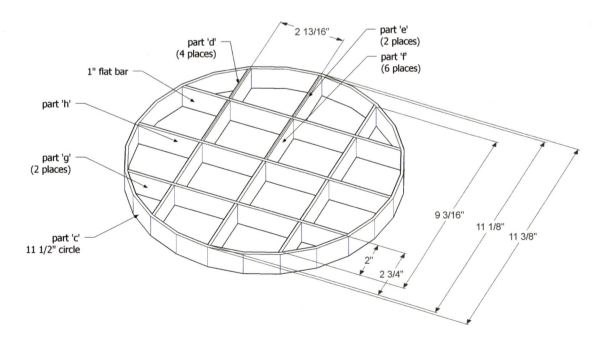

11

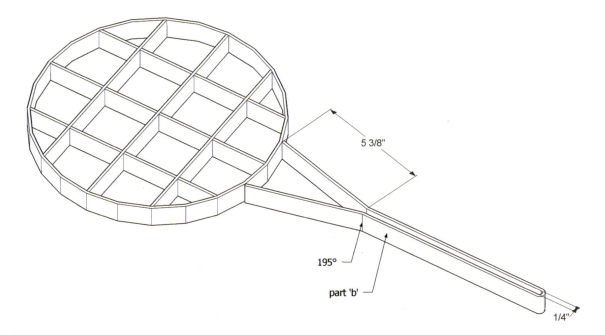

5 3/8"

195°

part 'b'

1/4"

12. For the feed chamber, cut 10¹³⁄₁₆-in hole in center top and bottom of a 55-gal plastic drum. Place drum on stand and pack (1) layer of cardboard in bottom and up sides 4 in (to prevent side drainage), followed by (3) layers of newspaper.

NOTE: In humid regions and to prevent moisture buildup, the larger the top hole the better. In cold or dry conditions, cut a smaller top hole and hinge for a lid.

WARNING: Don't cut ends completely off, or barrel will warp.

NOTE: If in predominantly humid and/or hot regions, drill ¾ in holes throughout a 3-4 x 32 in SDR35 EPDM pipe, wrap with weed barrier and center on cardboard for a drying and oxygenating center. Add (4) 1 L bottles of frozen water for cooling.

13. Add 1 in sand, 3 in peat moss, and 4 in aged compost (preferably from existing worm bin to jump start microbe reproduction) or 3 in compost and 1 in "Beneficial Micro-organisms" (page 74) and moisten. Use burro, horse, or cow manure if you don't have access to compost on 1 side only so worms have an area to escape the heat.

14. Begin adding organic matter (food, produce scraps, landscape cuttings) with a layer of bedding (2–3 layers newspaper plus 2–3 layers 1–2 in cardboard strips) on top, to allow worms to relocate to warm up, cool down, dry, or drink. In this manner, cardboard will soak up excess juices and act as a water reservoir (yes, worms need water). The traditional ratio is 2–1–1 (by mass) cardboard-organics-newspaper. Sprinkle a little sand once a week for grit.

NOTE: Balancing humidity levels, along with managing heat buildup is a constant problem in worm composters, as air at the bottom (where moisture collects) becomes stagnant since no fresh or dry air can replace it. In this design, internal heat (created by bacteria) causes air inside the material to rise, pulling cooler air in from the bottom, drying the content, supplying fresh oxygen to microbes and worms in the process, creating a well-balanced environment.

11

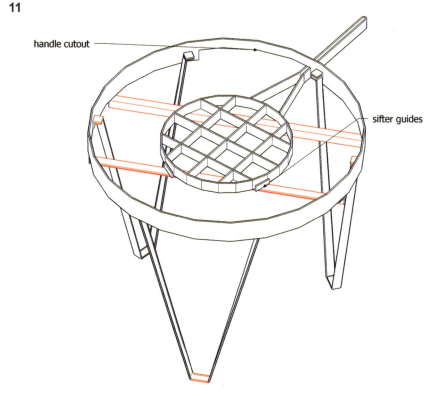

handle cutout

sifter guides

12

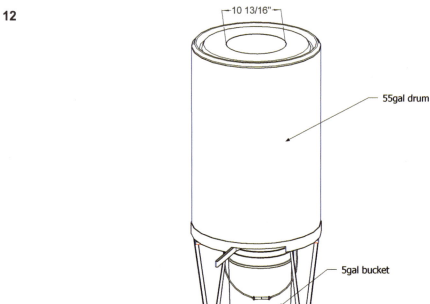

10 13/16"

55gal drum

5gal bucket

15. Once you've reached 1 ft, add blue (tolerate higher temps) or red worms at 100–500 or 1 lb (100) worms/ 1.5 lbs food a day, or 4–5 lbs of worms per person and another layer of moist bedding.
16. Weigh food and bedding added daily to determine your active processing rate and bioconversion capacity later, once fully established. This is shown in the 4:2:1 rule where you'll need 4 lbs of worms to process every 2 lbs you add (daily), which will produce 1 lb of castings.
17. To harvest your own red worms, fill a 5-gal bucket with food scraps, soak them down good and flip the bucket over upside down in a shady part of your backyard. After 5–10 days, the bucket contents should be crawling with red worms. For earthworms, simply lay a piece of cardboard in the back yard and keep damp. These worms can then be added to your worm farm.

18. To prevent removing worms and eggs, wait 3–4 months before first harvest. Don't worry about any falling out. Since there's no edible material in the lower half, there's no reason for them to be there.
19. OPERATION: When dumped, they'll eat their way down, turning around at the sand and head back up, leaving eggs and casings along the way. As these eggs and cocoons hatch, young naturally travel upwards to top, a 12–13 week process. To harvest material (castings and compost) place a 5 gal bucket or wheelbarrow underneath and ratchet sifter handle lever, only removing as much as added. You can also eat or feed worms to your animals. Collect worms from top in the morning (when coolest). On 2 people's waste, we pull 5 lb of worms in 8 months.

Silkworm Farm (9.3%)

Aaah, the ancient silkworm! Silk and silk making have a long and illustrious history stemming from ancient China. Silkworm farming all starts with the Bombyx mori larvae—not a worm, but an infant moth. This creature is able to manufacture one of the most precious materials known. Unfortunately, there are no silkworms in the wild. In fact, there never were. Todays' silkworm is the result of thousands of years of genetic modifications to induce a domesticated, flightless moth that mates instantly and dies immediately.

MATERIALS
mulberry leaves
silk worms

½-in mesh material (bird block netting, gutter guard)
1¼-in PVC pipe

TOOLS
Cake or other rectangle plastic trays with lid

1. Fill several cake or other rectangle plastic trays (brooders) with a layer of mulberry leaves leaving a 2-in border. Delicately place worms evenly spaced on top and remove any leaking sacks. Cover with cake cover to keep in humidity.

   WARNING: Do NOT feed silk worms any other leaves but mulberry leaves, it'll kill them!

2. To prevent a stuck or suffocated worm, don't touch or let other worms touch during this phase. For this reason, keep numbers limited to ¼ to ⅓ surface and food space . . . 6 to 8 worms a leaf or 125 to 150 worms on 15 to 20 leaves on a 1sq ft tray.

   IMPORTANT: If raising from eggs, feed only the newest and most tender growth or leaf mush. When I raised my first brood, I had a die-off due to their mouths being so small. Don't add water as they can drown in a drop. Silkworms get hydration from leaves, so keep leaves from drying.

3. When almost only stems remain, cover with a ½-in mesh material (bird block netting, gutter guard) with a layer of new leaves on top. With a never-ending supply of food during 5 molts, they'll double in size almost daily.

   IMPORTANT: If you miss even a single feeding your silkworms will starve to death. Pick enough leaves for 2 weeks. Place extra in Ziploc bags in the produce drawer to keep fresh. Pesticide free lettuce or shaved carrots work in a pinch.

4. Harvest for feed in 12 to 14 days (1 in long) or just before pupating (3 in). In 5 to 7 weeks worms will begin spinning cocoon silk. Place ¾-in sections of 1¼-in PVC pipe around each to make easy to unravel, wheel cocoons (page 228).
5. OPERATION: If allowed to hatch, they'll destroy the wheel, climb out and begin mating. Don't worry about providing food and water at this point since they don't own mouths. A female will lay 300 eggs every 3 weeks. The eggs hatch in 2 weeks and gain 10,000 x their weight (for humans, that equates to a 7.5 lb infant becoming a 75,000 lb person).

Black Soldier Fly Larvae Farm (35%)

MATERIALS

4-in shower drain
2½-in fpt PVC reducer bushing
shower pan or other wide container
½-in mpt to barb adapter
(1) 2 L plastic PET bottle or other capped container

½-in tubing
newspaper
cardboard or
carpet

TOOLS

drill with ½-in drill bit

spray bottle

Black Solder Fly Larvae (BSFL) aren't the larva we typically think of when we think of maggots.

BSF larva look more like roly polies than the squirmy little cream-colored pupae we see eating the innards of dead animals. Plus, they usually forage on rotting produce, though they will chow down on some protein as well.

1. Install a 4-in shower drain with 2-½ in fpt PVC reducer bushing in a shower pan or other wide container. Install a ½-in mpt to barb adapter. Unlike worms and maggots, BSFL aren't the best climbers. A simple slick shower pan works well at keeping them contained.
2. Drill a ½-in hole in a 2-L plastic PET bottle or other capped container and route ½-in tubing from barb to container. Add runoff to compost ("Composting," page 183).
3. Wrap scraps in newspaper and place inside in snaking rows. Keep moist (but not over moist) and cover with cardboard or carpet when not in use.
4. Harvest BSFL from earlier dropped food scraps and surrounding areas.

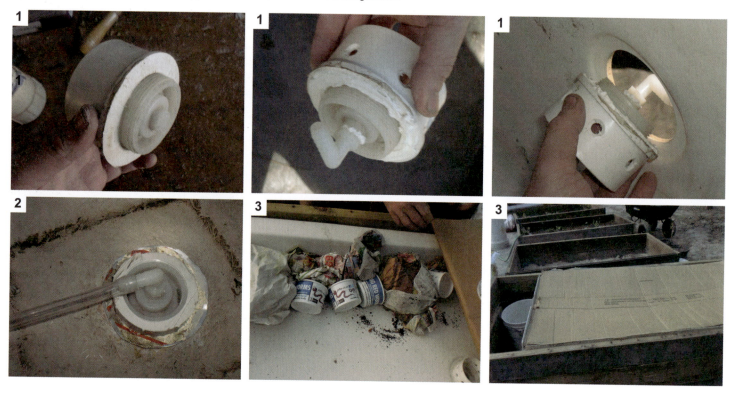

Beetle Farm (20% prortein)

MATERIALS

2-drawer plastic storage bin
nylon or vinyl window screen
corn or wheat meal
2 can top or lids
banana peels or quartered potatoes
meal worms or adult beetles

(1) egg carton
rolled oats
calcium
protein meal

TOOLS

utility knife or jigsaw
measuring tape
pencil or Sharpie
radius fillet gauge
hot glue gun
weight

fridge or turkey
  thermometer
gecko pooper
  scooper or
  window screen

Again, there are lots of designs floating around for meal worm habitats. When I started raising chickens and tilapia, meal worms were my protein supplement. It took 2 years to get a cheap, efficient, easy system going.

1. With utility knife or jigsaw, remove the top plastic drawer of a 2-drawer plastic storage bin. Flip and cut out (2) equally sized squares with ¼-in corner radiuses, leaving ½-in borders and a strip in the middle.
2. Using a utility knife or jigsaw, trace and cut drawer ID onto screen and hot glue on the top and the inside bottom. It helps to place a weight on top so that the screen makes contact with the plastic, gluing through the screen holes.

3. Replace drawer and add 1 in of corn or wheat meal, along with a can top with banana peels or quartered potatoes (for water). Dump meal worms or adult beetles into top drawer, and cover with (1) egg carton cut in half, placed loosely inside another for a nursery.

3. Replace drawer and add 1 in of corn or wheat meal, along with a can top with banana peels or quartered potatoes (for water). Dump meal worms or adult beetles into top drawer, and cover with (1) egg carton cut in half, placed loosely inside another for a nursery.

WARNING: If left out in the open, larger, older meal worms will eat the younger during their vulnerable pupae stage.

4. Fill bottom drawer with 2 in of rolled oats and another lid for a water and food source. Sprinkle 1 T of 1:1 calcium to protein meal (page 207) and drop an oven thermometer inside. Monitor consumption of water source, replacing every 2 to 3 days.
5. OPERATION: Weekly, check temp (70-85°). Opening, closing, and bouncing the drawer sieves the material, causing the tiny eggs to fall through screen into the lower drawer.

In 2 months, larvae will stop moving and turn into pale micro *Predator* (think movie) looking pupae. 1 to 4 weeks later, they'll hatch as light brown beetles, and in 10 days, turn black and mate (14 days). Both larvae and beetles eat the bedding. Harvest with a gecko pooper scooper or scooper and window screen.
6. At about the two-year mark, transfer a couple dozen meal worms to top drawer to resupply adult beetle population. Beetles live on average 2 years.

NOTE: If you get flour or grain mites, there's too much water source or moisture in bedding. For humid environments, place bin inside a tray of water as a trap. If your habitat is cold, place ¼ onto a sprouting heat mat.

PRODUCTION OF PROTEINS

Cricket Farm (20.5%)

MATERIALS
20 to 50-gal aquarium or storage tote
sand
(1) can top
protein meal or chicken mash
lettuce or fruit
crickets
toilet or paper towel rolls
fine screen or cloth

TOOLS
sponge
fridge or turkey thermometer
spray bottle

1. Fill bottom ½ in of a 20 to 50-gal aquarium or storage tote with sand, leaving corners empty. Place a can top in center, and fill corners with protein meal (page 207) or chicken mash.

2. Wet and microwave a ¾-in square piece of sponge for 30 secs (weekly) to kill bacteria. Moisten and place on lid with a lettuce leaf or fruit for food and water. Add crickets at 1:2 or 1:3 (males-females).

   NOTE: Sex females by their 3 antennae-like protrusions (ovipositor) in the rear and larger wings; males by their beautiful screeching vocal cords (actually legs).

3. Lay toilet or paper towel rolls for shading and refuge, making harvesting easy. Keep temps at high 80s, with natural daylight for about 3 hours a day. Mist lightly once every 3 days. Place fine screen or cloth over top for ventilation and to prevent cricket egress and predator ingress.

   IMPORTANT: The most prominent cause of die offs is over-watering, which quickly kills hatchlings.

4. OPERATION: Females lay 5-10 eggs a day or 100 total eggs, by inserting the ovipositor through sand. It takes 8 to 12 weeks to mature, so size habitat to maximum occupancy. This is determined by daily harvest quantity. For example, if pulling 300 a day, you'll need about 30 females for 2500 crickets. A good rule is 40–50 crickets a gallon.

   NOTE: If your males are eating eggs, hard pack another plastic jar lid with damp soil. As long as you keep it damp, the females will use it over the loose soil and the males won't be able to penetrate. This also makes removing eggs (after 7–10 days) simple.

Beekeeping (.3%)

There are tons of different ways of keeping and raising bees. I learned from an incredible keeper, Tim Hollmann out of Dante, SD, who's actually a major honey distributor with hundreds of thousands of hives throughout the U.S. (Hollmann Apiaries). Beekeeping isn't hard, but it does take a golden thumb, if you will, that can only be obtained through a seasoned keeper. Find one in your area and don't talk, just listen.

In a beehive tower or body, it's all about the supers. There are two types of supers: brood (2 typically large boxes located on the bottom of the tower) and honey (2 to 6 typically smaller boxes on top of brood boxes). The brood-rearing supers followed by a queen extractor in the hive body keep eggs separate from the honey supers. The remaining components are the bottom, queen extractor (optional), top, and weather cap (optional). I'd also highly suggest some form of hive beetle protection.

There are a couple types of hive configurations and designs. The first and easiest (to build and maintain) I ever built was a Japanese hive. I harvested a lot of honey, but it was very disruptive to the bees as harvesting requires cutting sections of hive away each time. The second, a traditional Langstroth hive, was slightly less disruptive, so I spent years harvesting from that. Finally, I discovered the Flow hive, which is a lot less destructive, and almost completely non-disruptive. The only problem with flow hives is they require a warm environment (about 80° is ideal) to extract honey, so they don't work as well in cooler areas.

Flow Hive Supers

When building supers, remember that bees will fill voids larger than ⅜ in with comb and smaller than ¼ in with propolis for weather seals. Therefore, voids of ⅜ to¼ in (¹⁵⁄₁₆ in being optimal) is a good gap for spaces for bee travel (i.e., vertical space separating frames, horizontal spaces separating supers, floors, lids, and all other spaces separating hive parts bees require access to).

MATERIALS

flow hive frames (see https://www.honeyflow.com/)
recycled cedar fence or pallet slats

tools
woodworking tools

1. For honey supers, construct (4 to 6) deep supers (brood chambers) with an ID of 14 x 18⅜ with an inside height of 9³⁄₁₆ in and a ⅝ in (high) x ⅜ in (wide) top or inside ledge using recycled cedar fence or pallet slats ("Pallets to Lumber" page 17) or other wood with dovetail or rabbet joints. (I use deep supers for honey supers. But you can reduce the height to 6⅝ in to accommodate 6 in shallow frame.) If using pine, treat outside with boiled linseed oil. Don't worry about something not being secure; bees glue everything with propolis.

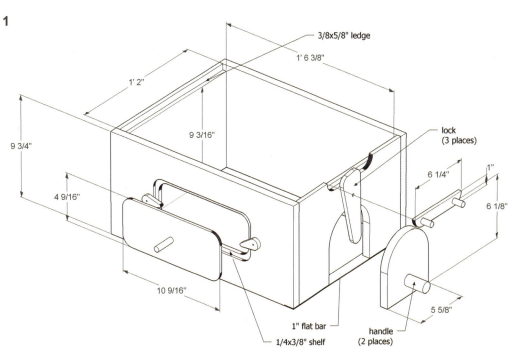

2. Cut out a 5⅝ x 6⅛ honey tube port access door in either side, along with a 6¼ x 1 in top lock door. Add handles and a barrel bolt lock, and a piece of ¹⁄₁₆ x 1 in flat bar, as long as the width of your box (to keep bees out of your honey extrusion area).

3. (Optional) In the front, cut a 4½ x 10½-in window with a ¼ x ⅜-in routed shelf and ⅛-in plexiglass viewing window glued in. Cut a ¼ in thick piece of wood to match for a door with a knob (centered) and locks on the sides.

4. For brood chambers, since brood chambers never need to be accessed, construct (2) deep Japanese style supers without side doors or flat bar.

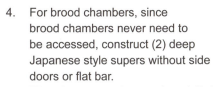

5. Place in an area that receives full shade in summer and full sun in winter. Fill with bees and queen (from online distributor, local beekeeper, or a wild hive).

Hive Bottoms

Bottoms can be made out of anything and only provide the bees with a protruding (an inch or so) platform to land on, as well as a guardable front door. The wasp, mortal foe of the bee, stands slightly taller than ⅜ in, so It's critical to keep door height at exactly ⅜ in.

MATERIALS

dog-eared fence slats or pallet wood

TOOLS

woodworking tools

measuring tape

pencil or Sharpie

1. Using dog-eared fence slats or pallet wood (page 17) construct a slat bottom and 1 x 2 top frame with a width equal to the width of your supers, and a depth equal to the depth of your supers plus 1½-in (landing platform).
2. Flip the bottom upside down, rip another set of 1 x 2s to ⅜ in, and nail all but the front to the bottom piece.
3. Cut the front piece into thirds, discard middle and place (don't nail) outside pieces in place.

Hive Tops

1. Construct a 1 x 1 frame with a width and depth equal to your super width and depth.
2. Cover with screen (staple) for hot climates, or nail ¼-in slats for cold climates.
3. Bees do a good job keeping their hives cooled and heated, going as far as sealing cracks, insulating walls, and creating in-house, whole house blower systems. If you're in hot regions where cold weather is non-existent, I'd highly suggest only using a screen for a top. In normal climates, cut a 1½-in hole in the center of the top slats and nail a 2-in piece of flashing on top that can be moved and closed in the winter and opened in the summer to let the heat out. In cold regions during winter months, I'd suggest adding a layer of insulation to the top, if not the exterior of the entire hive body.

Hive Weather Caps

MATERIALS

dog-eared fence slats, pallet wood, flashing or plastic garbage can lid

TOOLS

woodworking tools

measuring tape

pencil or Sharpie

A hive cap only serves to keep the rain out of the hive. In mild climes, the hive top (non-screen version) is enough to achieve this (the 1½-in door, even when open isn't enough to flood a hive).

However, in predominantly rainy or cold climates, flashing, wood, or even just a plastic garbage can lid is enough to keep the hive watertight.

Loading

MATERIALS
wine bottle
syrup
¾-in PVC elbow

TOOLS
5-gal bucket
funnel
drill with ⅛-in drill bit
hive tools
2-L plastic bottle

1. To start out, place your bottom. Then place the first super with half a dozen frames on top.
2. Place ordered or captured bees on top. Gently remove the syrup feed can, and douse the entire area and inside with syrup to keep bees calm.
3. Remove the queen; she has her own separate little wood box in the top of the box sent. Place her in between frames two and three. (You'll see the orange ribbon hanging by nail in photo.) The queen will eat herself out of her box within a day and begin building.

4. Douse the queen and the surrounding area with more syrup, turn the bee travel box upside down and shake out a few pounds of bees onto the queen. Place the boxes inside the super in the middle, hole up.
5. Place the top (flashing door open), place a second 6–frame super, and place the syrup can upside down over and in the hole.

NOTE: I like using a wine bottle with a .032 in hole drilled in the cap as a syrup dispenser as it's easy to fill or swap out each time for feeding.

6. Place a second top and weather cap and wait.
7. When the syrup can is empty, remove the can, and in a 5-gal bucket mix 163 oz sugar with 66.5 oz water ("Syrup," page 235). Pour through a funnel into a wine bottle, drill a few ⅛-in holes in the cap or cork, and place upside down in the hole.

NOTE: For different amounts of syrup, use the following formulas (at room temperature). For amount of sugar needed: $1.27 \times (CS)$ = cups of sugar. For amount of water: $.52 \times (CS)$ = cups of water, where CS = cups of syrup needed. A worker bee needs 11 mg of sugar a day. The rest goes to cells.

SBH infested hive

8. After 2 weeks, replace remaining frames.
9. Once the hive establishes (fills with comb) the first super, repeat for second super. Once hive grows enough so that it fills both brood supers, you can add honey supers as needed.
10. In warmer climates, dust tops of frames with cinnamon for mites and beetle barns or reusable oil beetle traps for small hive beetle (SHB) infestations.
11. OPERATION: After 1 week of making comb, the queen starts laying, while workers fill and cap cells with honey. The hive is weak, so close top and block entrance to 1½ in, allowing a few to defend the entrance. After 2 weeks, larvae will emerge and begin indoor fanner training. Monthly, enlarge entrance 1½ in, checking progress every 3 months until entrance is width of super. After first year, once super is 80% drawn and 75% filled, add a second deep super underneath. Towards the end of summer, check top brood box. If drawn and capped, place a third (honey) super on top to get them through the winter. To prevent queen from swarming (and taking half her bees), every spring add another brood chamber, building a new hive after 3 years so the queen can split the hive.

12. For harvesting Flow Hive Supers, it's a simple matter of removing the top and bottom side access doors, placing a container underneath (I like using 2-L plastic bottles with a ¾-in PVC elbow inserted in the Flow Hive spout), placing and turning the key (don't turn all at once) and allowing the honey to "flow" (see the project below, "Honey"). No smoke needed, no messy comb extraction, no breaking up hives, no disturbing of bees. Just remember, honey only flows at temps above 72°F.

Honey

Until recently, harvesting meant donning a sting proof suit and hood, smoking to disrupt scent, signaling or putting the bees into preservation mode, breaking the home's second story loose, and pulling the frames (rooms), and squashing residence upon reassembly, not to mention uncapping and centrifugal honey extraction. Don't get me wrong, this is fine, and if you prefer this method you have a source for wax (page 229). But it's hard work. Recently, I had the pleasure of participating in beta testing a new type of honey harvesting system: the Flow Hive.

Australian son/father duo inventors Stuart and Cedar Anderson crowd-funded the world's first automatic honey-on-tap hive. The campaign reached 1 million within minutes (a record), then 2 million, ultimately becoming the most successful Indiegogo campaign. No disturbing or killing bees, no suits, smoke, or work.

MATERIALS

1-gal milk jugs, jars or other suitable container

jars

1. Build a Flow Hive Super (page 216) and insert 7 Flow Hive frames.
2. At the start of summer, add a fourth deep (honey) super.
3. Harvest at nighttime (when bees aren't active), and temps are 80°F or higher. Remove doors and tube and tool plugs. Install frame tubes with hose directed into clean 2-L plastic bottles or 1-gal milk jugs, jars or other suitable container. To open honey comb, insert then turn valve tool, and walk away.

NOTE: If, after checking observation window and seeing honey is almost full, you don't have time to harvest, add another honey super and another ounce full (typically 2 to 6 weeks depending on hive strength and health and nectar flow), and harvest all together.

IMPORTANT: If you see uncapped comb, wait until it's capped. You can also test by igniting the honey. (Cured honey is flammable, nectar isn't.)

4. Wait until the honey stops flowing, close honey with tool, then remove tube and tool and immediately replace plugs. Move tube and container to next frame and repeat.

5. Repeat for all frames, then replace access doors.
6. Pour honey into clean (boiled) jars (jelly, jam, salsa, etc.) and store.
7. Depending on the weather/your location, you could get 2 or even 3 harvests. Store empty combed supers inside, protected from wax moth/larvae with mothballs.

MACRO PROTEINS

I won't go into (depth) on the societal stigma behind eating meats such as dog, cat, horse, rat, etc., but I will point out that these are only misnomers taught to you through media, family, and friends. Keep in mind other cultures as well as vegans in your own culture, cannot contemplate you eating things like cow. Once you break that mindset, you realize the absurdity of the notion that some types of animals you can eat while others you cannot. All meat is just as good or bad, with the same, worse and better nutritional values than others. You can choose not to eat dog or cow or hippo, but it must be your choice, not society's, and you must not look at others who choose to eat such things as being wrong. Right now, you don't eat dog meat because society has made that choice for you. I make my own choices, and dog (as well as cow) is tasty. To help break with this and other societal instilled mindsets, check out my YouTube series "Think About It!

Choosing the Best Macros

In the previous chapter, I covered homesteading in terms of animal husbandry or raising and housing poultry, bovine, caprine, swine and other larger animals. In this chapter the focus is on the proteins and protein by products of large animals such as the one's we discussed as well as small animals such as bees, ants, worms, and maggots. Some animals consume little and produce much. Others eat a ton and produce very little. To be efficient and not waste energy raising and reproducing animals that don't produce for us, it's good to understand what you need to put in (the animal) to get the maximum amounts of protein, either from the animal or from its byproducts. This is called *feed conversion ratio or rate* or FCR. Knowing an animal's FCR helps you make informed choices about what animals you choose to raise and rely on.

*PUFA—polyunsaturated fatty acids
*SFA—saturated fatty acids
*MUFA—monounsaturated fatty acids
O6:O3—omega 6 to omega 3 ratio

FEED CONVERSION RATIO/RATE

Type	Micronutrients	O6:O3* (PUFA)*	Fat cal % (SFA)*	Fat cal % (MUFA)*	Fat cal % (PUFA)*	Relative cost
Beef (grass-fed)	Iron, B vitamins, Vitamin D, Zinc, Selenium, Phosphorous, Potassium, Copper	2:1	51%	39%	2.40%	$$$
Beef (grain-fed)	Iron, B vitamins, Vitamin D, Zinc, Selenium, Phosphorous, Potassium, Copper	10:1	44%	47%	2.70%	$$
Chicken (with skin)	Niacin, Vitamin B6, Selenium	5:1	29%	41%	21%	$
Venison	Iron, B vitamins	1.7:1	48%	18%	6%	$$$
Ground lamb	B vitamins, Iron, Phosphorous, Potassium, Copper, Selenium, Magnesium	5:2	44%	42%	8%	$$
Salmon	Iodine, Selenium, B vitamins (especially B12), Potassium, Phosphorous, Copper	0.2:1	16%	33%	40%	$$
Tilapia	Iodine, Selenium	1:1	35%	29%	23%	$
Pork (retail cuts)	B vitamins, Niacin, Phosphorous, Zinc, Selenium	5:1	35%	44%	10%	$

Fostering Fowl (19% protein)

Chickens (and other poultry) are some of the only animals that produce two forms of protein (meat and egg) and are some of the easiest to raise and keep. You don't need cages, coops, or a big yard, as they'll find their own nests (and laying spots), usually up in a tree. And with 2.5 x the FCR than beef and ease of butchering, it's a no brainer.

Rearing Rabbits (33% protein)

Rabbits reproduce like, well, rabbits. The problem with rabbits is getting them to stop mating. You'll definitely need 2 sets of hutches or partitions. They have a 2 x more efficient FCR (at 4) than beef and are ready to butcher in 3 months. Although Flemish Giants are the largest, weighing up to 20 lbs, they tend to have higher bone, fat, meat ratios than the New Zealand whites, Satins, Cinnamons, Chinchillas, or Californian. Either way, rabbit is all white meat and lower in fat than beef, pork, or chicken. Also, raising rabbits in the city is permitted, whereas cows, chickens, or pigs, not so much.

Stocking Swine (28%)

How about some ham, ribs, sausage, and pork rinds with your bacon? The only bad thing about pigs is their FCR (3–4). Pigs have a lifespan of over 10 years and are capable of breeding 2 times a year with a gestation around 114 days and average litter of 10. They are omnivorous and scarf down insects, reptiles, rodents, birds, soured milk, grass, roots, tubers, acorns, bulbs, and any food scraps. For a treat, feed fruit, corn, rice, wheat, soybeans, peanuts, potatoes, watermelons, or cantaloupe. If you have access to dumpster food from a restaurant, cafeteria or grocery store, swine will eat it all (cook at 212° for 30 min to kill bacteria) and freeze the rest in 5-lb blocks. Durocs are a good choice as they gain weight quickly (5 months to butcher), but Yorkshires and Hampshires are also good large breeds.

For space, because of their lazy nature (pigs don't really move around much, and they sleep a lot) plan for a minimum of 10 sq ft per pig. Pigs can be a little more temperamental when it comes to temperatures. Pigs under 50 lbs need to be kept in temps above 70°F, whereas pigs over 150 lbs need to be kept cool when temps are above 70°. Also, heavier pigs (150 lbs and above) that are kept cool (50°–70°F) will eat more, while pigs that are in heat (above 70°) eat less.

Keep lean (legs apart) for meat. For lard, feed fatty foods and raise a butterball.

Bringing up Bovines (21% protein)

Boer is obviously my goat of preference; but I like the taste of Nubians, La Manchas, and Nigerians. Besides cattle (at 10–20 FCR—feed conversion rate), goats and sheep have one of the poorest FCRs at about 5. For every 5 lbs of feed they eat, they produce 1 lb of meat. Good thing they're only eating weeds!

Slaughter

We (usually) slaughter and eat 2 types: the very young and very old. The very young is slaughtered because the meat is in its prime, which leads it to be tender and rich. The old is butchered upon death, as long as death wasn't due to disease.

Critical elements to slaughtering:
- Never, ever kill just to kill or kill out of fear or without thinking!
- Never rush the process. Extinguishing something's life correctly, without pain is more important than anything else you have to do that day.
- Always provide a comfortable and happy environment before and during to ease and eliminate suffering. The animal doesn't need to be scared.
- Perform separated from other animals.
- Distract with treats.
- If the animal becomes scared, abstain and reschedule.
- Feel free to pray to your God/s for the animal's soul, or thank it for its life, whatever you prefer.
- Use everything. Don't waste anything.

killing cone

For small animals (fish, reptiles, rodents, and small birds), the quickest and easiest way I've found to terminate the life of a small creature is to simply grasp the body firmly in one hand, and with a sharp pair of game scissors, clip off the head at neck.

For larger birds like pheasant, duck, and chicken, use a killing cone (upside town 1-gal plastic container with the tip and base cut off or traffic cone with the tip cut off a few inches works well) to pacify and restrain the animal before slaughter. Place the bird upside down inside the cone, with its head and neck sticking out.

For larger game, use a 22 cal bullet shot at close range, to the back of the head (brain). 22s are the smallest caliber, but (and for the same reason) kill more efficiently than any others. This is because a 22 cal bullet, at close range, is just powerful enough to enter the skull but not enough to exit, bouncing around inside, mimicking several shots, causing as much damage as a 12-gage shotgun, without the surface destruction.

Hunting

I grew up in northern Utah where elk, deer, rabbit, bear, pheasant, duck and geese, to name just a few, are plentiful. Where schools are let out for opening weekend for hunting. Hunting is a very difficult subject to teach someone through a couple of paragraphs in a book. Anyone can point and shoot a gun. But it takes years of guided hands-on training to become an adequate, efficient hunter to the point where they can not only make a kill without suffering, but provide 100% of their family's protein needs with the activity. So, I'm not going to go to into the skills and techniques required to make a good kill, but I will touch on a few mandatory things not touched on enough in hunter's ed. The key here and NUMBER 1 RULE is to minimize suffering.

- Always use the right size weapon for the animal and distance. Don't go hunting a 1-ton elk with a .22-long rifle. For elk, I'd suggest a .30–.06 or higher, leaving .22s and 6 or 7½ shot (shotgun) for rabbit and smaller game.
- Never take a shot while the animal is moving, and always make sure you have a clear, clean shot of the animal's vitals.
- Never take a shot from farther away than your sights are honed in at.
- Always slit the throat of the animal (see "Butcher") immediately, just in case.
- Always eat what you kill, never kill something just for sport.
- Locate a resource. Mark off grids on a map, mark off creeks, lakes, ponds, springs, and stumble around the different areas until you find some resource worth coveting (water, shelter, food, or even just a well-worn or traveled path). Once you find an area, stay put. They're there, trust me.
- Don't be picky in what you kill. Everything's on the menu whether it be dog, cat, cow, deer, duck, rat, rabbit.
- Stalk your prey beforehand. Most kills in the wild aren't opportunity kills.

NOTICE: Some of the following methods may be illegal in your state or country. Research before you hunt and be sure to have needed permits and licenses for your area and season.

- Spotlighting—spotlights, car headlights, or powerful flashlights, allow humans to see almost as well at night as animals. The method comes with a second advantage: it removes the animal's ability to camouflage itself. Light shining on and reflecting off the animal's eyes creates a beacon in the dark. And finally, the effect even stuns the animal. In many cases, you get off a closer, better, non-moving and, therefore, cleaner shot.
- Feeders—by setting out highly desired food (corn, for some reason, is like candy to most herbivores and omnivores) in a specific location at specific times daily, you're able to lure the animal into a behavior of habit that you can now predict.
- Flushing—the critters of the forest already greatly outnumber us, but by lining up several dozen people in a straight line and traversing an area together, you'll push anything hidden in the brush into hunters on the other side.
- Circling—circling or circle flushing is when a group of people will surround an area, slowly working their way in towards the middle and the animals in towards each other.
- Dogs—dogs have been bred into all different types, sizes, shapes, and temperaments for thousands of years, specifically for our needs, hunting being the most predominant reason. The smaller breeds, such as Terriers, are meant for chasing rabbits and other small tunneling rodents out into the open, while scent hounds were manufactured for tracking foxes, cats, and those that don't fall for the human tricks listed above. Sighthounds are built lean and fast, able to chase down their prey, whereas Labradors and other retrievers were made for bringing back dove, quail, ducks, pheasants, and geese after a kill. Ridgebacks are bred for the 'Circling' technique.
- Decoys—decoys are fake, usually plastic or wood structures made to look like real birds which lure the duck or goose down to your location.
- Camouflage—we, too, can don blending clothes, blinds and other structures, to mask our highly noticeable shape. Most animals don't see with their eyes, but rather their nose, making masking our musk with the animal's urine (especially the armpits, groin area, feet, face and head) imperative. Clothing also releases odor (chemicals, dyes, detergents, and sweat), never use deodorants, soaps, shampoos, or any other man-made chemicals.
- Night hunting—birds won't usually fly once it's dark. So, if you can sneak up on a few floating in a pond after hours, you've made for an easy kill. In fact, waiting until after dark or just before dawn to hunt grazing animals is a critical tactic as well.
- Day hunting—conversely, carnivores sleep when the sun's out, making daytime a better time for finding and hunting them in their dens and caves.
- Vehicles—adding a truck to the mix can raise your land speed equally to that of most prey.
- Tree stands—comparably, tree stands, or other high spots, can provide you with a visual advantage while camouflaging you and your odor as well.
- Tracking—there are many methods of tracking, but all incorporate several of the same elements: keep quiet, travel slow, learn to identify tracks and read how old they may be. If you hunt the same area over and over, every day, you'll become accustomed to the daily soil conditions and be able to spot changes.
- Markers—you can set your own breakable and moveable identifiers. Running a string or fishing line across a well-worn path. Don't tie one end to anything, just drape across at about chest (animal chest) level; mist an area with ground-up drywall or other powder (see "Calcium Carbonate"), check every few hours for prints; fill a den, rabbit hole or fence hole with dry leaves. If they've been moved or dug out, the hole is active.

Finally, and this is the most important thing . . . *just wait*. Be patient, don't sleep, don't move, don't make noise, don't pee or poop in the area. Locate a high position downwind of the resource or path you found on previous scouting missions, and just wait: hours, maybe days, but wait. Eventually, whatever has come here before will come again.

When you finally find something moving around on four legs, you'll need to know where to aim. If it's a side shot, aim for the just behind the front armpits (see image). This way, if he moves forwards or backwards, you still have a kill shot on the vitals (heart, esophagus, trachea, lungs, and thoracic diaphragm). If the animal is facing you straight on, target the upper chest region just below the neck so that if you miscalculate your distance too close or too far, you'll still have a kill shot on the vitals. From the back, you can hit the vitals by aiming at the butt just below the tail, and from the top, aim between the shoulder blades. You never want to aim at the head unless it's the only appendage in view. When you're ready, lock everything in (arms, wrists, fingers, elbows, shoulders) so that you're not floating around, take a normal size breath, exhale half, hold and pull slowly back on the trigger until the gun fires.

Keep in mind, no matter if you do everything I've listed above right, animals seem to have a sixth sense about knowing when something's just not right.

Fishing

I consider fishing a form of hunting, without the backbreaking labor involved. And although I'm probably not an authority on the subject, I have quite an extensive amount of experience and upbringing in the field. Again, though, without taking you out and holding your hand through the process, there's very little I can do to fully prepare you to catch fish, other than relay several tricks I've learned over the years. Trying to fish with a pole is an inadequate and horribly inefficient form of fishing, generally only performed for sport or relaxation. There are much better, more efficient ways to provide needed protein for your family.

Trotlines— Using a trotline (not only for trout) can be the easiest way to obtain an unlimited source of protein. They're simple to make and use. It's like having dozens of full-time, non-eating, non-sleeping fisherman on the banks for several days, providing you with a 100% of their catch. Run a fishing line or rope (page 49) with dropper loops tied every 5 to 10 ft apart, from one side of the shore (river, pond, lake, lagoon, etc.) to the other side or from the shore out to an anchored milk jug. Tie a variety of different lengths of baited and weighted fishing lines to each loop, spanning the entire distance. This will provide bait for numerous different types of fish who live at different depths in the water. Daily, traverse the line, checking each individual hook for a catch.

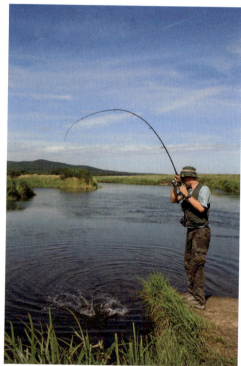

There are obviously hundreds of types of baits one can use to catch fish. Conversely, different baits work on different fish. The following are some typical baits.

- Insects—crickets, worms, grasshoppers, slugs, maggots, beetles, caterpillars, you name it, they'll eat it!
- Animal parts—save those guts and extras for bait, especially the liver.
- Bubble gum—if nothing else, bubblegum usually works well, not because it's tasty but because it's colorful, which for some reason draws a lot of fish in.
- Fly fishing—if you're crafty enough and have some spare thread, feathers, cotton and a whole lot of spare time, you can make your own handmade bait. Simply place a few small feathers, cotton, and blades of grass against a small hook, and wind with thread. The design should remain small enough to pass as a fly or other insect.
- Ticks—if your K9 fishing companion has ticks (which most due) he's constantly carrying around a tackle box of bait for you. Surprisingly, ticks live a long time when submerged underwater.
- Fish—smaller fish always attract larger fish. Hook placement is critical here, since you want the fish to remain living as long as possible. I usually pass the hook twice through the tail region for live bait. For dead bait, I'll pass it through the forehead (skull) and back out through the mouth or bridge of the nose.

Chumming—Chumming is similar to the deer feeder method mentioned, in that a plastic water bottle punched full of holes and filled with dog or cat food pellets (see "Dog Food"), scraps or guts and rocks, is submerged in an area you intend on fishing regularly. The food leaches out of the holes slowly, which attracts the fish into the region on a daily basis to wait for more food. When you're ready to fish, rather than submerging a bottle, drop a hook instead with the same bait, and—voila! They fall for it every time. You can also use a regular can of dog or cat food, with holes punched directly in it. Using this method is the only way I'd suggest for pole fishing as a daily source of food.

Spotlighting—I'm not sure what Mother Nature's obsession is with bright lights, but by keeping a light shining on the water all night, fish will begin congregating in the area daily. Partly, I assume, because it attracts bugs which die and fall into the water, becoming a food source for the aquatic varmints themselves.

Butchering Fowl

IMPORTANT: If butchering can't be carried out immediately, chill carcass at 33-35° to prevent spoiling.

1. For birds, if not using a killing cone, string the animal upside down from the legs and let the blood drain into a plastic container, then defeather (page 226).
2. Cut the head off (if it's still attached) and cut the legs off at the joint. Save these for stews ("Food Preparation and Preservation" page 231).

3. Place the bird on its belly and Cut off the oil gland (bump just above tail) and throw it out.
4. Place the bird on its back and Make a slight incision at the bottom of the neck (don't cut into the crop) and partially remove (don't cut) the esophagus and windpipe.

5. Spin the bird 180°, make a slight incision just above the vent and pull apart the skin to access the gizzard. Rip off the fat from the gizzard, pull out the esophagus and the connecting organs. Then the windpipe and lungs. Place these organs in another plastic container to be prepared ("Food Preparation and Preservation" page 231).
6. Make an incision down the middle of the breast and remove both breasts (or leave whole).

 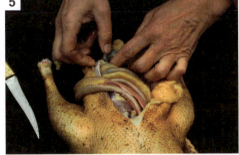 

7. Cut around both thigh and leg quarters, starting at the groin and both wings, starting at the armpit.
8. Finally fillet the meat off from the neck and back.

BY-PRODUCTS

When you can't go to town to purchase products, you learn how to use *everything* you have. Some animals, like chickens, produce a lot of by-products, while animals such as dogs—not so much.

Leather

MATERIALS

animal skin
container or garbage bag
water
1cup vinegar
1 c dish soap or potassium/sodium hydroxide

calcium carbonate or calcium sulfate
gray matter or emulsifying fat (egg yolks, vegetable oil, mayonnaise)
oil

TOOLS

rag and brush
smokehouse or fire
blender
drill with ½-in drill bit or ½-in punch and hammer
measuring tape
pencil or Sharpie

stretch rack
blunt/dull knife
hard-bristle brush
log, large diameter PVC pipe or other cylindrical object
dull curved piece of metal

1. As soon as the skin is removed, roll it up and place it in a container of water or tied garbage bag with the air removed to keep it from drying out.
2. Flesh the hide by placing it on a round long object like a log or large-diameter PVC pipe and running a dull curved piece of metal down and up with long hard strokes.
3. Decide if you want bare leather or hair/fur left on (hair-on). For hair-on, soak and wash in 1 c dish soap to 1 gal water. Dump and repeat, until water runs clear.
4. For bare leather, soak in a solution of potassium/sodium hydroxide (see "Chemical Compounds") and water at 1 c per gal water and 1 gal mixture to every 10 lbs of animal, for 2 to 3 days (more for deer/raccoons/opossums/skunk) until hair easily pulls out from roots.

WARNING: Once you start, don't let hide dry completely.

NOTE: If you're doing hair-on, don't leave material soaking for more than 1 to 2 days. For bare, you can double hydroxide mixture.

Scrub to remove oils and proteins with hard-bristle brush. Dump water, and repeat. Once thoroughly cleaned, repeat wash/scrub/rinse cycle in a solution of 10 gal water and 1 c vinegar to neutralize alkaline.

NOTE: I just throw them in a regular washing machine at this point. Neither the hide nor the light acid/alkaline will hurt the machine. A large washbasin or plastic garbage can will work as well.

5. Wring by twisting and pulling around a column or over a handrail. Lay flat on a clean work surface and pour then scrub calcium carbonate or calcium sulfate, working vigorously into pores. Flip and repeat (for bare).
6. Fill container again with 10 gal water, and let soak/bathe for 2 hrs, then wring again (optional). To remove hair, repeat hide fleshing, scrubbing and rubbing (not cutting) hair off. Soaking helps hide to retain water, causing it to swell and break up collagen fibers, making it softer.

NOTE: There's a layer of skin just underneath (epidermis) that will try to come off during the scraping process. This is okay. If the hide tries to slide around, it's too oily. Repeat washing and rinsing.

7. Once hair is removed, make ½-in holes around edge every 4 to 6 in, 1 in in and hang on a stretch rack (frame slightly larger than material) with cord so that you can access both sides. For hair-on, simply nail to a wall (hair facing wall).
8. Scrape off hypodermis layer on flesh side with a blunt/dull knife to dermis. For hair-on, or if you want rawhide, stop here and leave to dry. If you didn't get all of the epidermis off when scraping the hair, you'll need to now, but don't cut into the dermis. (The dermis layer is your leather.)

NOTE: Scraping will take time to master. Scraping too delicately will take all day. Too rough, and you'll cut through the dermis. The layer around the neck/face is thicker. Around the belly, thinner.

9. The next morning, blend gray matter (brain) in a blender with 1 c warm water per 10 lbs grey matter, then with the brush, work the solution in to each side (bare, 1-side hair-on).

NOTE: As a substitute for grey matter, use any emulsifying fat (water soluble) i.e., egg yolks (1/10 lbs), vegetable oil (3 T/10 lbs), mayonnaise, etc.

10. For our uses (furniture, bedding, comforters, coats, rugs, clothing, shoes, gloves, crafts), we want the hide really soft. To do this, crumple, twist, push, pull and rub it around a column or rail throughout the day, to break up existing protein fibers, and really work in our new proteins. The more you rough it up, the softer it'll be.

NOTE: I tumble it in the dryer (no heat/air) with a few softener sheets or concrete mixer with a few billiard balls (no blades). Also helpful is pressing and sliding a billiard ball or leg bone knob into the hide hard (without ripping) while hung.

11. Continue stretching and working until dry (no longer cold). Then hang in a smokehouse or over a smoking fire (no flames, just hot coals and punk wood) for 12 hrs (12 hours per side for fire smoking) or until golden brown. Smoking closes the pores, waterproofs and preserves leather. If you'd like to dye, do it now.
12. Finally, work enough oil (page 26) into hairless side/s with a rag and brush, so leather is soft, but not saturated.

You now have a beautiful, high quality piece of leather to make or do anything with. Search online for free patterns.

Feathers and Down

Since feathers come out effortlessly when meat is warm, you'll want to begin immediately after slaughter. As the bird's core body temperature drops, its pores close and make the task perpetually harder to the point that you'll need to soak it in hot water to raise the temperature and begin again.

1. With the body still warm, pluck all the feathers out by grabbing and pulling out handfuls. If there's any stubs left, burn them off with a torch.

   NOTE: If you wait too long to pluck, or if the body cools while plucking, you'll need to scald the skin by dunking the corpse head first (hold onto the legs) in a pot of 150-160°F (hot enough to allow easy release of feathers, but not hot enough to cook the bird) for 3 to 4 mins.

2. Separate down and small feathers from medium from quill (tail/primaries/tertials) in inside-out pillowcases. Hang all cases to breathe and dry for 3 days.

   IMPORTANT: For good growth but minimal pin (blood) feathers, butcher after 5 months, but after molt. If processing more than 10 birds at a time, to drop processing time from hours to seconds, build a drum or drill plucker (lots of free DIY designs online).

3. For live picking, at 2 months (then every 6 months, stopping 2 months before winter) just before or during molt (when feathers are loose or dropping), loop a wide piece of cotton around your knee, tied to the bird's feet.

4. Pull the down and small feathers from sides, belly, back, around wings and neck. (Don't pull after a molt; this will cause severe pain. If you're skinning or drawing blood, the feathers aren't ready. Stop immediately, wait a couple weeks and try again or wait to next molt.) Stuff pillowcases (as in step 1) and remove larger quills as necessary. No need to wash as they don't have bacteria/parasites (if you've adhered to the living/grooming conditions in Chapter 8). Store hanging in closet until ready to use.

   IMPORTANT: Live picking isn't to remove feathers, it's to clean discarded/discarding feathers to make the animal more comfortable. Like brushing a shedding cat/dog. So only light pressure is needed.

Wool/Angora and Mohair/Cashmere

You have to understand that shaving an animal isn't cruel if it's done correctly with compassion. In fact, not shaving them, I would argue, is animal cruelty, especially if you didn't match the animal to the environment as I advised. Any women with long hair knows what I'm talking about when summer hits. Imagine your entire body covered in wool.

Alpaca wool grows 5 to 6 inches per year (3 to 4 for llamas) and is 5x warmer than sheep. You may prefer rabbit wool (Angora) or Cashmere (goat) or mohair, all of which are sheered.

NOTE: If it's the animal's first time being sheared, you'll need several people to hold it down.

TOOLS

sharp shears, electric clippers, or large scissors

1. Place on its back, side, or butt with its shoulders and head resting and locked in between your knees (not necessary after a few shears).

2. With a pair of sharp shears, electric clippers, or large scissors, start from the belly (back/butt on a first timer), and cut a strip in a straight line, stopping where neck starts, leaving at least ¾ inch on the body.

   CAUTION: Electric shears are great because they're quick making the experience that much shorter, but they're more prone to nicking. A small nick won't kill the animal, but it will teach her that this process hurts, making her that much more skittish next time. To solve, I place the index finger of trimmer hand between skin and blade guide, which also guarantees my ¾-in spacing.

3. Working out from this strip, lift and cut blanket of one side away in one piece until you reach the back, paying special attention around leg pits. Repeat for the other side, then do the back.

4. In this fashion, cut away sections in basic accessible geometric shapes. This will result in numerous small patches of hair, but once you get the hang of how each section (britch, blanket, apron, etc.,) lays, you can work on bigger swaths.

   IMPORTANT: The first few times it's more important that you and the animal are comfortable, and that it's a pleasant experience, rather than it looking good or you coming out with a superior product. Otherwise, neither of you will want to do it again. If it's pleasant, comfortable and even feels good, even if it looks bad, a haircut can be a pleasant and an enjoyable thing!

Silk

We don't really make silk thread, we just unwind and then wind it. I should note that silk is just a protein and that there are many other creatures that build it. Some types of mayflies, midges, spiders, flies, raspy crickets, thrips, lacewings, silverfish, web-spinners, leafhoppers, beetles, and even fleas all make the protein fiber *fibroin*.

MATERIALS
wheel cocoons
small pot
ice water
black poster board or similar surface
popsicle stick or tongue depressor
large pot or bowl
copper wire or hanger
½-in PVC pipe

TOOLS
tape
spring clamp
slow cooker

magnifying or jewelers glass
vertical coarse bristle brush or ¾-in Dremel
wire cup brush

1. Remove 10 to 20 (start with 10, then try 20) wheel cocoons (more means thicker thread and vice versa) from your cultivation tray (see "Silkworm Farms") 1 week after they start spinning.

    NOTE: *If you wait too long or are breeding silkworms, spent cocoons can still be used for spinning or as a soft silk stuffing in mattresses and pillows.*

2. To avoid damaging the continuity of the single thread and remove the gum (sericin), boil for 1 sec. Once fizzing stops and water turns yellow from melted sericin, remove cocoons and place in ice water. This eases in removing the Keba (first floss) to access the long strands of fine silk.

3. Place on black posterboard or similar surface, (so you can see it) and carefully remove the outer layer (Keba) with a popsicle stick or tongue depressor (save for spinning, then place back in pot).

4. Set up your reeling pot by bending a loosely coiled (⅛-in gap works great) 2-in loop in the middle of a copper wire or hanger.

5. Attach 1 end to a spring clamp, and bend the other straight up so the 2-in loop will sit horizontally in the center of a slow cooker when clamped onto the side, with a final loosely coiled ½-in loop bent into the end.

6. Use a magnifying or jewelers glass to locate the single threads (filaments), or create a rotating whirlpool with a vertical coarse bristle brush (I use a ¾-in Dremel wire cup brush), causing ends to separate/attach to the brush.

7. After a few seconds, stop and lift. Balls that bob are connected. Remove and place in slow cooker filled with water, and repeat. Once all are transferred, feed filaments through loops and around the reel, securing with tape without ever letting go of the ends.

8. For the reel, I find ½-in PVC pipe works great. The wider the diameter, the faster you'll reel. Start reeling slowly, to make sure all balls are bobbing (unspooling) freely before picking up speed.

    NOTE: *The point in reeling is to a) harvest filament from cocoon and b) make usable thread by joining multiple filaments together. Reel the thread onto smaller empty spools later for sewing machine use.*

    IMPORTANT: *If a ball drops out or runs empty, it'll float to the side, away from the group and stop moving. No problem. Just place it in the first pot to relocate the end, thread through the loops again, and twist back into main body. Also, if a cocoon jumps (the filament doesn't unreel properly), stop and work out the issue (it's usually because the water isn't hot enough) or break and start again as described.*

9. When ⅓ (or more) are empty (resemble bubbles) and your thread's considerably thinner to the touch, you're finished. (Eat the silkworm or dispense as feed.)

    NOTE: *Even with 20 balls, your thread will still be exceptionally thin. Most sewing threads consist of 50 to 100 filaments. This means you'll have to reel more coils and either throw (spin) them ("Yarn," page 44) or right-hand lay (twist) together ("String," page 47).*

10. At this point, I'll remove the coil from the reel, twist slightly and tie into a large, loose single knot for further drying and store on a shelf. Dye or leave natural. If the thread feels sticky, re-boil and dry before use.

    Silk is sticky to work with, even after boiling numerous times. You'll have silk all over everything. Keep a clean area, free of distractions and a clean towel nearby to continuously wipe your fingers on.

Wax

1. For a separator, drill and cut a 1⅞-in hole ⅜ in up from the bottom of the side of a clean 5-gal bucket.
2. Install a honey gate.
3. Divide the bottom of a second bucket into quadrants, leaving a ¾-in border in between each, drill a ½-in hole in each quadrant and cut out each quadrant with a jigsaw and fine-tooth blade.
4. Place bottom of bucket on a piece of metal window screen, trace, cut circle and place inside bucket.

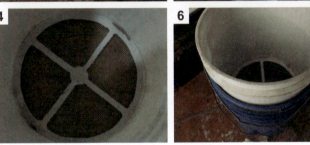

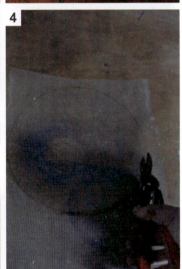

5. (Optional) Drill a ⅛-in hole in the top of the side and install a turkey thermometer.
6. Place second bucket inside the first bucket.
7. Smoke then pull *non flow hive* honey supers at honey extraction times ("Honey," page 220) using a painter's scrape pry bar for hive tool. Brush off bees and store supers in a cool area.
8. Pull frames, scrape comb into bucket with a plastic spatula, cover, and let sit to drip in the sun. To prevent melting wax, don't let interior temperature get above 100°.
9. Once honey stops dripping, pull bucket and lay screen with wax near hives for bees to clean the rest, then store wax until ready to use in 5-gal buckets or paper bags in a cool space. (Pour honey into jars and enjoy.)

NOTE: 8 kg of honey will produce 1 kg of wax.

Milk

Goats and llamas provide about 3 quarts of milk per day most of the year. For volume, you can't beat low-fat Saanens; select the dwarf progeny to make extraction easier. If you go with Boer, get a 75-25 cross with Nubian. This is a great milk and meat producing mix with little disease. Once a doe kids, allow the consumption of colostrum for 1 week. Then you can begin to milk. If milking more than 3 does at once, invest in a vacuum extractor to save hand strain. Udderly's EZ Hand Milker is the simplest I've come across.

1. Place a bucket upside down as a seat. Shave the tits (if necessary) and clean nipples with warm soapy water. Dry, then massage (or slam into them with your head as their kids do) the udder to induce oxytocin release, to drop milk.
2. Wrap your forefinger around top part of teat where it drops down from the body, pinching off with the help of the thumb, forming a circle with a balloon underneath.
3. With the other 3 fingers and bottom palm, squeeze into a clean container. If the teat is extremely large, pinch off the upper area with 1 entire hand while squeezing with the other. Once empty, massage again, then switch while milk drops, and repeat.

NOTE: If your goat is a mover (and shaker), place her in a stanchion. If she's a kicker, hobble by sliding the handle (slip knotted) of a dog leash to hock level, wrap around once, then tie off to back of stand or tie the two back legs together.

Eggs

Typically, Lucia looks for the eggs and puts them in a basket in a regular Easter egg hunt fashion. When free-ranging, fowl tend to pick places other than where convenient. Once you discover their hiding spots, though, they'll always use the same ones. The habit can be refocused by adding ceramic eggs in laying boxes.

Hens begin laying around 4 to 5 months, produce 1 egg a day for the first few years (except during molt), then 1 to 1.5 per day for 5 to 8 years when we provide: summer light hours (12–14 hrs) artificially in winter months; access to unlimited clean water, calcium, grit, and protein; and no extreme alterations or disturbances in routine.

When they're getting ready to lay, they become more vocal, talking and telling everyone and everything that passes that it's almost time. If you approach too fast, she'll lay submissively. If there's a rooster, this is when he'll mount her. This is also the time that you have to be really careful about predators, since they'll squat around anything. When they're actually laying, their pelvis widens dramatically (they look really fat), thighs swell, legs get light yellow (because nutrients from the pigmentation in their skin go into the yolk), and their crest gets swollen and turns a deep red.

Once she lays, she'll yell at the top of her lungs, telling everyone of her accomplishment (or for everyone to stay away, I really have no idea to be honest). If you think your hen may be laying but can't find the eggs, check her vent (butt). It will be glossy and wet. A dry vent signals no egg has passed. When her production days are coming to an end, the same changes (vocal, widened pelvis, swollen thighs, light yellow-colored legs, swollen deep red crest) will occur in reverse.

Ducks lay less but larger eggs and lay all year without light or feed. Guinea hens aren't great layers. They produce seasonally (March-May) at half the size; and turkeys are worthless. Emu and Ostrich, on the other hand, lay almost as frequently (every other day if eggs are removed daily for 50 to 80 days), and at 2 to 3 lbs per egg, they're comparable to 24 chicken eggs!

There are a lot of misconceptions surrounding eggs. The most common, so absurd it's hard for me to repeat, is that you need a rooster for hens to lay eggs. This is 100% false. Once hens are of egg-laying age, they'll produce an egg a day (depending on species). I say this because I see and hear about people butchering hens for meat (losing egg production) and keeping the rooster. Hens are like any other female mammal. Human eggs are produced and expelled at regular intervals without male assistance, existence, or participation of any kind. The only thing males do or do not do is fertilize them before they come out. So, if you have a bunch of birds and don't care about reproducing more, eat the males.

Chapter 13: Food Preparation and Preservation

I'm not trying to write a cookbook, but everyone should know how to make these common recipes and make food last.

CONCOCTIONS

Add 1 leech foot and (2) third eyes of toad to 3 gallons of field fog and mix for 4 minutes. Just kidding! The recipes here are much easier to follow than that, but some of them are just as magical.

Electrolytes

I don't profess to know exactly what electrolytes do on the cellular level, but I do know that if you're going to be working all day in the heat, drinking electrolytes is the best thing you can do to avoid dehydration. The following items are some of the best natural electrolytes I've found.

- **Sea salt:** magnesium, calcium, sodium, chloride
- **Honey:** immune booster, antibacterial, carbohydrate (instant and time release calories)
- **Baking soda:** sodium bicarbonate
- **Baking powder or salt substitute:** potassium, chloride
- **Lime or lemon:** vitamin C

When you mix them all together, you get an all-natural, homemade electrolyte concoction that is just as good or better than what you can buy at the store.

MATERIALS

8 c sea salt (page 233)

4 t baking soda

4 t baking powder

1 L water

1 lime or lemon

½ c honey ("Beekeeping," page 216)

TOOLS

airtight container

desiccant packet (page 248)

mixing spoon

1. Mix 8 c of sea salt, 4 t of baking soda, and 4 t of baking powder. Place the dry mixture in an airtight container with a desiccant packet, and when you're ready to use it, mix 1 t with 1 L of water, 1 squeezed lime or lemon, and ½ c of honey until dissolved.

Vinegar

Essentially, vinegar is just alcohol that's fermented a second time to become acetic acid through oxidation by acid bacteria, the two well-known vinegars being made from grape (balsamic vinegar) and apple (apple cider vinegar). But you can, and I encourage you to, make vinegar out of beets, pineapple, dates, figs, sugarcane, coconut, honey, grains, molasses, beer, whey, maple syrups, and even wood like beech. All can be used in, of course, salad dressings but also in mustard, ketchup, mayonnaise, and other sauces.

1. Fill a wide jar or pot (the wider the better) half full with the fruit of your choice.

   NOTE: To speed up the process, instead of fruit, add wine, mead, beer, etc.

2. Fill the remaining half with water and cover the pot with cheesecloth or cotton rag and place in a cupboard or other dark, warm location.

3. Stir or shake 1–2 times a week for 2 weeks to 2 months, depending on alcohol content. Higher alcohol content requires a longer fermentation period.

   NOTE: To speed up the process of higher alcohol content liquids, dilute 10–20% with water.

4. Siphon off the top vinegar, leaving the bottom gelatinous goo, "mother," intact on the bottom. Refill and repeat.

   NOTE: The process is much faster when kick-starting the batch with "mother." If when siphoning, the goo substance is still on top, your vinegar isn't ready yet. Wait until the top layer collapses and sinks to the bottom.

5. Bottle, cork, and store in a cool, dark location.

Emulsions

Emulsions are mixtures of liquids that are typically immiscible, or unmixable. Your typical emulsions are fish emulsions, cosmetics, mayonnaise, and, in the case of the following, vinaigrettes.

MATERIALS

1 c water or acid (e.g., vinegar [see above])

3 c oil

salt

pepper

herbs or other seasonings

3 T egg yolk, honey (page 220), mustard, soy lecithin, Pickering stabilization, DATEM

TOOLS

1-qt glass jar or salad dressing bottle with lid

mixing spoon

1. Add 1 c of external phase liquid, which is water or acid, in this case vinegar (page 232) and 3 c of internal phase liquid, an oil, in a 1-qt glass jar or salad dressing bottle.
2. Add salt and pepper, herbs, or (optional) other seasonings and stabilize the mixture to prevent separation by adding 3 T of emulsifier, such as egg yolk, honey (page 220), mustard, soy lecithin, Pickering stabilization, DATEM. Place the lid, shake the bottle, and add more emulsifier until the oil remains suspended.

Sea Salt (Sodium Chloride)

Before we lived on the ocean, I produced potassium salt from neutralized lactic acid (fermented milk) or from wood ash, which we produce when making potash (page 58)—but sea salt is much tastier.

MATERIALS
seawater

TOOLS
plastic pale/bucket
large pot
skimmer
spatula

1. In a 5-gal pail or bucket, collect seawater, skim off the top and let the rest sit, giving any sand and other sediment time to settle.

   NOTE: You can achieve the same results by passing the water through a few layers of a T-shirt or cloth filter (page 179) to remove sediment.

   IMPORTANT: Avoid shore water. It's full of sand, contaminants, and possible pollutants.

2. Boil all the water off in large stock pot, skimming until foam desists.
3. Let cool, then scrape pot bottom to retrieve salt crystals.
4. Place crystals in a pepper grinder/shaker or blend into a fine powder in blender or coffee bean grinder and, using a funnel, pour into a saltshaker.

   NOTE: 5 gallons of water will produce roughly 4 or 5 c of salt or a ratio of 1:28 salt–seawater, depending on the salinity of your location. In other words, seawater contains approximately 3%–3.5% salt. Also, the same results can be achieved by simply dehydrating the seawater in a solar dehydrator (page 137) or just flat cookie pans placed out in the sun.

Potassium Salt (Potassium Chloride)

If you'd like to try making potassium salt, aka reduced sodium salt like LoSalt, vegetable salt, Morton salt substitute, and Morton Lite Salt, which mitigates the risk of cardiovascular disease, hypertension, and high blood pressure, all you need is some ash and hydrochloric acid.

MATERIALS
ash ("Potash," page 58)   (optional) regular salt
hydrochloric acid

1. Filter ash, potassium carbonate, through a coffee filter and neutralize the potassium carbonate with hydrochloric acid (muriatic acid) to get potassium chloride.

   NOTE: Ash from corn, papaya, and seaweed produce more salt than others.

2. Wash and dehydrate. If the flavor's too bitter for you, mix regular salt in at 1:3 (potassium chloride–salt).

Pepper

To make pepper, all you have to know how to do is roast some peppercorns and grind them into powder.

MATERIALS
black Tellicherry peppercorns or other pepper berries

TOOLS
cookie sheet
spice mill or mortar and pestle
airtight container
desiccant packet (page 248)

1. Roast black Tellicherry peppercorns or other pepper berries for 5 minutes, or until popping and charring occurs.
2. Then mill in a spice mill or with a mortar and pestle as described in making meal (page 207) into coarse or fine meal, and store the powder in an airtight container with a desiccant packet.

Spices

Making spices from everyday plants is one of the easiest and most ancient of DIYs. You can either roast to dehydrate or dehydrate, your preference.

MATERIALS
spice seeds, buds, fruits, flowers, bark, or roots

TOOLS
spice grinder or mortar and pestle
airtight container
desiccant packet (page 248)

1. In a solar dehydrator (page 137), roast or dehydrate seeds, buds, fruits, flowers, bark, or roots of equivalent names.
2. Mill in a spice grinder or with a mortar and pestle, and store the powder in an airtight container with a desiccant packet (page 248).

Sugar

Glycerin is a sugar substitute. Instead, we can make real sugar with just a handful of ingredients.

MATERIALS
sugarcane, beet, agave, sorghum, or other high-sugar fruit
sugar crystals

TOOLS
juicer, cane mill, or oil press
clean cloth
hand mixer or mixing spoon
cookie sheet or molds
dehydrator or solar dehydrator (page 137)
container
desiccant packet (page 248)
large pot with lid
skimmer
candy thermometer

1. Extract juice from sugarcane, beet, agave, sorghum, or other fruit by running stalks through a juicer, mill, or oil press, which can be hand-cranked or animal powered, and filter the juice through a clean cloth or cloth filter (page 179).

   NOTE: Expect a yield of 40–50 kg per 100 kg of cane and a 20–25% sugar content.

2. Boil to draw off moisture, constantly skimming off impurities, until liquid crystalizes.
3. Measure with a candy thermometer and when it's reached over 90% syrup density or around 270°F, remove from heat.
4. Decant into a cookie sheet or molds, leaving bottom settlement in the pot.

5. Leave as is (panela) or seed with brown sugar crystals (page 235) and mix rapidly with a hand mixer or a wood spoon, which adds air, until crystals form.
6. Dehydrate the crystals, break and mill them in the same process as making meal (page 207), and store the sugar with a desiccant packet.

   NOTE: Expect a yield of 7–10 kg per 100 kg of cane.

Brown Sugar

I have some bad news for you . . . The "brown sugar" you purchase in grocery stores isn't brown sugar. It's just white sugar with coloring, disguised as brown sugar. With the exception of Billington's dark brown sugar and a couple others, all brown sugar manufactures, at least in the United States, grind white sugar slightly less fine, then add a little molasses during processing to give it that brown color, caramel flavor, and sticky texture. So, knowing that, here's how to make semifake brown sugar.

MATERIALS
1 c white sugar (page 234)
1–2 t molasses (treacle)

TOOLS
small mixing bowl
airtight container
desiccant packet (page 248)

1. In a small mixing bowl, using your hands, mix 1–2 t molasses with 1 c white sugar until the sugar turns completely brown. The more molasses you add, the darker the brown sugar.
2. Store in an airtight container with a desiccant packet (page 248).

Powdered Sugar

MATERIALS
1 c sugar (page 234)
1 c starch

TOOLS
blender
spice mill
sifter

1. Pulse 1 c of sugar and 1 c of starch in a blender until powdery; mill in the process described when making meal (page 207), and sift.

Honey

Honey is made up of 70% sugar, with vitamins, minerals, and anti-microbial agents, and it never spoils. Store it in a cupboard out of sunlight. If crystallization occurs, heat it until it's the right consistency.

See "Honey" on page 220 for harvesting.

Flavor Concentrates (Syrups)

Ever had those strawberry, blueberry syrups? Another bubble burster . . . they're not actually juice extracted from blueberries and strawberries, just sugar water with a little strawberry juice. So, we can definitely make our own.

MATERIALS
2 lbs fresh strawberries or other fruit
1 qt water
2 c sugar (page 234)

TOOLS
liquid water enhancer container or syrup container
skimmer
cloth
mixing spoon
medium pot
chopping knife

1. Hull and chop 2 lbs of fresh strawberries or other fruit and boil them with 1 qt of water for 5 minutes, then simmer for 15 minutes, skimming foam.

   NOTE: For fruit syrup to put on your french toast, pancakes, waffles, or anything else, simmer to 50% reduction instead.

2. Strain through a cloth, simmer again, and mix in 2 c of sugar (page 234) until it's dissolved. Let the syrup cool, then suction fill a liquid water enhancer container or syrup container.

   NOTE: For cane, beet, agave, or sorghum syrups, add respective sugars instead (page 234).

3. Operation: Add 1–2 short squirts of concentrate in 2 c of ice water.

Maple Syrup

Maple syrup comes from the sap of all maple trees (black, red, silver, sugar), even some non-maple trees like walnut and box elder trees. But the highest concentration of sugar is found in sugar maple.

MATERIALS
canning jars

TOOLS
measuring tape
cordless drill with ⁷⁄₁₆-in or ⁵⁄₁₆-in and ½-in bits
maple spout
small ball-peen hammer
1-gallon sterilized milk jug or other suitable container with lid
medium pot
stirring spoon
candy thermometer

1. Between March and mid-April, or when buds sprout, pick a maple tree that's 10 in thick or more at the 5-ft mark.

   NOTE: If the tree's diameter is 20–24 in, you can put in two taps; if it's larger than 24 in, you can do three.

2. Measure 2–4 ft up from the ground, drill a 2-in deep ⁷⁄₁₆-in hole (a 1½-in deep, ⁵⁄₁₆-in hole for a ⁵⁄₁₆-in spout) at a 10° upward angle. Tap in the maple spout.

3. Drill a ½-in hole in the top of the side of a 1-gallon sterilized milk jug or other suitable container and hang it on the tap hook, or if no hook is present, slide it over the spout, placing the lid on top to keep out debris and critters.

4. Once full, replace it with an empty, then immediately boil the sap in a shallow pan until runny, adding more as necessary. Only boil outdoors or in a vented room.

   NOTE: The barbs on the adapter will hold the jug in place, but if you have livestock or high winds, bungee the handle to the tree.

5. Check the temperature with a candy thermometer and remove from heat at 66–68.9% sugar content, 7.1°F above boiling. Let sit for 3 days, reheat to 180°F, then decant the syrup into canning jars, leaving sediment in the pot, and seal.

   NOTE: Expect 5–15 gallons of sap per tree and 40–80 gallons per year, depending on tree size. You can make 1 qt of syrup for every 10 gallons of sap.

FOOD

Skim Milk

There's actually little difference between whole, 2%, 1%, low-fat, fat-free, reduced-fat, and skim milk—"reduced-fat" equals 2%, "low-fat" equals 1%, "fat-free," which is the same as "skim" equals 0%, essentially meaning the fat has been removed, leaving minerals and water.

Here's the thing though. You think that whole milk is 100% fat milk, and therefore 2% is just 2% of the fat content of whole milk. And you'd be wrong. Whole milk isn't 100% fat, that would just be fat and probably look like butter. Whole milk is actually, in reality, only 3% fat. You've been misled. Milk coming straight out of the cow, bottled and placed on your grocery store shelf, only has 3% total fat. Remove 1%, you get reduced fat or "2%," remove another 1%, you get "1%" or "low fat," remove another 1%, you get 0% or "skim" or "fat-free."

And now that we know that these fats are actually good for you, if you're consuming 2-1-0%, you may actually be on the losing side of better health. Though again, it's a very minimal difference. Either way, we can make all three of them with one recipe.

MATERIALS
bottles

TOOLS
sun tea jar or other container with spigot
skimmer

NOTE: Since cow milk, unlike goat milk, isn't homogenized unless it's store bought, it will separate faster.

1. Fill a sun tea jar or other container with a spigot on the bottom with raw milk, and let sit in a dark cupboard at room temperature for 2–4 days or until fat, the cream, separates and rises to the top. Skim off the top and save by bottling the milk left over, or drain the milk from the spigot, stopping short of the fat layer. Since the fat is skimmed off, what's left is non-fat, or "skim" milk. Add some fat to your milk to create 2% or 3%.

Evaporated Milk

Evaporated milk is different than dried or powdered milk. Despite what the name implies, it's only slightly evaporated in that the water content is only partially removed.

MATERIALS
3½ c milk

TOOLS
small pot
stirring spoon
strainer
jars

1. Boil 2 c of milk while stirring, then set heat to low and add 2½ c more. Every 30 minutes, remove the top layer, stir, and repeat until volume is reduced by 60%, then strain, cool, and can (page 245).

Buttermilk

See step one in Butter on page 238.

Curds and Whey and Cream

When making curds and whey, you can also get cream out of the process.

MATERIALS
homemade skim milk (page 236)

TOOLS
skimmer
container with lid
two jars

1. Mix a batch of skim milk (page 236) and let sit for an additional 2–3 days or until 3 distinct layers form: top, white cream; middle, yellow whey; bottom, white curds.

2. Then to make cream, skim the cream with a skimmer and place it in a container with a lid.

NOTE: To make whipping or heavy cream, use 36–50% of the fat content that you skimmed while making skim milk.

3. To make curds and whey, pour off the other two layers, using two jars, and then can (page 245) and store.

Whipped Cream

MATERIALS
12 oz evaporated milk (page 237)
1 t vanilla extract
½–¾ c powdered sugar (page 235)

TOOLS
medium bowl
whisk
eggbeater

1. Chill 12 oz of evaporated milk in a bowl in the freezer for 30 minutes.
2. Remove and whisk for 30 minutes or more, and beat on high for about a minute or until foamy.
3. Add 1 t of vanilla extract, ½–¾ c of powdered sugar, and beat for another couple minutes or until the cream thickens.

Butter

Butter is just the fat of milk. When everything else (water, milk solids) is stripped away, what's left is butter.

MATERIALS
cream
tinfoil

TOOLS
jar with lid
cheesecloth
towel
small bowl

1. Fill a jar halfway with cream, replace the lid, and let the cream sit until it reaches room temperature.
2. Shake the jar for 15–20 minutes or until you hear or feel the butter ball/s knocking around inside. Open the jar and you'll see a large ball or several small balls of butter on the bottom. The longer you shake it, the more globular and cohesive and conglomerated the balls will become. The liquid that remains is buttermilk.

   NOTE: Expect a quarter jar of butter for half a jar of cream.

3. Filter through cheesecloth, then thoroughly rinse the butter ball until water flows clear. Place it on a towel and press firmly with both hands. Place the ball in a small bowl, then mold or cut it into rectangular cubes and wrap it in tinfoil. For it to fully solidify, store the butter in a cool dark place like you would regular butter.

   NOTE: Notice how white it is. This is the real color of butter since it comes from milk. Add artificial yellow food coloring and salt to match grocery store brands if you'd like.

Quick Bread

Quick breads are breads that are leavened via baking soda and powder rather than yeast.

MATERIALS

2 c flour
½ c sugar
1½ t baking powder
½ t baking soda
1 t salt
¼ c melted butter
1 c buttermilk
1 egg
oil
(optional) 1 c chopped fruit, nuts
(optional) cinnamon, cheese, jalapenos, or other toppings.

TOOLS

whisk
loaf pan

1. Mix 2 c of flour, ½ c of sugar, 1½ t of baking powder, ½ t of baking soda, 1 t of salt, then add ¼ c of melted butter, 1 c of buttermilk, and 1 egg, and whisk until thick.
2. Transfer batter into an oiled loaf pan. Place it in a preheated oven at 350°, and bake for 45–50 minutes, or until bread rises.
3. (Optional) Add 1 c of chopped fruit, nuts, cinnamon, cheese, jalapeno, or other toppings.

Tortillas

Living off the grid, corn tortillas were the easiest, fastest staple food we could make, while burning the least calories doing it. It really gave us the most bang for our buck.

MATERIALS

½ c water
3 c cornmeal or bread flour

TOOLS

(1) large ziplock bag or grocery bag
flat skillet or frying pan
(2) 1½-in hinges
(2) 1 x 10 x 10-in boards
cordless drill with ⅛-in drill bit
impact drill with apex adapter and #2 Phillips tip

1. Build a tortilla press by installing two 1½-in hinges on one side of two 1 x 10 x 10-in boards, leaving a ⅛-in gap in between.
2. Mix ½ c of water with 3 c of cornmeal or bread flour until it reaches dough consistency.
3. Place a large ziplock or grocery bag with sides cut inside the press, fold in the back.
4. Roll a hand-sized ball of dough and place it in the middle of either side of the press.
5. Close the tortilla press and press down on the dough.

6. Open the press, pull the plastic out, flip the tortilla into a flat skillet or frying pan, and cook it on medium-high for 2–3minutes until lightly browned. Flip and repeat.
7. Add butter (page 238), beans, chicken, cheese, beef, shrimp, cream, rice, guacamole, sour cream, salsa, or anything else.

Yogurt

Yogurt is just cultured milk. Bacteria ferment milk, converting lactose sugars into lactic acid, which causes it to thicken and have a tart flavor.

MATERIALS
raw or whole milk (page 236)
ice water
½ c starter culture (L. Bulgaricus, S. Thermophilus, L. Acidophilus, Bifidus, L. Casei).
dry milk or gelatin
(optional) fresh chopped fruit

TOOLS
stirring spoon
large bowl
whisk
yogurt containers with lids

1. In a medium pot, heat raw or whole milk to 200°F, while stirring. Let cool, or place in ice water, to 112–115°F. Continue stirring to prevent skin growth.
2. Add ½ c of starter culture. Cover the pot and store it in an ice chest or on a sprout heating mat at 110°F for 4–8 hours to cultivate, or you can dehydrate the mix to use later. Taste test the mix after 4 hours to see if it's tart enough for you. The longer yogurt sits, the thicker and more tart it becomes.

    NOTE: You can also use ½ c of unflavored yogurt with "live active yogurt cultures" in the ingredients to culture your yogurt. Also, the strain of yeast that cultures yogurt is also found in chili stems. Just dice them up and throw into the mix instead of using a culture.

3. Drain off or whisk in any surface whey, add dry milk or gelatin, 1 c at a time for body, then transfer the yogurt to containers with lids and refrigerate.
4. (Optional) Add fresh chopped fruit to flavor the yogurt.
5. Save ½ c of the yogurt to seed the next batch.

Cottage Cheese

When making cheese, keep everything sterile. Bacteria and mold spores that helped us to make penicillin (page 256) will hurt us making cheeses. The last thing you want is moldy cheese! . . . Unless you're making penicillin, that is!

MATERIALS
2 gal and 1 qt fresh milk
2–3 gallons of creamless curds and whey (page 237)
2 c starter culture
½ t rennet
½-in wood or plastic dowel
2 t salt
1 T cream

TOOLS
double boiler
rag
skimmer
stirring spoon
dicing knife
strainer
(2) airtight containers with lids
whisk

1. Boil water in the top pot of a double boiler, drain, add 1qt of fresh milk, cover with a rag, and let sit at room temperature for 1day or until sour.
2. Remove the top layer with a skimmer. Heat 2–3 gallons of creamless curds and whey to 185°F for 20 minutes, then let cool to 75–80°F before mixing into milk. Let sit for another 24 hours, stirring occasionally.

    NOTE: This is your starter culture, which can also be ordered online. If you make a lot of cheese, use part of this culture to inoculate a fresh batch of curds and whey (page 237) daily or weekly.

3. In the bottom pot, heat 2 gallons of milk to 85°F, stirring frequently. Mix in 2 c of starter culture, and let inoculate for 12–24 hours. Mix in ½ t of rennet, and let separate in a warm spot for another 12–24 hours.

    WARNING: If you add too little rennet, your milk won't curd; if you add too much, it'll be too dense.

4. Check by pressing a dowel into the curds. If the curds hold their shape, they're ready. Cut into ¼-in cubes and transfer to the top pot.

    WARNING: If you allow the milk to stand longer than necessary before cutting, your cheese will end up hard and tough.

5. Fill the bottom pot with water, place the top pot inside, and cook at 110°, stirring gently. Taste test after 30 minutes, then strain any remaining whey. Reserve 1 qt of whey for the rennet of your next batch to coagulate your milk. You can use it up to 15 times.

    NOTE: Substituting whey in pastry recipes that call for milk or water results in an excellent finished product.

6. Rinse the curds and dust them with 2 t of salt and 1 T of cream. (Optional) Whisk to get even distribution. Transfer to a container with a lid.

Mozzarella

For a cheese, mozzarella is one of the lower fat options. I first learned how to make mozzarella cheese using milk from a water buffalo.

MATERIALS
homemade cottage cheese (page 240)
water
1 c salt per 2 qt of water

TOOLS
large mixing bowl

1. In a large mixing bowl, make and cure cottage cheese in the fridge for 2 days or more by following steps 1–6 of "Cottage Cheese" (page 240). Be sure to cut the curds to ¼ x 2 in.
2. To test, cover a curd with water and heat to 175°F. If it starts melting in 15–30 seconds, or stretches under its own weight, it's ready. If not, chill another day and test again.
3. Soak the cheese for 5–15 minutes, mixing in 1 c of salt per 2 qt of water.
4. Remove the cheese, rinse it, and serve.

Jelly

Jelly, jam, fruit preserves, and other spreads are all made from fruit, sugar, and pectin. The difference between the three is merely the size of the fruit added, jelly being the smallest made from primarily the juice of the fruit, with no visible chunks, making it almost clear in transparency and the smoothest in consistency.

MATERIALS
fruit syrup ("Flavor Concentrates," page 235) or fruit puree
(optional) 1 T of citric acid and/or pectin per 2 c juice

TOOLS
medium pot
spoon

1. Cook fruit syrup until thick, as described in "Flavor Concentrates" (page 235). Taste test on a frozen spoon. Check consistency and flavor, and repeat, adding more sugar as needed.

    NOTE: For grapes, since pulp is ready before skins, separate skins from pulp and cook separately.

2. Most fruits contain all the pectin and acid needed to jell and thicken. Otherwise, to thicken, add 1 T of citric acid and/or pectin to 2 c of juice.

    NOTE: Fruits like blackberries, apples, and plums contain enough pectin that adding more isn't needed, whereas peaches, blueberries, and apricots require more. Always add more acid when adding more pectin since the carbohydrate pectin requires heat and acidity to gel.

3. Defoam, decant through a strainer into a jar to ¼ in from the top, and seal by canning (page 245).

Jam

Jam has the next smoothest consistency, being made from mostly fruit pulp or crushed fruit, with little liquid or visible fruit chunks, and therefore, it is almost opaque in transparency.

MATERIALS
2½ c fruit
¼ c sugar (page 234)
(optional) ¼ c lemon
pinch of salt

TOOLS
skimmer
potato masher
dicing knife
medium sauce pot
jars with lids

1. Dice 2½ c of fruit and pour them into a medium sauce pot, along with ¼ c of sugar, ¼ c of lemon (optional), and a pinch of salt. Heat on medium and mash, then bring to boil, stir for 5–10 minutes or until foam starts. Remove foam with a skimmer.

   NOTE: To set jam without cooking, add 1 T pectin and stir a lot.

2. Check consistency and taste, and repeat, then decant into jar and can (page 245).

Chutney

A chutney is, mostly, just a jam with fruits, sometimes vegetables, vinegar, and spices like cumin, fennel, cayenne, garam masala, onion, ginger, garlic, and mustard.

Marmalade

Marmalade is one step up in that the fruit chunks are slightly larger than in jam. I find the consistency to be of a jellied jam.

MATERIALS
1 lb oranges
¼ lemon
1½ c water
stirring spoon
1½ c sugar

TOOLS
dicing knife
candy thermometer
medium pot
spoon
small plate
jars with lids

1. Slice 1 lb of oranges (peels on) into quarters, adding ¼ of a lemon. Then cut those into thin slices. Discard the seeds.
2. In a medium pot, bring 1½ c water and the slices to a boil, then simmer covered for 20–30 minutes while stirring, and uncovered for an additional 10–15 minutes or until citrus is gelatin-like.
3. Now bring back to a boil, mix in 1½ c sugar and continue stirring until temperature on your candy thermometer reads 223ºF.
4. Test by placing a spoonful on a chilled plate for 20–30 seconds. If it's too runny, continue boiling in 5-minute increments, repeating testing until gel like consistency.
5. Once the correct consistency is reached, can (page 245).

Fruit Preserves

Fruit preserves are one step up the ladder from marmalades, being mostly made from whole or large chunks of fruit. These are the fillings you'll find in pies. You can also make preserves out of vegetables.

MATERIALS
¼ c sugar
3 lb fruit

TOOLS
slow cooker
dicing knife
jars with lids

1. In a slow cooker, sprinkle ¼ c sugar over 3 lb diced (for larger fruit) or whole fruit and cook on high for 2 hours.
2. Once they're finished cooking, can them (page 245).

Conserves

Conserves are similar to chunky jams, the difference being, typically more than one fruit is used, as well as even nuts and dried fruit.

Spreads

Spreads are similar in consistency to a jam that's more liquid-y. These are 100% fruit with no sugar, which explains why they are less sweet and have more fruit flavoring, and no pectin, which explains the lack of body, but with apple or grape juice.

Fruit Butters

No, not butter like dairy butter (page 238) or peanut butter, though peanuts being a fruit technically qualify, but butter from fruit. Fruit butters are typically made from berries, apple, mango, pear, nectarine, stone fruit, and even pumpkin. Anything but citrus.

MATERIALS
1 lb chopped fruit
⅛ c granulated sugar
salt
⅓ T lemon juice

TOOLS
vented crockpot
mixing stick
immersion blender

1. Mix 1 lb chopped fruit, ⅛ c granulated sugar, a pinch of salt in a vented crockpot (or keep the lid cracked) and simmer on low for 10–12 hours, or until dark and creamy to reduce, stirring every few hours.
2. Remove lid, mix in ⅓ T lemon juice, and let cool. Stir to desired consistency with an immersion blender.

Compote

Finally, we have the largest of the fruit concoctions, the compote, which uses whole, uncut fruit stewed in syrup.

Puree

Purees are similar in consistency to compotes, but they use fruits *or* vegetables. Once cooked, the materials are then ground, pressed, blended, and sieved to a creamy paste or liquid consistency.

PRESERVATION

Food doesn't just spoil, rot, or biodegrade on its own. Materials, living or dead, don't want to change. Something still wants to stay still; it doesn't want to move. Tiny microscopic animals eat food stuffs and other biological matter, degrading (bio-degrading) it into its smaller chemical components.

Preservation doesn't usually prevent spoilage or kill pathogenic bacteria but rather slows them by creating a very inhospitable environment for lifeforms to grow in. Like all living things, bacteria needs several things in order to survive, multiply, and thrive: food, air, water, warmth. By lowering the temperature, removing air or water, or changing the food to be too acidic, alkaline, salty, or sugary to consume, we remove one or several of these elements.

- Unless refrigerated, all foods should be stored in a cool, dry, dark place.
- Preserving doesn't add taste or freshness. However fresh the food was before, it will be slightly less after. This is why it's important to only use the freshest, best-tasting foods.
- Similarly, using the freshest food also extends preservation limits.
- Label all preserves with name, date, "eat by" date, and any special preparation instructions.
- Honey is a powerful antibacterial and antimicrobial. I suggest adding it to all preservation methods as a backup.

Curing

Curing, specifically salt packing or salting, is another method of preserving, usually for meat and fish.

MATERIALS
½ lb sea salt, sodium nitrate, or potassium nitrate
¼ c sugar
12 lb meat

TOOLS
wax, wax paper, or plastic wrap

1. Mix ½ lb sea salt, sodium nitrate, or potassium nitrate with ¼ c sugar, and dust 12 lb of meat that is cut into 4 in³.
2. Rub in with force, then pat until the excess salt falls off. Flip, repeat.
3. Place on wax paper in fridge uncovered for 24 hours (48 for fish) until particulates dissolve and soak in, then recoat daily until mix is used up. (Optional) Hang to dry for 3 weeks. Then coat with wax or wrap with wax paper or plastic.
4. To consume, soak in ice water for 12 hours.

Brining

Brining is similar to curing, the difference being instead of dusting with salt, we soak the food (again usually fish and meat) in a saltwater solution.

MATERIALS
5 c water
5 T salt

TOOLS
plastic container with lid

1. Mix 5 c water and 5 T salt until salt is fully dissolved, then fill a plastic container halfway with the solution.
2. Add meat or fish, then top off with solution. Place in refrigerator with lid on.

Dehydrating

Anything—fruit, veggies, roots, milk, seaweed, fish, snake—can be, and are dehydrated for a number of reasons from preservation to incense and spice (page 234) making.

MATERIALS
food of choice
marinade of choice

TOOLS
solar dehydrator (page 137) or air-driven dehydrator
jerky slicer or cheese grater
airtight container
desiccant packet (page 248)

1. Using a solar dehydrator (page 137) or an air-driven dehydrator, sterilize and preheat the chamber while you perform the prep work.
2. For meat, remove the fat and slice or roll material to ⅛–³⁄₁₆ in thick in a jerky slicer or cheese grater.
3. Marinate in salt and pepper, sugar, soy sauce, or your favorite seasonings, and place on the dehydrator shelf.

4. Once the top side looks fairly dried out, flip and repeat.
5. To test, pull a piece, let cool, and bend. Too much moisture and it'll fold, too dry and it'll break. It should be the consistency of dry leather, without an oily residue.
6. Package in an airtight container with adesiccant packet. Rehydrate with water or add to soups, stews, and chili.

NOTE: The process can also be achieved in a stove with the door cracked at temps under 170°.

Canning

Just as many things can be canned (jarred) as can be dehydrated… fruits, vegetables, meats, anything! Canning preserves foods by first killing off existing, harmful micro-organisms and spores, then acting as a barrier (the jar or can) to prevent further entry.

MATERIALS
jars with a beveled raised tab or mason jars
food of choice

TOOLS
large pot
tongs
towels
electric shaver, toothbrush, or other vibrating electrical device

1. Use a jar with a beveled raised tab in the center of the lid, a vacuum indicator, or use a mason jar. Boil the jar, along with any tools, towels, and lids separate, for 1 second to sterilize.
2. Remove any bones, stems, or seeds from the food product and simmer in a pot (in broth for cooked meat products), 10 minutes for fruits or vegetables in pint jars, or 75 minutes for meats. Simmer for 90 minutes if the fruits, vegetables, or meats are in quart-size jars.

IMPORTANT: Add 10 minutes for every 1000 ft of elevation. For raw meats, since they are a low acid, salt or sugar food, using a pressure canner is the only way to bring them up to a high enough pressure long enough to safely can.

3. Remove jars and fill to ⅛–¼ in from the top, place an electric shaver, toothbrush or other vibrating electrical device against the underside of the jar and vibrate to remove bubbles. Top with syrup, broth, or sterilized water using a spoon placed over contents to prevent water mixing, place the lid loosely on top with tongs.
4. Place jar on a towel, tighten the lid, and let cool for 24 hours. Check that the indicator tabs are now indented to verify vacuum, otherwise repeat.
5. To use regular jars without the vacuum indicator, prepare and cook as described in the above steps, but without the lid. Then using a spoon, top the jar contents with over ¼ in of melted wax (page 229), and store it without the lid, or with to prevent seal puncture.

NOTE: Unless the salt or sugar content of the canned food is extremely high (jars of honey have been found in pharaohs' tombs), the canning process doesn't preserve foods for eternity.

6. Operation: For foods in syrup like jams and fruits, you can expect them to last up to 2 years, as long as the seal is still intact. For everything else, plan for a year, with manufactured canned foods lasting 2–5 years. Once you break the seal or open the lid, you're re-exposing the food to bacteria. Drain off the water if applicable, and consume within 24 hours. Otherwise refrigerate. For cooked meats, boil for 10 minutes prior to consuming.

COLD STORAGE

Pot-in-Pot

Pot-in-Pot cold storage is an ancient technology used long before the invention of electricity and refrigeration.

1. Place a smaller terracotta pot inside a larger of the same shape, and fill in the difference, along the bottom and sides, with sand.
2. Operation: When the sand is wetted and left in the open, air cools the 2 pots through evaporative cooling, keeping the contents in the first cold and insulated. A leather or burlap bag or towel placed on top to keep the cold air in, and hot out, greatly hastens the process. This is known as a pot-in-pot cooler, or zeer pot.

Refrigerator

We can also build an entire fridge using the physics of evaporative cooling instead of electricity.

1. Position a metal or plastic open storage shelf system in the shade with a high cross breeze or fan, then flip the top shelf upside-down.
2. Drape a sheet or (4) pieces of burlap bags or cloth down the sides, front, and back, leaving at least 6 in lying in the top pan as a wick. Clip in place with plastic clothespins as needed, and fill the top shelf with water.
3. Place food on shelves.
4. Operation: As the material soaks up water from the top, it travels and covers the sides through wicking. Air passing through the material cools down the contents inside through evaporative cooling. Keep the top shelf topped off with water to prevent sides from drying.
5. If your shelf unit is too tall, the wicking action won't bring the water all the way down the walls. In this case, flip the bottom shelf upside down, place the bottom of the material inside, and fill it with water as well.

Root Cellar

All fruits and vegetables—even bread, meat, milk, and butter—last longer buried in plastic underground, or even better, in a root cellar. Root cellars also make great storm (and bomb) shelters, outfitted with all the food and wine you'll ever need.

1. Using a backhoe or trackhoe, dig a hole in your backyard 12–16 ft deep by 10 ft wide and 22 ft long, tapering up 1 end for a ramp.

   IMPORTANT: Often a pool permit is required.

2. Level and compact floor and backfill 4 in of 1-in crushed limestone or other rock. Place a 20-ft shipping container inside.

   IMPORTANT: Do not add insulation to the walls, floor, or ceiling. Because the shipping container walls are metal, they'll conduct heat and transfer it more easily to the surrounding earth, keeping the cellar cool, without any insulation holding heat in.

1

1

2

2

3. In 6-in high increments, backfill sides with soil, stopping 4 in from container wall. Add 1-in crushed limestone or other rock in the 4-in gap, then compact.

    WARNING: Despite what you've seen in TV shows and movies, shipping containers aren't load bearing and will crumble inwards under excessive weight. A few inches of dry earth won't cave in the top, but feet and feet will. It's imperative to keep surrounding dirt well aggregated with plenty of runoff for this reason. If you need to backfill with more dirt, I'd highly suggest reinforcing the box with a few inches of rebar-reinforced concrete.

2

3

4

4. Add rock or concrete stairs, and for the top, again add 4 in of rock (for drainage), then mound the dirt several inches high, planting sod to provide additional insulation, watershed, and thermal mass.
5. Add 4–6 in or more of rigid insulation to doors.

    IMPORTANT: In high rainfall locations I would cover the entire area extending 6–12 ft out with 10-mm pond liner, along with a 6-in wide by at least 12-in deep concrete or CMU wall around the stair's opening with storm doors to shed water away from the entrance.

PICKLING

Vinegar

So far we've talked about preserving food using salts, vacuum sealing, alcohol, and sugar, but we can also prevent bacterial growth by raising the acid content using something like vinegar as well, thereby preventing spoilage.

MATERIALS

1 c water
2 c vinegar (page 232)
½ t spice (page 234)
1 T salt (page 233)
wax (page 229)

TOOLS

(2) 1-qt containers

1. Wash, cut, and pack produce of choice into a sterilized, hot 1-qt container. Mix and boil 1 c of water, 2 c of vinegar (page 232), ½ t spice (page 234) of your choice, and 1 T of salt (page 233). Decant into a container to ¼ in from the top, and seal with wax like in step 5 of "Canning" (page 245).

Honey

Using honey is the easiest preservation method—and tastiest—by far.

MATERIALS
meats, vegetables, fruits, and nuts of your choice
honey (page 220)

TOOLS
container

1. In a sterilized container, add chopped, cooked, or dehydrated food and honey (page 220) at 1:1. No sealing, no cooking, and (kind of) no preservatives.

OTHER PRESERVATION METHODS

Many foods like honey, eggs, bread, coffee beans, nuts, garlic, onions, potatoes, apples, syrup, oils, mustard, ketchup, or hot sauce don't require refrigeration or any preservation. For example, as mentioned, eggs are pretty much airtight jars. Pickling can extend their natural protection, otherwise, date and place them in a bowl or basket. Typical shelf life is well over a month, which makes sense since it takes a month to hatch. Check quality by placing the egg in water. If it sinks, it's good.

Living

The easiest method of preserving produce or meat is to just not kill it until you're ready to eat it. It will not only save you a lot of work and hassle, but the food will keep better, is healthier—and fresh always tastes better.

Desiccant Packets

As you've likely noticed from purchasing stuff, desiccant packets are used for most dry storing in airtight containers to keep items fresh and dry. To recharge and recycle used packets, cook them on a baking pan in an oven at 200°F for 2 hours or 410°F for 1, and store in an airtight container with a fresh desiccant packet. (Ironic, right?)

EATING OFF THE GRID

Eat whatever you want. There's enough science-supported data to prove why each diet is better than the other. I have come to a few realizations in my life, though. Take them for what they're worth (genius!).

Raw foods

There are some benefits to cooking foods. For example, some proteins when heated go through denaturation, which breaks them down further, makes them more digestible, and makes more nutrients available, meaning there are more calories to consume. Eggs are one of these proteins. When eggs are eaten raw, the energy consumed is only approximately 60% of its potential; whereas when cooked, it jumps to 95%. Starchy foods act in a similar fashion, "opening up" when heated, separating sugars for easier digestion. The problem is that by heating food, you destroy some of other nutrients and enzymes contained.

That's not to say that all foods should be eaten raw. Some, such as alfalfa sprouts and kidney beans are toxic when raw and only edible when cooked. For the most part, however, the rule stands. Follow what the rest of nature does, and you'll be alright . . . We're the only animals on this entire planet that cook food before consuming, including and especially meat.

Soaking

Rather than boiling grains, pasta, and beans to soften, a simple soaking is effective in most cases. Wheat and oats, for example, are a perfect choice. Larger and harder grains like farro, barley, and rice, on the other hand, just sprout or ferment. Even these grains can benefit by some soaking though, speeding cooking times by up to two-thirds.

Place in a container with a lid, add water at 1:1, 4:1 for pasta, re-place lid, and store in the fridge overnight or until you're ready to eat.

Juicing

The logic behind eating meats for protein and calories rather than fruits and vegetables is the same as that behind juicing rather than eating fresh fruits and vegetables. In order to get enough of the correct vitamins and enzymes our bodies need from produce, you'd have to either eat 2 lbs of carrots, 10–12 apples, and 8 lbs of spinach, or drink a 16 oz glass of concentrated juice.

Drinking your food, be it animal or plant, greatly reduces digestion time. Which is why babies and elderly (and flies) do it and why we drink alcohol, allowing nutrients a streamline to the bloodstream, instead of eating fermented fruit and grains. For this reason, when trying to lose weight, juicing is not a good idea since your body will absorb all of that day's calories, but with an empty stomach, the "I'm hungry" signal will continue to be annoyingly sent.

That said, because you're breaking the fibers mechanically and not biologically, juicing should only be taken as a supplement to get all your nutrients, not a substitute of regular meals.

A raw veggie juice is a good way to start the day and get your vitamins without pills, especially if you're not going to eat your fruits and vegetables like mom told you to, anyway. Here is a recipe the missus recommends as a breakfast or dinner on light-activity days:

IMPORTANT: To avoid a false sense of energy from fructose, refrain from using too many fruits. Apple, pineapple, and kiwi are good bases. If you're looking to replace one of your meals with a juice, you must add high protein foods like kale, spirulina, duckweed, flax seed, chia seed, hemp seeds, etc.

1. If you have a juicer, just juice and combine all of the ingredients. If not, move to step 2.
2. Chop 1 thick pineapple slice with 1 celery spear, 5 baby kale leaves, 5 baby spinach leaves, and 1 ginger slice into ½-in pieces.
3. Blend on puree along with 1 c of coconut water, 1 t of spirulina or duckweed, and 1 t of seed of choice (flax, chia, hemp, etc.) for 1–2 minutes. Drink immediately.

Entomophagic Cuisine

WARNING: HUGE mindset breaker on the brink.

Throughout the world, at least everywhere other than the Unites States, people eat insects as part of their typical diet, especially snails (escargot), crickets (grillo) and worms (noke). According to recent studies, insects could account for over 60% of your daily protein requirements, which is higher than poultry and beef. 100 g of grasshoppers or crickets have more protein content than 100 g of red meat. Insects are also high in lysine and threonine, which would be equivalent to a diet of wheat, rice, cassava, or maize. Another analysis shows insects have a higher caloric value than soybeans, corn, beef, fish, lentils, beans, and wheat and rye grains.[7]

Then there are also other factors with insects like fatty acid count, vitamins, minerals, carbohydrates, and calcium, all individually equating to 100% of essential daily dietary requirements per 1–2 lb of substance.

These crucial nutrients are highly concentrated in egg and larvae form, which lack the indigestible chitin and exoskeleton, the outer shell-like coverings. From personal experience, not only are bugs a healthy food substitute, they're actually quite delectable, and semi nutty tasting, eaten raw or cooked—if you get past the fact you're eating creepy-crawlies, that is (which only takes a couple bites).

No special preparation methods are needed. Broil, cook, fry, dry, or mill insects into flour, with or without partial grain flours added for termite tortillas, beetle bread, praying mantis pastries, or buggy baked goods. See "Mezzo Proteins" on page 208 for insect farming.

Chapter 14: Health and Medicine

This chapter is going to be short since a) I experience more homesteading issues than health issues; b) society causes most of today's health problems, for example, lung disease, car accidents, stress, diabetes, obesity, high cholesterol, etc., so once you leave you actually become healthier; c) most times it's just about listening to your body; and d) you should always keep up on your emergency medical knowledge and get certified if possible.

And finally, when you're treating your ailments, remember that pain, even a headache or migraine, is the body's way of telling us that something's wrong, that we need to fix it. Now, not later. As soon as that problem—lack of water, sleep, food, or a cerebral hemorrhage—is fixed, the pain will subside.

MEDICAL

Cuts and Scrapes

Expect cuts, bruises, and even broken bones. When you work with your hands all day, with heavy, sharp things, power tools and heights, they hurt you *all* the time. I mean every single day, several times a day. The work is going to be hard, sweaty, and dirty; you're going to get angry, sad, let down, and absolutely hurt.

When your skin is broken, there are a lot of different bacteria to worry about, and one of the most common ways to preemptively combat them is through a tetanus vaccine. Turns out, most people nowadays don't get tetanus vaccines, at least more than once, despite the fact that Clostridium tetani covers everything from dirt, grass, and sticks to work surfaces and concrete. However, tetanus is rare. In fact, a doctor administering the inoculations told me she'd never even heard of a case. There are only around 50 cases a year in the U.S. That's 5.3 million to 1 odds. You're 320 million times more likely to die of something other than tetanus than to even get tetanus. So just wash with soap and water and clean with iodine, and don't be afraid of things that will never happen to you.

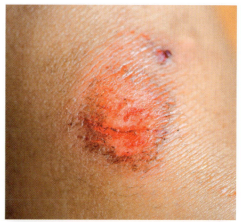

Punctures

Punctures are a bit more serious than a cut. Iodine's not going to cut it. In medieval times a puncture most likely meant death. They push germs into the meat and bloodstream where we can't clean. Cauterizing is one option if carried out immediately, but while it's effective, it's also painful. Otherwise, ingest penicillin (page 256), amoxicillin—basically any -cillins. Although you can make your own, breeding the culture takes 2–3 weeks.

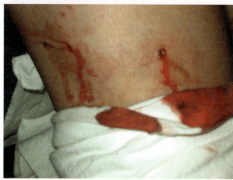

Bites and Stings

The stats for people dying from venomous animals are even more ridiculous than tetanus. I'm not sure where all the fear mongering comes from, but it's pushed on us since kindergarten. Because I'm out doing everything myself, stepping on and grabbing black widows, brown recluses, scorpions, centipedes, coral snakes, copperheads, diamondbacks, water moccasins, and other venomous things, I get bitten a lot more than normal—ten times a year, or three times that in close calls. Rattlesnake bites are extremely painful, but they won't kill you, no matter the type or size. Scorpion stings feel like a body-wide jolt from a 9-v battery—for those who've tongued one as a kid; it won't kill you, and it can even be euphoric.

From personal experience, if you're bitten or stung by any of the animals below, although it may not be fatal, without drugs you'll wish you were dead. Take off jewelry and restrictive clothing and ingest as much ibuprofen or aspirin as possible. For ingested poisons, consume activated carbon.

Scorpions

You're not going to die from a scorpion sting—unless you're allergic, and even then, you probably still wouldn't—so don't seek immediate medical attention. In the U.S., there have been four deaths in twelve years, and globally only 0.24% of people die from scorpion stings.

Bees and Wasps

I've been stung dozens, maybe hundreds of times by bees and wasps. Not the best feeling, but probably the least painful of the entire bunch. Immediately dose the area with a topical analgesic like Diphenhydramine, pop a couple Benadryl pills or the non-drowsy version, Claritin, and you'll most likely not feel any side effects or swelling.

Venomous Snakes

You have ten times more chance of dying from a scorpion than a snake! If you do get bitten, this is how I instruct my interns and volunteers:

MATERIALS
needleless syringe
tourniquets

1. Remove yourself from the area. The snake bit you for no reason other than you invaded its space. Never, in the history of homo sapiens, has a reptile or insect seen a human across the desert and made a beeline to attack them.
2. If performed instantly, some venom-enriched blood can be sucked out of each puncture with a needleless syringe. Don't suck it out with your mouth; ingestion of venom orally, sublingually, or buccally is just as lethal as subcutaneously or intramuscularly. Repeat 2 to 3 times. If it's not performed instantly though, skip to the next step.
3. Quickly restrict blood return by tying tourniquets above the bite, starting closest to the heart, working your way down and adding tourniquets towards the bite. This will allow for smaller doses to reach your heart at a time so that the heart doesn't receive the full shock.
4. Don't panic or run. This will only increase blood flow rate. Keep the bitten limb lower than the heart, remove any tight-fitting clothes and jewelry in preparation for extreme swelling, and ride out the pain comfortably, which will start in 5–10 minutes and shouldn't last more than 24 hours.

2
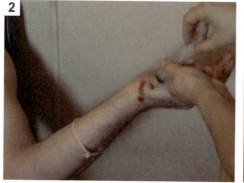

3
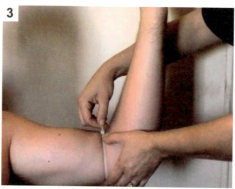

3

Spiders

Again, spider bites are not deadly but very uncomfortable:
- **Brown recluse:** nausea, vomiting, fever, rashes, and sometimes skin decay around bite.
- **Black widow:** acute pain around bite within 20 minutes, muscle and abdominal cramps, weakness, and tremors.

Centipede

The centipede is another misunderstood insect whose bite can only cause swelling, discomfort, and pain, which usually doesn't last for more than 8 hours.

Burns

Skin doesn't stop burning once you take your hand out of the heat. Even after taking your hand out of the fire, stove or other hot surface, the burning process can continue for up to an hour, depending on the degree. Often, by acting quickly, we can prevent a first degree burn from becoming a second or third. that's why in all three degrees, it's critical to *immediately* run very cold water over the area, or cover in sterile, cold, wet compress until the burning sensation subsides.

There are three degrees:

First degree: With first degree burns, the first layer of skin is reddish with small blistering. Most sunburns are first degree.

Treatment:

1. Rinse in cold water or cover with cold, wet compress until burning sensations subsides.
2. Remove jewelry from the burnt area.
3. Rotate applications of aloe and an antibacterial ointment like bacitracin or Neosporin, and cover with cling film or a sterile dressing.
4. Don't pop the blisters, but when they do pop, clean with saline solution.
5. Take max dosage of acetaminophen and ibuprofen. (Yes, you can take them both together.)

Second degree: With second degree burns, the burn has penetrated the first layer and affected the second, accompanied by swelling, blisters, and first layer skin loss.

Treatment:

1. Rinse in cold water or cover with cold, wet compress until burning sensations subsides.
2. Remove jewelry from the burnt area.
3. Clean with saline solution, then pat dry with sterile towel. Apply an antibacterial ointment like bacitracin or Neosporin, and cover with cling film or a sterile non-stick dressing. Leave for 12 hours.
4. Apply carbonate alginate. Dress with sterile dressing and cover with a second sterile dressing. Change dressing when moist.
5. Don't pop the blisters, but when they do pop, clean with saline solution.
6. Take max dosage and acetaminophen or ibuprofen. (Yes, you can take them both together.)

IMPORTANT: If burn percentage is larger than 20% TBSA (total body surface area), perform III degree burn treatment.

Third degree: Third degree is the most severe, having burned through all three layers. However, since the burn usually destroys underlying tissue and nerves, third degree burns are often the least painful, sometimes even painless. You should seek medical attention for these burns, but if you are unable to get outside attention, follow the below treatment plan.

Treatment:

1. Rinse in cold water or cover with cold, wet compress until burning sensations subsides.
2. Remove jewelry from the burnt area.
3. Clean with saline solution, then pat dry with sterile towel and apply carbonate alginate. Dress with sterile dressing and cover with a second sterile dressing.
4. Don't pop the blisters, but when they do pop, clean with saline solution.
5. Maintain an adequate airway and treat for shock (page 254).
6. For over 20% TBSA *(total body surface area)*, or over 10% TBSA for children, maintain proper levels of hemodynamic stability by providing fluid resuscitation with saline or sodium lactate solution at a rate of 2–4 mL per kg of body weight per the percentage of body surface burned, with 50% administered over the first 8 hours, and the remaining over the next 16 hours. (Warm as necessary to prevent heat loss.)

third degree burn

EXAMPLE: An adult weighing 100 kgs, with 20% body surface burns would be administered 4 x 100 x 20 = 8,000 mL. 4,000 mL in the first 8 hours, 4,000 mL over the next 16 hours.

7. Take max dosage of acetaminophen and ibuprofen. (Yes, you can take them both together.)

8. Perform hydrotherapy and hyperbaric oxygen therapy daily.

Fourth degree: Fourth degree burns are acid, alkaline, or chemical burns.
   Treatment:

1. Acids, alkalis, and chemicals are water dissolvable and should be washed off with water, pee, or any water-based liquid available immediately, to halt further reactions.
2. Then neutralize the burn with a chemical of equal and opposite pH value. For example, neutralize a base that has a pH of 10 with an acid that has a pH of 4.

Infections

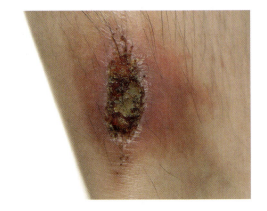

We never got sick after leaving society, but there are still some basic things you should know about infections:

- There are two main infection types: viral and bacterial.
- People get sick by being near sick people, their stuff, or animals.
- Along with antibacterial, there are antiviral medications that undermine the virus's ability to reproduce, despite what you're being told. These medications include oseltamivir phosphate (available as a generic version or under the trade name Tamiflu), zanamivir (trade name Relenza), peramivir (trade name Rapivab), and baloxavir marboxil (trade name Xofluza).
- Take immune system boosters weekly, especially when you're not sick.
- Pathogenic viruses generally don't hurt, and symptoms are widespread throughout your body, that is, sinus congestion, runny nose, body ache, cough, etc.
- Similar to getting a cut, pathogenic bacteria infections usually cause pain, swelling, redness, and heat, like a sore throat and earache.
- Phlegm, whether green, dark yellow, or white doesn't indicate whether an upper respiratory infection (URI) is bacterial or viral. It only indicates that your immune system—white blood cells and their green proteins—are fighting the invader.
- Antiseptics are applied to living tissue, that is, skin; antibiotics are ingested; antibacterials are formulated to kill bacteria; and antivirals are formulated for viruses.
- Disinfectants are applied to non-living surfaces, which kill both bacteria and viruses.

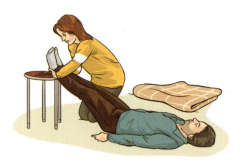

Shock

Shock occurs when an insufficient amount of blood reaches the brain. Without blood to the brain, death will occur.
- **Causes:** Allergic reaction, low blood pressure from blood loss or lack of food and water, a severe burn.
- **Symptoms:** Confusion, bluish lips, rapid breathing, clammy skin.
- **Treatment:** Stop bleeding and arrange the head to be lower than the body, allowing blood to flow toward the brain.

Choking

1. Look inside the patient's mouth, and if possible, remove any obstruction manually with a flashlight and a long pair of hemostats.
2. If not possible, perform the Heimlich maneuver. From behind a standing choking person, with one foot slightly in front of the other, make a fist with one hand, thumb side in, place the bottom of the hand touching the patients belly button.
3. Reach around the opposite side, grasp the fist with your other hand, and perform 5 abdominal thrusts by pulling both hands quickly, sharply, and firmly inwards and upwards.
4. Look inside the patient's mouth, and if possible, remove any obstruction.
5. If not possible, bend the patient over a table or chair and perform 5 back blows by delivering 5 firm, rapid blows in the center of the shoulder blades.
6. Look inside the patient's mouth, and if possible, remove any obstruction.
7. If not possible, from behind a standing choking person, with one foot slightly in front of the other, make a fist with one hand, thumb side in, place the top of the hand just under the rib cage sternum. Reach around the opposite side, grasp the fist with your other hand, and perform 5 chest thrusts.

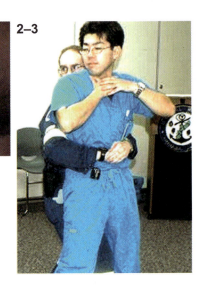

1

2–3

8. Look inside the patient's mouth, and if possible, remove any obstruction.
9. If the blockage has still not been removed, repeat abdominal and chest thrusts, back blows, and finger sweeps until the blockage is dislodged.
10. If patient loses consciousness at any point during the procedure, continue attempting to dislodge the obstacle while performing CPR.

Cardiac Arrest

Cardiac arrest is not the same as a heart attack. A heart attack is when blood and oxygen flow to the heart is blocked. Cardiac arrest on the other hand occurs when electrical signals that control the heart are interrupted or altered in some way, causing the heart to stop beating. In both conditions the patient stops breathing and loses consciousness.

- **Symptoms:** unconsciousness, no breathing, no pulse, sometimes shortness of breath or fast breathing, weakness, chest discomfort, heart palpitations.
- **Treatment:** Perform CPR or defibrillate.

Defibrillation

The process of electrocution to restart a heart is actually a viable one in that our body and brain start, run, and stop due to the presence or lack of electrical current. If cardiac arrest is a worry, or if you're planning to move off grid, keeping a defibrillator on hand is essential.

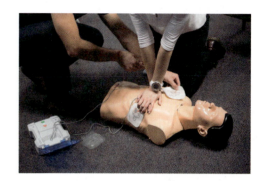

1. Confirm no breathing or pulse, open air passageways, and attempt CPR for 2 minutes, then remove adhesive backings from defibrillator pads. Stick pads to the patient's chest, 1 centered on the right, just above the right nipple, and the other just below the left nipple, left of the rib cage.
2. Set the level for electrical discharge at 200 J (Biphasic devices) or 360J (Monophasic). Press "charge" on the defibrillator and discharge by pressing "shock" on the unit. Perform another round of CPR and repeat.

DRUGS

Ever heard that saying, "a drug a day keeps the doctor away"? No? That's because I just made it up. First, all medicines and pills are natural. If you didn't just throw the book down because of that mindset breaker, then second, there's no such thing as a non-natural medication or anything for that matter. Everything on this planet is natural; it all comes from nature.

There are a few definitions of the word *nature*, all of which boil down to: Coming from nature and not made or caused by people, not containing anything artificial or made by humans. So, by definition, there's literally no way for humans to ever make anything "natural," for as soon as we start, it instantly becomes artificial. For example, if I were to take a dandelion and tie it into a knot, even gently, without killing or moving it, it's now artificial because I did it, not nature. This obviously includes smashing and mixing plants and extracting their oils and compounds, even though everything is still natural. So, below I've listed some perfectly natural drugs whose ingredients came from nature and their uses:

Ibuprofen

Ibuprofen (Advil, Motrin) is a nonsteroidal anti-inflammatory drug that relieves pain, tenderness, swelling and stiffness, fever, headaches, muscle aches, arthritis, toothaches, and backaches by halting the production of the substance that causes pain, fever, and inflammation. Acetaminophen (Tylenol) is also a analgesic and antipyretic used to relieve pain and fever.

Aspirin

Aspirin (acetylsalicylic acid) is a pain reliever and fever reducer that also reduces swelling and prevents heart attacks.

Morphine

Morphine is a narcotic pain reliever that completely dulls pain receivers and the perception center in the brain.

Disinfectant

Ethyl alcohol works as a disinfectant and antiseptic by denaturing the proteins of bacteria, fungi, and viruses.

Antiseptics

Because of the osmotic effect of its high sugar concentration and low water content, along with its high acidic content from gluconic acid, and along with containing H_2O_2, honey is an antibacterial, antifungal, and antiseptic all in one.

Bees add a glucose oxidase enzyme to nectar, producing hydrogen peroxide (H_2O_2) when honey is diluted. Apply honey directly to your wound; the wound's exudate will dilute it naturally.

NOTE: The highest H_2O_2 level is reached at a dilution of 30–60% honey–exudate.

Acetic acid also makes a great antiseptic.

Merbromin

Merbromin, originally Mercurochrome, is a topical antiseptic and is much more efficient than alcohol or hydrogen peroxide during surgical applications. You'll want the larger spray bottles, not the little drop bottles of iodine.

Antibiotics

Antibiotics fight both bacteria groups and can be purchased online without a prescription (look for any "-cillin" or "-cin"); in pet stores under the name Fish Pen (penicillin V potassium), Fish Mox (amoxicillin trihydrate) and Fish Flox (ciprofloxacin); or make your own:

IMPORTANT: Growing penicillin bacteria is actually a relatively easy process. It, like most bacteria, is everywhere. In lies the problem . . . to prevent growing an unwanted bacteria, total sterility at all time must be followed.

MATERIALS

bread, citrus or cantaloupe, or salami
ziplock bag
1 L water
sterile plastic forks or knives and paper plates
25 g cornstarch
44 g lactose monohydrate
2.75 g glucose monohydrate
0.5 g potassium phosphate monobasic

3 g sodium nitrate
0.25 g magnesium sulfate
0.044 g manganese sulfate
0.044 g zinc sulfate
citric acid
1 L ethyl or amyl acetate
aluminum oxide powder

TOOLS

glass or plastic container
measuring container
spray bottle
moisture meter
pH meter
medium pot

flask or sterile jar
measuring cups or spoons
thermostat
cloth or parachute silk
separatory funnel
large bowl of ice water

1. Using a spray bottle and moisture meter, spray a slice of bread so it has a moisture content of greater than 2.2%. You can also use citrus or cantaloupe or salami.
2. Place it in a dark room (indoor air spore count is usually around 15% higher than outdoor) with at least 85% humidity, and temperature of 70°F until a bluish green mold appears. If the mold doesn't appear in 14 days, wipe the top of a your fridge, cabinets, or the top of a door with the slice of bread, collecting dust, and repeat.
3. If the mold still doesn't appear, your humidity is most likely off. Place in a ziplock bag with 1 T water, store for another 14 days. If the mold still doesn't appear, repeat on a different location.

4. The mold will start out a gray, turning bright bluish green in a matter of days. This is not penicillin, just a mold (Penicillium chrysogenum) that's on all surfaces and even available to purchase online, along with other -cillins; however, this certain type of mold secretes penicillin.

5. To maximize yield during incubation, without touching anything with your hands, using sterile instruments, dissect into ½-in cubes, place inside a sterile glass or plastic container and store in the dark for another 5–14 days.

   NOTE: Plastic forks or knives and paper plates are sterile out of the box.

6. In a sterile measuring container, add 2 c sterile water, 25 g cornstarch, 44 g lactose monohydrate, 2.75 g glucose monohydrate, 0.5 g potassium phosphate mono, 3 g sodium nitrate, 0.25 g magnesium sulfate, 0.044 g manganese sulfate, 0.044 g zinc sulfate. Then fill to the 1 L mark with cold sterile water, adding citric acid as needed to obtain a pH of 5.0 to 5.5.

   NOTE: If you have limited resources, you can get away with 1 c milk, 2 T sugar, 5 T starch, 1 t salt and ½ t vinegar (to lower pH).

7. Boil to a paste-like consistency to kill any unwanted (harmful) fungus and bacteria. Once cooled, transfer to a flask or sterile jar using sterile instruments, and add 1 T penicillin spores.

8. With the lid off, rest the jar undisturbed, sideways for maximum air access, for 1 week at 70°F to further incubate. Shake contents twice a day.

9. Separate the liquids by passing the juice through a sterile cloth or parachute silk, then add citric acid until pH reaches 2.2. Shake vigorously and let sit until separation occurs.

   WARNING: Yes, at this point you have penicillin; you also probably have many other bacteria. Don't ingest before sterilizing.

10. Decant the clear water from the darker liquid. Then sterilize by heating to 212°F for 1 second.

11. To purify, decant into a separatory funnel, and mix 1:1 with ethyl or amyl acetate to separate the penicillin from the broth. Shake, let sit for a couple hours in an ice bath, then decant the ethyl acetate off the bottom and repeat.

12. The result will be semi-pure penicillin in a liquid state that could (though I wouldn't suggest it) be ingested at ½ t a day for 7 days. However, at this point, there are several pyrogens (fever producing agents) present.

   NOTE: The penicillin itself is a chemical ($C_{16}H_{18}N_2O_4S$) and can't go bad. Penicillin has been used decades after bottling. If you have trace amounts of cornstarch left in the mix though, it could.

13. To purify further to remove the pyrogens, fill separator funnel with aluminum oxide powder that we make when producing pigments (page 20), fill with penicillin juice, and let sit until separation occurs. There will be a brownish orange top layer that's mostly pyrogens and some penicillin; a pale-yellow middle layer that's mostly penicillin; and a dark red-violet bottom layer that's impurities. Decant, discarding the bottom layer and capturing middle.

14. (Optional) Use a buffer to wash the alumina.

15. The resulting liquid, a reddish orange color, is mostly penicillin. To dry for long-term storage, freeze dry or add 1% potassium acetate, shake, then decant into a cookie sheet or other flat container, and allow the ethyl acetate to evaporate off until you're left with potassium penicillin and potassium acetate crystals.

16. The measurement of Antibiotic properties can be measured in a petri dish containing agar-agar, introducing drops of penicillin, and inoculating dish with almost any gram-negative anaerobic bacteria, viewing the results under a microscope over a few days. Be sure to prepare a second dish in the same manner, substituting water for penicillin as a control.

17. Dosage for all penicillin types, synthetic or bacteria excretion-based, including amoxicillin and ciprofloxacin, are as follows. For severe cases 875 mg every 12 hours for 2 days after becoming asymptomatic. For mild cases, 500 mg every 12 hours for 2 days.

   NOTE: According to ncbi.nlm.nih.gov, neither antibiotics nor any other drug have an expiration date. Unlike organic compounds, chemical compounds don't "go bad" with time. Expiration dates are simply the date at which the manufacturers guarantee full potency and safety, not the expiration of the drug itself.

Antihistamines

Antihistamines stop nausea and dizziness.

Melatonin and Valerian

Melatonin and Valerian are good muscle relaxers and sleep aids.

Throat Lozenges and Cough Suppressants

Throat lozenges and cough suppressants are obviously great for sore throats and coughs, but what you may not know is they, like honey, protect mucus membranes from germs due to the osmotic nature of the syrup produced from cough suppressants. You can buy them, or you can mix 1 t of crystalized honey—let it sit in light to crystalize—with ½ of a key lime or a ¼ of a lemon. Ingest 1 t of the mix, hold it in your mouth a minute or two, swallow, and repeat.

Magnesium Hydroxide

Magnesium hydroxide can be used to help with digestion. For adult constipation, ingest 30–60 mL once a day, or smaller doses divided throughout the day. For dyspepsia in adults, ingest 5–15 mL between 1 and 4 times a day.

MEDICAL PROCEDURES

Sutures

Humans get banged up all the time. In most cases, there's no need to do anything. Every time I've ever heard "Eew, that's going to need stiches" it absolutely didn't need stiches. You'll know when to stitch if you hear "AAAAH, OMG!!!" and nothing else.

For small lacerations that require stitches but aren't life threatening, sterilize and have one person close the cut with gloved fingertips while applying superglue topically. Superglue was invented for this very procedure during the Vietnam War.

That said, if the wound keeps opening, or won't close on its own, follow the following steps:

MATERIALS

local anesthetic   3/0 to 4/0 suturing thread

TOOLS

FS2 needle   tweezers
hemostat   scissors

IMPORTANT: I highly advise getting familiar with suturing needles, suturing thread, and the following steps by practicing on pieces of raw bacon cut in half, or even sliced ham.

1. Boil everything, including the thread; sterilize the wound inside and out, and apply local anesthetic. Place base of an eye FS2 needle with 3/0 to 4/0 suturing thread perpendicularly in hemostat's tip.

   NOTE: Regular thread such as separated floss, which is already sterile, also works.

2. Hold either skin flap middle up with tweezers; then ¼ in away from edge, push needle through into subcutaneous layer, bisecting the wound, closing from the middle out, making sure not to puncture any muscular tissue.

3. Close tweezers on needle tip, release hemostat, reclamp hemostat on needle from the other side and pull through, leaving several inches of thread on both sides.

4. Repeat straight across on the other flap, this time from the inside out, again ¼ in from edge. Pull thread through, pick up thread in 1 hand, loop thread around hemostat tip, open hemostat, grab onto thread tail, and pull through loop just tight enough to butt skin edges together, but not enough to cause buckling.

5. Repeat 4–5 times in opposite directions. Cut thread to ¼ in and push knot to either side with tweezers. Repeat on either side, again starting from middle (quarter) and so on, until wound is closed or sutures are ¼ in apart.

6. After 1 week, sanitize area thoroughly. Hold thread with tweezers, and press down on skin slightly while pulling thread out 1/16 in. Cut flush with skin and remove. In this fashion, string covered in bacteria isn't pulled into tissue.

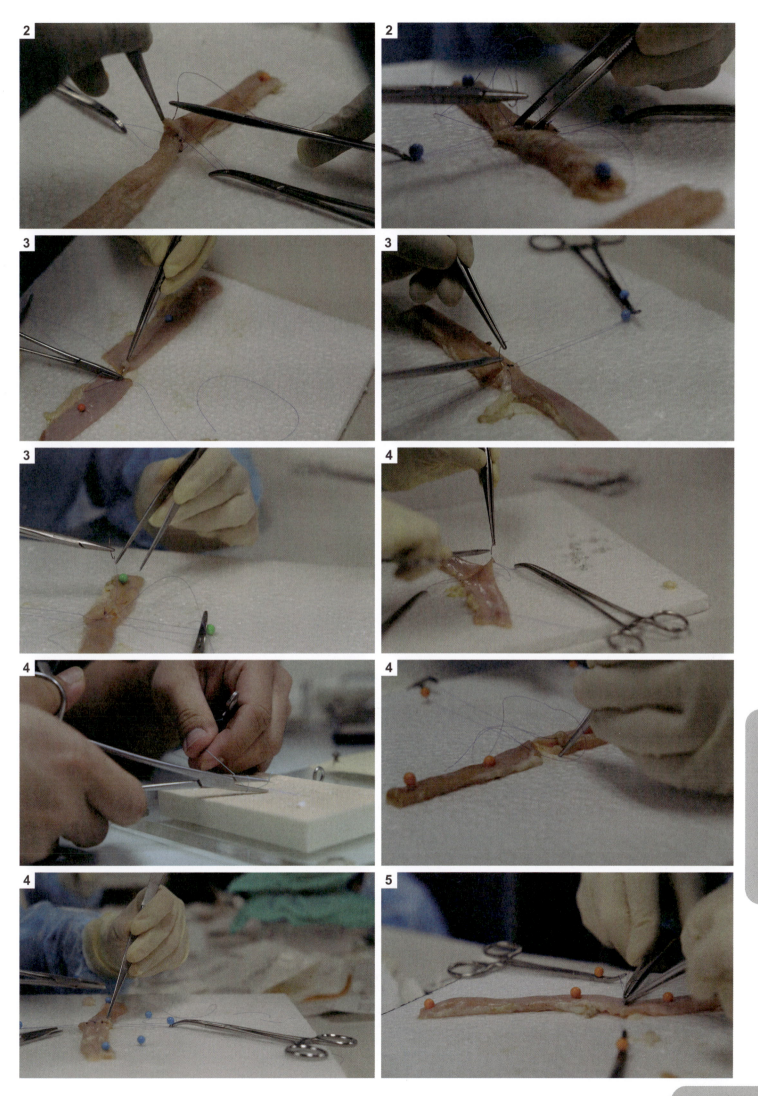

Chapter 15: Take the Plunge

If you are intrigued by what you've learned in these pages and are ready to exit the typical life, the ride that just never stops—until you STOP—it's time to make your first steps. I've laid out in the following chapter what I have found to work best, what we did wrong, and how to circumnavigate the process as effortlessly, efficiently, and on the least amount of money as possible.

MAKE A PLAN

The first thing to do is make a plan. Every good endeavor starts with a good plan, even if there's little to no chance it will go according to it. At least it provides a starting point. The following is what we did, which led to us being able to retire at twenty-five years old. Feel free to adapt or ignore.

Step 1: Prepare to Cash Out

It's a very strange concept, but you not only have to pay to play, you have to pay to leave the game, too. From your first day of work, put as much into savings and 401K as possible. At age fifteen when we get our first paper route or babysitting job, we don't have responsibilities or bills. Our lives are fluid. Saving early (even as a teenager) is the most important step, even if you don't plan on leaving society! What we save now won't last us for the rest of our lives and isn't meant to, but it will provide a tool, a stepping stone, later. Ever heard "it takes money to make money?" The bigger the savings, the bigger the tool and the more money you'll make.

I suggest staying away from university degrees. Unless you're planning on retiring from a long career (in which case you shouldn't be reading this), there's no point. I wasted years when I could have been working or learning skills needed for living. Those degrees are worthless now, and any education I received could have been acquired later for free. Stanford, Yale, MIT, Harvard, Berkeley, and Oxford offer free online courses for their *entire* curriculum and, of course, you can audit all classes at any school at no cost. (All university educations are free. It's the diploma that costs money.)

Education is great if it's done for the right reasons—to obtain a better income is the wrong reason. To obtain a paper that says you learned a lot is the wrong reason. For self-enrichment and academic exploration are the right reasons. These are the original reasons the first university, the Mouseion at Alexandria, was created.

I'm not saying don't learn. You'll need to learn as many trades as you can: foundry, forging, mechanics, carpentry, metal working, welding, electrical, plumbing, roofing, masonry, glass work, etc. Another option is military service. I recommend the Air Force or Coast Guard—and only a two-to-four-year stint. The military pays you to learn a trade (actually you're encouraged to learn all other trades as well), travel, live, and eat (room and board). They even pay your health insurance, give loans for land, and qualify you for tax breaks. If you manage your money well, you could save a lot over your two-to-four-year enrollment.

With money in hand, purchase or put a down payment on a fixer-upper home, preferably brick, in a decent neighborhood and get experience with construction as you remodel. Then you are ready to flip the home; aim to repeat this once a year. If you chose to remodel then rent, plan to repeat the process every three years with less than five year payoff plan (including your remodel costs). If necessary, get a signature, house, equity, or 401K loan. The renter will pay the loan and interest while you maintain value.

Step 2: Begin Researching Land

With your savings now working for you and your money growing, use the time to begin researching Land. Where do you want to live? Where are the best places to live? Where does it not get too cold nor too hot? What are the taxes, land costs, and accessibility? Decide on potential property locations based on your age, wants, and abilities to build and exist without outside assistance. For example, if you're older, you'd probably want the best possible healthcare and medical system, which would currently be in Cuba. Maybe you want safety and to be part of the next superpower, therefore China may be for you. Maybe extreme sports and nature is your thing, so I'd suggest Venezuela (all of which are strangely and unintentional non-capitalist suggestions). Americans and Canadians are leaving the polluted cities & clogged freeways by the hundreds of thousands to enjoy safer, stress-reduced, more comfortable, cheaper, and healthier life abroad.

Costa Rica, for example, contains 30,000 Americans. When you look at the conditions of the country, it's easy to see the attraction. A quarter of the country is national parks and protected environments. The literacy rate is 93%, and foreign residents are allowed to make up to $70,000 (US) without paying a local tax. If you stay outside the U.S. for two years, your US income tax drops to zero.

Choosing a temperate climate (not too cold in the winter, not too hot in the summer, not too dry, not too humid) should be important to you as well. Locations on a planet with two giant ice caps are few and far between. The following locations are reasonable options that I've been able to find with average highs ranging from 45° in the winter to 90° in the summer.

- Canary Islands: 62°–75°
- Cape Hatteras (NC): 55°–85°
- Costa Rica: 64°–75°
- Cuba: 70°–81°
- Mauritius: 60°–84°
- Honduras: 76°–83°
- Bolivia: 72°–59°
- El Salvador: 64°–73°
- Puerto Rico: 70°–83°
- Suriname: 70°–90°
- Guatemala: 56°–80°
- Peru: 57°–85°
- Belize: 70°–90°
- Uruguay: 45°–80°
- Paraguay: 56°–92°
- Argentina: 47°–83°
- Panama: 75°–90°
- French Guiana: 86° year round
- Venezuela: 79°–82°
- Tonga/Samoa/Vanuatu: 72°–79°
- Chile: 45°–62°

Options that don't meet the temperate criteria but that should still be explored are: northern Canada, Russia, Lithuania, Latvia, Germany, Solomon Islands, Morocco, Turkey, Syria, Tunisia, North Macedonia, North and South Korea, Brazil, Nicaragua, Armenia, Ecuador, Estonia, China, northern Spain.

Search Wikipedia or the county or town's website and read up on the flora, fauna, history, people, events, festivals, average temps, wind, sun, precipitation, population, topography, and etc. Google "[county, state or city name] news" for any fracking, drilling, pipelines, pollution, crime, hurricane, tornado, or other environmental and social data that may impact your decision.

Step 3: What's Next—Save and Sell

With income rolling in, a nice nest egg built up, and your spot picked out, you need to make a decision on whether you want to enjoy life now or later. If later, continue your current lifestyle, and retire and enjoy life when you're older (don't wait too long!). If now, make the trade-off and don't spend anything on comforts and other crap that bring you enjoyment now—things like movies, lattes, lunch, iPhone, Christmas/birthday presents, subscriptions, memberships, sunglasses, manicures, pizza, golf, beer, cigarettes, tattoos. Though they seem innocent, they add up to what will be the majority of your egg.

Let's look at just a small portion of these little costs for a BIG reality check. For a more accurate estimate, sit down, pull out the receipts from last week or month (an average week or month), and break down to forecast the long-term costs as shown in the following example. Then multiply the results by 520 (number of weeks in 10 years).

EXPENSES ADD UP[9]

Expense	Today	Over 10 years
Pizza delivery	$25 a week	$18,661
Coffee/donut	$4 a day	$22,389
Smoking	$35 a week	$26,125
Manicure	$40 a week	$29,857
Lunch at work	$10 a day*	$37,322
Golf	$75 a week	$55,983

NOTE: These are the small, needless things we waste money on every day as Americans. The bigger stuff like new cars, houses, trips, kids (American parents spend on average $267,233 on their children from birth to 18[1]) often takes a huge toll on your finances. Remember all these cost, whether the small or big, are choices you have control over.

*work days only

Next, it's time to get rid of all the junk that you have already bought. That was one of my mistakes. Not having a book to tell us what we would need and what we wouldn't, we kept too much. So, burn it, sell it, or give it away. Sell as much as possible, the expensive stuff online, in social media groups, Amazon and eBay, and the rest in garage sales. There's an art to garage selling, if you want to actually make real money. And it lies in the details:

Six months before:

- Don't throw away anything. Toss it into a box: pens, batteries, broken stuff, bags of used T-shirts (rags). Even if you think something's garbage, or that no one would buy it, someone will buy it. "One's man's trash is another man's treasure."
- Store up on plastic bags, boxes, and change (at least $100 in change 30-$1s, 20-$5s, 10-quarters).

One month before:

- Choose a date. The best time is the end of summer; the worst is the beginning (everyone has sales after spring cleaning).
- Try for a holiday weekend, under a shaded carport, on a main street and close to the road.

One week before:

- Place an ad in the newspaper, radio, and social media the day before and the day of (ads are event multipliers), with ad reading: "50% off everything. Huge, huge yard sale today only. Free stuff, tools, building materials, supplies, furniture, sporting goods, electronics, much more!" (even if you don't have it. If they ask, you sold it already). Don't waste ad space on clothes or books; they're implied.
- Get fold-out tables (rent or borrow) or use doors or plywood on saw horses.

One day before:

- Set up tables in aisles, with half the items facing each aisle. Place a cashier's table with chairs in back.
- Clean everything, wrap all cords and label everything with prices using orange painters' tape (CDs, DVDs, books $1).
- Add big paper printout prices on larger or more expensive items.
- Put everything out, right-side up (don't leave anything in boxes), but tell people you'll be bringing more out later today. Assemble if needed.
- Always under price, never over. Disconnect emotionally from all items.
- Separate items according to table (electronics, kitchen utensils, sporting goods); and don't pile stuff on top of each other.
- For cheap items erect dollar tables. Group lesser prices together, "5 for $1."
- Place bright colored items or balloons up high, out front and have a mirror for clothes.

Twelve hours before:

- Write out your signs using XL black marker in all caps: Top third "Huge yard sale, Friday, Saturday, and Sunday from sunrise to sunset. Free stuff." Start out the middle third with "tools" (so it looks like free tools), "building materials, supplies, furniture, sporting goods, electronics, more," with a GIANT solid arrow taking up the bottom third.
- Put your signs up next to other garage sale signs to take their traffic.
- Use staple gun on poles. Where there are no telephone poles, put signs on boxes with rocks.
- Use big bright orange signs all the same colors and size (full sheet), so that they don't confuse you with another garage sale.
- Put signs saying "great deal," "half off," "must sell" on expensive items and name and descriptions on items that are odd.

Sale days (Friday and Saturday):

- Start when the sun comes up (that's when you'll have the best-buying customers) until sunset.
- Have someone check signs every few hours. Tell friends to come just to visit. Offer them free items.
- Have fake shoppers walking around tables when slow. People never stop at empty sales.
- Be friendly, but make the sale no matter what.
- Say, "Hi, how are you," "Thanks for coming," "If you need any help let me know," "Thank you for your purchase," "Please come back later, we'll have more stuff."
- Don't be chatty while they're looking. But as soon as the buy is made or they're finished looking, talk, talk, talk to keep them longer.
- Treat every day as it's the last, and you need to get rid of everything. Don't hold onto something thinking you'll get a better deal later.
- With stuff you know won't sell, offer, "I'll throw in those . . . for free with that."
- Answer "yes or no" to every question, never "I don't know."
- Rotate items routinely to look like new stuff was put out, especially non-selling items.
- Counter-offer half of every offer. For example, the price is $10, they offer $5, counter $7.50, and you got yourself a deal.
- Flip a coin to make a sale. Often people will try to haggle the price down, not to beat you but to satisfy themselves. Counter half, and if they say no, or I don't know, offer to flip for it, their choice. "You win, I'll give it to you for $5. I win, $7.50. Either way, you win." And either way you were going to sell it for $5. And they're having fun!
- Ask someone to make an offer on what they're looking at, and then counter with an offer for half, "make it $5 and you got a deal!"

Final day (Sunday):

- Mark signs in bold "50% off EVERYTHING."
- Place ads in your social media and groups as well as freecycle.org that say you're giving away free stuff. Give away what you know won't sell, like reclaimed building materials, paint, books, clothes. It'll attract buying customers.

Day After (Monday):

- Either put everything back in boxes and have another sale one month later or freecycle, donate, or toss it.

Step 4: When's Best

Dreams without doing are just dreams and will stay just dreams. It's not okay to continue dreaming. There's no time like the present; since you've done nothing, it's the best time to start by making changes in this direction. The next best time, besides today, would be tomorrow.

Step 5: Game Over—Cash Out and "Retire"!

We're made to believe that retirement is when we're in our 60s, or 70s, not when we're in our 20s. But why not? Why can't I retire whenever I want? Well, you can, I did. Cash out. Put the rentals plus your house on the market. When they sell (which should give you well over $200k), roll the 401K into an IRA (IRAs pay interest monthly or annually) or cash out completely (with a 20 percent penalty); quit your job, cancel insurances, utilities, subscriptions and memberships, close bank accounts, turn off phones, and say your goodbyes. You're retired. It's the day. It's that easy!

Leaving your job may seem daunting, even scary. It's a new frontier. A path that not many (at least not in a very long time) have walked down. There's no one to ask for advice. You're making a huge leap of faith—faith in yourself, faith in your family, and faith that this is the right decision. Be confident in your decision and stick with it. You did the research, weighed all your options, and plotted a course. Many will laugh. They'll say, "You can't retire, you're only 25!" or "You're not really retired, you just quit." At least that's what they told me. When the federal government classified me as "retired," and I stopped paying income tax, well, that was good enough for me. I'm retired, have been for twenty years!

Retirement will take some time to adapt to. You'll learn new things about your family, and they'll learn things about you. If you have them, stay close to children, and explain that this will offer more time for you to be with them (instead of someone else raising them while you're at work). You can even homeschool. You have the time.

This plan gives you ten years to build a nest egg before retiring and leaving. If you start at age fifteen or twenty, you'll be ready at thirty, thirty-five years before everyone else. Even if you're forty or fifty, you're still ahead of the crowd. Whatever your age, the sooner the better, so you have time with your spouse, your children, and grandchildren.

Step 6: Begin Day 1 of Your New Life

With cash in hand, you're ready to begin planning your homestead. Make a list of wants based on country, climate, vegetation, resources, etc., then narrow it down using filters like acreage, wildlife, proximity to society, cost. Rate each 1-10, based on which has more wants, then relocate.

LOCATION CONSIDERATIONS

Climate*	Critical	>200dys sun	Important	No restrictions	Important	Existing quarries	Nice
Adult trees[2]	Critical	>200dys wind	Important	No or Low taxes	Critical	Neighboring land type	Nice
Water source	Critical	>6% grade	Important	No HOA	Important	On dirt road	Nice
Soil type	Important	Improvements[4]	Nice	At dead end	Nice	Timber or mineral rights[3]	Critical
10+ acres	Nice	Grazing land	Important	Square lot	Nice	Not landlocked	Critical

*Historically, poorer classes live near the equator since construction and cost of living are cheaper.

[2]⅔-¾ assiduous, ⅛-¼ deciduous

[3]No easements, rights-of-ways, liens or intrusive drilling

[4]Fencing, driveway, utilities, wells, electrical, and structures

Acreage required depends on terrain, flora, and animal type (see "Livestock Management"). A family living in Costa Rica, for example, could sustain themselves on half an acre with chickens, rabbits, etc., where the same family would need fifty acres in the desert raising goats or pigs. I haven't seen an environment where a single family would ever need more than fifty acres.

Most places that have everything you're looking for are going to cost a lot. To obtain cheap land, you'll have to sacrifice. The cheapest land available is free land, with many countries still giving away land (including Russia and the US) for different reasons. Some towns and counties will even pay you (through tax incentives) to move there and set up a homestead. There are even entire (modern) ghost towns available to purchase.

You really need to be in the area you've chosen (see step 2) in order to make connections, find the best deals, set up, and oversee transactions. This could mean living in a hotel (or camper) until you can find a rental to stay in while you are buying and closing on your land (and eventually building). If the area turns out to be not what you thought, this will mean relocating to the next area on your list, but this can only be found out by being there.

Once on-site, begin searching for the actual land, driving around or online using terms like: uninhabitable land, raw, unimproved, subdivided acreage, ranch land (not farmland), rough, hunting or grazing land. These are terms that, when attached, usually bring lower price margins.

Whether you desire immersion in society or to be on the edge or a hundred miles away, a trick is to look at a road map. More congested road networks mean more people. More people mean higher costs of living, zoning regulations, laws, taxes, regulations, associations, higher valued and priced land, etc. Fewer roads mean fewer people, materials, assistance or labor, availability, delivery, services, transportation, and fuel. But it also means dirt-cheap land. In other words, the closer or farther from society you live, the less or more self-reliant you'll need to be.

With the internet and tools like Google Maps, Google Earth, aerial drones, Trulia.com, Realty.com, and virtual tourist and the availability to search records, communicate and even complete transactions online, you don't really need a realtor. If you choose to use a realtor, have them sign a *buyer representation* contract before talking business, otherwise, they represent the seller. Next, realtors make a percent of final sale price, meaning it's in their best interest to not talk the seller down. So never say something they can use to drive up the cost like "looking for something to build a home on" and avoid terms like "beautiful, dream, nice, or need." Tell them you just want some "junk, garbage, or worthless" land. Otherwise, they may sell you the exact same land at a higher price with justification.

With the cost (and preference) of raw land skyrocketing, today's building costs and the decreased cost of already built houses, you can often find good deals on land with a fixer upper, foreclosure, trailers, or location next to a junkyard (great addition to any DIYer), graveyard, etc. State that the site requires bulldozing and that structure/s and hauling off the junk will cost money, so the price needs to be reduced accordingly. These eyesores reduce the land and neighborhood value (a good thing) and typically have been on the market for so long that owners are willing to come down considerably. In fact, when searching for land, sort by "longest time on market." You'll often find sellers dying to get rid of it and, therefore, bargain deals.

You can often get repossessed land at bank, sheriff, BLM, HOA, or tax quarterly auctions at the cost of paying off the debt or back taxes for pennies on the dollar. In an attempt to lure buyers (preferably young parents with children) some counties are offering free land, often with tax incentives. Some have stipulations like registering kids in school, so they receive federal funding or living or building on the land, so the county receives more income in the form of taxes. These resources change all the time, though, so when you're ready, Google terms like: homestead, redevelopment, free land or lots, or check out CFRA's (Center for Rural Affairs) website.

Once you have a few options, visit the property. For raw, untouched wild land, expect to travel by road, horse, air, or sea to get to it. The first visits when shopping for land meant a thirty-minute helicopter ride, and when we searched for land in Mexico, it more often than not was only accessible by boat. Once there, walk out the property lines and potential structure sites, especially the home, before committing. Take 360° video from possible locations. Take pictures of the area you actually want the house to be located, put it on a photo-editing program like Paint Shop Pro and photoshop a picture of a house in to see what it would look like. Do this for several potential areas. Share your results and all information with family and friends and compare before purchasing.

Step 7: Relax and Survey the Land

Set up some form of temporary lodging, be it in the form of a camper, a trailer house, tent, tepee, yurt, or tiny house. You're going to be working harder than you ever have in your life. You're going to be mentally, physically, and emotionally exhausted. The only remedy for these ailments is rest, comforts, and a good night's sleep. A tent might not fulfill that requirement.

Then, relax, get situated, get a feel for the land and enjoy the freedom as long as possible. Then, traverse your property to stake the corners with GPS, map the landscape with elevations using a hand site-level, annotating resources, topography (often you can find topography maps of your land at the country clerk's office), wind direction, compass headings, magnetic and true north, areas of thick and minimal vegetation, and clearings with approximate measurements using a measuring wheel or reel. Then draw up a homestead design and layout. Some elements to keep in mind during this process are that you want to: locate stables and pens downwind, wells and wind turbines uphill; be sure to think about placement for workshops, building site, and driveway; don't locate the house in the prettiest spot—build in any direction away from the prettiest spot, so that you always have a view of the prettiest spot; too rocky, too wet, or too steep makes everything harder. Share with friends and family to get input. It can only help to give you other perspectives and identify things you may not have noticed or thought about.

Step 8: Live, Work, and Play as a Self-Reliant Human

You're free! But you're not free. I worked harder being free from society, than I ever did working in society. And as the farmer, builder, surgeon, psychologist, and security to my wife, I suddenly was responsible for her very life, and in turn, she was responsible for mine. So, when it's time to get to work, do what needs to be done. These steps are just a rough guide. How long it will really take is dependent on many, many factors: the level of self-sufficiency you want to achieve, your location, free time, conditions, terrain, work ethic, drive, etc. For anyone, even me, to become 100% self-sufficient doesn't happen on day 1, or even by day 100. It's going to take time—years. The more knowledge, experience and money you go into it with, the less time wasted on the learning. When you add people to the equation, be it a spouse, children, family, or even friends or neighbors, that number goes down exponentially.

You can speed things up greatly by hiring out portions of work. You may find yourself needing and enlisting the help of friends, family, or even hired hands. Before I get into this too much, I will state that having someone help you doesn't mean you're not doing it yourself. There's nothing wrong with getting the help you need, and it can actually be a fun learning experience for everyone.

There are several factors to consider if you need helping hands, such as are they working for free; how well do *you* work with others (working with friends and family has the tendency to hurt relationships); or are they inexperienced or experienced? In reality, you'll be doing most of the work anyway. You have to understand the relationship between help, workload, and the number of people conducting that work. Help rendered isn't directly equal to the number of people helping. For example, on the surface, the math seems pretty simple: one person doing a forty-hour job would take forty hours, whereas two people doing a forty-hour job, would only take twenty hours, but, as I learned very quickly, two people working the job doesn't equate to the job getting done in half the time. It's strange—if you have one helper, even an inexperienced one, the job actually gets done in a fraction of the time, maybe even ten times faster. As you work more quickly with helpers, the most important advice I can share from my experience working with all kinds of people, in all kinds of countries is to 1) always talk to and treat others with respect, and 2) maybe more importantly, always make it fun, even if you don't get anything done. This actually has been proven to lead to more productive work and better relationships.

OTHER OPTIONS

Although I may have made it seem so, self-sufficient doesn't strictly mean being alone. We were self-sufficient, and even though I relied on my wife to do her share as she did me, we knew how to do, and often did, the other's chores. We can take this to the next level with small groups:

Join a Shared Community

A shared community can be an easier, more economical and far healthier way for families, individuals, and couples to achieve self-sufficiency. Building your own home, growing your own food, making your own fuel and electricity, and raising livestock, each in their own right are difficult things to do. But when you enlist the help of others in the community, or when most of the work is carried out by others, this workload is drastically lessened, leading to an easier and more enjoyable self-sufficient experience, one where more necessities and higher levels of luxuries can be achieved than what can be achieved on your own. Co-operation can drastically raise everyone's level of living when done in small communities, proving just how simple life can become when you cooperate and share.

Shared communities or Seed Communities, Co-Housing Developments, and Eco-Villages are multifamily cooperative housing developments, that are driven towards contributing to the collaborative sharing economy by offering private or shared living quarters, multiple family areas like community kitchens, gyms, and game rooms. These features not only encourage camaraderie, cooperation, shared chores, and collective child development and interaction but cut costs as well.

For example, maybe you're a single parent who'd like to purchase or build a $15k in-ground pool so the kids can beat the heat. Since actual usage averages less than eight hours a week, justifying such an investment is hopeless. However, if fifteen families chip in and share pool time, each only pays $1000, leaving $14,000 for other amenities. In this type of community, the buck doesn't stop there. The same savings encompasses all elements of not only a home but life as well (babysitting, clothes washing, food production, security) not only saving money but time and energy.

Living together, in smaller self-sufficient communities, is a more economical, social, and far healthier option for families, individuals, and couples. It's an easier first step toward self-sustainability, and an enjoyable way of building, growing, producing, and sharing the necessities and luxuries of life with family and friends, drastically raising everyone's level of living. This system relies on equal participant contribution, skill, intelligence, creativity, and teamwork instead of money, power, position, and systems of law. It's a place where co-workers really care about you because they're also your neighbors, friends, and/or family. Those producing your water and food care because their children are eating and drinking the same stuff. Unlike today's society, there's also a place for the elderly to help take care of the children, passing on knowledge, cooking, and other tasks while adults work on building the community.

If you are looking to leave the rat race and contribute to something bigger—if you enjoy talking, spending time, having fun and working with other like-minded individuals and families, or just want something better, healthier, and more educational for your children than what society has to offer—a co-op may be for you. There are hundreds, maybe thousands of cooperative communities around the world. Make sure to research locations, practices, rules, and relationships, and find one that best fits. I would even suggest asking to join on a temporary basis in order to test the water. Or join up with others in your area who have similar goals, and start or build your own. Feel free to contact me for pointers! I have one in Texas (Imladris) and one starting up in Oregon.

Build a Shared Community

If you don't find any worth joining, why not build your own? I've had the pleasure of designing and overseeing the development of communities in or near Iquitos, Peru, Monkey River, Belize, Oregon, and East Texas as well as working for The Mars Project and on PayPal founder Peter Theil's The Seasteading Institute. Unfortunately, largely because of human nature and what these communities strive to abolish (rules, laws, government), they can have short life spans, which can be disappointing when so much is invested in building them. In order to create a strong foundation, key aspects should be presented and decided beforehand including:

- your system of government and decision making
- your capital source (initial construction and sustaining)
- your desired level of self-sufficiency
- the best, most efficient self-sufficiency systems

- residents' roles and jobs
- quantity of residents
- methods of harnessing energy in your location
- methods of growing and raising food
- purposes and methods of producing fuel
- additional required sustainable living elements options

- methods of producing additional required elements
- types, materials, and methods of required structures
- distinguishing the "doers" from the "talkers"
- building teams and assigning tasks
- determining the first steps

Notice that I didn't put anything about community beliefs or charter. Often, at least in my experience, when these are included either written or behind closed doors, it becomes a religion or cult, no matter how innocent the idea.

Create a High End Community

Another option would be to purchase a large cut of land, build all support systems first, then sell off lots geared towards higher-end demographic, just like developers, along with yearly dues—an eco-subdivision. This is what we were able to do in two off-the-grid subdivisions on the outskirts of Las Vegas, Nevada, and Edinburg, Texas. Like any subdivision, sell the concept first and obtain deposits up front to pay for the venture. Your listing may look something like this.

Now Available - Extremely energy efficient, zero-carbon, zero-waste, renewable energy-powered solar homes, built with local natural green materials, located in a self-sufficient gated community with 24/7 security.

How It Works: Fresh groceries are delivered weekly (or enjoy hand picking your meals), fresh water via 3 private on-site wells, and flex-fuel vehicles are fueled and ready to go every evening. Daily housekeeping, lawn maintenance, childcare, pet care.

Other amenities include: indoor gym and fitness center with weights, treadmills, separate exercise, Zumba and yoga rooms (classes every Sat. and Wed.), movie theater, meeting rooms, educational lectures, medical and first-aid center, racquetball courts, sauna, 2 swimming pools (1 indoor, 1 outdoor) with whirlpools, basketball and volleyball courts, community game room with pool tables; on-site tennis courts, horseback riding, petting zoo, playground, community garden, hair and nail salon, walking and running tracks, soccer and football field, 9-hole golf course, miniature golf course, 5-acre stocked lake, clubhouse and events pavilion with stage, nature areas with wooded hiking, biking trails and ultimate frisbee course, 12 table picturesque picnic areas and dog and cat (separate) parks, all with complete high-speed Wi-Fi coverage, all accessible by your own private solar powered golf cart and all included free.

Seasteading

In the extreme opposite direction is seasteading. The concept revolves around the fact that all land has already been conquered and is presently being ruled or governed, leaving the vast open seas, outside the Exclusive Economic Zone of 200 nautical miles (territory not claimed or under the jurisdiction by any government) to set up a permanent, self-sustainable dwelling. This is achieved either by modifying cruise ship vessels (capable of holding thousands), abandoned oil rigs, or constructing floating and/or partially submerged platforms or islands.

Currently, The Seasteading Institute (a modular concept started by PayPal founder Peter Thiel), Blue Seed (floating cruise vessel off San Francisco), and Spiral Island (floating island off Cancun) are in the works in this area.

General Advice Worth Passing On

Keep it fun!

Whatever choices you made, always, always keep things fun! You chose to make this change because you didn't like how your life in society was going—because you wanted your life to be better. So don't make your life off the grid worse. Choose your hours, play your favorite music—heck blast it for all nature to enjoy. Work when you feel like it. If you don't feel like doing something, YOU will make it a miserable experience by doing it anyway. Try (I say try because sometimes you just need to buckle down and get a job done) to only work when the following are met:
- You have enough light and space.
- The work environment is clean and dry.
- You have the right tool for the job, and ALWAYS use power tools—you'll thank me.
- It's not too cold/hot.
- You're not being rushed.
- Your work space is set up so you're not running back and forth.
- You have enough knowledge on what you're doing.
- You have support.

When you have fun doing something, you do it better, people around you work harder/longer and you appreciate a job well done. Remember, you control and create your environment. You can create a utopia, or you can create a hell—it's up to you.

There are lots of things I would have done differently; the good news is you get to benefit from my mistakes. I would strongly advise you doing (or not doing) the following:
- **Do** keep connected to the internet for as long as possible. It's a source of entertainment, communication, parts and supplies sourcing, and manuals, DIY guides and videos.
- **Don't** be too close to society, but don't be too far away either.

- **Don't** fight nature; it always wins.
- **Don't** force things; don't break things. You'll just make twice as much work for yourself.
- **Don't** use your teeth as tools. You can never get them back. And don't put nails in your mouth when working.
- **Do** landscape last because you'll destroy it all during construction if you don't.
- **Do** implement some kind of a support person/system that can handle everything except the physical working, so that you can devote 100% of your time to work. Otherwise, you'll get nothing done.
- **Don't** bring pets or animals because you don't need any extra work or distractions when building your homestead.
- **Don't** bring your former life's clutter off the grid!
- **Do** remember to stay calm in emergencies! In most cases, no one is going to die and nothing will be destroyed in the few minutes it will take to stop and think things through to come up with a plan.
- **Do** put plenty of time into the design phase. Know and plan for what you really want and need.
- **Do** give up (sometimes). When things are going bad, when everything's just going wrong in your life, you're not on your path. Stop, quit, reorganize your thoughts or plans, and start again. If things go smoother, you're on your path.
- **Do** work smarter rather than work harder.
- **Don't** do it alone. In survival school you're taught you can go 3 hours without shelter, 3 days without water, 30 days without food, and 3 months without people.

A Few Last Words

I watched and even tried to fit in for a long time as people walked away from their families every day to a place they thought would provide them a means to a better life. If you listen to nothing else in this book, and if you decide in the end to continue with your current path, please take these two things to heart: 1) There is *nothing* more important to your family than their family! Not the toys, jewelry, cars, vacations, or even food. The only thing they really care about, even if they don't know it, is to have you around more! 2) You only get one life, make it a good one, even if that means doing things differently than everyone else!

Good luck, and most of all, treat each other well, treat everything else on this planet well, and have fun!

References

1. LaPonsie, Maryalene. "How Much Does It Cost to Raise a Child?" *U.S. News and World Report*. Published September 7, 2021. https://money.usnews.com/money/personal-finance/articles/how-much-does-it-cost-to-raise-a-child.

2. Leblanc, Rick. "The Importance of Tire Recycling: Old Tires Are Being Increasingly Utilized." The Balance Small Business. Last modified December 29, 2018. https://www.thebalancesmb.com/the-importance-of-tire-recycling-2878127.

3. "As a matter of Fact . . . : Fun Tidbits About Recycling, Energy and Climate Change." CT.gov. Last modified February 2020. https://portal.ct.gov/DEEP/Reduce-Reuse-Recycle/Municipal-Recycling-Resource-Center/As-A-Matter-of-Fact.

4. "Fix a Leak Week." EPA.gov. Last modified August 13, 2021. https://www.epa.gov/watersense/fix-leak-week.

5. Nunez, Christina. "Climate 101: Deforestation." National Geographic. Published February 7, 2019. https://www.nationalgeographic.com/environment/article/deforestation.

6. Rostagno, Horacio, L.F.T. Albino, Juarez Lopes Donzele, P.C. Gomes, R.F. DE Oliveira, D.C.Lopes, A.S. Ferreira, S.L. De Toledo Barreto, R.F. Euclides. "30-Daily Nutritional Requirements of Gestating Swine Breeders." Research Gate. Published January 2011. https://www.researchgate.net/figure/30-Daily-Nutritional-Requirements-of-Gestating-Swine-Breeders-kcal-day-or-g-day_tbl51_285909167.

7. Ramos-Elorduy, Julieta, Jose Manuel Pino Moreno, Esteban Escamilla Prado, Manuel Alvarado Perez, Jaime Lagunez Otero, Oralia Ladronde Guevara. "Nutritional Value of Edible Insects from the State of Oaxaca, Mexico." *The Journal of Food Composition and Analysis* 10, no. 2 (1997). https://doi.org/10.1006/jfca.1997.0530.

8. Gikonyo, Dan, Anthony Gikonyo, Duncan Luvayo, and Premanand Ponoth. "Drug Expiry Debate: The Myth and the Reality." *African Health Sciences* 19, no. 3 (2019). https://doi.org/10.4314/ahs.v19i3.49.

9. Kristof, Kathy. "6 Little Things That Cost a Lot." Last modified on April 6, 2011. http://www.cbsnews.com/news/6-little-things-that-cost-a-lot/.

Additional Resources

Books

1997 *NDS National Design Specification for Wood Construction* by American Forest and Paper Association

ACI-318 *Building Code Requirements for Structural Concrete*

ACI-530 *Building Code Requirements for Masonry Structures*

Apocalypse: How to Survive a Global Crisis by Dan Martin

ASCE 7-98 *Minimum Design Loads for Buildings and Other Structures*

ASM International's *Heat Treater's Guide* by Harry Chandler

Back to Basics published by Readers Digest in 1981

Ball Complete Book of Home Preserving by Judi Kingry

The Complete Guide to Water Storage by Julie Fryer

Concrete and Masonry, FM 5-742 by Headquarters, Department of the Army

Construction and Home Repair Techniques Simply Explained by the United States Naval Education and Training Command

Convert It! by Michael P. Brown

Create an Oasis With Greywater by Art Ludwig

Ecovillages: A Practical Guide to Sustainable Communities by Jan Martin Bang

Henley's Twentieth Century Formulas, Recipes and Processes by Gardner D. Hiscox

The Joy of Juicing by Gary Null

Manual de Autoconstrucción by Carlos Rodriguez R.

PATH's *Residential Structural Design Guide* by the U.S. Department of Housing and Urban Development

Physicians' Desk Reference by PDR Staff

The Pill Book by Harold M. Silverman

Pocket Ref by Thomas J. Glover

Practical Handbook of Photovoltaics: Fundamentals and Applications by Augustin McEvoy, Tom Markvart, and Luis Castaner

The Solar House: Passive Heating and Cooling by Daniel D. Chiras

Steelworker 3 & 2, NAVEDTRA 10653-G by Naval Education and Training Program Management Support Activity

The Ultimate Dehydrator Cookbook by Tammy Gangloff, Steven Gangloff, and September Ferguson

US Department of Agriculture Publications: www.nal.usda.gov/publications

General Books for Reference

Farmers' almanac
The Foxfire Books
Local building code
NASA Hydroponics Database and Handbook for Advanced Life: ntrs.nasa.gov/citations/19990063466

Websites

fao.org/3/x5738e/x5738e09.htm
infonet-biovision.org/AnimalHealth/Animal-nutrition-and-feed-rations
ndvsu.org/images/StudyMaterials/Nutrition/NUTRIENT.pdf

General Websites for Reference

AskExpertsNow.com
Communa.org.il
EcoVillage.org
Free online courses from Yale, Harvard, MIT, Princeton (visit individual university websites for online enrollment): ClassCentral.com/universities
Hugh Piggott's Blog (work in wind turbines): scoraigwind.co.uk
IC.org
instructables.com
JustAnswer.com
LifeHacker.com
Reddit.com
YouTube.com

Magazines, Catalogs, and Online News Media

BackHome
Backwoods Home
Grit
Harbor Freight Tools catalog
Hobby Farms
Home Power
Homesteading magazine
JC Whitney catalog
Mother Earth News
Northern Tools catalog
Treehugger

Self-Sufficient and Homesteading Organizations

Alberta Ministry of Agriculture, Forestry, and Rural Economic Development: Alberta.ca/agriculture-forestry-and-rural-economic-development.aspx
Auroville.org
Blue Frontiers
Dan Martin Does Everything (youtube channel)
DIYsufficient.com
Free Food Factory
The Land Pavilion or Living with the Land at Epcot, Disney World
Local food bank
Mars-one.com
The Seasteading Institute

Places to Find Products

Amazon
AmishAmerica.com/store
eBay

Facebook Marketplace
Freecycle.org
GoodsStores.com/collections/amish-mennonite-goods
Goodwill
GreenMagicHomes.com (underground home kit)
Habitat for Humanity
HoneyFlow.com
Salvation Army
Unirac.com/solarmount
WindAndSolar.com/wind-turbine-tower-locking-collar/

Services

123D Design
Adobe Illustrator
AutoCAD
Autodesk
Blender
mfg.com
NextFab
Shopify
SketchUp
TaskRabbit
TechShop
Tinkercad
Volusion

3D Printing Services

OpenSourceEcology.org
Shapeways
Skillshare.com
uShip

Online Calculators

Conduit size calculator: www.southwire.com/calculator-conduit
Engineering calculators: www.engineersedge.com/calculators.htm
Friction head loss calculator: www.dutypoint.com/friction-head-loss-2020
Mechanical calculators: www.omnicalculator.com/physics
Pipe size table: www.engineersedge.com/pipe_schedules.htm
Solar position calculator: gml.noaa.gov/grad/solcalc/azel.html
Wide array of math and physics calculators: calculatorsoup.com/calculators/physics/index.php
Wire size calculator: www.paigewire.com/pumpWireCalc.aspx

Apps

Autodesk BIM 360
Bubble Level
Compass
Construction Master Pro Calculator
FingerCAD
Measuring Tape
Rogers Mushrooms or Shroomify
Seek
Solocator
Toolshare

Index

Acknowledgments

First and foremost, there's no other person in this world that has or could ever have helped in the making of this book more than my wife, Lucia. She not only bought me my first sustainable living book, sparking the fire that led us to move off the grid (which ultimately led to this book), but was brave enough to accept and believe in the ludicrous notion that we *could* live cut off from any and all forms of society indefinitely. She left her country, family, friends, and a high-paying career as a computer engineer with AT&T and abandoned all of the many material possessions society had to offer in order to live on an unknown, inhospitable, "uninhabitable" mountain while we built our home together, entirely alone.

If that wasn't enough, for the last three years she's not only encouraged me to travel around the world but accompanied and assisted in helping and teaching others in disaster-stricken areas how to rebuild sustainably and be self-reliant. Lucia also built and runs all aspects of our non-profit Agua-Luna.

The sacrifices and contributions she's made are remarkable, if not superhuman. It takes a very special type of person to not only support but drive, motivate, and inspire someone to do such things with their life, and I love her for that. And although those years we spent sustaining each other were physically demanding, spending twenty-four hours a day, seven days a week for six years completely alone in an area where no one even knew we existed, they were honestly the best years of my life. We accomplished more than we ever had dreamed, making this book, my prior books, and the ones that will follow possible, and I truly couldn't and wouldn't have done it without her.

I'd also like to thank my preliminary editor, Barbara Seiden, who is an award-winning journalist and an incredible writer with over forty years in the field. A Hopwood Award winner, her list of Hollywood credits includes Writer on Columbia Studio's series *Bewitched*, Story Analyst for ABC-TV's *Movie of the Week*, and News Associate at ABC-TV. She played a huge role, and I'm lucky to have been able to utilize her expert skills as an editor, experience as a writer, and support as my biggest fan. She stood by our decision to leave society, offering insight before and after, while patiently awaiting our return. Her editorial skills bring a comprehensive breath of fresh air to my clumsy and often confusing writing style.

I'd also like to thank my final edition editor Shaelyn Topolovec, who, with her degree in editing and publishing and her experience in writing and editing, helped get this book to where it is now.

And I can't forget my father, Craig Martin, who encouraged me to join the military and taught me about nature, hunting, fishing, shooting, and tracking, along with mechanics and construction. And of course, I'd like to thank my father's brother, Robert, and Robert's wife, Jo, who on several occasions, way up in the mountains, out in the desert, well into many nights, enlightened me on how the government and world should be.

Many thanks to the entire and incredibly beautiful country of Mexico who still live off and with the land and who gave me a place to live when the US wouldn't cut it, but especially to my in-laws Sergio, Socorro, Sergio Sr., extended family, friends, and neighbors.

I would also like to thank you, the reader, for buying my books and continuing to request the information I have amassed through our website. Your interest, need, and desire to be enlightened, self-sufficient, and independent energizes and motivates me to continue to construct and pass on these lessons to you. I appreciate your past feedback and loyalty, which inspires me to make each book better than the last.

About the Author

In his twenties, Dan Martin and his wife, Lucia, quit their careers as engineers; got rid of their cookie-cutter suburban home, vehicles, boat, and jet skis; burned their phones, computers, and belongings (and wads of cash); and left society. For the next eight years they lived off the grid, 100% self-sufficient, entirely cut off, not leaving their homestead once and not seeing or speaking with another person the entire time.

There were no electric or water lines; no internet, cell, or emergency services; no calendars, clocks, or TVs; and there wasn't even a road to the property. Dan built their home from available materials, and they lived on caught rainwater, hydroponically grown produce, and hand-raised livestock. He made his own ethanol, solar and wind power, alcohol still, furniture, dishes, pots, pans, and even an indoor swimming pool, eliminating mortgages, bills, expenses, and the need for money or income of any kind.

His journey was inspired by a thought he'd had one day: "Even though we're born in a herd of sheep, maybe we don't need to continue as one. Maybe we could stop . . . leave." And so he had split from the herd, leaving all comforts, materialism, and capitalism behind.

In 2010, Dan returned and moved to Mexico to form a global nonprofit that enabled him to enter catastrophe zones so he could provide second response relief to survivors of natural and man-made catastrophes (of which we seem to be having a lot of lately).

Dan grew up in Detroit when the city was labeled the homicide capital of the world. At thirteen, as the child of divorced parents, he went to live with his father and learned to hunt, track, trap, and work with animals. At eighteen, he fought in the Gulf War and was awarded several medals. Upon returning, he spent years volunteering with Habitat for Humanity and traveled throughout Latin America. He prepared himself by learning everything, receiving educations in agriculture, medicine, and engineering while attending trade schools in heating/AC, electrical, and welding. At the same time, he attended community workshops in woodworking, pottery, leather, glass working, and canning/preserving, and took unpaid apprenticeships in masonry, construction, carpentry, and metalworking.

Dan now lives in a 6,400 ft² hand-built bunker/seed vault on an animal refuge, and he consults on the subject of self-sustainability and societal collapse for Hollywood movies and prime time TV shows like AMC's *The Walking Dead*, TNT's *Falling Skies*, NatGeo's *Doomsday Preppers*, Fox's *Utopia* and Discovery's *The Colony*. He teaches workshops and gives lectures on self-sustainability and has even built several self-sufficient shared living eco-villages around the world (and off of it), including The Mars Project; Paypal Founder Peter Thiel's floating self-sufficient community, the Seasteading Institute; Monkey River Eco Village; Espíritu de Anaconda near Iquitos, Peru, in the Amazon rain forest; and his very own communities (which are now accepting residents) near Portland, Oregon, and East Texas.

In 2012, he published his best seller, *Apocalypse: How to Survive a Global Crisis*; in 2018, *The End: Survivors*; and now the 300-pager, *Breaking the Grid*, a guide to self-sufficiency. Dan has been the hot topic of CNN, MSNBC, *Men's Journal*, *Men's Health*, *The Huffington Post*, *Esquire*, and The Travel Channel to name a few. Martin is widely considered one of the foremost experts on the topic of self-sufficiency due to being "boots on the ground" in places like Haiti after the earthquake and cholera outbreaks, New Orleans after Katrina, Colombia during the floods, Japan for Fukushima, Detroit and Venezuela during their societal collapses, the Middle East during the war, Mexico during the cartel wars, and Puerto Rico, Morocco, the US, and several other countries during the global pandemic, all of which amounts to over 100,000 hours in the field.

He knows firsthand the ins and outs of day-to-day life in environments when humanity is at its lowest and society stops or can no longer provide for us. He possesses that on-site, eyewitness account only imprinted on someone by actually being there, seeing firsthand the trauma and chaos-induced behaviors, reactions, and horrific chain of events that unfold during and in the aftermath of catastrophic events. Through his books, Martin provides eye-opening views of us at our worst, and his insight into future events, forecasted by his wide variety of past experiences, are incredible at least, lifesaving at best. Dan says it best: "I'm not a writer; I didn't even learn to read until I was seventeen. I don't live life to write, I just write about my life."

Haiti tent city after earthquake

Connect with Dan Martin

Website: www.diysufficient.com
Instagram: @danmartinhuman
Facebook: facebook.com/DanMartinHuman
Twitter: @DanMartinHuman
YouTube: youtube.com/DanMartinHuman
Email: DanMartinHuman@outlook.com

About Familius

Visit Our Website: www.familius.com

Familius is a global trade publishing company that publishes books and other content to help families be happy. We believe that the family is the fundamental unit of society and that happy families are the foundation of a happy life. We recognize that every family looks different, and we passionately believe in helping all families find greater joy. To that end, we publish books for children and adults that invite families to live the Familius Ten Habits of Happy Family Life: *love together, play together, learn together, work together, talk together, heal together, read together, eat together, give together* and *laugh together*. Founded in 2012, Familius is located in Sanger, California.

FAMILIUS

Connect

Facebook: www.facebook.com/familiustalk
Twitter: @familiustalk, @paterfamilius1
Pinterest: www.pinterest.com/familius
Instagram: @familiustalk

The most important work you ever do will be within the walls of your own home.